W9-BYP-882

ROGER CARAS'
TREASURY OF GREAT
HORSE STORIES

ROGER CARAS'
TREASURY OF GREAT
HORSE STORIES

Galahad Books · New York

Copyright © Roger Caras and Martin H. Greenberg, 1990.

All rights reserved. No part of this work may be
reproduced, transmitted in any form or by any means,
electronic or mechanical, including photocopying,
recording, or any information storage and retrieval
system, without permission in writing from the publisher.
All requests for permission to reproduce material from
this Work should be directed to Dutton, an imprint of
New American Library, a division of Penguin Books USA
Inc., 375 Hudson Street, New York, NY 10014.

Published in 1993 by

Galahad Books
A division of Budget Book Service, Inc.
386 Park Avenue South
New York, NY 10016

Published by arrangement with Dutton, an imprint of
New American Library, a division of Penguin Books USA Inc.

Library of Congress Catalog Card Number: 89-38832

ISBN: 0-88365-840-2

Printed in the United States of America.

Grateful acknowledgment is given for permission to reprint the following works:

Max Brand: "The Miniature." Copyright 1939 by Frederick Faust; copyright renewed © 1967
by Jane F. Easton, Judith Faust, and John Frederick Faust. Reprinted by permission of Brandt &
Brandt Literary Agents, Inc.

Clay Fisher: "The Trap." From *The Oldest Maiden Lady in New Mexico,* copyright © 1962 by The
Macmillan Company, Inc. Reprinted by permission of the author.

Erle Stanley Gardner: "Carved in Sand." Copyright 1933 by Erle Stanley Gardner. Reprinted by permission of Curtis Brown, Ltd

Deborah Moulton: "Nordeth" and "Those Who Wear the Medallion," reprinted here as "The Wingèd Foal." From *The First Battle of Morn.* copyright © 1988 by Deborah Moulton. Reprinted by permission of the publisher, Dial Books for Young Readers.

Larry Niven: "The Flight of the Horse." From *The Magazine of Fantasy and Science Fiction.* copyright © 1969 by Mercury Press, Inc. Reprinted by permission of the author.

William F. Nolan: "Shadow Quest." Copyright © 1990 by William F. Nolan. Used by permission of the author.

James Powell: "The Kidnap of Bounding Mane." Copyright © 1988 by James Powell. Reprinted by permission of the Scott Meredith Literary Agency, Inc., 845 Third Avenue, New York, N.Y. 10022.

CONTENTS

Contents

CONTENTS

Contents

Roger Caras

INTRODUCTION

There is no denying the fact that man arrived at his present high station in life on the back of a horse. Of all the Earth's continents only Antarctica was not opened up for the most part by mounted men with their necessities pulled and carried behind them by still other horses. And the ill-fated Robert Falcon Scott expedition trying to be the first to reach the South Pole even tried horses there. (It was the wrong place and a bad idea. Horses require too much food. Scott and all of his companions died as a result of that tragic miscalculation.)

Through all of *recorded* history, whenever man set out to

expand his horizons, he went by ship or by horse and very often he carried horses on his ships to help him conquer the new worlds he felt sure he would discover. On his second voyage Christopher Columbus carried enough horses to establish a stud farm on the island of Hispaniola. They and their issue were later used to invade Mexico and to terrorize the Aztecs and the other high but horseless cultures the Spaniards encountered.

Horses have always been at the core of human expansion, exploration, and later agriculture, as well as the management of large numbers of meat animals. We could not have managed herds of cattle without horses, and in many places this has been true of sheep as well. What horses have meant to the military is legend (right up to World War II and the heroic but foolish use of the Polish cavalry against German tanks) and in sport, pleasure, and easy personal transportation they have been the absolutely essential animal around the world. The history of man would have been altered by the absence of the horse more than the loss of any other single species of domestic animal. Quite simply, we would live different lives today had we not had ancestors with the courage and imagination, not to mention the stamina, to subdue and selectively breed horses.

All of this has not gone unnoticed in the cultures of man. No matter where we turn, we find horses as symbols. In real life the emperor of Japan rides a white horse. The samurai were legendary horsemen as were the Cossacks. In movies the bad guy rides a black horse. Where chance is an element the unexpected winner is called the *dark horse.* In art there is even a code for equestrian statues. The number of feet the horse has on the ground tells us how its rider died: in battle, from wounds after the battle, or from more natural causes. The more heroic the rider and the more epic his death the more the marble or bronze horse seems to be pawing the air with its forefeet.

Literature, of all the arts, has never been outdone in its tribute to the long-suffering horse. People have written more about the horse, perhaps, than about any other species of animal. And it all goes rather far back in time and quite deep in cultural tradition. Muhammad, after all, rose from the Dome of the Rock in Jerusalem all the way to heaven on horseback, and the gods of war have thundered across our heavens in their chariots of fire drawn by horses of enormous size and power. The eternal symbol of nobility and honor, the knight, gained his station and his power only when mounted on a prancing steed. The mounted Plains Indians and the cowboys of the American West are two of the most durable figures in the lexicon of the adventurous and courageous whether you live in Texas, Turkey, or Tokyo. There are equally exciting figures in the fact and fiction of Australia, Argentina, and North Africa.

Interestingly, there have been authentic historical figures who recorded their love or, somewhat surprisingly, their hatred of dogs and cats, but I personally do not know of even one who hated his horse. Not every larger-than-life hero loved his horse as much as Robert E. Lee, Henry VIII, George Washington, Geronimo, Jeb Stuart, or George Armstrong Custer, but no one seems to have hated his horse or even took it for granted. It wasn't very long ago in America when you might have been hanged if you killed a man in a gunfight, but you sure as shootin' were hanged if you stole his horse. Priorities then were basic and pragmatic.

A strange symbology has grown up around the heroic horses of history. It is often stated even in authoritative history books that the only survivor of the July 1876 battle known as Custer's Last Stand was a horse called Comanche—a "fact" repeated endlessly despite the fact that history knows better. At least four Crow scouts working for Custer got away (Charlie, Curley, Hairy Moccasin, and White-Man-Runs-Him), and it is almost certain that some troopers did as well.

And Lady Godiva was not the only woman in history to ride to fame on a horse. In modern times women, whether as veterinarians or show riders or riding instructors and judges, virtually dominate the world of horses.

Martin Greenberg, that master anthologist, and I have tried to bring together in this collection a sampling of relatively recent writings that did not need to be edited down or severely compressed. We thought it better to allow longer works, some of them the absolute classics of the literature of the horse, to stand on their own with the suggestion that the readers of the shorter stories included here may want to explore or reread those volumes themselves. People in general and writers in particular reveal a lot of themselves in the comments they make about things that are important to them. Horses have long been extremely important to man, and in the things he has said about the bond between man and mount there is more than just a little cultural anthropology as well as a good bit of individual psychology.

ROGER CARAS'
TREASURY OF GREAT
HORSE STORIES

Mark Twain

A HORSE'S TALE

Part I

1 SOLDIER BOY—PRIVATELY TO HIMSELF

I am Buffalo Bill's horse. I have spent my life under his saddle—with him in it, too, and he is good for two hundred pounds, without his clothes; and there is no telling how much he does weigh when he is out on the warpath and has his batteries belted on. He is over six feet, is young, hasn't an ounce of waste flesh, is straight, graceful, springy in his motions, quick as a cat, and has a handsome face, and black hair dangling down on his shoulders, and is beautiful to look at; and nobody is braver than he is, and nobody is stronger, except myself. Yes, a person that doubts that he is fine to see should see him in his beaded buckskins, on my back and his rifle peeping above his shoulder, chasing a hostile trail, with me going like the wind and his hair streaming out behind from the shelter of his broad slouch. Yes, he is a sight to look at then—and I'm part of it myself.

I am his favorite horse, out of dozens. Big as he is, I have carried him eighty-one miles between nightfall and sunrise on the scout; and I am good for fifty, day in and day out, and all the time. I am not large, but I am built on a business basis. I have carried him thousands and thousands of miles on scout duty for the army, and there's not a gorge, nor a pass, nor a valley, nor a fort, nor a trading post, nor a buffalo range in the whole sweep of the Rocky Mountains and the Great Plains that we don't know as well as we know the bugle calls. He is chief of scouts to the Army of the Frontier, and it makes us very important. In such a position as I hold in the military service, one needs to be of good family and possess an education much above the common to be worthy of the place. I am the best-educated horse outside of the hippodrome, everybody says, and the best-mannered. It may be so, it is not for me to say; modesty is the best policy, I think. Buffalo Bill taught me the most of what I know, my mother taught me much, and I taught myself the rest. Lay a row of moccasins before me—Pawnee, Sioux, Shoshone, Cheyenne, Blackfoot, and as many other tribes as you please—and I can name the tribe every moccasin belongs to by the make of it. Name it in horse talk, and could do it in American if I had speech.

I know some of the Indian signs—the signs they make with their hands, and by signal fires at night and columns of smoke by day. Buffalo Bill taught me how to drag wounded soldiers out of the line of fire with my teeth; and I've done it, too; at least I've dragged *him* out of the battle when he was wounded. And not just once, but twice. Yes, I know a lot of things. I remember forms, and gaits, and faces; and you can't disguise a person that's done me a kindness so that I won't know him thereafter wherever I find him. I know the art of searching for a trail, and I know the stale track from the fresh. I can keep a trail all by myself, with Buffalo Bill asleep in the saddle; ask him—he will tell you so. Many a time, when he has ridden all night, he has said to me at dawn, "Take the watch, boy; if the trail freshens, call me." Then he goes to sleep. He knows he can trust me, because I have a reputation. A scout horse that has a reputation does not play with it.

My mother was all American—no alkali spider about *her*, I can tell you; she was of the best blood of Kentucky, the bluest bluegrass aristocracy, very proud and acrimonious—or maybe it is ceremonious. I don't know which it is. But it is no matter; size is the main thing about a word, and that one's up to standard. She spent her military life as colonel of the Tenth Dragoons, and saw a deal of rough service—distinguished service it was, too. I mean, she *carried* the Colonel; but it's all the same. Where would he be without his horse? He wouldn't arrive. It takes two to make a colonel of dragoons. She was a fine dragoon horse, but never got above that. She was strong enough for the scout service and had the endurance, too, but she couldn't quite come up to the speed required; a scout horse has to have steel in his muscle and lightning in his blood.

My father was a bronco. Nothing as to lineage—that is, nothing as to recent lineage—but plenty good enough when you go a good way back. When Professor Marsh was out here hunting bones for the chapel of Yale University, he found skeletons of horses no bigger than a fox, bedded in the rocks, and he said they were ancestors of my father. My mother heard him say it; and he said those skeletons were two million years old, which astonished her and made her Kentucky pretensions look small and pretty antiphonal, not to say oblique. Let me see. . . . I used to know the meaning of those words, but . . . well, it was years ago, and 'tisn't as vivid now as it was when they were fresh. That sort of words doesn't keep, in the kind of climate we have out here. Professor Marsh said those

3

skeletons were fossils. So that makes me part bluegrass and part fossil; if there is any older or better stock, you will have to look for it among the Four Hundred, I reckon. I am satisfied with it. And am a happy horse, too, though born out of wedlock.

And now we are back at Fort Paxton once more, after a forty-day scout, away up as far as the Big Horn. Everything quiet. Crows and Blackfeet squabbling—as usual—but no outbreaks, and settlers feeling fairly easy.

The Seventh Cavalry still in garrison here; also the Ninth Dragoons, two artillery companies, and some infantry. All glad to see me, including General Alison, commandant. The officers' ladies and children well, and called upon me—with sugar. Colonel Drake, Seventh Cavalry, said some pleasant things; Mrs. Drake was very complimentary; also Captain and Mrs. Marsh, Company B, Seventh Cavalry; also the Chaplain, who is always kind and pleasant to me, because I kicked the lungs out of a trader once. It was Tommy Drake and Fanny Marsh that furnished the sugar—nice children, the nicest at the post, I think.

That poor orphan child is on her way from France—everybody is full of the subject. Her father was General Alison's brother; married a beautiful young Spanish lady ten years ago, and has never been in America since. They lived in Spain a year or two, then went to France. Both died some months ago. This little girl that is coming is the only child. General Alison is glad to have her. He has never seen her. He is a very nice old bachelor, but is an old bachelor just the same and isn't more than about a year this side of retirement by age limit; and so what does he know about taking care of a little maid nine years old? If I could have her it would be another matter, for I know all about children, and they adore me. Buffalo Bill will tell you so himself.

I have some of this news from overhearing the garrison gossip, the rest of it I got from Potter, the General's dog.

Potter is the Great Dane. He is privileged all over the post, like Shekels, the Seventh Cavalry's dog, and visits everybody's quarters and picks up everything that is going, in the way of news. Potter has no imagination, and no great deal of culture, perhaps, but he has a historical mind and a good memory, and so he is the person I depend upon mainly to post me up when I get back from a scout. That is, if Shekels is out on depredation and I can't get hold of him.

2 LETTER FROM ROUEN—TO GENERAL ALISON

My dear Brother-in-law,

Please let me write again in Spanish, I cannot trust my English, and I am aware, from what your brother used to say, that army officers educated at the Military Academy of the United States are taught our tongue. It is as I told you in my other letter: Both my poor sister and her husband, when they found they could not recover, expressed the wish that you should have their little Catherine—as knowing that you would presently be retired from the army—rather than that she should remain with me, who am broken in health, or go to your mother in California, whose health is also frail.

You do not know the child, therefore I must tell you something about her. You will not be ashamed of her looks, for she is a copy in little of her beautiful mother—and it is that Andalusian beauty which is not surpassable, even in your country. She has her mother's charm and grace and good heart and sense of justice, and she has her father's vivacity and cheerfulness and pluck and spirit of enterprise, with the affectionate disposition and sincerity of both parents.

My sister pined for her Spanish home all these years of exile; she was always talking of Spain to the child, and tending and nourishing the love of Spain in the little thing's heart as a precious flower; and she died happy in

5

the knowledge that the fruitage of her patriotic labors was as rich as even she could desire.

Cathy is a sufficiently good little scholar, for her nine years; her mother taught her Spanish herself, and kept it always fresh upon her ear and her tongue by hardly ever speaking with her in any other tongue; her father was her English teacher, and talked with her in that language almost exclusively; French has been her everyday speech for more than seven years among her playmates here; she has a good working use of governess-German and -Italian. It is true that there is always a faint foreign fragrance about her speech, no matter what language she is talking, but it is only just noticeable, nothing more, and is rather a charm than a mar, I think. In the ordinary child studies Cathy is neither before nor behind the average child of nine, I should say. But I can say this for her: in love for her friends and in high-mindedness and good-heartedness she has not many equals, and in my opinion no superiors. And I beg of you, let her have her way with the dumb animals—they are her worship. It is an inheritance from her mother. She knows but little of cruelties and oppressions—keep them from her sight if you can. She would flare up at them and make trouble, in her small but quite decided and resolute way; for she has a character of her own, and lacks neither promptness nor initiative. Sometimes her judgment is at fault, but I think her intentions are always right. Once when she was a little creature of three or four years she suddenly brought her tiny foot down upon the floor in an apparent outbreak of indignation, then fetched it a backward wipe, and stooped down to examine the result. Her mother said:

"Why, what is it, child? What has stirred you so?"

"Mamma, the big ant was trying to kill the little one."

"And so you protected the little one."

"Yes, Mamma, because he had no friend, and I wouldn't let the big one kill him."

"But you have killed them both."

Cathy was distressed, and her lip trembled. She picked up the remains and laid them upon her palm, and said:

"Poor little anty, I'm so sorry; and I didn't mean to kill you, but there wasn't any other way to save you, it was such a hurry."

She is a dear and sweet little lady, and when she goes it will give me a sore heart. But she will be happy with you, and if your heart is old and tired, give it into her keeping; she will make it young again, she will refresh it, she will make it sing. Be good to her, for all our sakes!

My exile will soon be over now. As soon as I am a little stronger I shall see my Spain again; and that will make *me* young again!

Mercedes

3 GENERAL ALISON TO HIS MOTHER

I am glad to know that you are all well, in San Bernardino.

. . . That grandchild of yours has been here—well, I do not quite know how many days it is; nobody can keep account of days or anything else where she is! Mother, she did what the Indians were never able to do. She took the Fort—took it the first day! Took me, too; took the colonels, the captains, the women, the children, and the dumb brutes; took Buffalo Bill, and all his scouts: took the garrison—to the last man; and in forty-eight hours the Indian encampment was hers, illustrious old Thunderbird and all. Do I seem to have lost my solemnity, my gravity, my poise, my dignity? You would lose your own, in my circumstances. Mother, you never saw such a winning little devil. She is all energy and spirit and sunshine, and interest in everybody and everything, and pours out her prodigal love upon every creature that will take it, high or low, Christian or pagan, feathered or furred; and none has declined it to date, and none ever will, I think. But she has a temper, and sometimes it catches fire and flames up, and is likely to burn whatever is near it; but it is soon over, the passion goes as quickly as it comes. Of course she has an Indian name already; Indians always rechristen a stranger early. Thunderbird attended to her case. He gave her the Indian equivalent for firebug, or firefly. He said:

" 'Times, ver' quiet, ver' soft, like summer night, but when she mad she blaze."

Isn't it good? Can't you see the flare? She's beautiful, mother, beautiful as a picture; and there is a touch of you in her face, and of her father—poor George!—and in her unresting activities, and her fearless ways, and her sunbursts and cloudbursts, she is always bringing George back to me. These impulsive natures are dramatic. George was dramatic, so is this Lightning Bug, so is Buffalo Bill. When Cathy first arrived—it was in the forenoon—Buffalo Bill was away, carrying orders to Major Fuller, at Five Forks, up in the Clayton Hills. At midafternoon I was at my desk, trying to work, and this sprite had been making it impossible for half an hour. At last I said:

"Oh, you bewitching little scamp, *can't* you be quiet just a minute or two, and let your poor old uncle attend to a part of his duties?"

"I'll try, uncle; I will, indeed," she said.

"Well, then, that's a good child—kiss me. Now, then, sit up in that chair, and set your eye on that clock. There—that's right. If you stir—if you so much as wink—for four whole minutes, I'll bite you!"

It was very sweet and humble and obedient she looked, sitting there, still as a mouse; I could hardly keep from setting her free and telling her to make as much racket as she wanted to. During as much as two minutes there was a most unnatural and heavenly quiet and repose, then Buffalo Bill came thundering up to the door in all his scout finery, flung himself out of the saddle, said to his horse, "Wait for me, Boy," and stepped in, and stopped dead in his tracks—gazing at the child. She forgot orders, and was on the floor in a moment, saying:

"Oh, you are so beautiful! Do you like me?"

"No, I don't, I love you!" and he gathered her up with a hug, and then set her on his shoulder—apparently nine feet from the floor.

She was at home. She played with his long hair, and admired his big hands and his clothes and his carbine, and asked question after question, as fast as he could answer, until I excused them both for half an hour, in order to have a chance to finish my work. Then I heard Cathy exclaiming over Soldier Boy; and he was worthy of her raptures, for he is a wonder of a horse, and has a reputation which is as shining as his own silken hide.

4 CATHY TO HER AUNT MERCEDES

Oh, it is wonderful here, auntie dear, just paradise! Oh, if you could only see it! everything so wild and lovely; such grand plains, stretching such miles and miles and miles, all the most delicious velvety sand and sagebrush, and rabbits as big as a dog, and such tall and noble jackassful ears that that is what they name them by; and such vast mountains, and so rugged and craggy and lofty, with cloud shawls wrapped around their shoulders, and looking so solemn and awful and satisfied; and the charming Indians, oh, how you would dote on them, auntie dear, and they would on you, too, and they would let you hold their babies, the way they do me, and they *are* the fattest, and brownest, and sweetest little things, and never cry, and wouldn't if they had pins sticking in them, which they haven't, because they are poor and can't afford it; and the

horses and mules and cattle and dogs—hundreds and hundreds and hundreds, and not an animal that you can't do what
you please with, except Uncle Thomas, but *I* don't mind him,
he's lovely; and oh, if you could hear the bugles: *too—too—too-
too—too—too,* and so on—per-fectly beautiful! Do you recognize that one? It's the first toots of the reveille; it goes, dear
me, *so* early in the morning!—then I and every other soldier
on the whole place are up and out in a minute, except Uncle
Thomas, who is most unaccountably lazy, I don't know why,
but I have talked to him about it, and I reckon it will be better
now. He hasn't any faults much, and is charming and sweet,
like Buffalo Bill, and Thunderbird, and Mammy Dorcas, and
Soldier Boy, and Shekels, and Potter, and Sour Mash, and—
well, they're *all* that, just angels, as you may say.

The very first day I came, I don't know how long ago it
was, Buffalo Bill took me on Soldier Boy to Thunderbird's
camp, not the big one which is out on the plain, which is
White Cloud's, he took me to *that* one next day, but this one
is four or five miles up in the hills and crags, where there is
a great shut-in meadow, full of Indian lodges and dogs and
squaws and everything that is interesting, and a brook of the
clearest water running through it, with white pebbles on the
bottom and trees all along the banks cool and shady and good
to wade in, and as the sun goes down it is dimmish in there,
but away up against the sky you see the big peaks towering
up and shining bright and vivid in the sun, and sometimes an
eagle sailing by them, not flapping a wing, the same as if he
was asleep; and young Indians and girls romping and laughing
and carrying on, around the spring and the pool, and not
much clothes on except the girls, and dogs fighting, and the
squaws busy at work, and the bucks busy resting, and the old
men sitting in a bunch smoking, and passing the pipe not to
the left but to the right, which means there's been a row in
the camp and they are settling it if they can, and children

playing *just* the same as any other children, and little boys
shooting at a mark with bows, and I cuffed one of them
because he hit a dog with a club that wasn't doing anything,
and he resented it but before long he wished he hadn't—but
this sentence is getting too long and I will start another.
Thunderbird put on his Sunday-best war outfit to let me see
him, and he was splendid to look at, with his face painted red
and bright and intense like a fire coal and a valance of eagle
feathers from the top of his head all down his back, and he
had his tomahawk, too, and his pipe, which has a stem which
is longer than my arm, and I never had such a good time in
an Indian camp in my life, and I learned a lot of words of the
language, and next day B.B. took me to the camp out on the
Plains, four miles, and I had another good time and got acquainted with some more Indians and dogs; and the big chief,
by the name of White Cloud, gave me a pretty little bow and
arrows and I gave him my red sash ribbon, and in four days
I could shoot very well with it and beat any white boy of my
size at the post; and I have been to those camps plenty of times
since; and I have learned to ride, too, B.B. taught me, and
every day he practices me and praises me, and every time I
do better than ever he lets me have a scamper on Soldier Boy,
and *that's* the last agony of pleasure! for he is the charmingest
horse, and so beautiful and shiny and black, and hasn't another color on him anywhere, except a white star in his forehead, not just an imitation star, but a real one, with four
points, shaped exactly like a star that's handmade, and if you
should cover him all up but his star you would know him
anywhere, even in Jerusalem or Australia, by that. And I got
acquainted with a good many of the Seventh Cavalry, and the
dragoons, and officers, and families, and horses, in the first
few days, and some more in the next few and the next few and
the next few, and now I know more soldiers and horses than
you can think, no matter how hard you try. I am keeping up

11

my studies every now and then, but there isn't much time for it. I love you so! and I send you a hug and a kiss.

Cathy

P.S.—I belong to the Seventh Cavalry and Ninth Dragoons; I am an officer, too, and do not have to work on account of not getting any wages.

5   GENERAL ALISON TO MERCEDES

She has been with us a good nice long time now. You are troubled about your sprite because this is such a wild frontier, hundreds of miles from civilization, and peopled only by wandering tribes of savages? You fear for her safety? Give yourself no uneasiness about her. Dear me, she's in a nursery! and she's got more than eighteen hundred nurses. It would distress the garrison to suspect that you think they can't take care of her. They think they can. They would tell you so themselves. You see, the Seventh Cavalry has never had a child of its very own before, and neither has the Ninth Dragoons; and so they are like all new mothers, they think there is no other child like theirs, no other child so wonderful, none that is so worthy to be faithfully and tenderly looked after and protected. These bronzed veterans of mine are very good mothers, I think, and wiser than some other mothers; for they let her take lots of risks, and it is a good education for her; and the more risks she takes and comes successfully out of, the prouder they are of her. They adopted her, with grave and formal military ceremonies of their own invention—solemnities is the truer word; solemnities that were so profoundly solemn and earnest that the spectacle would have been comical if it hadn't been so touching. It was a good show, and as stately and complex as guard mount and the trooping of the colors; and it had its own special music, composed for the occasion by the bandmaster of the Seventh; and the child was as serious as the most serious war-worn soldier of them all;

and finally when they throned her upon the shoulder of the oldest veteran, and pronounced her "well and truly adopted," and the bands struck up and all saluted and she saluted in return, it was better and more moving than any kindred thing I have seen on the stage, because stage things are make-believe, but this was real and the players' hearts were in it.

It happened several weeks ago, and was followed by some additional solemnities. The men created a couple of new ranks, thitherto unknown to the army regulations, and conferred them upon Cathy, with ceremonies suitable to a duke. So now she is Corporal General of the Seventh Cavalry, and Flag Lieutenant of the Ninth Dragoons, with the privilege (decreed by the men) of writing U.S.A. after her name! Also, they presented her a pair of shoulder straps—both dark blue, the one with F.L. on it, the other with C.G. Also, a sword. She wears them. Finally, they granted her the *salute.* I am witness that that ceremony is faithfully observed by both parties—and most gravely and decorously, too. I have never seen a soldier smile yet, while delivering it, nor Cathy in returning it.

Ostensibly I was not present at these proceedings, and am ignorant of them; but I was where I could see. I was afraid of one thing—the jealousy of the other children of the post; but there is nothing of that, I am glad to say. On the contrary, they are proud of their comrade and her honors. It is a surprising thing, but it is true. The children are devoted to Cathy, for she has turned their dull frontier life into a sort of continuous festival; also they know her for a staunch and steady friend, a friend who can always be depended upon and does not change with the weather.

She has become a rather extraordinary rider, under the tutorship of a more than extraordinary teacher—B.B., which is her pet name for Buffalo Bill. She pronounces it *beeby.* He has not only taught her seventeen ways of breaking her neck, but twenty-two ways of avoiding it. He has infused into her the best and surest protection of a horseman—*confidence.* He did it gradually, systematically, little by little, a step at a time, and each step made sure before the next was essayed. And so he inched her along up through terrors that had been discounted by training before she reached them, and therefore were not recognizable as terrors when she got to them. Well, she is a daring little rider now, and is perfect in what she knows of horsemanship. By and by she will know the art like a West Point cadet, and will exercise it as fearlessly. She doesn't know anything about sidesaddles. Does that distress you? And she is a fine performer, without any saddle at all. Does that discomfort you? Do not let it; she is not in any danger, I give you my word.

You said that if my heart was old and tired she would refresh it, and you said truly. I do not know how I got along without her before. I was a forlorn old tree, but now that this blossoming vine has wound itself about me and become the life of my life, it is very different. As a furnisher of business for me and for Mammy Dorcas she is exhaustlessly competent, but I like my share of it and of course Dorcas likes hers, for Dorcas "raised" George, and Cathy is George over again in so many ways that she brings back Dorcas's youth and the joys of that long-vanished time. My father tried to set Dorcas free twenty years ago, when we still lived in Virginia, but without success; she considered herself a member of the family, and wouldn't go. And so, a member of the family she remained, and has held that position unchallenged ever since, and holds it now; for when my mother sent her here from San Bernardino when we learned that Cathy was coming, she only changed from one division of the family to the other. She has the warm heart of her race, and its lavish affections, and when Cathy arrived the pair were mother and child in five minutes, and that is what they are to date and will continue. Dorcas really thinks she raised George, and that is one of her prides, but perhaps it was a mutual raising, for their ages were the same—thirteen years short of mine. But they were playmates, at any rate; as regards that, there is no room for dispute.

Cathy thinks Dorcas is the best Catholic in America except herself. She could not pay anyone a higher compliment than that, and Dorcas could not receive one that would please her better. Dorcas is satisfied that there has never been a more wonderful child than Cathy. She has conceived the curious idea that Cathy is *twins,* and that one of them is a boy twin and failed to get segregated—got submerged, is the idea. To argue with her that this is nonsense is a waste of breath—her mind is made up, and arguments do not affect it. She says:

"Look at her; she loves dolls, and girl plays, and every-thing a girl loves, and she's gentle and sweet, and ain't cruel to dumb brutes—now that's the girl twin, but she loves boy plays, and drums and fifes and soldiering, and rough-riding, and ain't afraid of anybody or anything—and that's the boy twin; 'deed you needn't tell *me* she's only *one* child; no, sir, she's twins, and one of them got shet up out of sight. Out of sight, but that don't make any difference, that boy is in there, and you can see him look out of her eyes when her temper is up."

Then Dorcas went on, in her simple and earnest way, to furnish illustrations.

"Look at that raven, Marse Tom. Would anybody be-friend a raven but that child? Of course they wouldn't; it ain't natural. Well, the Injun boy had the raven tied up, and was all the time plaguing it and starving it, and she pitied the po' thing, and tried to buy it from the boy, and the tears was in her eyes. That was the girl twin, you see. She offered him her thimble, and he flung it down; she offered him all the dough-nuts she had, which was two, and he flung them down; she offered him half a paper of pins, worth forty ravens, and he made a mouth at her and jabbed one of them in the raven's back. That was the limit, you know. It called for the other twin. Her eyes blazed up, and she jumped for him like a wildcat, and when she was done with him she was rags and he wasn't anything but an allegory. That was most undoubtedly the other twin, you see, coming to the front. No, sir; don't tell *me* he ain't in there. I've seen him with my own eyes—and plenty of times, at that."

"Allegory? What is an allegory?"

"I don't know, Marse Tom, it's one of her words; she loves the big ones, you know, and I pick them up from her; they sound good and I can't help it."

"What happened after she had converted the boy into an allegory?"

"Why, she untied the raven and confiscated him by force and fetched him home, and left the doughnuts and things on the ground. Petted him, of course, like she does with every creature. In two days she had him so stuck after her that she—well, *you* know how he follows her everywhere, and sets on her shoulder often when she rides her breakneck rampages—all of which is the girl twin to the front, you see—and he does what he pleases, and is up to all kinds of devilment, and is a perfect nuisance in the kitchen. Well, they all stand it, but they wouldn't if it was another person's bird."

Here she began to chuckle comfortably, and presently she said:

"Well, you know, she's a nuisance herself, Miss Cathy is, she *is* so busy, and into everything, like that bird. It's all just as innocent, you know, and she don't mean any harm, and is so good and dear; and it ain't her fault, it's her nature; her interest is always a-working and always red-hot, and she *can't* keep quiet. Well, yesterday it was 'Please, Miss Cathy, don't do that'; and, 'Please, Miss Cathy, let that alone'; and, 'Please, Miss Cathy, don't make so much noise'; and so on and so on, till I reckon I had found fault fourteen times in fifteen minutes; then she looked up at me with her big brown eyes that can plead so, and said in that odd little foreign way that goes to your heart:

" 'Please, Mammy, make me a compliment.' "

"And of course you did it, you old fool?"

"Marse Tom, I just grabbed her up to my breast and says, 'Oh, you po' dear little motherless thing, you ain't got a fault in the world, and you can do anything you want to, and tear the house down, and yo' old black mammy won't say a word!' "

"Why, of course, of course—*I* knew you'd spoil the child."

She brushed away her tears, and said with dignity:

"Spoil the child? spoil *that* child, Marse Tom? There can't *anybody* spoil her. She's the king bee of this post, and everybody pets her and is her slave, and yet, as you know, your own self, she ain't the least little bit spoiled." Then she eased her mind with this retort: "Marse Tom, she makes you do anything she wants to, and you can't deny it; so if she could be spoilt, she'd been spoilt long ago, because you are the very *worst*! Look at that pile of cats in your chair, and you sitting on a candle box, just as patient; it's because they're her cats."

If Dorcas were a soldier, I could punish her for such large frankness as that. I changed the subject, and made her resume her illustrations. She had scored against me fairly, and I wasn't going to cheapen her victory by disputing it. She proceeded to offer this incident in evidence on her twin theory:

"Two weeks ago when she got her finger mashed open, she turned pretty pale with the pain, but she never said a word. I took her in my lap, and the surgeon sponged off the blood and took a needle and thread and began to sew it up; it had to have a lot of stitches, and each one made her scrunch a little, but she never let go a sound. At last the surgeon was so full of admiration that he said, 'Well, you *are* a brave little thing!' and she said, just as ca'm and simple as if she was talking about the weather, 'There isn't anybody braver but the Cid!' You see? it was the boy twin that the surgeon was a-dealing with."

"Who is the Cid?"

17

"I don't know, sir—at least only what she says. She's always talking about him, and says he was the bravest hero Spain ever had, or any other country. They have it up and down, the children do, she standing up for the Cid, and they working George Washington for all he is worth."

"Do they quarrel?"

"No; it's only disputing, and bragging, the way children do. They want her to be an American, but she can't be anything but a Spaniard, she says. You see, her mother was always longing for home, po' thing! and thinking about it, and so the child is just as much a Spaniard as if she'd always lived there. She thinks she remembers how Spain looked, but I reckon she don't, because she was only a baby when they moved to France. She is very proud to be a Spaniard."

Does that please you, Mercedes? Very well, be content; your niece is loyal to her allegiance: her mother laid deep the foundations of her love for Spain, and she will go back to you as good a Spaniard as you are yourself. She had made me promise to take her to you for a long visit when the War Office retires me.

I attend to her studies myself; has she told you that? Yes, I am her schoolmaster, and she makes pretty good progress, I think, everything considered. Everything considered— being translated—means holidays. But the fact is, she was not born for study, and it comes hard. Hard for me, too; it hurts me like a physical pain to see that free spirit of the air and the sunshine laboring and grieving over a book; and sometimes when I find her gazing far away toward the plains and the blue mountains with the longing in her eyes, I have to throw open the prison doors; I can't help it. A quaint little scholar she is, and makes plenty of blunders. Once I put the question:

"What does the czar govern?"

She rested her elbow on her knee and her chin on her hand and took that problem under deep consideration. Presently she looked up and answered, with a rising inflection implying a shade of uncertainty,

"The dative case?"

Here are a couple of her expositions, which were delivered with tranquil confidence:

"*Chaplain,* diminutive of chap. *Lass* is masculine, *lassie* is feminine."

She is not a genius, you see, but just a normal child; they all make mistakes of that sort. There is a glad light in her eye which is pretty to see when she finds herself able to answer a question promptly and accurately, without any hesitation; as, for instance, this morning:

"Cathy dear, what is a cube?"

"Why, a native of Cuba."

She still drops a foreign word into her talk now and then, and there is still a subtle foreign flavor or fragrance about even her exactest English—and long may this abide! for it has for me a charm that is very pleasant. Sometimes her English is daintily prim and bookish and captivating. She has a child's sweet tooth, but for her health's sake I try to keep its inspirations under check. She is obedient—as is proper for a titled and recognized military personage, which she is—but the chain presses sometimes. For instance, we were out for a walk, and passed by some bushes that were freighted with wild gooseberries. Her face brightened and she put her hands together and delivered herself of this speech, most feelingly:

"Oh, if I was permitted a vice it would be the *gourmandise!*"

Could I resist that? No. I gave her a gooseberry.

You ask about her languages. They take care of themselves; they will not get rusty here; our regiments are not made up of natives alone—far from it. And she is picking up Indian tongues diligently.

6   SOLDIER BOY AND THE MEXICAN PLUG

"When did you come?"

"Arrived at sundown."

"Where from?"

"Salt Lake."

"Are you in the service?"

"No. Trade."

"Pirate trade, I reckon."

"What do you know about it?"

"I saw you when you came. I recognized your master. He is a bad sort. Trap robber, horse thief, squaw man, renegado —Hank Butters—I know him very well. Stole you, didn't he?"

"Well, it amounted to that."

"I thought so. Where is his pard?"

"He stopped at White Cloud's camp."

"He is another of the same stripe, is Blake Haskins." (*Aside.*) They are laying for Buffalo Bill again, I guess. (*Aloud.*) "What is your name?"

"Which one?"

"Have you got more than one?"

"I get a new one every time I'm stolen. I used to have an honest name, but that was early; I've forgotten it. Since then I've had thirteen aliases."

"Aliases? What is alias?"

"A false name."

"Alias. It's a fine large word, and is in my line; it has quite a learned and cerebrospinal incandescent sound. Are you educated?"

"Well, no, I can't claim it. I can take down bars, I can distinguish oats from shoe pegs, I can blaspheme a saddle boil with the college-bred, and I know a few other things—not many; I have had no chance, I have always had to work; besides, I am of low birth and no family. You speak my dialect like a native, but you are not a Mexican plug, you are a gentleman, I can see that; and educated, of course."

"Yes, I am of old family, and not illiterate. I am a fossil."

"A which?"

"Fossil. The first horses were fossils. They date back two million years."

"Gr-eat sand and sagebrush! do you mean it?"

"Yes, it is true. The bones of my ancestors are held in reverence and worship, even by men. They do not leave them exposed to the weather when they find them, but carry them three thousand miles and enshrine them in their temples of learning, and worship them."

"It is wonderful! I knew you must be a person of distinction, by your fine presence and courtly address, and by the fact that you are not subjected to the indignity of hobbles, like myself and the rest. Would you tell me your name?"

"You have probably heard of it—Soldier Boy."

"What!—the renowned, the illustrious?"

"Even so."

"It takes my breath! Little did I dream that ever I should stand face to face with the possessor of that great name. Buffalo Bill's horse! Known from the Canadian border to the deserts of Arizona, and from the eastern marches of the Great Plains to the foothills of the Sierra! Truly this is a memorable day. You still serve the celebrated Chief of Scouts?"

"I am still his property, but he has lent me, for a time, to the most noble, the most gracious, the most excellent, her Excellency Catherine, Corporal General Seventh Cavalry and Flag Lieutenant Ninth Dragoons, U.S.A.—on whom be peace!"

"Amen. Did you say *her* Excellency?"

"The same. A Spanish lady, sweet blossom of a ducal house. And truly a wonder; knowing everything, capable of everything; speaking all the languages, master of all sciences, a mind without horizons, a heart of gold, the glory of her race! On whom be peace!"

"Amen. It is marvelous!"

"Verily. I knew many things, she has taught me others. I am educated. I will tell you about her."

"I listen—I am enchanted."

"I will tell a plain tale, calmly, without excitement, without eloquence. When she had been here four or five weeks she was already erudite in military things, and they made her an officer—a double officer. She rode the drill every day, like any soldier; and she could take the bugle and direct the evolutions herself. Then, on a day, there was a grand race, for prizes—none to enter but the children. Seventeen children entered, and she was the youngest. Three girls, fourteen boys—good riders all. It was a steeplechase, with four hurdles, all pretty high. The first prize was a most cunning half-grown silver bugle, and mighty pretty, with red silk cord and tassels. Buffalo Bill was very anxious; for he had taught her to ride, and he did most dearly want her to win that race, for the glory of it. So he wanted her to ride me, but she wouldn't; and she reproached him, and said it was unfair and unright, and taking advantage; for what horse in this post or any other could stand a chance against me? and she was very severe with him, and said, 'You ought to be ashamed—you are proposing to me conduct unbecoming an officer and a gentleman.' So he just tossed her up in the air about thirty feet and caught her as she came down, and said he *was* ashamed; and put up his handkerchief and pretended to cry, which nearly broke her heart, and she petted him, and begged him to forgive her, and said she would do anything in the world he could ask but that; but he said he ought to go hang himself, and he *must,* if he could get a rope; it was nothing but right he should, for he never, never could forgive himself; and then *she* began to cry, and they both sobbed, the way you could hear him a mile, and she clinging around his neck and pleading, till at last he was comforted a little, and gave his solemn promise he wouldn't hang himself till after the race; and wouldn't do it at all if she

won it, which made her happy, and she said she would win
it or die in the saddle; so then everything was pleasant again
and both of them content. He can't help playing jokes on her,
he is so fond of her and she is so innocent and unsuspecting;
and when she finds it out she cuffs him and is in a fury, but
presently forgives him because it's *him;* and maybe the very
next day she's caught with another joke; you see she can't
learn any better, because she hasn't any deceit in her, and that
kind aren't ever expecting it in another person.

"It was a grand race. The whole post was there, and there
was such another whooping and shouting when the seventeen
kids came flying down the turf and sailing over the hurdles—
oh, beautiful to see! Halfway down, it was kind of neck and
neck, and anybody's race and nobody's. Then, what should
happen but a cow steps out and puts her head down to munch
grass, with her broadside to the battalion, and they a-coming
like the wind; they split apart to flank her, but *she?*—why, she
drove the spurs home and soared over that cow like a bird!
and on she went, and cleared the last hurdle solitary and
alone, the army letting loose the grand yell, and she skipped
from the horse the same as if he had been standing still, and
made her bow, and everybody crowded around to congratu-
late, and they gave her the bugle, and she put it to her lips
and blew 'Boots and Saddles' to see how it would go, and
B.B. was as proud as you can't think! And he said, 'Take
Soldier Boy, and don't pass him back till I ask for him!' and
I can tell you he wouldn't have said that to any other person
on this planet. That was two months and more ago, and nobody has been on my back since but the Corporal General,
Seventh Cavalry and Flag Lieutenant of the Ninth Dragoons,
U.S.A.—on whom be peace!"

"Amen. I listen—tell me more."

"She set to work and organized the sixteen, and called
it the First Battalion, Rocky Mountain Rangers, U.S.A., and
she wanted to be bugler, but they elected her Lieutenant

General *and* Bugler. So she ranks her uncle the commandant, who is only a Brigadier. And doesn't she train those little people! Ask the Indians, ask the traders, ask the soldiers; they'll tell you. She has been at it from the first day. Every morning they go clattering down into the plain, and there she sits on my back with her bugle at her mouth and sounds the orders and puts them through the evolutions for an hour or more; and it is too beautiful for anything to see those ponies dissolve from one formation into another, and waltz about, and break, and scatter, and form again, always moving, always graceful, now trotting, now galloping, and so on, sometimes nearby, sometimes in the distance, all just like a state ball, you know, and sometimes she can't hold herself any longer, but sounds the charge, and turns me loose! And you can take my word for it, if the battalion hasn't *too* much of a start we catch up and go over the breastworks with the front line.

"Yes, they are soldiers, those little people; and healthy, too, not ailing anymore, the way they used to be sometimes. It's because of her drill. She's got a fort now—Fort Fanny Marsh. Major General Tommy Drake planned it out, and the Seventh and Dragoons built it. Tommy is the Colonel's son, and is fifteen and the oldest in the Battalion; Fanny Marsh is Brigadier General, and is next oldest—over thirteen. She is daughter of Captain Marsh, Company B, Seventh Cavalry. Lieutenant General Alison is the youngest by considerable; I think she is about nine and a half or three-quarters. Her military rig, as Lieutenant General, isn't for business, it's for dress parade, because the ladies made it. They say they got it out of the Middle Ages—out of a book—and it is all red and blue and white silks and satins and velvets; tights, trunks, sword, doublet with slashed sleeves, short cape, cap with just one feather in it; I've heard them name these things; they got them out of the book; she's dressed like a page, of old times, they say. It's the daintiest outfit that ever was—you will say so, when you see it. She's lovely in it—oh, just a dream! In some ways she is just her age, but in others she's as old as her uncle, I think. She is very learned. She teaches her uncle his book. I have seen her sitting by with the book and reciting to him what is in it, so that he can learn to do it himself.

"Every Saturday she hires little Injuns to garrison her fort; then she lays siege to it, and makes military approaches by make-believe trenches in make-believe night, and finally at make-believe dawn she draws her sword and sounds the assault and takes it by storm. It is for practice. And she has invented a bugle call all by herself, out of her own head, and it's a stirring one, and the prettiest in the service. It's to call *me*—it's never used for anything else. She taught it to me, and told me what it says: 'It is I, Soldier—come!' and when those thrilling notes come floating down the distance I hear them without fail, even if I am two miles away; and then—oh, then you should see my heels get down to business!

"And she has taught me how to say good morning and good night to her, which is by lifting my right hoof for her to shake; and also how to say good-bye; I do that with my left foot—but only for practice, because there hasn't been any but make-believe good-byeing yet, and I hope there won't ever be. It would make me cry if I ever had to put up my left foot in earnest. She has taught me how to salute, and I can do it as well as a soldier. I bow my head low, and lay my right hoof against my cheek. She taught me that because I got into disgrace once, through ignorance. I am privileged, because I am known to be honorable and trustworthy, and because I have a distinguished record in the service; so they don't hobble me nor tie me to stakes or shut me tight in stables, but let me wander around to suit myself. Well, trooping the colors is a very solemn ceremony, and everybody must stand uncovered when the flag goes by, the commandant and all; and once I was there, and ignorantly walked across right in front of the band, which was an awful disgrace. Ah, the Lieutenant General was so ashamed, and so distressed that I should have done such a thing before all the world, that she couldn't keep the tears back; and then she taught me the salute, so that if I ever did any other unmilitary act through ignorance I could do my salute and she believed everybody would think it was apology enough and would not press the matter. It is very nice and distinguished; no other horse can do it; often the men salute me, and I return it. I am privileged to be present when the Rocky Mountain Rangers troop the colors and I stand solemn, like the children, and I salute when the flag goes by. Of course when she goes to her fort her sentries sing out 'Turn out the guard!' and then . . . do you catch that refreshing early-morning whiff from the mountain pines and the wildflowers? The night is far spent; we'll hear the bugles before long. Dorcas, the black woman, is very good and nice; she takes care of the Lieutenant General, and is Brigadier General Alison's mother, which makes her mother-in-law to the Lieutenant General. That is what Shekels says. At least it is what I think he says, though I never can understand him quite clearly. He—"

"Who is Shekels?"

"The Seventh Cavalry dog. I mean, if he *is* a dog. His father was a coyote and his mother was a wildcat. It doesn't really make a dog out of him, does it?"

"Not a real dog, I should think. Only a kind of a general dog, at most, I reckon. Though this is a matter of ichthyology, I suppose; and if it is, it is out of my depth, and so my opinion is not valuable, and I don't claim much consideration for it."

"It isn't ichthyology; it is dogmatics, which is still more difficult and tangled up. Dogmatics always are."

"Dogmatics is quite beyond me, quite; so I am not competing. But on general principles it is my opinion that a colt out of a coyote and a wildcat is no square dog, but doubtful. That is my hand, and I stand pat."

"Well, it is as far as I can go myself, and be fair and conscientious. I have always regarded him as a doubtful dog, and so has Potter. Potter is the Great Dane. Potter says he is no dog, and not even poultry—though I do not go quite so far as that."

"And I wouldn't, myself. Poultry is one of those things which no person can get to the bottom of, there is so much of it and such variety. It is just wings, and wings, and wings, till you are weary: turkeys, and geese, and bats, and butterflies, and angels, and grasshoppers, and flying fish, and—well, there is really no end to the tribe; it gives me the heaves just to think of it. But this one hasn't any wings, has he?"

"No."

"Well, then, in my belief he is more likely to be dog than poultry. I have not heard of poultry that hadn't wings. Wings is the *sign* of poultry; it is what you tell poultry by. Look at the mosquito."

"What do you reckon he is, then? He must be something."

"Why, he could be a reptile; anything that hasn't wings is a reptile."

"Who told you that?"

"Nobody told me, but I overheard it."

"Where did you overhear it?"

"Years ago. I was with the Philadelphia Institute expedition in the Badlands under Professor Cope, hunting mastodon bones, and I overheard him say, his own self, that any plantigrade circumflex vertebrate bacterium that hadn't wings and was uncertain was a reptile. Well, then, has this dog any wings? No. Is he a plantigrade circumflex vertebrate bacterium? Maybe so, maybe not; but without ever having seen him, and judging only by his illegal and spectacular parentage, I will bet the odds of a bale of hay to a bran mash that he looks it. Finally, is he uncertain? That is the point—is he uncertain? I will leave it to you if you have ever heard of a more uncertainer dog than what this one is."

"No, I never have."

"Well, then, he's a reptile. That's settled."

"Why, look here, whatsyourname—"

"Last alias, 'Mongrel.'"

"A good one, too. I was going to say, you are better educated than you have been pretending to be. I like cultured society, and I shall cultivate your acquaintance. Now as to Shekels, whenever you want to know about any private thing that is going on at this post or in White Cloud's camp or Thunderbird's, he can tell you; and if you make friends with him he'll be glad to, for he is a born gossip, and picks up all the tittle-tattle. Being the whole Seventh Cavalry's reptile, he doesn't belong to anybody in particular, and hasn't any military duties; so he comes and goes as he pleases, and is popular with all the house cats and other authentic sources of private information. He understands all the languages, and talks them all, too. With an accent like gritting your teeth, it is true, and with a grammar that is no improvement on blasphemy—still, with practice you get at the meat of what he says, and it serves . . . Hark! That's the reveille. . . .

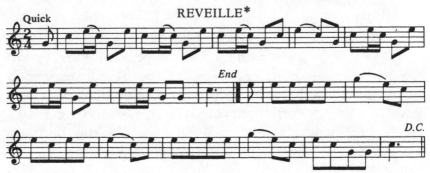

REVEILLE*

"Faint and far, but isn't it clear, isn't it sweet? There's no music like the bugle to stir the blood, in the still solemnity of the morning twilight, with the dim plain stretching away to

*At West Point the bugle is supposed to be saying:
    "I can't get 'em up,
    I can't get 'em up,
    I can't get 'em up in the morning!"

nothing and the spectral mountains slumbering against the sky. You'll hear another note in a minute—faint and far and clear, like the other one, and sweeter still, you'll notice. Wait . . . listen. There it goes! It says, 'It is I, Soldier—come!' . . .

SOLDIER BOY'S BUGLE CALL

. . . Now then, watch me leave a blue streak behind!"

7 SOLDIER BOY AND SHEKELS

"Did you do as I told you? Did you look up the Mexican plug?"

"Yes, I made his acquaintance before night and got his friendship."

"I liked him. Did you?"

"Not at first. He took me for a reptile, and it troubled me, because I didn't know whether it was a compliment or not. I couldn't ask him, because it would look ignorant. So I didn't say anything, and soon I liked him very well indeed. Was it a compliment, do you think?"

"Yes, that is what it was. They are very rare, the reptiles; very few left, nowadays."

"Is that so? What is a reptile?"

"It is a plantigrade circumflex vertebrate bacterium that hasn't any wings and is uncertain."

"Well, it—it sounds fine, it surely does."

"And it *is* fine. You may be thankful you are one."

"I am. It seems wonderfully grand and elegant for a person that is so humble as I am; but I am thankful, I am indeed, and will try to live up to it. It is hard to remember. Will you say it again, please, and say it slow?"

"Plantigrade circumflex vertebrate bacterium that hasn't any wings and is uncertain."

"It *is* beautiful, anybody must grant it; beautiful, and of a noble sound. I hope it will not make me proud and stuck-up—I should not like to be that. It is much more distinguished and honorable to be a reptile than a dog, don't you think, Soldier?"

"Why, there's no comparison. It is awfully aristocratic. Often a duke is called a reptile; it is set down so, in history."

"Isn't that grand! Potter wouldn't ever associate with me, but I reckon he'll be glad to when he finds out what I am."

"You can depend upon it."

"I will thank Mongrel for this. He is a very good sort, for a Mexican plug. Don't you think he is?"

"It is my opinion of him; and as for his birth, he cannot help that. We cannot all be reptiles, we cannot all be fossils; we have to take what comes and be thankful it is no worse. It is the true philosophy."

"For those others?"

"Stick to the subject, please. Did it turn out that my suspicions were right?"

"Yes, perfectly right. Mongrel has heard them planning. They are after B.B.'s life, for running them out of Medicine Bow and taking their stolen horses away from them."

"Well, they'll get him yet, for sure."

"Not if he keeps a sharp lookout."

"*He* keep a sharp lookout! He never does; he despises them, and all their kind. His life is always being threatened, and so it has come to be monotonous."

"Does he know they are here?"

"Oh, yes, he knows it. He is always the earliest to know who comes and who goes. But he cares nothing for them and their threats; he only laughs when people warn him. They'll shoot him from behind a tree the first he knows. Did Mongrel tell you their plans?"

"Yes. They have found out that he starts for Fort Clayton day after tomorrow, with one of his scouts; so they will leave tomorrow, letting on to go south, but they will fetch around north all in good time."

"Shekels, I don't like the look of it."

8   THE SCOUT START: B.B. AND LIEUTENANT GENERAL ALISON

B.B. (*saluting*): "Good! handsomely done! The Seventh couldn't beat it! You do certainly handle your Rangers like an expert, General. And where are you bound?"

"Four miles on the trail to Fort Clayton."

"Glad am I, dear! What's the idea of it?"

"Guard of honor for you and Thorndike."

"Bless—your—*heart*! I'd rather have it from you than from the commander in chief of the armies of the United States, you incomparable little soldier!—and I don't need to take any oath to that, for you believe it."

"I *thought* you'd like it, B.B."

"*Like* it? Well, I should say so! Now then—all ready— sound the advance, and away we go!"

9   SOLDIER BOY AND SHEKELS AGAIN

Well, this is the way it happened. We did the escort duty; then we came back and struck for the plain and put the Rangers through a rousing drill—oh, for hours! Then we sent them home under Brigadier General Fanny Marsh; then the Lieutenant General and I went off on a gallop over the plains for about three hours, and were lazying along home in the middle of the afternoon, when we met Jimmy Slade, the drummer-boy, and he saluted and asked the Lieutenant General if she had heard the news, and she said no, and he said:

" 'Buffalo Bill has been ambushed and badly shot this

side of Clayton, and Thorndike the scout, too; Bill couldn't travel, but Thorndike could, and he brought the news, and Sergeant Wilkes and six men of Company B are gone, two hours ago, hotfoot, to get Bill. And they say—'

" '*Go!*' she shouted to me—and I went."

"Fast?"

"Don't ask foolish questions. It was an awful pace. For four hours nothing happened, and not a word said, except that now and then she said, 'Keep it up, Boy, keep it up, sweetheart; we'll save him!' I kept it up. Well, when the dark shut down, in the rugged hills, that poor little chap had been tearing around in the saddle all day, and I noticed by the slack knee pressure that she was tired and tottery, and I got dreadfully afraid; but every time I tried to slow down and let her go to sleep, so I could stop, she hurried me up again; and so, sure enough, at last over she went!

"Ah, that was a fix to be in! for she lay there and didn't stir, and what was I to do? I couldn't leave her to fetch help, on account of the wolves. There was nothing to do but stand by. It was dreadful. I was afraid she was killed, poor little thing! But she wasn't. She came to, by and by, and said, 'Kiss me, Soldier,' and those were blessed words. I kissed her—often; I am used to that, and we like it. But she didn't get up, and I was worried. She fondled my nose with her hand, and talked to me, and called me endearing names—which is her way—but she caressed with the same hand all the time. The other arm was broken, you see, but I didn't know it, and she didn't mention it. She didn't want to distress me, you know.

"Soon the big gray wolves came, and hung around, and you could hear them snarl, and snap at each other, but you couldn't see anything of them except their eyes, which shone in the dark like sparks and stars. The Lieutenant General said, 'If I had the Rocky Mountain Rangers here, we would make those creatures climb a tree.' Then she made believe that the Rangers were in hearing, and put up her bugle and blew the

'Assembly'; and then, 'Boots and Saddles'; then the 'Trot'; 'Gallop'; *'Charge!'* Then she blew the 'Retreat,' and said, 'That's for you, you rebels; the Rangers don't ever retreat!'

"The music frightened them away, but they were hungry, and kept coming back. And of course they got bolder and bolder, which is their way. It went on for an hour, then the tired child went to sleep, and it was pitiful to hear her moan and nestle, and I couldn't do anything for her. All the time I was laying for the wolves. They are in my line; I have had experience. At last the boldest one ventured within my lines, and I landed him among his friends with some of his skull still on him, and they did the rest. In the next hour I got a couple more, and they went the way of the first one, down the throats of the detachment. That satisfied the survivors, and they went away and left us in peace.

"We hadn't any more adventures, though I kept awake all night and was ready. From midnight on the child got very restless, and out of her head, and moaned, and said, 'Water, water—thirsty'; and now and then, 'Kiss me, Soldier'; and sometimes she was in her fort and giving orders to her garrison; and once she was in Spain, and thought her mother was with her. People say a horse can't cry; but they don't know, because we cry inside.

"It was an hour after sunup that I heard the boys coming, and recognized the hoofbeats of Pomp and Caesar and Jerry, old mates of mine; and a welcomer sound there couldn't ever be.

"Buffalo Bill was in a horse litter, with his leg broken by a bullet, and Mongrel and Blake Haskins's horse were doing the work. Buffalo Bill and Thorndike had killed both of those toughs.

"When they got to us, and Buffalo Bill saw the child lying there so white, he said, 'My God!' and the sound of his voice brought her to herself, and she gave a little cry of pleasure and struggled to get up, but couldn't, and the soldiers gathered her up like the tenderest women, and their eyes were wet and they were not ashamed, when they saw her arm dangling; and so were Buffalo Bill's, and when they laid her in his arms he said, 'My darling, how does this come?' and she said, 'We came to save you, but I was tired, and couldn't keep awake, and fell off and hurt myself, and couldn't get on again.' 'You came to save me, you dear little rat? It was too lovely of you!' 'Yes, and Soldier stood by me, which you know he would, and protected me from the wolves; and if he got a chance he kicked the life out of some of them—for you know he would, B.B.' The sergeant said, 'He laid out three of them, sir, and here's the bones to show for it.' 'He's a grand horse,' said B.B.; 'he's the grandest horse that ever was! and has saved your life, Lieutenant General Alison, and shall protect it the rest of his life—he's yours for a kiss!' He got it, along with a passion of delight, and he said, 'You are feeling better now, little Spaniard—do you think you could blow the Advance?' She put up the bugle to do it, but he said wait a minute first. Then he and the sergeant set her arm and put it in splints, she wincing but not whimpering; then we took up the march for home, and that's the end of the tale; and I'm her horse. Isn't she a brick, Shekels?''

"Brick? She's more than a brick, more than a thousand bricks—she's a reptile!''

"It's a compliment out of your heart, Shekels. God bless you for it!''

10   GENERAL ALISON AND DORCAS

"Too much company for her, Marse Tom. Betwixt you, and Shekels, and the Colonel's wife, and the Cid—''

"The Cid? Oh, I remember—the raven.''

"—and Mrs. Captain Marsh and Famine and Pestilence the baby coyotes, and Sour Mash and her pups, and Sardanapalus and her kittens—hang these names she gives the creatures, they warp my jaw—and Potter: you—all sitting around *in* the house, and Soldier Boy at the window the entire time, it's a wonder to me she comes along as well as she does. She—"

"You want her all to yourself, you stingy old thing!"

"Marse Tom, you know better. It's too much company. And then the idea of her receiving reports all the time from her officers, and acting upon them, and giving orders, the same as if she was well! It ain't good for her, and the surgeon don't like it, and tried to persuade her not to and couldn't; and when he *ordered* her, she was that outraged and indignant, and was very severe on him, and accused him of insubordination, and said it didn't become him to give orders to an officer of her rank. Well, he saw he had excited her more and done more harm than all the rest put together, so he was vexed at himself and wished he had kept still. Doctors *don't* know much, and that's a fact. She's too much interested in things— she ought to rest more. She's all the time sending messages to B.B., and to soldiers and Injuns and whatnot, and to the animals."

"To the animals?"

"Yes, sir."

"Who carries them?"

"Sometimes Potter, but mostly it's Shekels."

"Now come! who can find fault with such pretty make-believe as that?"

"But it ain't make-believe, Marse Tom. She does send them."

"Yes, I don't doubt that part of it."

"Do you doubt they get them, sir?"

"Certainly. Don't you?"

"No, sir. Animals talk to one another. I know it perfectly well, Marse Tom, and I ain't saying it by guess."

"What a curious superstition!"

"It ain't a superstition, Marse Tom. Look at that Shekels—look at him, *now*. Is he listening, or ain't he? *Now* you see! He's turned his head away. It's because he was caught—caught in the act. I'll ask you—could a Christian look any more ashamed than what he looks now?—*Lay down!* You see? he was going to sneak out. Don't tell *me*, Marse Tom! If animals don't talk, I miss *my* guess. And Shekels is the worst. He goes and tells the animals everything that happens in the officers' quarters; and if he's short of facts, he invents them. He hasn't any more principle than a blue jay; and as for morals, he's empty. Look at him now; look at him grovel. He knows what I am saying, and he knows it's the truth. You see, yourself, that he can feel shame; it's the only virtue he's got. It's wonderful how they find out everything that's going on—the animals. They—"

"Do you really believe they do, Dorcas?"

"I don't only just believe it, Marse Tom, I know it. Day before yesterday they knew something was going to happen. They were that excited, and whispering around together; why, anybody could see that they—But my! I must get back to her, and I haven't got to my errand yet."

"What is it, Dorcas?"

"Well, it's two or three things. One is, the doctor don't salute when he comes. . . . Now, Marse Tom, it ain't anything to laugh at, and so—"

"Well, then, forgive me; I didn't mean to laugh—I got caught unprepared."

"You see, she don't want to hurt the doctor's feelings, so she don't say anything to him about it; but she is always polite, herself, and it hurts that kind for people to be rude to them."

"I'll have that doctor hanged."

"Marse Tom, she don't *want* him hanged. She—"

"Well, then, I'll have him boiled in oil."

"But she don't *want* him boiled. I—"

"Oh, very well, very well, I only want to please her; I'll have him skinned."

"Why, *she* don't want him skinned; it would break her heart. Now—"

"Woman, this is perfectly unreasonable. What in the nation *does* she want?"

"Marse Tom, if you would only be a little patient, and not fly off the handle at the least little thing. Why, she only wants you to speak to him."

"Speak to him! Well, upon my word! All this unseemly rage and row about such a—a—Dorcas, I never saw you carry on like this before. You have alarmed the sentry; he thinks I am being assassinated; he thinks there's a mutiny, a revolt, an insurrection; he—"

"Marse Tom, you are just putting on; you know it perfectly well; *I* don't know what makes you act like that—but you always did, even when you was little, and you can't get over it, I reckon. Are you over it now, Marse Tom?"

"Oh, well, yes; but it would try anybody to be doing the best he could, offering every kindness he could think of, only to have it rejected with contumely and . . . Oh, well, let it go; it's no matter—I'll talk to the doctor. Is that satisfactory, or are you going to break out again?"

"Yes, sir, it is; and it's only right to talk to him, too, because it's just as she says; she's trying to keep up discipline in the Rangers, and this insubordination of his is a bad example for them—now ain't it so, Marse Tom?"

"Well, there *is* reason in it, I can't deny it; so I will speak to him, though at bottom I think hanging would be more lasting. What is the rest of your errand, Dorcas?"

"Of course her room is Ranger headquarters now, Marse Tom, while she's sick. Well, soldiers of the cavalry and the dragoons that are off duty come and get her sentries to let them relieve them and serve in their place. It's only out of affection, sir, and because they know military honors please her, and please the children too, for her sake; and they don't bring their muskets; and so—"

"I've noticed them there, but didn't twig the idea. They are standing guard, are they?"

"Yes, sir, and she is afraid you will reprove them and hurt their feelings, if you see them there; so she begs, if—if you don't mind coming in the back way—"

"Bear me up, Dorcas; don't let me faint."

"There—sit up and behave, Marse Tom. You are not going to faint; you are only pretending—you used to act just so when you was little; it does seem a long time for you to get grown up."

"Dorcas, the way the child is progressing, I shall be out of my job before long—she'll have the whole post in her hands. I must make a stand, I must not go down without a struggle. These encroachments. . . . Dorcas, what do you think she will think of next?"

"Marse Tom, she don't mean any harm."

"Are you sure of it?"

"Yes, Marse Tom."

"You feel sure she has no ulterior designs?"

"I don't know what that is, Marse Tom, but I know she hasn't."

"Very well, then, for the present I am satisfied. What else have you come about?"

"I reckon I better tell you the whole thing first, Marse Tom, then tell you what she wants. There's been an *émeute,* as she calls it. It was before she got back with B.B. The officer of the day reported it to her this morning. It happened at her fort. There was a fuss betwixt Major General Tommy Drake and Lieutenant Colonel Agnes Frisbie, and he snatched her doll away, which is made of white kid stuffed with sawdust, and tore every rag of its clothes off, right before them all, and is under arrest, and the charge is conduct un—"

"Yes, I know—conduct unbecoming an officer and a gentleman—a plain case, too, it seems to me. This is a serious matter. Well, what is her pleasure?"

"Well, Marse Tom, she has summoned a court-martial, but the doctor don't think she is well enough to preside over it, and she says there ain't anybody competent but her, because there's a major-general concerned; and so she—she—well, she says, would you preside over it for her? . . . Marse Tom, *sit* up! You ain't any more going to faint than Shekels is."

"Look here, Dorcas, go along back, and be tactful. Be persuasive; don't fret her; tell her it's all right, the matter is in my hands, but it isn't good form to hurry so grave a matter as this. Explain to her that we have to go by precedent, and that I believe this one to be new. In fact, you can say I know that nothing just like it has happened in our army, therefore I must be guided by European precedents, and must go cautiously and examine them carefully. Tell her not to be impatient, it will take me several days, but it will all come out right, and I will come over and report progress as I go along. Do you get the idea, Dorcas?"

"I don't know as I do, sir."

"Well, it's this. You see, it won't ever do for me, a brigadier in the regular army, to preside over that infant court-martial—there isn't any precedent for it, don't you see. Very well. I will go on examining authorities and reporting progress until she is well enough to get me out of this scrape by presiding herself. Do you get it now?"

"Oh, yes, sir, I get it, and it's good, I'll go and fix it with her. *Lay down!* and stay where you are."

"Why, what harm is he doing?"

"Oh, it ain't any harm, but it just vexes me to see him act so."

"What was he doing?"

"Can't you see, and him in such a sweat? He was starting

out to spread it all over the post. *Now* I reckon you won't deny anymore that they go and tell everything they hear, now that you've seen it with yo' own eyes."

"Well, I don't like to acknowledge it, Dorcas, but I don't see how I can consistently stick to my doubts in the face of such overwhelming proof as this dog is furnishing."

"There, now, you've got in yo' right mind at last! I wonder you can be so stubborn, Marse Tom. But you always was, even when you was little. I'm going now."

"Look here; tell her that in view of the delay, it is my judgment that she ought to enlarge the accused on his parole."

"Yes, sir, I'll tell her. Marse Tom?"

"Well?"

"She can't get to Soldier Boy, and he stands there all the time, down in the mouth and lonesome; and she says will you shake hands with him and comfort him? Everybody does."

"It's a curious kind of lonesomeness; but, all right, I will."

11   SEVERAL MONTHS LATER. ANTONIO AND THORNDIKE

"Thorndike, isn't that plug you're riding an asset of the scrap you and Buffalo Bill had with the late Blake Haskins and his pal a few months back?"

"Yes, this is Mongrel—and not a half-bad horse, either."

"I've noticed he keeps up his lick first-rate. Say—isn't it a gaudy morning?"

"Right you are!"

"Thorndike, it's Andalusian! and when that's said, all's said."

"Andalusian *and* Oregonian, Antonio! Put it that way, and you have my vote. Being a native up there, I know. You being Andalusian-born—"

"Can speak with authority for that patch of paradise? Well, I can. Like the Don! like Sancho! This is the correct Andalusian dawn now—crisp, fresh, dewy, fragrant, pungent—"

" 'What though the spicy breezes
Blow soft o'er Ceylon's isle—'

—*git* up, you old cow! Stumbling like that when we've just been praising you! Out on a scout and can't live up to the honor any better than that? Antonio, how long have you been out here in the Plains and the Rockies?"

"More than thirteen years."

"It's a long time. Don't you ever get homesick?"

"Not till now."

"Why now, after such a long cure?"

"These preparations of the retiring commandant's have started it up."

"Of course. It's natural."

"It keeps me thinking about Spain. I know the region where the Seventh's child's aunt lives; I know all the lovely country for miles around; I'll bet I've seen her aunt's villa many a time; I'll bet I've been in it in those pleasant old times when I was a Spanish gentleman."

"They say the child is wild to see Spain."

"It's so; I know it from what I hear."

"Haven't you talked with her about it?"

"No. I've avoided it. I should soon be as wild as she is. That would not be comfortable."

"I wish I was going, Antonio. There's two things I'd give a lot to see. One's a railroad."

"She'll see one when she strikes Missouri."

"The other's a bullfight."

"I've seen lots of them; I wish I could see another."

"I don't know anything about it, except in a mixed-up, foggy way, Antonio, but I know enough to know it's grand sport."

"The grandest in the world! There's no other sport that begins with it. I'll tell you what I've seen, then you can judge. It was my first, and it's as vivid to me now as it was when I saw it. It was a Sunday afternoon, and beautiful weather, and my uncle, the priest, took me as a reward for being a good boy and because of my own accord and without anybody asking me I had bankrupted my savings box and given the money to a mission that was civilizing the Chinese and sweetening their lives and softening their hearts with the gentle teachings of our religion, and I wish you could have seen what we saw that day, Thorndike.

"The amphitheater was packed, from the bullring to the highest row—twelve thousand people in one circling mass, one slanting, solid mass—royalties, nobles, clergy, ladies, gentlemen, state officials, generals, admirals, soldiers, sailors, lawyers, thieves, merchants, brokers, cooks, housemaids, scullery maids, doubtful women, dudes, gamblers, beggars, loafers, tramps, American ladies, gentlemen, preachers, English ladies, gentlemen, preachers, German ditto, French ditto, and so on and so on, all the world represented: Spaniards to admire and praise, foreigners to enjoy and go home and find fault—there they were, one solid, sloping, circling sweep of rippling and flashing color under the downpour of the summer sun—just a garden, a gaudy, gorgeous flower garden! Children munching oranges, six thousand fans fluttering and glimmering, everybody happy, everybody chatting gaily with their intimates, lovely girl-faces smiling recognition and salutation to other lovely girl-faces, gray old ladies and gentlemen dealing in the like exchanges with each other—ah, such a picture of cheery contentment and glad anticipation! not a mean spirit, nor a sordid soul, nor a sad heart there—ah, Thorndike, I wish I could see it again.

"Suddenly, the martial note of a bugle cleaves the hum and murmur—clear the ring!

"They clear it. The great gate is flung open, and the

procession marches in, splendidly costumed and glittering: the marshals of the day, then the picadores on horseback, then the matadores on foot, each surrounded by his quadrille of *chulos*. They march to the box of the city fathers, and formally salute. The key is thrown, the bull gate is unlocked. Another bugle blast—the gate flies open, the bull plunges in, furious, trembling, blinking in the blinding light, and stands there, a magnificent creature, center of those multitudinous and admiring eyes, brave, ready for battle, his attitude a challenge. He sees his enemy: horsemen sitting motionless, with long spears in rest, upon blindfolded broken-down nags, lean and starved, fit only for sport and sacrifice, then the carrion heap.

"The bull makes a rush, with murder in his eye, but a picador meets him with a spear thrust in the shoulder. He flinches with the pain, and the picador skips out of danger. A burst of applause for the picador, hisses for the bull. Some shout 'Cow!' at the bull, and call him offensive names. But he is not listening to them, he is there for business; he is not minding the cloak bearers that come fluttering around to confuse him; he chases this way, he chases that way, and hither and yon, scattering the nimble banderillos in every direction like a spray, and receiving their maddening darts in his neck as they dodge and fly—oh, but it's a lively spectacle, and brings down the house! Ah, you should hear the thundering roar that goes up when the game is at its wildest and brilliant things are done!

"Oh, that first bull, that day, was great! From the moment the spirit of war rose to floodtide in him and he got down to his work, he began to do wonders. He tore his way through his persecutors, flinging one of them clear over the parapet; he bowled a horse and his rider down, and plunged straight for the next, got home with his horns, wounding both horse and man; on again, here and there and this way and that; and one after another he tore the bowels out of two horses

43

so that they gushed to the ground, and ripped a third one so badly that although they rushed him to cover and shoved his bowels back and stuffed the rents with tow and rode him against the bull again, he couldn't make the trip; he tried to gallop, under the spur, but soon reeled and tottered and fell, all in a heap. For a while, that bullring was the most thrilling and glorious and inspiring sight that ever was seen. The bull absolutely cleared it, and stood there alone! monarch of the place. The people went mad for pride in him, and joy and delight, and you couldn't hear yourself think, for the roar and boom and crash of applause."

"Antonio, it carries me clear out of myself just to hear you tell it; it must have been perfectly splendid. If I live, I'll see a bullfight yet before I die. Did they kill him?"

"Oh, yes; that is what the bull is for. They tired him out, and got him at last. He kept rushing the matador, who always slipped smartly and gracefully aside in time, waiting for a sure chance; and at last it came. The bull made a deadly plunge for him—was avoided neatly, and as he sped by, the long sword glided silently into him, between left shoulder and spine—in and in, to the hilt. He crumpled down, dying."

"Ah, Antonio, it *is* the noblest sport that ever was. I would give a year of my life to see it. Is the bull always killed?"

"Yes. Sometimes a bull is timid, finding himself in so strange a place, and he stands trembling, or tries to retreat. Then everybody despises him for his cowardice and wants him punished and made ridiculous; so they hough him from behind, and it is the funniest thing in the world to see him hobbling around on his severed legs; the whole vast house goes into hurricanes of laughter over it; I have laughed till the tears ran down my cheeks to see it. When he has furnished all the sport he can, he is not any longer useful, and is killed."

"Well, it is perfectly grand, Antonio, perfectly beautiful. Burning a nigger don't begin."

12 MONGREL AND THE OTHER HORSE

"Sagebrush, you have been listening?"

"Yes."

"Isn't it strange?"

"Well, no, Mongrel, I don't know that it is."

"Why don't you?"

"I've seen a good many human beings in my time. They are created as they are; they cannot help it. They are only brutal because that is their make; brutes would be brutal if it was *their* make."

"To me, Sagebrush, man is most strange and unaccountable. Why should he treat dumb animals that way when they are not doing any harm?"

"Man is not always like that, Mongrel; he is kind enough when he is not excited by religion."

"Is the bullfight a religious service?"

"I think so. I have heard so. It is held on Sunday."

(*A reflective pause, lasting some moments.*) Then:

"When we die, Sagebrush, do we go to heaven and dwell with man?"

"My father thought not. He believed we do not have to go there unless we deserve it."

Part II   In Spain

13 GENERAL ALISON TO HIS MOTHER

It was a prodigious trip, but delightful, of course, through the Rockies and the Black Hills and the mighty sweep of the Great Plains to civilization and the Missouri border—where the railroading began and the delightfulness ended. But no one is the worse for the journey; certainly not Cathy, nor Dorcas, nor Soldier Boy; and as for me, I am not complaining.

Spain is all that Cathy had pictured it—and more, she says. She is in a fury of delight, the maddest little animal that ever was, and all for joy. She thinks she remembers Spain, but that is not very likely, I suppose. The two—Mercedes and Cathy—devour each other. It is a rapture of love, and beautiful to see. It is Spanish; that describes it. Will this be a short visit?

No. It will be permanent. Cathy has elected to abide with Spain and her aunt. Dorcas says she (Dorcas) foresaw that this would happen; and also says that she wanted it to happen, and says the child's own country is the right place for her, and that she ought not to have been sent to me, I ought to have gone to her. I thought it insane to take Soldier Boy to Spain, but it was well that I yielded to Cathy's pleadings; if he had been left behind, half of her heart would have remained with him, and she would not have been contented. As it is, everything has fallen out for the best, and we are all satisfied and comfortable. It may be that Dorcas and I will see America again some day; but also it is a case of maybe not.

We left the post in the early morning. It was an affecting time. The women cried over Cathy, so did even those stern warriors the Rocky Mountain Rangers; Shekels was there, and the Cid, and Sardanapalus, and Potter, and Mongrel, and Sour Mash, Famine, and Pestilence, and Cathy kissed them all and wept; details of the several arms of the garrison were present to represent the rest, and say good-bye and God bless you for all the soldiery; and there was a special squad from the Seventh, with the oldest veteran at its head, to speed the Seventh's Child with grand honors and impressive ceremonies; and the veteran had a touching speech by heart, and put up his hand in salute and tried to say it, but his lips trembled and his voice broke, but Cathy bent down from the saddle and kissed him on the mouth and turned his defeat to victory, and a cheer went up.

The next act closed the ceremonies, and was a moving

surprise. It may be that you have discovered, before this, that
the rigors of military law and custom melt insensibly away and
disappear when a soldier or a regiment or the garrison wants
to do something that will please Cathy. The bands conceived
the idea of stirring her soldierly heart with a farewell which
would remain in her memory always, beautiful and unfading,
and bring back the past and its love for her whenever she
should think of it; so they got their project placed before
General Burnaby, my successor, who is Cathy's newest slave,
and in spite of poverty of precedents they got his permission.
The bands knew the child's favorite military airs. By this hint
you know what is coming, but Cathy didn't. She was asked to
sound the "Reveille," which she did.

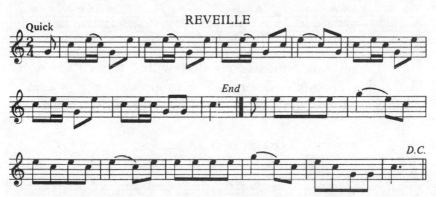

With the last note the bands burst out with a crash: and
woke the mountains with the "Star-Spangled Banner" in a
way to make a body's heart swell and thump and his hair rise!
It was enough to break a person all up, to see Cathy's radiant
face shining out through her gladness and tears. By request
she blew the "Assembly," now. . . .

THE ASSEMBLY

47

. . . Then the bands thundered in, with "Rally round the flag, boys, rally once again!" Next, she blew another call ("To the Standard") . . .

TO THE STANDARD

. . . and the bands responded with "When We Were Marching Through Georgia." Straightway she sounded "Boots and Saddles," that thrilling and most expediting call. . . .

BOOTS AND SADDLES

. . . and the bands could hardly hold in for the final note; then they turned their whole strength loose on "Tramp, Tramp, Tramp, the Boys Are Marching," and everybody's excitement rose to blood heat.

Now an impressive pause—then the bugle sang "Taps"—translatable, this time, into "Good-bye, and God keep us all!" for taps is the soldier's nightly release from duty, and farewell: plaintive, sweet, pathetic, for the morning is never sure, for him; always it is possible that he is hearing it for the last time. . . .

TAPS

Slow

. . . Then the bands turned their instruments toward
Cathy and burst in with that rollicking frenzy of a tune, "Oh,
we'll all get blind drunk when Johnny comes marching
home—yes, we'll all get blind drunk when Johnny comes
marching home!" and followed it instantly with "Dixie," that
antidote for melancholy, merriest and gladdest of all military
music on any side of the ocean—and that was the end. And
so—farewell!

I wish you could have been there to see it all, hear it all,
and feel it: and get yourself blown away with the hurricane
huzza that swept the place as a finish.

When we rode away, our main body had already been on
the road an hour or two—I speak of our camp equipage; but
we didn't move off alone: when Cathy blew the "Advance"
the Rangers cantered out in column of fours, and gave us
escort, and were joined by White Cloud and Thunderbird in
all their gaudy bravery, and by Buffalo Bill and four subordinate scouts. Three miles away, in the Plains, the Lieutenant
General halted, sat her horse like a military statue, the bugle
at her lips, and put the Rangers through the evolutions for
half an hour; and finally, when she blew the "Charge," she led
it herself. "Not for the last time," she said, and got a cheer,
and we said good-bye all around, and faced eastward and rode
away.

Postscript. A Day Later. Soldier Boy was stolen last night.
Cathy is almost beside herself, and we cannot comfort her.
Mercedes and I are not much alarmed about the horse, although this part of Spain is in something of a turmoil politi-
cally, at present, and there is a good deal of lawlessness. In
ordinary times the thief and the horse would soon be captured. We shall have them before long, I think.

14   SOLDIER BOY—TO HIMSELF

It is five months. Or is it six? My troubles have clouded my memory. I think I have been all over this land, from end to end, and now I am back again since day before yesterday, to that city which we passed through, that last day of our long journey, and which is near her country home. I am a tottering ruin and my eyes are dim, but I recognized it. If she could see me she would know me and sound my call. I wish I could hear it once more; it would revive me, it would bring back her face and the mountains and the free life, and I would come—if I were dying I would come! She would not know *me,* looking as I do, but she would know me by my star. But she will never see me, for they do not let me out of this shabby stable—a foul and miserable place, with most two wrecks like myself for company.

How many times have I changed hands? I think it is twelve times—I cannot remember; and each time it was down a step lower, and each time I got a harder master. They have been cruel, every one; they have worked me night and day in degraded employments, and beaten me; they have fed me ill and some days not at all. And so I am but bones, now, with a rough and frowsy skin humped and cornered upon my shrunken body—that skin which was once so glossy, that skin which she loved to stroke with her hand. I was the pride of the mountains and the Great Plains; now I am a scarecrow and despised. These piteous wrecks that are my comrades here say we have reached the bottom of the scale, the final humiliation; they say that when a horse is no longer worth the weeds and discarded rubbish they feed to him, they sell him to the bull-ring for a glass of brandy, to make sport for the people and perish for their pleasure.

To die—that does not disturb me; we of the service never care for death. But if I could see her once more! If I could hear her bugle sing again and say, "It is I, Soldier—come!"

15 GENERAL ALISON TO MRS. DRAKE, THE COLONEL'S WIFE

To return, now, to where I was, and tell you the rest. We shall never know how she came to be there; there is no way to account for it. She was always watching for black and shiny and spirited horses—watching, hoping, despairing, hoping again; always giving chase and sounding her call, upon the meagerest chance of a response, and breaking her heart over the disappointment; always inquiring, always interested 'in sales stables and horse accumulations in general. How she got there must remain a mystery.

At the point which I had reached in a preceding paragraph of this account, the situation was as follows: two horses lay dying; the bull had scattered his persecutors for the moment, and stood raging, panting, pawing the dust in clouds over his back, when the man that had been wounded returned to the ring on a remount, a poor blindfolded wreck that yet had something ironically military about his bearing—and the next moment the bull had ripped him open and his bowels were dragging upon the ground and the bull was charging his swarm of pests again. Then came pealing through the air a bugle call that froze my blood—"It is I, Soldier—come!" I turned; Cathy was flying down through the massed people; she cleared the parapet at a bound, and sped toward that riderless horse, who staggered forward toward the remembered sound; but his strength failed, and he fell at her feet, she lavishing kisses upon him and sobbing, the house rising with one impulse, and white with horror! Before help could reach her the bull was back again—

She was never conscious again in life. We bore her home, all mangled and drenched in blood, and knelt by her and listened to her broken and wandering words, and prayed for her passing spirit, and there was no comfort—nor ever will be, I think. But she was happy, for she was far away under another sky, and comrading again with her Rangers, and her animal friends, and the soldiers. Their names fell softly and caressingly from her lips, one by one, with pauses between. She was not in pain, but lay with closed eyes, vacantly murmuring, as one who dreams. Sometimes she smiled, saying nothing; sometimes she smiled when she uttered a name—such as Shekels, or B.B., or Potter. Sometimes she was at her fort, issuing commands; sometimes she was careering over the plains at the head of her men; sometimes she was training her horse; once she said, reprovingly, "You are giving me the wrong foot; give me the left—don't you know it is good-bye?"

After this, she lay silent some time; the end was near. By and by she murmured, "Tired . . . sleepy . . . take Cathy, Mamma." Then, "Kiss me, Soldier." For a little time she lay so still that we were doubtful if she breathed. Then she put out her hand and began to feel gropingly about; then said, "I cannot find it; blow 'Taps.' "* It was the end.

TAPS

*"Lights Out"

Larry Niven

THE FLIGHT
OF THE HORSE

The year was 750 A.A. (Ante Atomic) or 1200 A.D. (Anno Domini), approximately. Hanville Svetz stepped out of the extension cage and looked about him.

To Svetz the atomic bomb was eleven hundred years old and the horse was a thousand years dead. It was his first trip into the past. His training didn't count; it had not included actual time travel, which cost several million commercials a shot. Svetz was groggy from the peculiar gravitational side effects of time travel. He was high on preindustrial-age air, and drunk on his own sense of destiny; while at the same time he was not really convinced that he had *gone* anywhere. Or anywhen. Trade joke.

He was not carrying the anesthetic rifle. He had come to get a horse; he had not expected to meet one at the door. How big was a horse? Where were horses found? Consider what the Institute had had to go on: a few pictures in a salvaged children's book, and an old legend, not to be trusted, that the horse had once been used as a kind of animated vehicle!

In an empty land beneath an overcast sky, Svetz braced himself with one hand on the curved flank of the extension cage. His head was spinning. It took him several seconds to realize that he was looking at a horse.

It stood fifteen yards away, regarding Svetz with large intelligent brown eyes. It was much larger than he had expected. Further, the horse in the picture book had had a glossy brown pelt with a short mane, while the beast now facing Svetz was pure white, with a mane that flowed like a woman's long hair. There were other differences . . . but no matter, the beast matched the book too well to be anything but a horse.

To Svetz it seemed that the horse watched him, waited for him to realize what was happening. Then, while Svetz wasted more time wondering why he wasn't holding a rifle, the horse laughed, turned, and departed. It disappeared with astonishing speed.

Svetz began to shiver. Nobody had warned him that the horse might have been sentient! Yet the beast's mocking laugh had sounded far too human.

Now he knew. He was deep, deep in the past.

Not even the horse was as convincing as the emptiness the horse had left behind. No reaching apartment towers clawed the horizon. No contrails scratched the sky. The world was trees and flowers and rolling grassland, innocent of men.

The silence—it was as if Svetz had gone deaf. He had heard no sound since the laughter of the horse. In the year

1100 Post Atomic, such silence could have been found nowhere on Earth. Listening, Svetz knew at last that he had reached the British Isles before the coming of civilization. He had traveled in time.

The extension cage was the part of the time machine that did the traveling. It had its own air supply, and needed it while being pushed through time. But not here. Not before civilization's dawn; not when the air had never been polluted by fission wastes and the combustion of coal, hydrocarbons, tobaccos, wood, et al.

Now, retreating in panic from that world of the past to the world of the extension cage, Svetz nonetheless left the door open behind him.

He felt better inside the cage. Outside was an unexplored planet, made dangerous by ignorance. Inside the cage it was no different from a training mission. Svetz had spent hundreds of hours in a detailed mockup of this cage, with a computer running the dials. There had even been artificial gravity to simulate the peculiar side effects of motion in time.

By now the horse would have escaped. But he now knew its size, and he knew there were horses in the area. To business, then . . .

Svetz took the anesthetic rifle from where it was clamped to the wall. He loaded it with what he guessed was the right size of soluble crystalline anaesthetic needle. The box held several different sizes, the smallest of which would knock a shrew harmlessly unconscious, the largest of which would do the same for an elephant. He slung the rifle and stood up.

The world turned gray. Svetz caught a wall clamp to stop himself from falling.

The cage had stopped moving twenty minutes ago. He shouldn't still be dizzy! But it had been a long trip. Never before had the Institute for Temporal Research pushed a cage beyond zero P.A. A long trip and a strange one, with gravity

55

pulling Svetz's mass uniformly toward Svetz's navel . . .

When his head cleared, he turned to where other equipment was clamped to a wall.

The flight stick was a lift field generator and power source built into five feet of pole, with a control ring at one end, a brush discharge at the other, and a bucket seat and seat belt in the middle. Compact even for Svetz's age, the flight stick was a spinoff from the space-flight industries.

But it still weighed thirty pounds with the motor off. Getting it out of the clamps took all his strength. Svetz felt queasy, very queasy.

He bent to pick up the flight stick, and abruptly realized that he was about to faint.

He hit the door button and fainted.

"We don't know where on Earth you'll wind up," Ra Chen had told him. Ra Chen was the director of the Institute for Temporal Research, a large round man with gross, exaggerated features and a permanent air of disapproval. "That's because we can't focus on a particular time of day—or on a particular year, for that matter. You won't appear underground or inside anything because of energy considerations. If you come out a thousand feet in the air, the cage won't fall; it'll settle slowly, using up energy with a profligate disregard for our budget. . . ."

And Svetz had dreamed that night, vividly. Over and over his extension cage appeared inside solid rock, exploded with a roar and a blinding flash.

"Officially the horse is for the Bureau of History," Ra Chen had said. "In practice it's for the secretary-general, for his twenty-eighth birthday. Mentally he's about six years old, you know. The royal family's getting a bit inbred these days. We managed to send him a picture book we picked up in 130 P.A. and now the lad wants a horse. . . ."

Svetz had seen himself being shot for treason, for the crime of listening to such talk.

". . . Otherwise we'd never have gotten the appropriation for this trip. It's in a good cause. We'll do some cloning from the horse before we send the original to the UN. Then—well, genes are a code, and codes can be broken. Get us a male, and we'll make all the horses anyone could want."

But why would anyone want even one horse? Svetz had studied a computer duplicate of the child's picture book that an agent had pulled from a ruined house a thousand years ago. The horse did not impress him.

Ra Chen, however, terrified him.

"We've never sent anyone this far back," Ra Chen had told him the night before the mission, when it was too late to back out with honor. "Keep that in mind. If something goes wrong, don't count on the rule book. Don't count on your instruments. Use your head. Your head, Svetz. Gods know it's little enough to depend on. . . ."

Svetz had not slept in the hours before departure.

"You're scared stiff," Ra Chen had commented just before Svetz entered the extension cage. "And you can hide it, Svetz. I think I'm the only one who's noticed. That's why I picked you, because you can be terrified and go ahead anyway. Don't come back without a horse. . . ."

The director's voice grew louder. "Not without a horse, Svetz. Your *head,* Svetz, your HEAD . . ."

Svetz sat up convulsively. The air! Slow death if he didn't close the door! But the door was closed, and Svetz was sitting on the floor holding his head, which hurt.

The air system had been transplanted intact, complete with dials, from a Martian sandboat. The dials read normally, of course, since the cage was sealed.

Svetz nerved himself to open the door. As the sweet, rich air of twelfth-century Britain rushed in, Svetz held his breath and watched the dials change. Presently he closed the door and waited, sweating, while the air system replaced the heady poison with its own safe, breathable mixture.

When next he left the extension cage, carrying the flight stick, Svetz was wearing another spinoff from the interstellar exploration industries. It was a balloon, and he wore it over his head. It was also a selectively permeable membrane, intended to pass certain gases in and others out, to make a breathing-air mixture inside.

It was nearly invisible except at the rim. There, where light was refracted most severely, the balloon showed as a narrow golden circle enclosing Svetz's head. The effect was not unlike a halo as shown in medieval paintings. But Svetz didn't know about medieval paintings.

He wore also a simple white robe, undecorated, constricted at the waist, otherwise falling in loose folds. The Institute thought that such a garment was least likely to violate taboos of sex or custom. The trade kit dangled loose from his sash: a heat-and-pressure gadget, a pouch of corundum, small vials of additives for color.

Lastly he wore a hurt and baffled look. How was it that he could not breathe the clean air of his own past?

The air of the cage was the air of Svetz's time, and was nearly 4 percent carbon dioxide. The air of 750 Ante Atomic held barely a tenth of that. Man was a rare animal here and now. He had breathed little air, he had destroyed few green forests, he had burnt scant fuel since the dawn of time.

But industrial civilization meant combustion. Combustion meant carbon dioxide thickening in the atmosphere many times faster than the green plants could turn it back to oxygen. Svetz was at the far end of two thousand years of adaptation to air rich in CO_2.

It takes a concentration of carbon dioxide to trigger the autonomic nerves in the lymph glands in a man's left armpit.

Svetz had fainted because he wasn't breathing.

So now he wore a balloon, and felt rejected.

He straddled the flight stick and twisted the control knob on the fore end. The stick lifted under him, and he wriggled into place on the bucket seat. He twisted the knob further.

He drifted upward like a toy balloon.

He floated over a lovely land, green and untenanted, beneath a pearl-gray sky empty of contrails. Presently he found a crumbling wall. He turned to follow it.

He would follow the wall until he found a settlement. If the old legend was true—and, Svetz reflected, the horse had certainly been *big* enough to drag a vehicle—then he would find horses wherever he found men.

Presently it became obvious that a road ran along the wall. There the dirt was flat and bare and consistently wide enough for a walking man, whereas elsewhere the land rose and dipped and tilted. Hard dirt did not a freeway make; but Svetz got the point.

He followed the road, floating at a height of ten meters.

There was a man in worn brown garments. Hooded and barefoot, he walked the road with patient exhaustion, propping himself with a staff. His back was to Svetz.

Svetz thought to dip toward him to ask concerning horses. He refrained. With no way to know where the cage would alight, he had learned no ancient languages at all.

He thought of the trade kit he carried, intended not for communication, but instead of communication. It had never been field-tested. In any case it was not for casual encounters. The pouch of corundum was too small.

Svetz heard a yell from below. He looked down in time to see the man in brown running like the wind, his staff forgotten, his fatigue likewise.

Something scared him, Svetz decided. But he could see nothing fearful. Something small but deadly, then.

The Institute estimated that man had exterminated more

than a thousand species of mammal and bird and insect—some casually, some with malice—between now and the distant present. In this time and place there was no telling what might be a threat. Svetz shuddered. The brown man with the hairy face might well have run from a stinging thing destined to kill Hanville Svetz.

Impatiently Svetz upped the speed of his flight stick. The mission was taking far too long. Who would have guessed that centers of population would have been so far apart?

Half an hour later, shielded from the wind by a paraboloid force field, Svetz was streaking down the road at sixty miles per hour.

His luck had been incredibly bad. Wherever he had chanced across a human being, that person had been just leaving the vicinity. And he had found no centers of population.

Once he had noticed an unnatural stone outcropping high on a hill. No law of geology known to Svetz could have produced such an angular, flat-sided monstrosity. Curious, he had circled above it—and had abruptly realized that the thing was hollow, riddled with rectangular holes.

A dwelling for men? He didn't want to believe it. Living within the hollows of such a thing would be like living underground. But men tend to build at right angles, and this thing was *all* right angles.

Below the hollowed stone structure were rounded, hairy-looking hummocks of dried grass, each with a man-sized door. Obviously they must be nests for very large insects. Svetz had left that place quickly.

The road rounded a swelling green hill ahead of him. Svetz followed, slowing.

A hilltop spring sent a stream bubbling downhill to break the road. Something large was drinking at the stream. Svetz jerked to a stop in midair. *Open water: deadly poison.*

He would have been hard put to say which had startled him more: the horse, or the fact that it had just committed suicide.

The horse looked up and saw him.

It was the same horse. White as milk, with a flowing abundance of snowy mane and tail, it almost had to be the horse that had laughed at Svetz and run. Svetz recognized the malignance in its eyes, in the moment before it turned its back.

But how could it have arrived so fast?

Svetz was reaching for the gun when the situation turned upside down.

The girl was young, surely no more than sixteen. Her hair was long and dark and plaited in complex fashion. Her dress, of strangely stiff blue fabric, reached from her neck to her ankles. She was seated in the shadow of a tree, on dark cloth spread over the dark earth. Svetz had not noticed her, might never have noticed her. . . .

But the horse walked up to her, folded its legs in alternate pairs, and laid its ferocious head in her lap.

The girl had not yet seen Svetz.

"Xenophilia!" Svetz snarled the worst word he could think of. Svetz hated aliens.

The horse obviously belonged to the girl. He could not simply shoot it and take it. It would have to be purchased, somehow.

He needed time to think! And there was no time, for the girl might look up at any moment. Baleful brown eyes watched him as he dithered.

He dared waste no more time searching the countryside for a wild horse. There was an uncertainty, a Finagle factor in the math of time travel. It manifested itself as an uncertainty in the energy of a returning extension cage, and it increased with time. Let Svetz linger too long, and he could be roasted alive in the returning cage.

Moreover, the horse had drunk open water. It would die,

and soon, unless Svetz could return it to 1100 Post Atomic. Thus the beast's removal from this time could not change the history of Svetz's own world. It was a good choice—if he could conquer his fear of the beast.

The horse was tame. Young and slight as she was, the girl had no trouble controlling it. What was there to fear?

But there was its natural weaponry—of which Ra Chen's treacherous picture book had shown no sign. Svetz surmised that later generations routinely removed it before the animals were old enough to be dangerous. He should have come a few centuries later.

And there was the look in its eye. The horse hated Svetz, and it knew Svetz was afraid.

Could he shoot it from ambush?

No. The girl would worry if her pet collapsed without reason. She would be unable to concentrate on what Svetz was trying to tell her.

He would have to work with the animal watching him. If the girl couldn't control it—or if he lost her trust—Svetz had little doubt that the horse would kill him.

The horse looked up as Svetz approached, but made no other move. The girl watched too, her eyes round with wonder. She called something that must have been a question.

Svetz smiled back and continued his approach. He was a foot above the ground, and gliding at dead slow. Riding the world's only flying machine, he looked impressive as all hell, and knew it.

The girl did not smile back. She watched warily. Svetz was within yards of her when she scrambled to her feet.

He stopped the flight stick at once and let it settle. Smiling placatorially, he removed the heat-and-pressure device from his sash. He moved with care. The girl was on the verge of running.

The trade kit was a pouch of corundum, Al_2O_3, several vials of additives, and the heat-and-pressure gadget. Svetz poured corundum into the chamber, added a dash of chromic oxide, and used the plunger. The cylinder grew warm. Presently Svetz dropped a pigeon's-blood star ruby into his hand, rolled it in his fingers, held it to the sun. It was red as dark blood, with a blazing white six-pointed star.

It was almost too hot to hold.

Stupid! Svetz held his smile rigid. Ra Chen should have warned him! What would she think when she felt the gem's unnatural heat? What trickery would she suspect?

But he had to chance it. The trade kit was all he had.

He bent and rolled the gem to her across the damp ground.

She stooped to pick it up. One hand remained on the horse's neck, calming it. Svetz noticed the rings of yellow metal around her wrist; and he also noticed the dirt.

She held the gem high, looked into its deep red fire.

"Ooooh," she breathed. She smiled at Svetz in wonder and delight. Svetz smiled back, moved two steps nearer, and rolled her a yellow sapphire.

How had he twice chanced on the same horse? Svetz never knew. But he soon knew how it had arrived before him.

He had given the girl three gems. He held three more in his hand while he beckoned her onto the flight stick. She shook her head; she would not go. Instead she mounted the animal.

She and the horse, they watched Svetz for his next move.

Svetz capitulated. He had expected the horse to follow the girl while the girl rode behind him on the flight stick. But if they both followed Svetz it would be the same.

The horse stayed to one side and a little behind Svetz's flight stick. It did not seem inconvenienced by the girl's weight. Why should it be? It must have been bred for the task. Svetz notched his speed higher, to find how fast he could conveniently move.

Faster, he flew, and faster. The horse must have a limit.

He was up to eighty before he quit. The girl lay flat along the animal's back, hugging its neck to protect her face from the wind. But the horse ran on, daring Svetz with its eyes.

How to describe such motion? Svetz had never seen ballet. He knew how machinery moved, and this wasn't it. All he could think of was a man and a woman making love. Slippery-smooth rhythmic motion, absolute single-minded purpose, motion for the pleasure of motion. It was terrible in its beauty, the flight of the horse.

The word for such running must have died with the horse itself.

The horse would never have tired, but the girl did. She tugged on the animal's mane, and it stopped. Svetz gave her the jewels he held, made four more, and gave her one.

She was crying from the wind, crying and smiling as she took the jewels. Was she smiling for the jewels, or for the joy of the ride? Exhausted, panting, she lay with her back against the warm, pulsing flank of the resting animal. Only her hand moved, as she ran her fingers repeatedly through its silver mane. The horse watched Svetz with malevolent brown eyes.

The girl was homely. It wasn't just the jarring lack of makeup. There was evidence of vitamin starvation. She was short, less than five feet in height, and thin. There were marks of childhood disease. But happiness glowed behind her homely face, and it made her almost passable, as she clutched the corundum stones.

When she seemed rested, Svetz remounted. They went on.

He was almost out of corundum when they reached the extension cage. There it was that he ran into trouble.

The girl had been awed by Svetz's jewels, and by Svetz himself, possibly because of his height or his ability to fly. But the extension cage scared her. Svetz couldn't blame her. The side with the door in it was no trouble: just a seamless spherical mirror. But the other side blurred away in a direction men could not visualize. It had scared Svetz spitless the first time he saw the time machine in action.

He could buy the horse from her, shoot it here, and pull it inside, using the flight stick to float it. But it would be so much easier if . . .

It was worth a try. Svetz used the rest of his corundum. Then he walked into the extension cage, leaving a trail of colored corundum beads behind him.

He had worried because the heat-and-pressure device would not produce facets. The stones all came out shaped like miniature hen's eggs. But he was able to vary the color, using chromic oxide for red and ferric oxide for yellow and titanium for blue; and he could vary the pressure planes, to produce cat's-eyes or star gems at will. He left a trail of small stones, red and yellow and blue. . . .

And the girl followed, frightened, but unable to resist the bait. By now she had nearly filled a handkerchief with the stones. The horse followed her into the extension cage.

Inside, she looked at the four stones in Svetz's hand: one of each color, red and yellow and light blue and black, the largest he could make. He pointed to the horse, then to the stones.

The girl agonized. Svetz perspired. She didn't want to give up the horse . . . and Svetz was out of corundum.

She nodded, one swift jerk of her chin. Quickly, before she could change her mind, Svetz poured the stones into her hand. She clutched the hoard to her bosom and ran out of the cage, sobbing.

The horse stood up to follow.

Svetz swung the rifle and shot it. A bead of blood appeared on the animal's neck. It shied back, then sighted on Svetz along its natural bayonet.

Poor kid, Svetz thought as he turned to the door. But she'd have lost the horse anyway. It had sucked polluted water from an open stream. Now he need only load the flight stick aboard. . . .

Motion caught the corner of his eye.

A false assumption can be deadly. Svetz had not waited for the horse to fall. It was with something of a shock that he realized the truth. The beast wasn't about to fall. It was about to spear him like a cocktail shrimp.

He hit the door button and dodged.

Exquisitely graceful, exquisitely sharp, the spiral horn slammed into the closing door. The animal turned like white lightning in the confines of the cage, and again Svetz leapt for his life.

The point missed him by half an inch. It plunged past him and into the control board, through the plastic panel, and into the wiring beneath.

Something sparkled and something sputtered.

The horse was taking careful aim, sighting along the spear in its forehead. Svetz did the only thing he could think of. He pulled the home-again lever.

The horse screamed as it went into free fall. The horn, intended for Svetz's navel, ripped past his ear and tore his breathing-balloon wide open.

Then gravity returned; but it was the peculiar gravity of an extension cage moving forward through time. Svetz and the horse were pulled against the padded walls. Svetz sighed in relief.

He sniffed again in disbelief. The smell was strong and strange, like nothing Svetz had ever smelled before. The animal's terrible horn must have damaged the air plant. Very likely he was breathing poison. If the cage didn't return in time . . .

But would it return at all? It might be going anywhere, anywhen, the way that ivory horn had smashed through anonymous wiring. They might come out at the end of time, when even the black infrasuns gave not enough heat to sustain life.

There might not even be a future to return to. He had left the flight stick. How would it be used? What would they make of it, with its control handle at one end and the brush-style static discharge at the other and the saddle in the middle? Perhaps the girl would try to use it. He could visualize her against the night sky, in the light of a full moon . . . and how would that change history?

The horse seemed on the verge of apoplexy. Its sides heaved, its eyes rolled wildly. Probably it was the cabin air, thick with carbon dioxide. Again, it might be the poison the horse had sucked from an open stream.

Gravity died. Svetz and the horse tumbled in free fall, and the horse queasily tried to gore him.

Gravity returned, and Svetz, who was ready for it, landed on top. Someone was already opening the door.

Svetz took the distance in one bound. The horse followed, screaming with rage, intent on murder. Two men went flying as it charged out into the Institute control center.

"It doesn't take anesthetics!" Svetz shouted over his shoulder. The animal's agility was hampered here among the desks and lighted screens, and it was probably drunk on hyperventilation. It kept stumbling into desks and men. Svetz easily stayed ahead of the slashing horn.

A full panic was developing.

"We couldn't have done it without Zeera," Ra Chen told him much later. "Your idiot tanj horse had the whole Center terrorized. All of a sudden it went completely tame, walked up to that frigid bitch Zeera and let her lead it away."

"Did you get it to the hospital in time?"

Ra Chen nodded gloomily. Gloom was his favorite expression and was no indication of his true feelings. "We found over fifty unknown varieties of bacteria in the beast's bloodstream. Yet it hardly looked sick! It looked healthy as a . . . healthy as a . . . it must have tremendous stamina. We managed to save not only the horse, but most of the bacteria too, for the zoo."

Svetz was sitting up in a hospital bed, with his arm up to the elbow in a diagnostician. There was always the chance that he too had located some long-extinct bacterium. He shifted uncomfortably, being careful not to move the wrong arm, and asked, "Did you ever find an anesthetic that worked?"

"Nope. Sorry about that, Svetz. We still don't know why your needles didn't work. The tanj horse is simply immune to tranks of any kind.

"Incidentally, there was nothing wrong with your air plant. You were smelling the horse."

"I wish I'd known that. I thought I was dying."

"It's driving the interns crazy, that smell. And we can't seem to get it out of the Center." Ra Chen sat down on the edge of the bed. "What bothers me is the horn on its forehead. The horse in the picture book had no horns."

"No, sir."

"Then it must be a different species. It's not really a horse, Svetz. We'll have to send you back. It'll break our budget, Svetz."

"I disagree, sir—"

"Don't be so tanj polite."

"Then don't be so tanj stupid, sir." Svetz was *not* going back for another horse. "People who kept tame horses must have developed the habit of cutting off the horn when the animal was a pup. Why not? We all saw how dangerous that horn is. Much too dangerous for a domestic animal."

"Then why does our horse have a horn?"

"That's why I thought it was wild, the first time I saw it. I suppose they didn't start cutting off horns until later in history."

Ra Chen nodded in gloomy satisfaction. "I thought so too. Our problem is that the secretary-general is barely bright enough to notice that his horse has a horn, and the picture-book horse doesn't. He's bound to blame me."

"Mmm." Svetz wasn't sure what was expected of him.

"I'll have to have the horn amputated."

"Somebody's bound to notice the scar," said Svetz.

"Tanj it, you're right. I've got enemies at court. They'd be only too happy to claim I'd mutilated the secretary-general's pet." Ra Chen glared at Svetz. "All right, let's hear *your* idea."

Svetz was busy regretting. Why had he spoken? His vicious, beautiful horse, tamely docked of its killer horn. . . . He had found the thought repulsive. His impulse had betrayed him. What could they do but remove the horn?

He had it. "Change the picture book, not the horse. A computer could duplicate the book in detail, but with a horn on every horse. Use the Institute computer, then wipe the tape afterward."

Morosely thoughtful, Ra Chen said, "That might work. I know someone who could switch the books." He looked up from under bushy black brows. "Of course, you'd have to keep your mouth shut."

"Yes, sir."

"Don't forget." Ra Chen got up. "When you get out of the diagnostician, you start a four-week vacation."

"I'm sending you back for one of these," Ra Chen told him four weeks later. He opened the bestiary. "We picked up the book in a public park around ten Post Atomic; left the kid who was holding it playing with a corundum egg."

Svetz examined the picture. "That's *ugly*. That's really

ugly. You're trying to balance the horse, right? The horse was so beautiful, you've got to have one of these or the universe goes off balance."

Ra Chen closed his eyes in pain. "Just go get us the Gila monster, Svetz. The secretary-general wants a Gila monster."

"How big is it?"

They both looked at the illustration. There was no way to tell.

"From the looks of it, we'd better use the *big* extension cage."

Svetz barely made it back that time. He was suffering from total exhaustion and extensive second-degree burns. The thing he brought back was thirty feet long, had vestigial batlike wings, breathed fire, and didn't look very much like the illustration; but it was as close as anything he'd found.

The secretary-general loved it.

Richard Harding Davis

MR. TRAVERS'S FIRST HUNT

Young Travers, who had been engaged to a girl down on Long Island for the last three months, only met her father and brother a few weeks before the day set for the wedding. The brother is a master of hounds near Southampton and shared the expense of importing a pack from England with Van Bibber. The father and son talked horse all day and until one in the morning; for they owned fast Thoroughbreds, and entered them at the Sheepshead Bay and other racetracks. Old Mr. Paddock, the father of the girl to whom Travers was engaged, had often said that when a young man asked him for his daughter's hand he would ask him in return, not if he had lived straight, but if he could ride straight. And on his answering this question in the affirmative depended his gaining her parent's consent. Travers had met Miss Paddock and her mother in Europe, while the men of the family were at home. He was invited to their place in the fall when the hunting season opened, and spent the evening most pleasantly and satisfactorily with his fiancée in a corner of the drawing room. But as soon as the women had gone, young Paddock joined him and said, "You ride, of course?" Travers had never ridden; but he had been prompted how to answer by Miss Paddock, and so said there was nothing he liked better. As he expressed it, he would rather ride than sleep.

"That's good," said Paddock. "I'll give you a mount on Satan tomorrow morning at the meet. He is a bit nasty at the start of the season; and ever since he killed Wallis, the second groom, last year, none of us care much to ride him. But you can manage him, no doubt. He'll just carry your weight."

Mr. Travers dreamed that night of taking large, desperate leaps into space on a wild horse that snorted forth flames, and that rose at solid stone walls as though they were hayricks.

He was tempted to say he was ill in the morning—which was, considering his state of mind, more or less true—but concluded that as he would have to ride sooner or later during his visit, and that if he did break his neck it would be in a good cause, he determined to do his best. He did not want to ride at all, for two excellent reasons—first, because he wanted to live for Miss Paddock's sake, and, second, because he wanted to live for his own.

The next morning was a most forbidding and doleful-looking morning, and young Travers had great hopes that the meet would be declared off; but, just as he lay in doubt, the servant knocked at his door with his riding things and his hot water.

He came downstairs looking very miserable indeed. Satan

had been taken to the place where they were to meet, and Travers viewed him on his arrival there with a sickening sense of fear, as he saw him pulling three grooms off their feet.

Travers decided that he would stay with his feet on solid earth just as long as he could, and when the hounds were thrown off and the rest had started at a gallop he waited, under the pretense of adjusting his gaiters, until they were all well away. Then he clinched his teeth, crammed his hat down over his ears, and scrambled up onto the saddle. His feet fell quite by accident into the stirrups, and the next instant he was off after the others with an indistinct feeling that he was on a locomotive that was jumping the ties. Satan was in among and had passed the other horses in less than five minutes, and was so close on the hounds that the whippers-in gave a cry of warning. But Travers could as soon have pulled a boat back from going over the Niagara Falls as Satan, and it was only because the hounds were well ahead that saved them from having Satan ride them down. Travers had taken hold of the saddle with his left hand to keep himself down, and sawed and swayed on the reins with his right. He shut his eyes whenever Satan jumped, and never knew how he happened to stick on; but he did stick on, and was so far ahead that no one could see in the misty morning just how badly he rode. As it was, for daring and speed he led the field, and not even young Paddock was near him from the start. There was a broad stream in front of him, and a hill just on its other side. No one had ever tried to take this at a jump. It was considered more of a swim than anything else, and the hunters always crossed it by the bridge, toward the left. Travers saw the bridge and tried to jerk Satan's head in that direction; but Satan kept right on as straight as an express train over the prairie. Fences and trees and furrows passed by and under Travers like a panorama run by electricity, and he only breathed by accident. They went on at the stream and the hill beyond as though they were riding at a stretch of turf, and, though the whole field set up a shout of warning and dismay, Travers could only gasp and shut his eyes. He remembered the fate of the second groom and shivered. Then the horse rose like a rocket, lifting Travers so high in the air that he thought Satan would never come down again; but he did come down, with his feet bunched, on the opposite side of the stream. The next instant he was up and over the hill, and had stopped panting in the very center of the pack that were snarling and snapping around the fox. And then Travers showed that he was a thoroughbred, even though he could not ride, for he hastily fumbled for his cigar case, and when the field came pounding up over the bridge and around the hill, they saw him seated nonchalantly on his saddle, puffing critically at a cigar and giving Satan patronizing pats on the head.

"My dear girl," said old Mr. Paddock to his daughter as they rode back, "if you love that young man of yours and want to keep him, make him promise to give up riding. A more reckless and more brilliant horseman I have never seen. He took that double jump at the gate and that stream like a centaur. But he will break his neck sooner or later, and he ought to be stopped." Young Paddock was so delighted with his prospective brother-in-law's great riding that that night in the smoking room he made him a present of Satan before all the men.

"No," said Travers, gloomily, "I can't take him. Your sister has asked me to give up what is dearer to me than anything next to herself, and that is my riding. You see, she is absurdly anxious for my safety, and she has asked me to promise never to ride again, and I have given my word."

A chorus of sympathetic remonstrance rose from the men.

"Yes, I know," said Travers to her brother. "It is rough, but it just shows what sacrifices a man will make for the woman he loves."

Hugh Johnson

LEVANT

In "L" Troop of the Nth Cavalry there is a horse that is sixteen years old. He does no work, he eats candy and carrots to his heart's content, and he will never be condemned. The story of these honors is worth knowing. It is unofficial history.

When "L" Troop took the field in the Philippines, its commander was a brand-new second lieutenant, fresh from West Point, for its captain was on distant duty. This might have been a calamity to any troop but "L." The father of Lieutenant Grinnell had commanded the troop before him, and the older sergeants had yanked the boy from beneath the horses' feet on the picket line when he could no more than toddle. He had ridden with them as a lank, awkward twelve-year-old, and slept between their blankets on the Geronimo campaign. They called him Bobbie then, to his face, and Bobbie he would remain to them, even if he became field-marshal-general commanding the allied armies of six nations, as they fondly hoped he some day would. Nothing could have pleased the troop more than his return to it as an officer, and what he did not know about commanding a troop in campaign they would shortly show him.

They did. "L" Troop painted its letter in vivid colors over a large part of the Island of Luzon. It rode through twenty battles, skirmishes, and engagements in the earlier war; it endured a cholera epidemic at Bato-bato, and at last it took station at Bontoc to guard its particular section of a partly pacified country and to await eventualities. It was proud of itself as a whole, but no one was prouder than First Sergeant Dale, who, as the veteran of the troop, the guardian of its traditions, and the rider of the storied horse Levant, was herein forever justified in many extravagant prophecies.

"Didn't we tell 'em—didn't we tell 'em?" he used to chuckle into the silken mane of his horse, for Levant was his chief confidant. "Of *course* the boy's a *soldier*. It's in the blood, an' he's the spit of his daddy before him. They couldn't fool *us*—could they, old Daisy-Crusher? Praise be that we lived to serve under him!" Levant did not understand these effusions, but he did know that his sides were plump with fat and his hide was clean and comfortable.

This—or its equivalent—the whole of "L" Troop knew. They were looked after, and they were commanded. When the unreasoning cholera had descended upon them, and a fear that they had not known in the field gripped them uncannily, their lieutenant had gone among them, his cheeks as fresh and smiling, his eye as clear and cool and pleasant as ever; and thus, through it all—"bloody war and sickly season"—they had found him without flaw.

This service-born confidence, you must understand, is the beginning and the end and all between with a company of soldiers. If they have it, the efficiency of the officer is the efficiency of the troop without one iota of discount. "L" Troop believed that it could have whipped the entire armed force of insurrection. Believing so, and led as it was, it was probably right.

But into this confident calm of self-gratulation three horrors descended. In the order of their coming, they were: the rainy season, El General Pedro Gerónimo Aguilar Borda y Pradillo, and First Lieutenant Harrison Wentworth.

The rains began as a gentle afternoon shower and settled into a three weeks' deluge. Roads and trails disappeared in rivers and brooklets and lagoons and narrow chasms of liquid mud. The jungle took on new strength of life in the fetid air and threatened to engulf the town. Just when all movement of troops through the swimming country seemed impossible, movement became suddenly imperative. The mail brought Grinnell a simple order:

> The Insurrecto leader, Aguilar, has transferred his activities to your section. With the force at your command the General looks to you to capture him without delay.
>
> Milton, *Adjutant General*

Pedro Aguilar was a little brown guerrilla and his activities were no myth. Day after day, "L" Troop rode on wild chases and day after day it returned disheartened and finally almost hopeless. It received no grace from Aguilar. Now he sacked the hacienda of a friendly Filipino to westward, burning the sugar mills, killing the carabao, and ruining the rice dikes. When the troop arrived at the scene of destruction, he would be blowing up a bridge twenty miles away. It chased him for a month and, at the end of it, seemed no nearer success than when it began. Once it sent a scattering volley after a line of white cotton-clad backs, scuttling through a banana grove, and once it was itself fired into in a narrow gorge, but that was all. Aguilar grew daily bolder. Headquarters became at first insistent, then sarcastic, and finally scathing. The troop thought and dreamed nothing but Aguilar and his capture. Its reputation was at stake and in very apparent danger. The men became peaked and worn and thin and the horses showed signs of grievous suffering. Another organization would have been in a state of incipient mutiny, but these men could still grin and take up new holes in their belts in their ignorance of what was still to come.

First Lieutenant Wentworth came to take the command of the troop from Bobbie Grinnell at a most unfortunate time. For a subaltern, he was an oldish man (perhaps thirty-eight) with a high, narrow forehead and small, close-set, myopic eyes. His captaincy had been too long coming and he was a little soured. He was as neat and pernickety as an old maid, his perspective was not broader than a barn door, and he had no sense of humor whatever. He did not like the appearance of Bontoc Sonoyta, and he was shocked by the childlike appearance of Bobbie Grinnell.

"You young fellows shouldn't be given command of troops," he told Bobbie, judicially. "You have no experience and you let things go to the dogs. *Look* at these horses."

Grinnell flushed and said nothing. Sergeant Dale was making wry faces, and the men, grooming on the picket line, poised their brushes in midair, expecting to see their lieutenant fall upon and quite obliterate the opinionated interloper. But most of the heart had been taken out of Bobbie. The coming of Wentworth was an official expression of lost confidence, and he had scarcely recovered from the shock when the new lieutenant, passing critically along the line of horses, stopped behind Levant.

"Mister Grinnell," he said decisively (subalterns call each other mister only for discipline or "squelching")—"Mister Grinnell, in the future I will ride this horse."

Now, in most cavalry troops, and certainly in "L," the assignment of any horse to any soldier is considered the beginning of a relation terminable only by death or discharge. Picture, then, the sacrilege here. Dale had trained Levant as an awkward colt recruit. Bobbie was incautious.

"Why, Wentworth—that is—Lieutenant," he stammered, "*that* is Levant—Sergeant Dale's horse. You can't do that. Surely you've heard of Dale and Levant. Why, that would break the old man's heart." The troop had frankly stopped grooming as its lares and penates came tumbling about its ears. Wentworth drew himself to his full height, and fixed Grinnell with a stare, pitying, haughty, and inquiring.

"Mister Grinnell," he began in a weary voice—"*Mister* Grinnell, perhaps you didn't understand me. In the future, *I* will ride *this* horse." Grinnell's fingers straightened to their full length, then they closed in such knotty, painful fists that the cords on the knuckles stood out white and trembling. Once he drew in breath to speak (his face had grown ashen), but turned away, and an hour later shuddered at the thought of what he had been about to do.

"L" Troop's condition became a tragedy. Poor Wentworth was a conscientious man. In theory he was excellent, but he had not served two days with a troop in the field, and he knew as much about men in the abstract as he did about the plumbing system of the sacred city of Lhasa. His idea of discipline was nagging; of firmness, meanness; and of fighting Malay guerrillas, blank and pitiful nothing.

A troop of cavalry is a human machine and this sort of

thing may not go on forever. The rainy season was drawing to a close. A burning ball of a sun now popped into a cloudless sky at dawn and seared its way across, sucking the steam from the soaked earth, and literally cooking what it touched. The men off duty lay in their bunks through the sweltering day, fighting swarms of big, vigorous mosquitoes, venomous with malaria. The jungle hummed by day and screamed by night with million-throated insect choruses and Aguilar woke to a fiendish activity like nothing he had done before. A sullen silence fell over the squad rooms. The men no longer laughed and joked. They were growing ugly with that black ugliness that comes to white men in the tropics and outcrops in the horrible things that people at home read about and do not understand. Bobbie, who was as sensitive to the undercurrent of life in the barracks as a delicate thermometer is to heat, wrote to his father:

"If we don't get Aguilar and get rid of Wentworth soon, something—I don't even dare to think what—but something very terrible is going to happen—"

Bobbie did not finish his letter at that sitting. While he was writing, the bugles on the hill sounded a frantic "To Horse" (which is to a troop quite what an alarm is to a fire company), the barrack yard was alive with half-dressed men dragging saddles and equipment toward the stables, and ten minutes later the troop was formed, with Wentworth, pale and nervous, seated on Levant, in its front. He and Bobbie were scarcely on speaking terms and, anyway, he did not care to tell that he had just received the most audacious message ever penned by a guerrilla Malay to a troop of United States cavalry—namely, to come into the open and fight it out. It was an insult and Wentworth knew it.

He wheeled the troop into column and started down the jungle road at a trot without a word of explanation. This was a grievous error.

For Wentworth had never been under fire. He was going through that stage of mental panic that comes to every man on the eve of his first battle. For no one knows how he may act, and every man fears that he *may* act as he shouldn't. This is to be expected, but it is no state of mind for a troop commander in the face of the enemy. Wentworth forgot his advance guard, and neither Bobbie nor any of the men suspected the imminence of danger. The road dropped into the throat of a little valley between two outlying foothills of the Zambalesian mountains. There was a rustle in the bamboo on each side, and, with no further word of warning, a horizontal sheet of Mauser fire ripped out and emptied six saddles. It was a perfect ambuscade, and the next moment the narrow road was a chaos of rearing, plunging horses and swearing men. A mortally wounded charger, at the head of the column, turned and went careening back through the ruck, screaming and blind with agony. He knocked the remaining semblance of formation into ruin and completed the fearful confusion. From both sides of the road now came a furious fusillade that lacked only accuracy to make it annihilating.

In his panicky state of nerves, Wentworth had shredded Levant's mouth with the bit and lathered his flanks with bloody foam. The old horse for once failed in his steadiness and completed his rider's panic. Bobbie spurred toward them furiously.

"What's the matter with you?" he yelled. "Why don't you deploy and answer? Don't you see the troop is being murdered?" Wentworth was shaking in frank terror.

"Oh, Grinnell," he chattered, "I know it. They're being killed. Oh, what'll we do? They're all around. Oh, please tell 'em to stop shooting. Tell 'em I surrender. I surrender." He had torn the handkerchief from his neck and was waving it about his head. Bobbie jerked it angrily from his hand.

"Surrender—hell!" he said. "You can't surrender to

them. They don't know what it means. Surrender if *you* want to. I'm going to fight!" and he turned to take command of the troop.

There are limits, even to the patience of a veteran troop horse, and Levant had quite arrived at his. Just as Bobbie turned, a Mauser bullet whipped like a lash across the old horse's haunches and something within his head seemed to snap. He reared in a mighty effort and came down, boring on the bit, and then, nose poked square to the front, sweat-blinded eyes unseeing, he was off, running like a wild horse, anywhere, anyhow, to escape the stinging pain in his haunches—but straight for the insurrecto lines. Wentworth was no horseman. In the presence of this new peril from his runaway mount (for the thorny bamboo switched his face and tore it cruelly), he forgot all other danger, leaned forward, gripping the mane, and yelled:

"Oh, stop him—please, for the love of heaven, stop him!"

The prayer was answered. Levant came counter of a bamboo fence and stopped because he could go no farther and for no other reason. Wentworth could and did go farther. He smashed against the fence and rolled to the ground. A swarm of little brown men appeared and pounced upon him. They trussed him as peak-backed pigs are trussed for the San Fernando Market. They caught Levant's bridle reins and they took both to Pedro Aguilar, who was hugely pleased, but who had little time to enjoy his pleasure.

Bobbie somehow formed the troop, unlimbered his pistols and charged the far flank, breaking through and pursuing it until it melted away in the ten-foot-high grass where the horses could not follow. He was returning now to his wounded. Aguilar had no mind to meet a charge on his side of the road, and he had other plans in view. He mounted the captured horse in sinful pride and he saw to it that poor Wentworth was hustled through the brush.

Pedro Aguilar had lost much of his respect for the fighting power of "L" Troop in the preceding weeks. He had prepared the ambuscade, keenly foreseeing exactly what happened. Five miles farther up the gorge he had prepared a place where, if he could lure "L" Troop, he could also destroy it. He had sown the ground cunningly with mantraps, automatic arrows, staked foot-pits, and fiendish land mines. Above these snares lay his trenches in tiers, where the main force of his command was already waiting. Cautiously he began his feigned retreat.

When Bobbie returned to the road, he found that the other half of the ambuscade had quietly disappeared. He spent perhaps an hour with his wounded. Then he found and took up the trail. But "L" Troop was living under a new regime. It moved cautiously, with its scouts (who had learned their business from the White Mountain Apaches) far to the front, Sergeant Dale commanding. It was these scouts who discovered Aguilar's "position" and Aguilar himself, impudently mounted on Levant, waiting impatiently for the first signs of pursuit, and impudently outlined against the skyline of a little hill. Dale swore. Then a very shrewd look came into his wrinkle-tanned old eyes. He motioned his men to dismount—all save one, who rode with a whispered message back to the troop commander. Bobbie heard it and grinned. Then he halted the troop and called a trumpeter.

At his position on the hilltop, Levant was becoming uneasy. The wind was bringing up odors that disturbed him. Aguilar jerked the reins and told him to be still, but the voice was strange and the words were stranger. Suddenly Levant *was* still—as still as a marble horse on a pedestal—ears pricked sharply forward, nose thrust out, and nostrils dilated. From some place in the flatlands below tinkled a sound, so faint and distant that Aguilar hardly heard it. Levant heard and knew it well. He had heard it twice a day for years. It means the same thing to every horse in the cavalry, and it is the first thing a recruit horse learns, for it calls to grateful grooming, water, and feed. It was stable call, and nine times out of ten it will stop a stampeded herd, and always it will bring the horses in a paddock galloping breakneck to the gate. Levant lunged, and Aguilar did an unwise thing. He struck the old horse over the ears and poll with the flat of his bolo.

"Kitty, *bar* the door!" old Dale always puts it. "It was all off. Fer at that minute, the trumpeter blowed 'Charge,' an' Levant knows the calls as well as he knows me. He was off like a bat from the bad place. He 'charged' all right, an' Ageelar! He ain't over bein' scared yet. He makes a fall fer the mane and he hangs on fer all he knows. Levant was a-foggin' like a quarter horse at the stretch—nose an' tail in a straight line an' belly nigh touchin' the ground at every jump. He didn't stop till he got to the troop an' the men had Aggie off a' that an' up before Bobbie quicker 'n the cook can say, 'Come an' git it.' "

"L" Troop went wild. There was little food for a feast and only soggy dog tents for comfort in camp that night, but they had more than food and shelter. They made a fire and danced about it like the lesser demons of the pit. They forgot discipline and carried their lieutenant about on their shoulders, mauling him without mercy. They put the old horse in the center of a ceremonial circle, about which they marched, first with yells that dropped to a sort of delirious chant, lapsed into hoarseness, and then to squeaking, when their voices were quite gone.

"No," explains Sergeant Dale, "we didn't attack that position. Aggie *was* the insurrection in our parts. Levant here had captured him, an' that was all we wanted. It was dangerous—but all them ain't the main reasons. You see," here his eyes closed to shrewd sparkling slits—"we *might*—they was jest that *shade* of chancet, that we'd recapture that Wentworth man, *but* we didn't."

84

George Pattullo

THE MAN-KILLER

All this happened in the Bad Year, which was not so many months ago. The outfit issued daily from their camps—riding bog, skinning cattle, and driving in the helpless to the home pastures to be fed on oil cake and alfalfa. The cows were walking skeletons, wild of eye, ready to wheel in impotent anger on their rescuers; or sinking weakly to the ground at the least urging, never to rise again. Every creek was dry. Springs that were held eternal became slimy mudholes and a trap. A well-grown man could easily step across the San Pedro, oozing sluggishly past mauled carcasses.

Wherever one rode he found bones of hapless creatures or starved cows stretched flat on their sides, waiting for death to end their sufferings. And the flies settled in sickening, heaving clusters. Each mire held its victim. Wobbly-legged calves wandered over the range, crying for mothers that could never come. And the sun blazed down out of a pale sky.

Even the saving mesquite in the draws and on the ridges was failing as sustenance; of grass there was none. The country lay bleak and gasping from Tombstone to the border. Not even a desert cow, accustomed to slake her water hunger by chewing cactus, could have long survived such blighting months. How we prayed for rain!

Manuel Salazar gave heed to the comet where he lay on his tarp, and crossed himself to avert the death curse which was come upon the land. This weird luminary portended dire events and Manuel began, like a prudent man, to take thought of his religion. There might be nothing in religion, as Chico contended; but a man never knows, and it is the part of wisdom to be on the safe side.

Then, one evening, when the mountains were taking on their blue sheen and the beauty of these vast stretches smote one with a feeling akin to pain, Archie Smith rode up to headquarters and tossed a human hand on the porch.

"Found it in the far corner of the Zacatón Bottom," he said.

Jim Floyd recognized it at once by the triangular scar on the palm. The hand had been gnawed off cleanly at the wrist. Floyd wrapped the gruesome thing in a sack, wishful to give it decent interment when opportunity should offer.

"It's ol' man Greer's," he said. "You remember ol' man Greer? He used to dig postholes for the Lazy L. Where's the rest of him, Smith?"

"I aim to go and see. Ki-yotes eat him up, don't you reckon, Jim?"

"It sure looks that way. Pore ol' Greer—he could dig

postholes right quick," the boss answered.

What Archie found of the digger of postholes established nothing of the manner of death. Both arms were gone, and wolves had dragged the body; hence, there was no real argument against the theory that old man Greer, who indulged a taste for tequila, had sustained a fall from his horse and had perished miserably within sight of the ranch. Yet Archie found this hard to believe. Wolves do not crush in the skull of a man, and it was the cowboy's conviction that anyone could fall off Hardtimes, the digger's mount, twice or thrice a day with no other injury than the blow to his pride.

Two days later Manuel Salazar brought in Greer's horse, shockingly gaunt and worried, and swelled as to the head. But what interested the outfit, when the saddle and bridle had been removed from Hardtimes, were long, parallel wales along neck and flank. Archie pronounced them to be the marks of a horse's teeth.

"That don't show anything. He wandered off and got into a fight with another horse," Floyd asserted. "Yes, sir, it's like that he done just that."

After which he dismissed the unfortunate Greer from his mind. The outfit shook its head and expressed sorrow for the lonely digger, but opined that his fate surely went to show how injurious steady application to tequila could be, more especially in cruel weather. The Mexicans and the nesters in outlying parts were not satisfied with the explanation put forward. They discussed the mystery during protracted pauses in work and in the dark of the night. When two men met on a trail and halted to pass the time of day, old man Greer was the subject of talk. There were rumors of a snug fortune the digger had amassed and buried—sixty-six thousand dollars in gold, it was. Joe Toole, who made a nice, comfortable living by systematic theft of calves from the cattle company, did not hesitate to hint that Greer had died a victim to its professional gunfighter for reasons best known to the rich corporation;

but, then, Joe was prejudiced. Soon the death grew to a murder, and no man not of white blood would ride the Zacatón Bottom after nightfall.

Tommy Floyd talked of these and other matters to his father as the boss was feeding Apache.

"Pshaw!" Floyd said contemptuously. "Don't you put no stock in them stories, Tommy boy. Some people in this here country can smell a skunk when they sight a dead tree."

"But what do you guess killed him, Dad?"

"I don't know, son. I sure wish I did," was the troubled reply.

He punched Apache in the ribs to make him move over. The huge jack laid back his ears and his tail whisked threateningly, but he gave place with an awkward flop, and Floyd laughed. Others might fear Apache, but he knew there was not the least particle of viciousness lurking in that hammerlike head. Of all the ranch possessions—blooded horses, thoroughbred Herefords and cow ponies—he liked the jack best. It pandered to his vanity that others should avoid the monster, or approach him in diffidence, with suspicion and anxiety; and, in truth, Apache's appearance was sufficiently appalling. Great as was his blue-gray bulk, it was dwarfed by the ponderous head; his knees were large and bulbous, and when he opened his mouth to bray, laying bare the powerful teeth, Apache was a spectacle to scare the intrepid. Horses would run at sight of him; an entire pasture would squeal with fear and flee on his approach. Yet there was not a gentler animal to handle in the million acres of the company's range.

Toward the fag end of a day Tommy was eating *panocha* on the steps of the porch, a favorite diversion with him. While removing some particles thereof from his cheek, in the region of his ear, he espied his father riding homeward from the Zacatón Bottom. Something in the way the boss swayed in the saddle brought Tommy's head up alertly. Floyd was clinging to the horn and the reins trailed on the ground. The boy threw his crust away and ran to meet him. A dozen yards from the house the horse stopped, as though he knew that the end of the journey had come for his master.

"That black devil, Tommy!" his father gasped, and lurched outward and to the ground.

Two of the boys came running and bore Floyd to his bed. That he had contrived to ride home filled them with wonder at his endurance and fortitude—nearly the whole of his right side was torn away, one arm swung limply, and there were ragged cuts on the head. Tommy hovered near, crying to him to open his eyes.

The boss never regained consciousness, and died at midnight.

A Mexican doctor was summoned from a border village—his American competitor was off in the Dragoons, assisting at an increase to the population. After a minute examination the man of medicine announced that five ribs were broken. It was his opinion that Señor Floyd had met with an accident, from the effects of which he had passed away. Nobody was inclined to dispute this finding.

"Something done tromped him," Dan Harkey asserted. "It's like one of them bulls got into the Bottom and went for him when he got down to drink."

"No," said Archie positively, "a bull couldn't have tore him up that way. It looks to me like teeth done that."

Then Tommy awoke from the benumbed state in which he had moved since the tragedy and repeated his father's dying words. They were very simple of interpretation. A black man had drifted into the country from eastern Texas, and lived, an outcast, on a place not fifteen miles from headquarters. It was well known that Floyd had had trouble with him, being possessed of a prejudicial contempt for Negroes, and twice had made threats to run the newcomer off.

"A nigrah could easy have beat him up thataway," Dan

declared. "A nigrah could do most anything. Yes, sir, he beat him to death—that's what he done. It's like he used that old hoe of his'n."

Word of the killing flew over the land in the marvelous fashion news is carried in the cow country. Within twelve hours men knew of it in the most remote canyons of the Huachucas, and a party of nine set forth from headquarters. But somebody had carried warning, for the lonely hut was untenanted and the door swung loose on its rawhide hinges.

They buried Floyd on top of a hill where the wind had a free sweep, and piled a few stones atop. Tommy fashioned a cross out of two rough boards; and the boss sleeps there today. The sheriff was deeply stirred and had notices posted throughout the territory.

$250 REWARD

For the arrest, dead or alive, of the man who brutally murdered James Floyd, boss of the Tumbling K, sixteen miles from here, sometime yesterday evening. This man is supposed to be a Negro; about forty years of age; black; about six feet in height and weighing close to two hundred pounds. Has a razor scar above the left ear.

He has in his possession a .35 caliber autoloading rifle, No. 5096, and a .32-30 pistol. He may be riding a sorrel horse with a roached mane, branded 93 on left hip.

This crime is one of the most dastardly in the criminal annals of the Territory, and I earnestly urge every officer and other person receiving this circular to do everything in his power to effect the capture of this human fiend.

The above reward is only a preliminary reward, which may be increased later to one thousand dollars, when the governor, with whom the matter will be taken up, is heard from.

Wire me if any suspect is arrested, or if any information is obtained whatever concerning this Negro, at my expense.

Two months passed, and nothing was heard or seen of the black man. The rains held off. North and east the ranges were deluged. A blight appeared to have fallen upon the Tumbling K. The land grew a shade grayer, the dust spurts whirled in gleeful, savage dance, and the cattle gave up the effort of living and lay down to die. All that the boys could do was to distribute salt and feed and work frantically to maintain the water supply. The emaciated brutes would eat of the oil cake and hay, and sweat profusely on the nose, then stiffen out and expire with a sigh. Those that clung to life carried swollen underjaws from the strain of tearing at the short grass.

"Poor bastard!" Archie grunted, tailing up a cow he had already helped to her feet three times. "It fair makes a man sick at the stummick to see 'em. Here, you doggone ol' she-devil! Why don't you try for to help yourself? Up you come! That's it; try to hook me."

It was no use. He shot her where she lay, and skinned her. Then, with the wet hide dragging at the end of a rope and her calf thrown over the fork of the saddle, he set out for headquarters. The orphan was a lusty youngster, and Archie made him many promises, accompanied by many strange oaths.

"Li'l' dogie," he said, "I'll find a mammy for you tonight if I have to tie up the old milch cow. Do you think you can suck a milch cow, dogie? Sure you can. Man alive, feel of him kick! He's a stout rascal. You'll be a fine steer some day, dogie."

On a black-dark night flames leaped above the rim of the mountain, and the Tumbling K were roused from bed to go forth with wet sacks, and rage in their hearts, for the scum of humanity who would fire a range. Twenty-six hours in the saddle and six more fighting the leaping, treacherous enemy; then two hours of sweating sleep on saddle blankets beside their hobbled horses, and back a score of miles on desperate trails for fresh mounts—three separate times they beat out the blaze with sacks and backfiring. Once more, rising heavy-lidded and dripping from the stupor of utter exhaustion, they saw it licking hungrily through the Gap. No unlucky cigarette stub thrown amid parched grass, no abandoned campfire, had done this. It was the deliberate work of an enemy.

Orders came to move the cattle down into the valley, lest they perish to the last horn, to the last torn hoof.

"It'll take you three days to move 'em ten miles," the manager said, "but never mind. Ease 'em. Ease 'em careful. The man who yells at a cow, or pushes her along, gets his time right there. The only real way to handle cattle is to let 'em do what they want and work 'em as you can. Think that over, boys."

Manuel Salazar remembered this warning as he moved his tired horse at a snail's pace behind a bunch of sick ones in the Zacatón Bottom. Manuel made twenty dollars a month with consummate ease, working only seven days in the week and only thirteen hours a day; and he would not throw his job away lightly. Therefore he permitted the gaunt cows to straggle as pleased them, humming to himself while they nibbled at tufts here and there. If one turned its head to look at him, it fell from sheer weakness; therefore he held aloof. So the sad procession crept along.

It was in Manuel's mind to save a mile by moving the bunch through the horse pasture. He put them through the gate with no trouble and was dreamily planning how he might steal back a hair rope Chico had stolen from him, when the quirt slipped out of his fingers. The vaquero got down to pick it from the ground.

"Hi! Hi!" he yelled in panic, and ducked just in time.

A black shape towered above him, striking with forefeet, reaching for the nimble Manuel with its teeth. Its mouth yawned agape; Salazar swore he could have rammed a lard bucket into it. The vaquero swerved from under the deadly hoofs and hit out blindly with the quirt. The stallion screamed his rage for the first time and lunged at him, head swinging low, the lips flicking back from the ferocious teeth. Manuel seized a stone, put to his hand by the blessed saints, and hurled it with precision, striking the horse on the nose. Midnight blared from pain and shook his royal mane in fury, but the shock stayed him and Salazar gained his horse.

"Now," he yelled, pulling his gun and maneuvering his mount that he might be ready to flee, "come on, you! You want to fight? That's music to me."

But Midnight did not want to fight. He had employed craft in stealing up on the man, and now he moved off sulkily, the whites of his eyes rolled back, a thin stream of blood trickling from his muzzle. Salazar longed to shoot holes through his shiny black hide, but contented himself with abuse instead. Was not the stallion worth five thousand dollars? Who was he—Manuel, a poor vaquero—to be considered in the same thought with so noble a beast?

"Tommy," he said as he unsaddled at headquarters, "I've found who killed your pore father. Yes, and old man Greer, too. Don't look so pale, Tommy."

Tommy stalked into the manager's office next forenoon, a very solemn and very determined, if a short and somewhat dirty figure. He was white under his freckles and he talked through his teeth, jerkily, his eyes fixed unwaveringly on the manager's face.

"Midnight!" the manager exclaimed. "Nonsense! Why, he wouldn't harm a fly. That horse would never kill a man. He's worth five thousand dollars. Since we got him from Kentucky, two years ago, a woman could handle him, Tommy boy. Salazar must have been teasing him. You'll have to look somewhere else, Tommy."

"You mean you ain't going to do nothing, Mr. Chalmers?" Tommy asked in a dry voice.

"Of course not. Midnight? Impossible. Why, that horse is worth five thousand dollars. He couldn't have done it."

Tommy went back home very slowly. That night he sat beside Manuel's candle and cleaned and oiled a sawed-off .25-30 rifle, inherited from the man who slept on the hill. Salazar smoked lazily and watched him through drooping lids. The boy finished his task and leaned forward on the stool, staring at the tiny flame, the weapon across his knees.

Of what avail to shoot Midnight? Of course it would be easy. Tommy had acquired some degree of skill by blowing the heads off chickens whenever any were desired for the dinner table, and he felt assured that at two hundred yards he could pick off the stallion with one pressure of his finger. It would be mere child's work to distinguish Midnight from the mares, even on the murkiest night. But, after all—had the stallion done the killing? He had only Manuel's experience and suspicions to go on. Moreover, if he took punishment into his own hands, they might throw him into a jail. Midnight was worth five thousand dollars; assuredly, Mr. Chalmers would cast Tommy out into the world to shift for himself. He put the rifle back under his bunk.

Very discreetly Tommy entered the horse pasture at sunup—he had been unable to sleep for scheming—and made his way down the mile-long fence toward the corner where the mares usually grazed at that hour. He had a six-shooter in his pocket for an emergency, but he hoped that he would not use it. Midnight sighted him and stood rigid a full minute, twenty paces in advance of the mares, gazing at the boy. He was a regal animal; Tommy thought he had never seen so glorious a horse. Then the stallion advanced with mincing steps, his head bobbing, the ears laid back. He sidled nearer, without haste, whinnying softly. The boy waited until he was a dozen feet distant, then threw himself flat and rolled under the barbed-wire fence. With a rending scream Midnight reared and plunged for him, his forefeet battering the ground where Tommy had fallen. He tore at the earth in discomfiture and wrath, and raved up and down on the other side of the fence, his nostrils flaring, his eyes a glare of demoniacal hate. Tommy surveyed him in deathly quiet.

The dark came warm, with puffs of hot wind, so that the Tumbling K men reviled the discomfort joyously, since it presaged rain. So long as the cold nights endured there could be no relief. Tommy slipped from the bunkhouse for a breath of air, though it was past bedtime and they had told him to turn in.

"Apache!" he called in a low tone, gliding into the stall.

The jack cocked his monstrous ears and listened, knowing well the voice. Tommy put a halter over his head and opened the stall door. It was gnawed and scarred by Apache's teeth and hooves, and the boy wrenched it from the hinges and laid it aslant on the ground.

"You done bust your way out, Apache," he whispered. "You hear me, you ol' devil?"

He led him out into the corral and thence into the lane, talking softly as they went. Apache raised his nose and sniffed of the wind. When they reached the horse pasture, the boy tore out the strands of wire at a spot near the corner of the fence.

"You was fond of my dad, wasn't you, Apache?" Tommy quavered, working with nervous fingers to unbuckle the halter. "Then go to it."

The jack required no bidding. He wrenched free and stepped carefully over the wire into Midnight's domain. Apache never did anything in ill-judged haste. A blur, two hundred yards off, attracted him and he headed toward it eagerly. A moment, and he stopped; then went forward with caution.

Midnight had seen him coming. He trotted out from his band of mares and halted expectantly. Next instant he had recognized Apache for what he was, and shrilled a challenge. The jack brayed like a fiend and went forward slowly to meet him.

Now, a capable jack can whip any stallion that ever breathed. It is really an education to watch a jack like the mighty Apache fight. There exists the same difference between the methods of a stallion and a jack as between those of a nervous amateur boxer and the seasoned champion. A jack has no fear that anyone can detect, and is practically insensible to pain. One can see at a glance what an advantage this gives him over an opponent with any lingering predilection for longevity.

Also, a jack never fights for glory, never fights for the gallery. His sole object is to win. Wherefore, no idle and frivolous prancing about for him—no swift rush in, a blind striking with hooves, a tearing with the teeth, then out again. A jack is not constructed that way. Fighting is a business—a serious, albeit a pleasurable, business, and he attends to that side of it with passionate singleness of purpose. He will watch his opportunity with the alert coolness of the professional, wasting not an ounce of energy. When the opening comes, he goes to it like the stroke of a rattler, gets his grip, and shuts his eyes and hangs on. There is considerable of the bulldog in a jack, and if he is to be gotten off at all, one must pry him off with a crowbar; in fact, next to a Shetland stallion, which is the darlingest little fighter that ever tore at an enemy's ribs, nothing more instructive can be witnessed than a full-size jack in a fair field and no interruptions.

Apache had fought before—many, many times. Therefore, he made for the foe with circumspection, his head jerking sideways, his tail tucked, ears laid flat on his neck, and his feet barely touching the ground, so lightly did his tense muscles carry him. One evil eye measured the giant horse with venomous composure.

Vastly different was Midnight's attack. The stallion had

pluck to spare, but his temper was overhasty and his skill slight. Rage forever clouded his judgment in encounter. He had learned only one plan of battle and that was to rush and bear down his opponent. There was his rival. He would kill him. Midnight's was a simple creed.

His harsh scream rent the night silence, and the fight was on. Another horse would have circled so formidable an adversary in an endeavor to create an opening, but the black's temper was too imperious for delay. Straight was his rush. He bore down on the jack at the top of his speed, his wonderful, supple body aquiver with eagerness and anger.

Then Apache did a remarkable thing—a thing almost human in ingenuity. What Apache didn't know about fighting is best forgotten. Swerving ever so slightly as the black came, he lunged to meet him, crashing shoulder to shoulder with all the strength of his tough sinews behind the impact. Hit sideways, taken off his balance, the force of Midnight's own charge contributed to his overthrow. Down he tumbled, scrambling with his feet as he fell. Before his body touched the ground, the jack whirled and lashed with both heels into his sides. With the same appalling speed, Apache drove for the throat of his prostrate enemy, secured his grip, and shut his eyes, wrenching frenziedly from side to side and upward.

It is well not to tell further what Apache did to the man-killer. A jack has about as much sense of mercy as he has of fear, and he has never been taught any rules of warfare. When he gets his enemy where his enemy would like to get him, he does his utmost to obliterate him from the face of the earth. So it was that next day the Tumbling K men were barely able to recognize the Kentucky stallion in the torn, broken, black pulp they found in the horse pasture.

All night long Apache brayed and screeched. The noise of his triumph would set a soul to quaking. It pierced Manuel's dreams and he muttered in his sleep a prayer for protection from the Evil One. The jack pranced around and around his victim, and up and down the pasture, wild with the joy of battle, magnificent in his superb strength and the pride of victory. Toward dawn he abandoned the carcass and drove off the terror-stricken mares as the just spoils of the conqueror.

Big white clouds boiled up back of the mountains that afternoon, with a stiff wind from the southeast behind them; and at sunset the heavens opened of their blessed treasure. Manuel and Tommy lay in the bunkhouse listening to the thunder of rain on the sod roof. A burro came to the door and poked his patient head inside, seeking warmth and a friendly dry spot.

"Come in!" cried Manuel cheerily. "Take a chair. Tommy, give him your bed. Ain't that music, though? Hark! Oh, the cattle! Can't you see them soaking in it, boy?"

A yellow mongrel ousted the doubtful burro from the doorway and began nosing about for a place to rest his uneasy rump. The roof was leaking in strong, hearty streams, and Salazar sprawled on his back, letting the water run onto his chest. He was smiling placidly. Tommy snuggled into the blankets and pictured to himself a new land of much grass, and clear-eyed, contented cows and high-tailed calves.

"The curse is lifted," Manuel observed piously. "Yes, sir. The dear God sent the jack to kill that stallion. How else could it be? What do you think, Tommy, boy?"

"I reckon so," said Tommy.

Cloudesley Johns

SKYROCKET AND THE BLUE STUFF

I

The Colt Arrives

The colt's dam had been a crack cow pony in her time, and, when turned into a herd of broncos which were to be driven four hundred miles, she seemed to consider herself in duty bound, though unridden, to help keep the bunch compact; she swung round and round it in a rhythmic single-foot, crashing through the light bunches of sagebrush in her path, utterly ignoring her offspring the while. Only during the halts did she display any recognition of her maternity. The colt, imitating his dam's single-foot when the pace was not too fast, and galloping when he must, kept close at her heels, leaping the brush barriers, throughout the long days for two hundred miles of the drive—nearly four hundred miles of actual travel for him; then he weakened, and was left behind in one of the canyons in a spur of the Sierra Madre range.

Inconsiderate as his parent had been, he mourned her, sulking, whinnying incessantly in sorrow and anger at his bereavement, kicking wickedly at his genial elders in the corral where he had been placed, and sniffing disgustedly at the pail of cow's milk with which Dolly Hazeltine fed him when he became hungry enough to accept the service. With his rages and his chafing, and by the nature of his life tragedy, he won the heart of Dolly. She had had a mother, too; she was impatient, oppressed by her environment; and so she loved the little restless waif, and wept over him while he drank churlishly, or ungratefully bit at her with his dripping pink mouth.

Jem Harley liked the colt, too, maintaining that he was going to be a devil. Jem Harley had an admiring fondness for all honest devils.

But the tender petting of Dolly and the rough play of Jem aroused the colt's ire equally; his temper had been soured by overstrain, and all his struggle had availed only to get him to a place he was determined not to like. From force of habit and restlessness he spent much of his time wheeling rapidly about the enclosure he was in; and, as his young heart had hardened, his expanding muscles continued to do the same.

"Certainly a devil," chuckled Jem, one day, as the colt whirled sharply and landed both pointed heels against the already sore ribs of a big plow horse that had strayed into the beaten path around which the youngster was doing his mile in about 3:04. "I'll have lots of fun breaking you some day, old boy," he added, addressing the colt.

"I won't let you, Jem Harley," protested Dolly. "You're too rough with him, and that's what makes him mean."

Jem laughed. "There are horses and horses, Dolly, and you have no practical knowledge of either kind. This little fellow sucked meanness with his first milk, and he'll drop some of it only when fully satisfied that it's not good for him."

"Oh, of course, girls don't know anything. I suppose I make him mean by being good to him, don't I?" she challenged.

Jem laughed again, in good-natured reproof. "Wait, Dolly; see which of us he likes best and minds quickest when he's a yearling," he said.

Dolly frowned impatiently: Jem never would submit to being quarreled with, not even a little.

As the pair turned back from the corral, where Jem had found Dolly with the colt, they met Robert Hazeltine coming in from some part of the ranch. His was not so strong a face as Jem Harley's; his smile of greeting—tender and wistful as he looked at Dolly, but fading altogether when her glance met his—was weak. His manner showed that he expected her to speak.

"You should see that colt, Papa," she said, but with less animation than she had displayed in fencing with Jem. "He bosses those broncos around as if he were born a prince." She walked on slowly, leaving the men standing together.

"Well, how's the mine, Jem?" asked Hazeltine, with cheerfulness a little forced.

"I'm beginning to be afraid 'mine' isn't the name for it at all, and that it's about done as a prospect. The gold's less and less, and harder and harder to separate."

"More of the blue stuff?"

"Lots more; worse every foot we go in. If it wasn't for that cursed blue stuff, that mine would be worth twenty thousand easy; as it is—*quién sabe*? Maybe in another week it won't pay to work at all."

"I've often wondered what it can be—the blue stuff—and if it might be good for something."

"Good for nothing! It's too common and forward for that. About as good for a mine as Russian thistles are for a ranch, I guess. Heavy as it is, I'm quite sure it's not metal; it's no sort of cyanide, either, and I don't know what it is besides a confounded nuisance. It's coming so thick now that it takes less than half an hour to clog the riffles, and even when we're cleaning up it's still with us: the small grains stick in a gold pan lots worse than black sand, and we lose a lot of colors scraping them out. I wish it was some good; there's more than six tons of it in the dump alongside our sluice, and it looks like the ledge was stuffed full of it.''

"Well, when you fellows are forced to quit up there, I dare say I'll soon be giving up ranching in the canyon. It's a lonely place here, Jem—for a young girl,'' he ended wistfully, questioningly.

Jem did not perceive that it was half a question, and he had not heard the stories which had been rife in Parkersfield and San Francisco five years before, giving the name of Hazeltine a wider notoriety than the cautious and timid Robert—or the well-balanced Dolly, if he could only have known—could ever have gained for it. Then it was that Hazeltine, left alone with Dolly, had gone to make a home in the hills.

"But Dolly would make any lonely place jolly,'' Jem cried impulsively.

"A host in herself?'' said Hazeltine, smiling sadly. "Perhaps, and perhaps she feels that her talents should be employed for a purpose more august, if quite indefinite. Jem, it is Dolly wants to go—to town.''

II

"Mucha Bother"

Several times the colt, by persistent and sometimes painful effort, had splintered away the top rail of the corral fence, lightly leaping the three-foot barrier which remained, and enjoyed a wider freedom for a while—a freedom, however, which was not without its disadvantages, and he had always returned to the ranch of his own accord, if uncaptured during the first day or so. He was an epicure; the total absence of bran mush in the wild hills shocked him during his first evasion, and its periodical appearance at the corral drew him back there. Later it was green alfalfa and rolled barley that his mind dwelled upon while he wandered over the mountain ridges, springing like a goat from rock to rock, and absence made his heart grow fonder. Yet liberty is sweet, and he compromised between that and the succulent provender of which it deprived him. A time came when he did not need to kick off a section of cottonwood rail, at the risk of bruises when hooves missed, as a preliminary to his cherished outing: the five-foot fence could be cleared at a bound. But Dolly was not going to have the colt break his neck, she said; he was her chief source of recreation now, the prospectors being gone and the rancher folk of the mountains quite uninteresting, in her opinion; so another rail was added to the corral fence. Disgustedly the colt examined the whole two hundred feet of it, tried to kick away a portion, but found the height so great that accurate aim was impossible; with his slim legs damaged in the process of acquiring knowledge, he desisted. Then the Mexican came; he gave a name to the colt, but Dolly would not accept it: Diablo was the name.

The Mexican had come out of the mountains, wearing spurs and carrying a bridle, the Spanish bit of which was heavily mounted with silver; yet his boots were badly worn through walking long and far over the jagged rocks. When asked questions of a personal nature he did not understand English; at other times he understood it tolerably well. Hazeltine did not exactly employ this man, but somehow he insinuated himself into the economy of things at the ranch, and stayed.

Dolly distrusted the Mexican, slinking of body and eye,

yet delighted in commanding him imperiously. The neighbors—half a dozen families within eight miles—professed to fear the Mexican, some even opining that he would burn the house over Hazeltine's head if discharged and cut his throat some night if retained. Naturally, when this man dashed wildly down through the canyons one afternoon, his normally swarthy face livid and his eyes glaring, he was shot to death by a rancher, on suspicion, and so he never told his story. The colt had a little to do with it.

Again and again had the colt planted his rear against the fence, gazing at the side opposite, and summoning all his courage for the great feat; then he would dash across the enclosure, gather his slim legs under him for the leap, only to lose heart at the last instant, crashing into the fence and hurting himself, instead of flying over it. One day he made two attempts, retreating after the first with a red trickle down his breast from a nasty gash torn by a long splinter, his little body quivering with rage and pain. Squealing angrily, he whirled about, ran straight at the fence again, and with a mighty leap he cleared the top rail, only his hind hooves encountering it heavily. Almost on his nose he fell; his forelegs doubled under him, but were not broken; and after a whimpering whinny of distress at his numerous wounds and bruises, he paced away into the hills.

"Ramón!" called Dolly, a few moments later, at the corral gate.

"Yess, mees?" and the Mexican appeared.

"Where's the colt?" she demanded.

The Mexican stared blankly into the corral.

"I now have find heem?" he queried sullenly.

"Of course you must, and be quick. He's hurt; I know he's hurt himself."

As a matter of fact, the hurt colt had before this forgotten his hurts, having discovered certain objects of curiosity which had been overlooked in his previous wanderings. It was an abandoned prospect where a ridge of thoroughly rotted quartz had been worked as placer ground and sluiced; beside the sluice lay heaps of crumbled rock filled with a hard bluish substance. The colt ignored the blue stuff, giving his attention to the flume; obviously this thing had been constructed by human beings, doubtless with a view to the discomfort of horses; at any rate, it would be well to demolish it, and it looked easy. The light pine boxes flew in splinters from the sharp hooves, and when the work was finished, the colt held his head high, whinnying a loud challenge to all the world. That whinny brought the Mexican, and he began creeping up behind the ridges so that he might get close enough to throw a rope on the colt. Quite close he came—the colt was nipping at new bunchgrass which had forced its way out of the old dump—almost close enough to throw; but a jagged bit of quartz hurt his knee, and he looked down with an impreca-tion, gasped, screamed frantic oaths, and danced about like a madman, his bulging black eyes searching out the blue stuff in the dump. The colt paced away unnoticed. Ten minutes later the Mexican ran past the corral, shouted something to Dolly which at first puzzled her and then caused her eyes to flash with anger, and on he ran, down the canyon and the long foothill road, to where he was suddenly to die through a misapprehension.

"Impudence!" Dolly half soliloquized, when she saw her father. "And he's gone now, and he was lots of fun," she ended fretfully.

"What impudence? Who?" asked Hazeltine.

"The Mexican. I sent him after the colt—he jumped out again, after all—and presently he came back, running, and yelled at me over his shoulder, 'Mucha bother!' and then kept on down the road. What's he for but to be bothered?" she concluded indignantly.

III

All's Fair

Though half satisfied that he ought to fall in with Dolly's dearest wishes, or that he must do so eventually, Hazeltine procrastinated; Dolly said little, showing only by her manner and actions how weary she was of the mountain life. But circumstances were presently to make the situation tolerable again for a while.

The next arrival at the ranch gave the colt a name, which all acquaintances of the daring little animal adopted for him. This man was a government surveyor, by virtue of a little technical knowledge, some wealthy and influential relatives, and a charming manner. Tired of camping, he concluded that his imaginary surveys could be platted and his salary earned far more pleasantly in some comfortable mountain ranchhouse. In Hazeltine he found an old acquaintance of San Francisco days, and remembered Dolly as a ten-year-old girl; she remembered Percy Laurel, too, and was delighted.

When Laurel, having heard of the colt's exploits, was taken to the corral to see the creature, he cried:

"Hello, Skyrocket!"

Dolly laughed. Dolly knew how to laugh, and when, intuitively; she was born to charm and entertain, and her father was really inconsiderate in clinging to the mountain ranch.

Then Jem came back, after a five months' absence, and Dolly's days were filled with interest and joy. Jem had come ostensibly for a very brief visit, yet stayed and stayed, apparently because the surveyor did the same, though Jem did not seem overfond of the surveyor. Jem was dignified and frank; Laurel was very polite and most thoughtful of Jem's convenience, but there was something hidden in all this which the prospector did not like. The undeclared rivalry was not openly encouraged or even recognized by Dolly, but she found means to punish either for any hint of malice toward the other.

The young men talked much to each other in the evenings—exhibition dialogues—of things they knew and did not know, had done or had not done, and many of their half lies were amusing. Hazeltine listened critically to these performances, Dolly with delight.

Then the rivals went on bear hunts together, seeking opportunities to save each other's life, and they undertook to break Skyrocket. He acted more like a fancy reverse pinwheel than a skyrocket when they tried to ride him, and Jem kept his seat only a very little longer than Laurel did. On each occasion Skyrocket continued his whiplash contortions till, strand after strand parting, the cinch broke and the saddle was whirled high in the air. Dolly forbade further efforts in this direction, truly saying that the horse would kill himself, at least, in another turn or two; so they hitched him to a stout buckboard, without preparing his mind for it, and hung on together while he snaked it over ridges and canyons, trailing it in the air behind him as he leaped the gulches. Skyrocket returned to the ranch alone, some harness and two bits of shaft hanging to him, and Dolly, very pale, rode well ahead of a relief expedition which followed the trail. They met Jem trying to carry Laurel to the ranch; he had done half a mile of it.

For many days Jem limped around the ranch, avoiding all moving objects which might come in contact with spots where the doctor from Alpine had done some needlework on him, cursing Skyrocket from a distance for his own injuries, but yet more for Percy Laurel's broken leg. Dolly devoted most of her time and talent to the entertainment of the helpless one. Finally Jem, somewhat recovered and craving excitement, harnessed Skyrocket and drove him from the back of Dolly's saddle horse; the latter galloped, Skyrocket paced. Next the strenuous youngster was hitched double to a heavy farm wagon, and did not succeed in leaving the road for the brush; he wore himself out dragging the wagon and the other horse, with the strength of Jem's arms on the lines, and thereafter Jem was his master.

While Jem was improving the time, which had become a burden to him, certain developments were in progress in the invalid's room. For one thing, the broken bone had knit, and the patient would soon be able to stand and to walk with care; for another, he must then be leaving the ranch, to make his reports; also, Dolly showed indications of restlessness, and so far from insisting that the sufferer must not be disturbed when Jem came in to chaff the companion of his adventure, she now welcomed the prospector—so Laurel had concluded that the most auspicious moment for what he intended was at least not in the future, and even feared he had waited overlong.

Dolly had come in from a short but exciting ride with Jem behind Skyrocket; the broken but not tamed horse had given the driver little time to talk to his companion, but Dolly had seen a look in his eyes in an instant of apparent danger, as he half turned toward her, which caused her heart to flutter more than Skyrocket's plunges could, and then she had insisted on going back to the ranchhouse. With her nerves still vibrant, before reaction began, she came upon Laurel and his crutches in the deepest shadow on the ranchhouse porch.

"Stay, Dolly, and entertain me, please," he cried lightly, as she started back and would have retreated. "Please, Dolly," he begged as she hesitated. "Now that I'm no longer really an invalid, I can't expect to have you playing nurse for me, of course; but I'm still too nearly helpless to be the companion of your wild adventures, so please sit here and talk to me a little while."

Dolly dropped weakly into the chair he drew up close to

his, leaning back into the shadows to hide the flush which overspread her face.

"Wild adventures?" she echoed.

"I heard you drive out, and recognized the hoofbeats of that little gray fiend. Oh, Dolly, why do you take such reckless chances?" Yet it was not of the "little gray fiend" that he was thinking. "If anything should happen to you, Dolly—" Her manner warned him and he broke off. Discomfited he was, but not unhopeful, for he saw that she was only flustered and uncertain in her mind. Laurel's heart still beat thickly, but his mind was cool.

The pause was only momentary, but it was Dolly that ended it.

"Oh, Skyrocket is quite well broken, and doesn't try many of his tricks in harness now."

"Jem is certainly a wonder," commented Laurel.

Dolly felt uneasy, and thought to change the subject as Laurel paused, yet she did not speak. Presently Laurel went on:

"I can easily understand the attraction prospecting has for him: it holds all the fascination of gambling for great stakes and all the charm of adventure. Hardship and disappointment cannot awe a man of such strength and courage as our friend Jem."

Dolly was filled with conflicting emotions—of delight at Laurel's recognition of Jem's qualities in this encomium, and an uneasy feeling that it was an encomium in appearance only. She had not learned that no thing or person is either wholly bad or wholly good, but may be the one or the other according to circumstances or the point of view. She believed, vaguely, that every trait and action may be judged by fixed standards of morality and wisdom; she had only dreamed of life, she did not know. The modulated voice of Laurel broke in upon her reverie:

"I've told him of a place I ran across a few weeks ago,

where it seems to me the croppings look promising—though I know little of minerals myself—and he's going after it presently. I suppose the delight of great hopes repays him for all he has to endure, for the never-ending seesaw of fortune."

"Oh, but someday . . ." began Dolly, and paused.

" 'Someday,' " said Laurel, "is the prospector's motto and coat of arms: someday he'll win millions, and then? *Quién sabe?* Perhaps a hundred deep holes and tunnels in the mountains, dreams of other millions to be won, and then a pack and burro and the trail again. The life does not breed contentment, Dolly." He left the abstract now. "I hope it will not be so with Jem; I hope his someday extends beyond the bonanza which may be his, not only because of what he has done for me and my regard for him, but because he deserves it. Yet there are some things I do not wish him, Dolly." Dolly flushed crimson, and though her face was in the shadow, Laurel again stopped abruptly, but took up the thread of his discourse at once.

"But what are the probabilities? He and his partner took two thousand apiece from the place up here before that strange blue stuff drove them out, and Jem sank his share in five months on wildcat prospects. That's the way it goes, Dolly."

Dolly's hands were tightly clasped in her lap; her face was pale now.

"Why do you tell me this?" she demanded moodily.

Laurel laughed lightly. "Why, I'm sure I don't know, now that you call my attention to it. It is a rather melancholy subject we got started on, at least from our point of view; I imagine Jem would laugh at us if he had heard it."

Dolly felt chilled. She stood up and walked slowly down the porch. Laurel did not seek to detain her then.

IV

Base Metal?

Hazeltine had yielded to Dolly's will at last: two months after Percy Laurel had returned to San Francisco and Jem Harley to his prospecting, he sold the ranch and stock and went to Parkersfield to live. And it was five months after this that Jem, having opened five prospects—one of which paid the expenses of the four unsuccessful ones, leaving him two hundred dollars for his five months' work—arrived at the ranch. He found Skyrocket in disgrace and in danger of a sentence of death for having exuberantly gone mountain climbing with a buggy, to the terror and distress of his new owner, who had clung to the conveyance as long as it lasted. Jem bought the horse, led him down the canyon till he found a buckboard for sale, and then drove off for Parkersfield.

Skyrocket, after a few tentative plunges, for which he was well punished with whip and rein, paced quietly along the rough foothill road, allowing Jem's thoughts to stray again to some glittering croppings he had stumbled upon during his late wanderings. He had not sunk a prospect shaft there, being content for the moment with locating the claim; he was not sure his find would prove to be of value, for he kept telling himself he did not know what it was. That it was metal of some sort he had sufficient knowledge to know; that it was not gold was manifest, for he did have a very good working knowledge of gold; and if it did not prove to be silver, there was bitter disappointment in store for Jem Harley. Another thought possessed his mind, coupled with that of the hypothetical silver lead: he would tell Dolly of his hopes, and then of that greater hope he had held so long. And would she—if the rock carried silver? He hoped to hear her say that silver mines were nothing to her—though well aware that this would be untrue—and that Jem was all her world. Yet, with this last intoxicating thought in his mind, he drew out his specimens from the pocket of his canvas coat and examined them for the thousandth time. The metal in the ore shone and sparkled as he turned the rock in his hand till all its surfaces had caught the light of the sun.

Jem received his letters at Alpine post office, the accumulation of seven months, and drove on. Skyrocket was inclined to be frisky, and Jem presently stopped and tied him to a juniper, then he opened his mail.

Dolly's letters vaguely troubled him. She seemed too happy; what he would have wished her he did not ask himself. It caused him a jealous pang. He reread the six letters, searching for some hint of incompleteness in the life of the writer, but could find none. Two letters remained to be read; he opened the one from Hazeltine, and glanced over it. Laurel! Laurel there! In Hazeltine's letter there was a suggestion of uneasiness, a strange urgency in the invitation to Jem to visit them. But why? Hazeltine had seemed to like and admire Laurel more than Jem in the days on the canyon ranch. jem glanced at the date, and was relieved to find that it was only two weeks old—more may sometimes happen in two weeks than in two years, but Jem was seeking comfort. What little he found was short-lived: Dolly's last letter, more joyous than the rest, bore a later date by two days; Laurel had been there then, and Dolly had not told him.

There was one more letter, addressed in a hand he recognized but could not place; that could have no bearing on the existing situation, he thought, and opened it listlessly. However, it held its momentary sensation for him, for it was from Percy Laurel, flippantly urging Jem to join the "festive party" in Parkersfield at his earliest convenience. It was a sarcastic fling, yet a reckless act of honor. Jem felt neither despondent nor apathetic after that; his blood leaped hotly in his veins, and his eyes shone brightly. In a moment more Skyrocket was being allowed to gather the impression that he was running away, though held closely to the rocky stage road through the long pass.

V

What the Mexican Said

"Hello!" cried Laurel, who was walking alone along the main street of Parkersfield. "Just in time, old man."

"For what?" demanded Jem, savagely.

"Why, everything that's going; but I meant supper. Hello, Skyrocket! He's been abusing you, hasn't he? What was the matter, Jem? Been hurrying, I should say."

Jem flushed under the banter. "Skyrocket doesn't care about slow travel," he mumbled, "and I let him come through."

"Well, Dolly's saddle horse and mine fill the bit of stable at the place, but if you'll give me a lift down there I'll take Transit to a boarding stable and make room for Skyrocket. Oh, that's all right, I've had the stall three weeks, and it's proper I vacate for you. Don't worry, Jem; I'll have my share."

Jem scowled darkly, and made little reply to the running fire of comment upon things in general which Laurel kept up.

"Dolly's the forefront of everything in this place," he was saying. "There was never any social life in the wretched little town as I remember it; but, say!—well, 'Frisco'd be a lot too small for her, I say." He broke off to direct the morose Jem, and the buckboard swung through Hazeltine's gate.

"I'm glad, very glad to see you, Jem, my boy," said Hazeltine, gravely. "Any good news?"

"I don't know," answered Jem, thinking of the bright

metal and trying to feel sure it was silver. "Prospects," he added, "but I haven't gone down on them much yet."

"Well, I'm glad you've come. I don't know what to do about your horse; our—"

"Transit yields to Skyrocket," interrupted the surveyor, and went to saddle his horse.

"Skyrocket? So it is!" cried Hazeltine.

"I bought him at the ranch. I didn't know you'd gone till I got there," explained Jem. "How's Dolly?"

"Quite well, and seems very happy, but I fear not altogether content," he said, with an unconscious sigh.

"How'll you swap plugs, Jem?" asked Laurel, riding up. "Mine's a good saddle horse, and fast; a good stayer, too."

"I'm going to keep Skyrocket," said Jem.

"Then I keep Transit; you've got the only horse I'd trade him for."

Dolly did not come out to meet Jem; her greeting, when he went in, was not effusive, as it had been on other occasions. She seemed to study him reflectively, while he talked with her father or Laurel.

Dolly appeared to be a little tired. Through the supper hour she remained soberly contemplative, rousing only once to frown impatiently at Jem's attempt to emulate Laurel in his brilliant banter. Later in the evening they went out, and with Dolly as his rather passive sponsor and Laurel exerting himself to win general attention to the wanderer, Jem became a lion in the petty social circle which had formed about Dolly Hazeltine. He enjoyed it, too, though always with an uneasy feeling that Laurel was doing it all. Dolly seemed surprised at Jem's complacency, and scarcely pleased.

The interest in the new life, such as he found it in its freshness, and the presence of Dolly made Jem forget or ignore the problem which had perplexed him when he came, but finally he sent his specimens to be assayed. Having done this, he began to fear that the report would leave him without even the doubtful prospect of fortune to offer Dolly, and he hastened to tell her of his hopes; then he would tell of the hope he cherished.

"Silver!" cried Dolly, excitedly, but Jem checked her, explaining that it might not be.

"Then you'll be prospecting over the mountains again, months and years," she said. "What is the use, Jem? Look at those old men that used to come to the ranch, twisted with rheumatism so that it made my bones ache to see them, prospecting all their lives and dying in the mountains. I don't want ever to live in the mountains anymore. Do you like them? Why don't you stop it, Jem?"

Then a soft flush overspread her face and throat, deepening as he began:

"I would Dolly, if—"

"If everything was just as you wanted it," she interrupted hastily, "which it can't ever be, for you don't know what you want."

"Oh, Dolly! I do know, and—"

Dolly laughed nervously. "You're too unreasonable and absurd to talk to today, Jem," she protested, and would have retreated but that he caught her hand and held it.

"If it is silver, Dolly," he said, "if I can leave the mountains forever and take you wherever you care to go—Dolly, will you marry me then?"

Dolly whimpered, hanging weakly back from him. "Don't, Jem!" she pleaded. "Don't ask me that." Then her trepidation passed and she laughed. "I don't want to marry a silver mine, Jem," she said.

In his surprise he released her, but as she backed away from him he cried:

"Marry me, then! Oh, Dolly, I love you so!"

"No, Jem," she answered gravely. "I won't be a prospector either." Again she tried to laugh, but failed. He let her go.

The following day the assayer's report came. It showed the rock to go twenty cents per ton in silver, fifty cents in gold, and about eleven dollars in lead: a very valuable prospect if the ore could be milled at the mine, but it could not.

Laurel, in his sympathy, was a little less flippant than usual; Hazeltine was manifestly grieved; Dolly had nothing to say. Jem then declined Laurel's suggestion that they pay some calls and get cheered up, Dolly likewise refusing, and Jem retired into a corner of the parlor with a work on metallurgy, the leaves of which he began moodily turning. He knew it could not tell him how to run a mill without water, and that twelve dollars a ton would not pay for hauling and shipping the ore, yet he began reading passages in the chapters on lead. The metal was bright and shiny in the ore, he saw it stated. All he read was almost new to him, for, like many another prospector with some knowledge of gold-bearing rocks, he knew almost nothing of other ores.

"Well, then, what does silver look like?" the question formed itself in his mind.

Angrily, as if he had a grievance against nature for deceiving him by appearances, he turned to the chapters on silver ores, reading several pages absently, the words making no impression on his mind; but suddenly something impelled him to fix his attention on the book—something he had just read, with his mind far away, vaguely suggested some elusive memory. What was it? He ran his eye up along the page.

". . . of a dull blue color," that was it; but what—why, it was silver he was reading about!

"Blue in the ore!" he gasped, and then, throwing down the book, he leaped across the room and seized Dolly's wrist.

"What was it he said?" he demanded wildly.

The girl shrank back from him, terrified.

"The Mexican," ejaculated Jem. "He was from the mines of Mexico, I'm sure of it, and he knew. Tell me what it was he said. Listen! Think! You said it was 'mucha bother'; remember? Wasn't it 'mucha plata'? Dolly, tell me!"

"Why, that was it!" she answered, amazed. "But what is it? What did he mean? Jem, what is it?"

"Silver! Virgin silver by the ton!"

"Well"—in an imperturbable drawl Laurel spoke—"I'll race you for that silver, Jem."

"You have no right!" cried Dolly. "It's Jem's; he mined it for months."

"Location expired some six months ago, I believe," demurred Laurel, easily; "but if you say so, Dolly, Jem shall go for the silver alone."

Dolly turned white, leaning back against the wall. Laurel laughed lightly, but there was a hard gleam in his eyes.

"I guess we race, Jem. Boots and saddles, old man, or—er—possibly you prefer to drive?"

VI

The Race for the Blue Stuff

"Shall I help you hitch up, Jem? No? Well, you're wise: I'd cut the tugs for you. This is war, Jem. By the way, shall you pack a gun?"

"Gun! No!" snorted Jem, contemptuously.

"Well, so long as it's even, I won't. *Au revoir.* You'll get a little lead before Transit takes the trail, but we'll pass you this side of Round Top in spite of Skyrocket's wiry legs." The last words came faintly to Jem through the darkness, and Laurel was gone.

Jem harnessed Skyrocket quickly, but with great care. Hazeltine had lighted a lantern and come out as Laurel started off, and lighted Jem at his work.

"Good-bye," he said as his guest drove slowly out, "and good luck to you."

Jem held in his pawing horse at the gate, though it was open; he could see nothing and knew nothing, yet his heart beat as heavily as it might in a close finish to the race which was to be run that night.

"Dolly!" he called softly.

She stepped out from the shadow of a peppertree and stood beside the buckboard.

"I didn't want to keep you, Jem," she panted. "Go!"

He leaned down and kissed her, and her arms clung about his neck for a moment; then Skyrocket was off.

Dark clouds smothered the stars and moon; the reins Jem held were damp with moisture from the heavy air. Mud in the long pass, of which there seemed to be every promise now, would clog even the light wheels of a buckboard far more than it would hamper a saddle horse, yet Jem was laughing silently as Skyrocket fell into his stride along the valley road. He tightened the reins a little.

Once the cloud banks lifted in the east. Round Top loomed shadowy against the dark mass of the towering Sierra, and beyond, above, the sky was for a moment filled with a soft opalescent light from the hidden moon; then they thickened again and a driving mist swept across the valley.

Rain behind that, thought Jem. My race is with the storm, and if I beat it I'll tire his Transit in the last ten miles. Skyrocket knows the road.

Round Top, a dark blur in the mist, came in sight again, close ahead on the right, as the buckboard swung around the curve and whirled away straight for the mouth of the long pass; but out of the wet night behind came a loping horse, drawing slowly up to the pacer, and, with the isolated mountain still fifty yards in front, passed him. A cynical chuckle, an unspoken I told you, came back from the rider; it was answered by a peal of laughter so triumphant that the chuckle died in Laurel's throat. Yet he called out to the driver:

"Rain with yours, Jem; I'll beat it to the summit and leave you and it in the pass behind: prophecy number two. With my location made in the morning, and you left with your precious lead mine, I'll have another prophecy for you." The mist swallowed him. Jem drew the lines still tighter as Skyrocket tried to bolt after the saddle horse.

Round Top faded into the thick night behind, and close before the buckboard a huge black post suddenly appeared— an old dead oak the fallen branches of which had been replaced by two rough pine boards, one pointing back the way they had come, the other to the right.

"Ten miles," said Jem.

Straight away they went. Jem slackened the lines a little, and trees, rocks, fences, and ranchhouses rushed at them out of the murky nearer distance and scurried away behind.

The blanketed landscape changed, and they passed through a brush-grown country, where the road now rose before them like a white signboard in the distorting gray mist, or fell away like a chalk-marked precipice; but only to the eyes of the man was the way so strange. And now appeared a vast wall before them through the thinning mist, rising far above them and shading away into the somber sky, darkening with every mile covered by the beating hooves, seeming to bend over them at last. Against the black wall Jem saw a blacker line, and soon it sank away before them, deep into the great mountain range, and the buckboard swayed and rattled over the loose stones of the long pass.

A yellow bar of light lay over the road at the second turn, and here Jem brought Skyrocket to a standstill.

"Hello!" he called, while Skyrocket drank at the trough before the mountain saloon.

"Hello!" came the response. "A drink? Feller hoss-back ahead said to say there'd be no arsenic in it, if you wanted some; nor there wouldn't be, nohow, for I ain't that kind. What's the row?"

"I've no time to tell you now. No, I won't drink, thanks. How long gone?"

"Half an hour, 'bout— Whew! that's a hoss an' a half!"

Skyrocket was off through the pass.

Click-click, click-click, click-click. For hours of the long climb the rhythmic beat of the steel-shod hooves never flagged, and at last, on the final curve of the upward way, Skyrocket paced out of the heavy mist, out and above the lowering clouds, and stood still on the summit, under the twinkling stars.

Jem looked back and listened; the gray smother filled all the canyons below him—a fantastic, flimsy sea in the blue-white light of the moon—while out of it rose the taller peaks of the range like islands; but up from its depths came a swishing, screeching sound, for the storm had followed close, and was roaring up the narrow pass behind. And Jem laughed loudly, there on the crest of the range, looking down in the soft moonlight at the rain-whipped mountains below.

"Second prophecy wrong!" he cried.

Down the mountain, tugs loose, paced Skyrocket, breathing hard, but with no nerveless jerking of the knees. Alpine, all dark, was left behind, and the flying hooves rang loudly on the foothill road.

Fifty miles away, now, was the drenched city of Parkersfield, where Dolly shivered at the sound of wind and rain; and here, in the light of stars and the setting moon, Skyrocket entered the last long stretch of the race.

Mile after mile he paced steadily, his sharp ears held stiffly back, while Jem watched fearfully for the sinking and rising of the flanks, the spasmodic heave of the ribs, which should tell him the pace was too fast and the race lost; but the dreaded signs had not appeared when Rattlesnake Rocks were passed. Nine miles more to the blue stuff. Where was Laurel?

Jem no longer watched the flanks of his horse, but fixed

his eyes on the outstretched head, for the regular beat of the hooves told him that now Skyrocket would last to the end; but the sharp ring of the steel shoes could not prevent his heart from sinking as the miles spun away behind, for he had not seen what he watched for so eagerly.

Tight on the slopes and loose on the levels were the reins over Skyrocket's back, and Jem urged him forward every moment with his voice; pebbles rattled in the spokes of the wheels as the buckboard slid and jumped over the stones. Jem's eyes were on Skyrocket's head, but the sign he hoped for had not come.

The only ranchhouse close beside the foothill road— here the Mexican had died two years before—flashed into sight and was gone, and a mile beyond that the buckboard slid sidewise for a yard as Skyrocket wheeled sharply into the byroad to the old Hazeltine ranch. Three miles more to the silver lead! Jem's eyes were glassy, and he no longer shouted to the horse; but still he watched his head.

And suddenly Skyrocket's ears shot forward; Jem stood up in the plunging, staggering buckboard and yelled. The buckboard leaped forward drunkenly, pounding the ground like a triphammer, and Jem was sprayed by a shower of foam from the horse's mouth; Skyrocket was galloping.

One more mile and Laurel was in sight, swinging his long quirt till the writhing lash circled Transit's body and bit through the rider's clothes, drawing blood from horse and man: Laurel's sangfroid had deserted him.

Skyrocket leaped over the ground, flinging the buckboard into the air over the hollows, pounding it against the ridges. Jem was silent now, watching Laurel.

It was a savage finish.

The white dawn had come, unnoticed by the racers. In the growing light the rancher who had bought from Hazeltine stood beside the old corral where Skyrocket had spent the fretful months of his babyhood; he saw them flash past, saw Transit stagger ten feet to one side of the trail and fall like a stone, and Skyrocket go tearing away into the hills with a shattered buckboard behind him.

An hour later Jem came down, thin and haggard. Laurel was at breakfast.

"Hello!" he cried. The tone was cheery, but it was a forced note. "Where's Skyrocket?"

"Dead!" groaned Jem, and dropped heavily into a chair.

"Whew!" whistled Laurel. "Transit, too. What brutes we are, and what fools! Why didn't you stop when you saw Transit down?"

"I didn't think about how things were going," answered Jem, slowly, his eyes looking far away at nothing, his awed mind dwelling on the madness that had passed. "I'd have killed you up there, Percy, if Transit had stuck it out," he ended wonderingly.

Laurel laughed nervously. "And you're surprised at getting that way?" he asked. "I was wishing for a gun when you passed me. Didn't I say we're fools?"

Jem was weakly angry at everything, especially at Laurel for seeming to understand things.

"Well, here I am," he blurted: "now your third prophecy!"

"What wretched bad taste you have, Jem!" complained Laurel, rising. "Well, here: I named the horse that won the race for you; I'll name your mine; I'll describe the nature of the greatest felicity you now hope for in life—all!" Laurel's lips were white; he no longer sneered with placid politeness, but with the rage of a netted wasp: *"Skyrocket! Skyrocket! Skyrocket!"* he cried.

"I understand," said Jem. "But that prophecy is wrong, too," he added, with conviction.

Laurel laughed jeeringly, slammed the door shut as he passed out, and walked unsteadily down the trail.

Jem looked after him for a moment, and many thoughts of the past, of the present, and of the future rose in his mind, and there was a tightness in his throat. Something seemed to be going out of his life; much had come into it, but the sense of loss was none the less keen for that.

"Percy!" he called. Jem could not know all his tone might tell.

Laurel stopped short and stood still for an instant without turning; then he laughed and looked back at Jem.

"*Adiós!*" he cried, waving his hand.

Rudyard Kipling

THE MALTESE CAT

They had good reason to be proud, and better reason to be afraid, all twelve of them; for though they had fought their way, game by game, up the teams entered for the polo tournament, they were meeting the Archangels that afternoon in the final match; and the Archangels men were playing with half a dozen ponies apiece. As the game was divided into six quarters of eight minutes each, that meant a fresh pony after every halt. The Skidars' team, even supposing there were no accidents, could only supply one pony for every other change; and two to one is heavy odds. Again, as Shiraz, the gray Syrian, pointed out,

they were meeting the pink and pick of the polo ponies of
Upper India, ponies that had cost from a thousand rupees
each, while they themselves were a cheap lot gathered, often
from country carts, by their masters, who belonged to a poor
but honest native infantry regiment.

"Money means pace and weight," said Shiraz, rubbing
his black-silk nose dolefully along his neat-fitting boot, "and
by the maxims of the game as I know it—"

"Ah, but we aren't playing the maxims," said the Maltese
Cat. "We're playing the game; and we've the great advantage
of knowing the game. Just think a stride, Shiraz! We've pulled
up from bottom to second place in two weeks against all those
fellows on the ground here. That's because we play with our
heads as well as our feet."

"It makes me feel undersized and unhappy all the same,"
said Kittiwynk, a mouse-colored mare with a red brow band
and the cleanest pair of legs that ever an aged pony owned.
"They've twice our style, these others."

Kittiwynk looked at the gathering and sighed. The hard,
dusty polo ground was lined with thousands of soldiers, black
and white, not counting hundreds and hundreds of carriages
and drags and dogcarts, and ladies with brilliant-colored para-
sols, and officers in uniform and out of it, and crowds of
natives behind them; and orderlies on camels, who had halted
to watch the game, instead of carrying letters up and down the
station; and native horse dealers running about on thin-eared
Baluchi mares, looking for a chance to sell a few first-class
polo ponies. Then there were the ponies of thirty teams that
had entered for the Upper India Free-for-All Cup—nearly
every pony of worth and dignity, from Mhow to Peshawar,
from Allahabad to Multan; prize ponies, Arabs, Syrian, Barb,
country-bred, Deccanee, Waziri, and Kabul ponies of every
color and shape and temper that you could imagine. Some of
them were in mat-roofed stables, close to the polo ground, but
most were under saddle, while their masters, who had been

defeated in the earlier games, trotted in and out and told the world exactly how the game should be played.

It was a glorious sight, and the come and go of the little, quick hooves, and the incessant salutations of ponies that had met before on other polo grounds or racecourses were enough to drive a four-footed thing wild.

But the Skidars' team were careful not to know their neighbors, though half the ponies on the ground were anxious to scrape acquaintance with the little fellows that had come from the North, and, so far, had swept the board.

"Let's see," said a soft-gold-colored Arab, who had been playing very badly the day before, to the Maltese Cat; "didn't we meet in Abdul Rahman's stable in Bombay, four seasons ago? I won the Paikpattan Cup next season, you may remember?"

"Not me," said the Maltese Cat, politely. "I was at Malta then, pulling a vegetable cart. I don't race. I play the game."

"Oh!" said the Arab, cocking his tail and swaggering off.

"Keep yourselves to yourselves," said the Maltese Cat to his companions. "We don't want to rub noses with all those goose-rumped half-breeds of Upper India. When we've won this Cup they'll give their shoes to know *us.*"

"We shan't win the Cup," said Shiraz. "How do you feel?"

"Stale as last night's feed when a muskrat has run over it," said Polaris, a rather heavy-shouldered gray; and the rest of the team agreed with him.

"The sooner you forget that the better," said the Maltese Cat, cheerfully. "They've finished tiffin in the big tent. We shall be wanted now. If your saddles are not comfy, kick. If your bits aren't easy, rear, and let the *saises* know whether your boots are tight."

Each pony had his *sais,* his groom, who lived and ate and slept with the animal, and had betted a good deal more than he could afford on the result of the game. There was no chance of anything going wrong, but to make sure, each *sais* was shampooing the legs of his pony to the last minute. Behind the *saises* sat as many of the Skidars' regiment as had leave to attend the match—about half the native officers, and a hundred or two dark, black-bearded men with the regimental pipers nervously fingering the big, beribboned bagpipes. The Skidars were what they call a Pioneer regiment, and the bagpipes made the national music of half their men. The native officers held bundles of polo sticks, long cane-handled mallets, and as the grandstand filled after lunch they arranged themselves by ones and twos at different points round the ground, so that if a stick were broken the player would not have far to ride for a new one. An impatient British Cavalry Band struck up "If you want to know the time, ask a policeman!" and the two umpires in light dustcoats danced out on two little excited ponies. The four players of the Archangels' team followed, and the sight of their beautiful mounts made Shiraz groan again.

"Wait till we know," said the Maltese Cat. "Two of 'em are playing in blinkers, and that means they can't see to get out of the way of their own side, or they *may* shy at the umpires' ponies. They've *all* got white web reins that are sure to stretch or slip!"

"And," said Kittiwynk, dancing to take the stiffness out of her, "they carry their whips in their hands instead of on their wrists. Hah!"

"True enough. No man can manage his stick and his reins and his whip that way," said the Maltese Cat. "I've fallen over every square yard of the Malta ground, and I ought to know."

He quivered his little, flea-bitten withers just to show how satisfied he felt; but his heart was not so light. Ever since he had drifted into India on a troop ship, taken, with an old rifle, as part payment for a racing debt, the Maltese Cat had played and preached polo to the Skidars' team on the Skidars' stony polo ground. Now, a polo pony is like a poet. If he is born with a love for the game, he can be made. The Maltese Cat knew that bamboos grew solely in order that polo balls might be turned from their roots, that grain was given to ponies to keep them in hard condition, and that ponies were shod to prevent them slipping on a turn. But, besides all these things, he knew every trick and device of the finest game in the world, and for two seasons had been teaching the others all he knew or guessed.

"Remember," he said for the hundredth time, as the riders came up, "you *must* play together, and you *must* play with your heads. Whatever happens, follow the ball. Who goes out first?"

Kittiwynk, Shiraz, Polaris, and a short high little bay fellow with tremendous hocks and no withers worth speaking of (he was called Corks) were being girthed up, and the soldiers in the background stared with all their eyes.

"I want you men to keep quiet," said Lutyens, the captain of the team, "and especially not to blow your pipes."

"Not if we win, Captain Sahib?" asked the piper.

"If we win you can do what you please," said Lutyens with a smile, as he slipped the loop of his stick over his wrist and wheeled to canter to his place. The Archangels' ponies were a little bit above themselves on account of the many-colored crowd so close to the ground. Their riders were excellent players, but they were a team of crack players instead of a crack team; and that made all the difference in the world. They honestly meant to play together, but it is very hard for four men, each the best of the team he is picked from, to remember that in polo no brilliancy in hitting or riding makes up for playing alone. Their captain shouted his orders to them by name, and it is a curious thing that if you call his name aloud in public after an Englishman you make him hot and fretty. Lutyens said nothing to his men, because it had all been said before. He pulled up Shiraz, for he was playing back, to guard the goal. Powell on Polaris was halfback, and Macnamara and Hughes on Corks and Kittiwynk were forwards. The tough bamboo ball was set in the middle of the ground, one hundred and fifty yards from the ends, and Hughes crossed sticks, heads up, with the captain of the Archangels, who saw fit to play forward; that is a place from which you cannot easily control your team. The little click as the cane shafts met was heard all over the ground, and then Hughes made some sort of quick wrist stroke that just dribbled the ball a few yards. Kittiwynk knew that stroke of old, and followed as a cat follows a mouse. While the Captain of the Archangels was wrenching his pony round, Hughes struck with all his strength, and next instant Kittiwynk was away, Corks following close behind her, their little feet pattering like raindrops on glass.

"Pull out to the left," said Kittiwynk between her teeth. "It's coming your way, Corks!"

The back and halfback of the Archangels were tearing down on her just as she was within reach of the ball. Hughes leaned forward with a loose rein, and cut it away to the left almost under Kittiwynk's foot, and it hopped and skipped off to Corks, who saw that if he was not quick it would run beyond the boundaries. That long bouncing drive gave the Archangels time to wheel and send three men across the ground to head off Corks. Kittiwynk stayed where she was; for she knew the game. Corks was on the ball half a fraction of a second before the others came up, and Macnamara, with a backhanded stroke, sent it back across the ground to Hughes, who saw the way clear to the Archangels' goal, and smacked the ball in before any one quite knew what had happened.

"That's luck," said Corks, as they changed ends. "A goal in three minutes for three hits, and no riding to speak of."

"Don't know," said Polaris. "We've made 'em angry too soon. Shouldn't wonder if they tried to rush us off our feet next time."

"Keep the ball hanging, then," said Shiraz. "That wears out every pony that is not used to it."

Next time there was no easy galloping across the ground. All the Archangels closed up as one man, but there they stayed, for Corks, Kittiwynk, and Polaris were somewhere on the top of the ball, marking time among the rattling sticks, while Shiraz circled about outside, waiting for a chance.

"We can do this all day," said Polaris, ramming his quarters into the side of another pony. "Where do you think you're shoving to?"

"I'll—I'll be driven in an *ekka* if I know," was the gasping reply, "and I'd give a week's feed to get my blinkers off. I can't see anything."

"The dust is rather bad. Whew! That was one for my off-hock. Where's the ball, Corks?"

"Under my tail. At least, the man's looking for it there! This is beautiful. They can't use their sticks, and it's driving 'em wild. Give old Blinkers a push and then he'll go over."

"Here, don't touch me! I can't see. I'll—I'll back out, I think," said the pony in blinkers, who knew that if you can't see all round your head, you cannot prop yourself against the shock.

Corks was watching the ball where it lay in the dust, close to his near foreleg, with Macnamara's shortened stick tap-tapping it from time to time. Kittiwynk was edging her way out of the scrimmage, whisking her stump of a tail with nervous excitement.

"Ho! They've got it," she snorted. "Let me out!" and she galloped like a rifle bullet just behind a tall lanky pony of the Archangels, whose rider was swinging up his stick for a stroke.

"Not today, thank you," said Hughes, as the blow slid off his raised stick, and Kittiwynk laid her shoulder to the tall pony's quarters, and shoved him aside just as Lutyens on Shiraz sent the ball where it had come from, and the tall pony went skating and slipping away to the left. Kittiwynk, seeing that Polaris had joined Corks in the chase for the ball up the ground, dropped into Polaris' place, and then "time" was called.

The Skidars' ponies wasted no time in kicking or fuming. They knew that each minute's rest meant so much gain, and trotted off to the rails, and their *saises* began to scrape and blanket and rub them at once.

"Whew!" said Corks, stiffening up to get all the tickle of the big vulcanite scraper. "If we were playing pony for pony, we would bend those Archangels double in half an hour. But they'll bring up fresh ones and fresh ones and fresh ones after that—you see."

"Who cares?" said Polaris. "We've drawn first blood. Is my hock swelling?"

"Looks puffy," said Corks. "You must have had rather a wipe. Don't let it stiffen. You'll be wanted again in half an hour."

"What's the game like?" said the Maltese Cat.

"Ground's like your shoe, except where they put too much water on it," said Kittiwynk. "Then it's slippery. Don't play in the center. There's a bog there. I don't know how their next four are going to behave, but we kept the ball hanging, and made 'em lather for nothing. Who goes out? Two Arabs and a couple of country-breds! That's bad. What a comfort it is to wash your mouth out!"

Kitty was talking with a neck of a lather-covered soda-water bottle between her teeth, and trying to look over her withers at the same time. This gave her a very coquettish air.

"What's bad?" said Grey Dawn, giving to the girth and admiring his well-set shoulders.

"You Arabs can't gallop fast enough to keep yourselves warm that's what Kitty means," said Polaris, limping to show that his hock needed attention. "Are you playing back, Grey Dawn?"

"Looks like it," said Grey Dawn, as Lutyens swung himself up. Powell mounted the Rabbit, a plain bay country-bred much like Corks, but with mulish ears. Macnamara took Faiz-Ullah, a handy, short-backed little red Arab with a long tail, and Hughes mounted Benami, an old and sullen brown beast, who stood over in front more than a polo pony should.

"Benami looks like business," said Shiraz. "How's your temper, Ben?" The old campaigner hobbled off without answering, and the Maltese Cat looked at the new Archangel ponies prancing about on the ground. They were four beautiful blacks, and they saddled big enough and strong enough to eat the Skidars' team and gallop away with the meal inside them.

"Blinkers again," said the Maltese Cat. "Good enough!"

"They're chargers—cavalry chargers!" said Kittiwynk, indignantly. "*They'll* never see thirteen-three again."

"They've all been fairly measured, and they've all got their certificates," said the Maltese Cat, "or they wouldn't be here. We must take things as they come along, and keep your eyes on the ball."

The game began, but this time the Skidars were penned to their own end of the ground, and the watching ponies did not approve of that.

"Faiz-Ullah is shirking—as usual," said Polaris, with a scornful grunt.

"Faiz-Ullah is eating whip," said Corks. They could hear the leather-thonged polo quirt lacing the little fellow's well-rounded barrel. Then the Rabbit's shrill neigh came across the ground.

"I can't do all the work," he cried, desperately.

"Play the game—don't talk," the Maltese Cat whickered;

and all the ponies wriggled with excitement, and the soldiers and the grooms gripped the railings and shouted. A black pony with blinkers had singled out old Benami, and was interfering with him in every possible way. They could see Benami shaking his head up and down, and flapping his under lip.

"There'll be a fall in a minute," said Polaris. "Benami is getting stuffy."

The game flickered up and down between goalpost and goalpost, and the black ponies were getting more confident as they felt they had the legs of the others. The ball was hit out of a little scrimmage, and Benami and the Rabbit followed it, Faiz-Ullah only too glad to be quiet for an instant.

The blinkered black pony came up like a hawk, with two of his own side behind him, and Benami's eye glittered as he raced. The question was which pony should make way for the other, for each rider was perfectly willing to risk a fall in a good cause. The black, who had been driven nearly crazy by his blinkers, trusted to his weight and his temper; but Benami knew how to apply his weight and how to keep his temper. They met, and there was a cloud of dust. The black was lying on his side, all the breath knocked out of his body. The Rabbit was a hundred yards up the ground with the ball, and Benami was sitting down. He had slid nearly ten yards on his tail, but he had had his revenge, and sat cracking his nostrils till the black pony rose.

"That's what you get for interfering. Do you want any more?" said Benami, and he plunged into the game. Nothing was done that quarter, because Faiz-Ullah would not gallop, though Macnamara beat him whenever he could spare a second. The fall of the black pony had impressed his companions tremendously, and so the Archangels could not profit by Faiz-Ullah's bad behavior.

But as the Maltese Cat said when time was called, and the four came back blowing and dripping, Faiz-Ullah ought to have been kicked all round Umballa. If he did not behave better next time the Maltese Cat promised to pull out his Arab tail by the roots and—eat it.

There was no time to talk, for the third four were ordered out.

The third quarter of a game is generally the hottest, for each side thinks that the others must be pumped; and most of the winning play in a game is made about that time.

Lutyens took over the Maltese Cat with a pat and a hug, for Lutyens valued him more than anything else in the world; Powell had Shikast, a little gray rat with no pedigree and no manners outside polo; Macnamara mounted Bamboo, the largest of the team; and Hughes Who's Who, alias the Animal. He was supposed to have Australian blood in his veins, but he looked like a clotheshorse, and you could whack his legs with an iron crowbar without hurting him.

They went out to meet the very flower of the Archangels' team; and when Who's Who saw their elegantly booted legs and their beautiful satin skins, he grinned a grin through his light, well-worn bridle.

"My word!" said Who's Who. "We must give 'em a little football. These gentlemen need a rubbing down."

"No biting," said the Maltese Cat, warningly; for once or twice in his career Who's Who had been known to forget himself in that way.

"Who said anything about biting? I'm not playing tiddlywinks. I'm playing the game."

The Archangels came down like a wolf on the fold, for they were tired of football, and they wanted polo. They got it more and more. Just after the game began, Lutyens hit a ball that was coming toward him rapidly, and it rolled in the air, as a ball sometimes will, with the whirl of a frightened partridge. Shikast heard, but could not see it for the minute, though he looked everywhere and up into the air as the

Maltese Cat had taught him. When he saw it ahead and over-head he went forward with Powell as fast as he could put foot to ground. It was then that Powell, a quiet and levelheaded man as a rule, became inspired and played a stroke that some-times comes off successfully after long practice. He took his stick in both hands, and, standing up in his stirrups, swiped at the ball in the air, Munipore fashion. There was one second of paralyzed astonishment, and then all four sides of the ground went up in a yell of applause and delight as the ball flew true (you could see the amazed Archangels ducking in their saddles to dodge the line of flight, and looking at it with open mouths), and the regimental pipes of the Skidars squealed from the railings as long as the pipers had breath.

Shikast heard the stroke; but he heard the head of the stick fly off at the same time. Nine hundred and ninety-nine ponies out of a thousand would have gone tearing on after the ball with a useless player pulling at their heads; but Powell knew him, and he knew Powell; and the instant he felt Pow-ell's right leg shift a trifle on the saddle flap, he headed to the boundary, where a native officer was frantically waving a new stick. Before the shouts had ended, Powell was armed again.

Once before in his life the Maltese Cat had heard that very same stroke played off his own back, and had profited by the confusion it wrought. This time he acted on experience, and leaving Bamboo to guard the goal in case of accidents, came through the others like a flash, head and tail low—Lutyens standing up to ease him—swept on and on before the other side knew what was the matter, and nearly pitched on his head between the Archangels' goalpost as Lutyens kicked the ball in after a straight scurry of a hundred and fifty yards. If there was one thing more than another upon which the Maltese Cat prided himself, it was on this quick, streaking kind of run half across the ground. He did not believe in taking balls round the field unless you were clearly overmatched. After this they gave the Archangels five-minuted football; and an expensive fast pony hates football because it rumples his temper.

Who's Who showed himself even better than Polaris in this game. He did not permit any wriggling away, but bored joyfully into the scrimmage as if he had his nose in a feed box and was looking for something nice. Little Shikast jumped on the ball the minute it got clear, and every time an Archangel pony followed it, he found Shikast standing over it, asking what was the matter.

"If we can live through this quarter," said the Maltese Cat, "I shan't care. Don't take it out of yourselves. Let them do the lathering."

So the ponies, as their riders explained afterward, "shut up." The Archangels kept them tied fast in front of their goal, but it cost the Archangels' ponies all that was left of their tempers; and ponies began to kick, and men began to repeat compliments, and they chopped at the legs of Who's Who, and he set his teeth and stayed where he was, and the dust stood up like a tree over the scrimmage until that hot quarter ended.

They found the ponies very excited and confident when they went to their *saises*; and the Maltese Cat had to warn them that the worst of the game was coming.

"Now *we* are all going in for the second time," said he, "and *they* are trotting out fresh ponies. You think you can gallop, but you'll find you can't; and then you'll be sorry."

"But two goals to nothing is a halter-long lead," said Kittiwynk, prancing.

"How long does it take to get a goal?" the Maltese Cat answered. "For pity's sake, don't run away with a notion that the game is half won just because we happen to be in luck *now*. They'll ride you into the grandstand, if they can; you must not give 'em a chance. Follow the ball."

"Football, as usual?" said Polaris. "My hock's half as big as a nose bag."

"Don't let them have a look at the ball, if you can help it. Now leave me alone. I must get all the rest I can before the last quarter."

He hung down his head and let all his muscles go slack, Shikast, Bamboo, and Who's Who copying his example.

"Better not watch the game," he said. "We aren't playing, and we shall only take it out of ourselves if we grow anxious. Look at the ground and pretend it's fly time."

They did their best, but it was hard advice to follow. The hooves were drumming and the sticks were rattling all up and down the ground, and yells of applause from the English troops told that the Archangels were pressing the Skidars hard. The native soldiers behind the ponies groaned and grunted, and said things in undertones, and presently they heard a long-drawn shout and a clatter of hurrahs!

"One of the Archangels," said Shikast, without raising his head. "Time's nearly up. Oh, my sire—and *dam*."

"Faiz-Ullah," said the Maltese Cat, "if you don't play to the last nail in your shoes this time, I'll kick you on the ground before all the other ponies."

"I'll do my best when my time comes," said the little Arab, sturdily.

The *saises* looked at each other gravely as they rubbed their ponies' legs. This was the time when long purses began to tell, and everybody knew it. Kittiwynk and the others came back, the sweat dripping over their hooves and their tails telling sad stories.

"They're better than we are," said Shiraz. "I knew how it would be."

"Shut your big head," said the Maltese Cat. "We've one goal to the good yet."

"Yes, but it's two Arabs and two country-breds to play now," said Corks. "Faiz-Ullah, remember!" He spoke in a biting voice.

As Lutyens mounted Grey Dawn he looked at his men, and they did not look pretty. They were covered with dust and sweat in streaks. Their yellow boots were almost black, their wrists were red and lumpy, and their eyes seemed two inches deep in their heads; but the expression in the eyes was satisfactory.

"Did you take anything at tiffin?" said Lutyens; and the team shook their heads. They were too dry to talk.

"All right. The Archangels did. They are worse pumped than we are."

"They've got the better ponies," said Powell. "I shan't be sorry when this business is over."

That fifth quarter was a painful one in every way. Faiz-Ullah played like a little red demon, and the Rabbit seemed to be everywhere at once, and Benami rode straight at anything and everything that came in his way; while the umpires on their ponies wheeled like gulls outside the shifting game. But the Archangels had the better mounts—they had kept their racers till late in the game—and never allowed the Skidars to play football. They hit the ball up and down the width of the ground till Benami and the rest were outpaced. Then they went forward, and time and again Lutyens and Grey Dawn were just, and only just, able to send the ball away with a long, spitting backhander. Grey Dawn forgot that he was an Arab; and turned from gray to blue as he galloped. Indeed, he forgot too well, for he did not keep his eyes on the ground as an Arab should, but stuck out his nose and scuttled for the dear honor of the game. They had watered the ground once or twice between the quarters, and a careless waterman had emptied the last of his skinful all in one place near the Skidars' goal. It was close to the end of the play, and for the tenth time

Grey Dawn was bolting after the ball, when his near hind foot slipped on the greasy mud, and he rolled over and over, pitching Lutyens just clear of the goalpost; and the triumphant Archangels made their goal. Then time was called—two goals all; but Lutyens had to be helped up, and Grey Dawn rose with his near hind leg strained somewhere.

"What's the damage?" said Powell, his arm around Lutyens.

"Collarbone, *of* course," said Lutyens, between his teeth. It was the third time he had broken it in two years, and it hurt him.

Powell and the others whistled.

"Game's up," said Hughes.

"Hold on. We've five good minutes yet, and it isn't my right hand. We'll stick it out."

"I say," said the captain of the Archangels, trotting up, "are you hurt, Lutyens? We'll wait if you care to put in a substitute. I wish—I mean—the fact is, you fellows deserve this game if any team does. Wish we could give you a man, or some of our ponies—or something."

"You're awfully good, but we'll play it to a finish, I think."

The captain of the Archangels stared for a little. "That's not half bad," he said, and went back to his own side, while Lutyens borrowed a scarf from one of his native officers and made a sling of it. Then an Archangel galloped up with a big bath sponge, and advised Lutyens to put it under his armpit to ease his shoulder, and between them they tied up his left arm scientifically; and one of the native officers leaped forward with four long glasses that fizzed and bubbled.

The team looked at Lutyens piteously, and he nodded. It was the last quarter, and nothing would matter after that. They drank out the dark golden drink, and wiped their mustaches, and things looked more hopeful.

The Maltese Cat had put his nose into the front of Lutyens' shirt and was trying to say how sorry he was.

"He knows," said Lutyens, proudly. "The beggar knows. I've played him without a bridle before now—for fun."

"It's no fun now," said Powell. "But we haven't a decent substitute."

"No," said Lutyens. "It's the last quarter, and we've got to make our goal and win. I'll trust the Cat."

"If you fall this time, you'll suffer a little," said Macnamara.

"I'll trust the Cat," said Lutyens.

"You hear that?" said the Maltese Cat proudly, to the others. "It's worthwhile playing polo for ten years to have that said of you. Now then, my sons, come along. We'll kick up a little bit, just to show the Archangels this team haven't suffered."

And, sure enough, as they went on to the ground, the Maltese Cat, after satisfying himself that Lutyens was home in the saddle, kicked out three or four times, and Lutyens laughed. The reins were caught up anyhow in the tips of his strapped left hand, and he never pretended to rely on them. He knew the Cat would answer to the least pressure of the leg, and by way of showing off—for his shoulder hurt him very much—he bent the little fellow in a close figure-of-eight in and out between the goalposts. There was a roar from the native officers and men, who dearly loved a piece of *dugabashi* (horse-trick work), as they called it, and the pipes very quietly and scornfully droned out the first bars of a common bazaar tune called "Freshly Fresh and Newly New," just as a warning to the other regiments that the Skidars were fit. All the natives laughed.

"And now," said the Maltese Cat, as they took their place, "remember that this is the last quarter, and follow the ball!"

"Don't need to be told," said Who's Who.

"Let me go on. All those people on all four sides will begin to crowd in—just as they did at Malta. You'll hear people calling out, and moving forward and being pushed back; and that is going to make the Archangel ponies very unhappy. But if a ball is struck to the boundary, you go after it, and let the people get out of your way. I went over the pole of a four-in-hand once, and picked a game out of the dust by it. Back me up when I run, and follow the ball."

There was a sort of an all-round sound of sympathy and wonder as the last quarter opened, and then there began exactly what the Maltese Cat had foreseen. People crowded in close to the boundaries, and the Archangels' ponies kept looking sideways at the narrowing space. If you know how a man feels to be cramped at tennis—not because he wants to run out of the court, but because he likes to know that he can at a pinch—you will guess how ponies must feel when they are playing in a box of human beings.

"I'll bend some of those men if I can get away," said Who's Who, as he rocketed behind the ball; and Bamboo nodded without speaking. They were playing the last ounce in them, and the Maltese Cat had left the goal undefended to join them. Lutyens gave him every order that he could to bring him back, but this was the first time in his career that the little wise gray had ever played polo on his own responsibility, and he was going to make the most of it.

"What are you doing here?" said Hughes, as the Cat crossed in front of him and rode off an Archangel.

"The Cat's in charge—mind the goal!" shouted Lutyens, and, bowing forward, hit the ball full, and followed on, forcing the Archangels toward their own goal.

"No football," said the Maltese Cat. "Keep the ball by the boundaries and cramp 'em. Play open order, and drive 'em to the boundaries."

Across and across the ground in big diagonals flew the

ball, and whenever it came to a flying rush and a stroke close to the boundaries the Archangel ponies moved stiffly. They did not care to go headlong at a wall of men and carriages, though if the ground had been open they could have turned on a sixpence.

"Wriggle her up the sides," said the Cat. "Keep her close to the crowd. They hate the carriages. Shikast, keep her up this side."

Shikast and Powell lay left and right behind the uneasy scuffle of an open scrimmage, and every time the ball was hit away Shikast galloped on it at such an angle that Powell was forced to hit it toward the boundary; and when the crowd had been driven away from that side, Lutyens would send the ball over to the other, and Shikast would slide desperately after it till his friends came down to help. It was billiards, and no football, this time—billiards in a corner pocket; and the cues were not well chalked.

"If they get us out in the middle of the ground they'll walk away from us. Dribble her along the sides," cried the Maltese Cat.

So they dribbled all along the boundary, where a pony could not come on their right-hand side; and the Archangels were furious, and the umpires had to neglect the game to shout at the people to get back, and several blundering mounted policemen tried to restore order, all close to the scrimmage, and the nerves of the Archangels' ponies stretched and broke like cobwebs.

Five or six times an Archangel hit the ball up into the middle of the ground, and each time the watchful Shikast gave Powell his chance to send it back, and after each return, when the dust had settled, men could see that the Skidars had gained a few yards.

Every now and again there were shouts of "Side! Off side!" from the spectators; but the teams were too busy to care, and the umpires had all they could do to keep their maddened ponies clear of the scuffle.

At last Lutyens missed a short easy stroke, and the Skidars had to fly back helter-skelter to protect their own goal, Shikast leading. Powell stopped the ball with a backhander when it was not fifty yards from the goalposts, and Shikast spun round with a wrench that nearly hoisted Powell out of his saddle.

"Now's our last chance," said the Cat, wheeling like a cockchafer on a pin. "We've got to ride it out. Come along."

Lutyens felt the little chap take a deep breath, and, as it were, crouch under his rider. The ball was hopping toward the right-hand boundary, an Archangel riding for it with both spurs and a whip; but neither spur nor whip would make his pony stretch himself as he neared the crowd. The Maltese Cat glided under his very nose, picking up his hind legs sharp, for there was not a foot to spare between his quarters and the other pony's bit. It was as neat an exhibition as fancy figure skating. Lutyens hit with all the strength he had left, but the stick slipped a little in his hand, and the ball flew off to the left instead of keeping close to the boundary. Who's Who was far across the ground, thinking hard as he galloped. He repeated stride for stride the Cat's maneuvers with another Archangel pony, nipping the ball away from under his bridle, and clearing his opponent by half a fraction of an inch, for Who's Who was clumsy behind. Then he drove away toward the right as the Maltese Cat came up from the left; and Bamboo held a middle course exactly between them. The three were making a sort of Government-broad-arrow-shaped attack; and there was only the Archangels' back to guard the goal; but immediately behind them were three Archangels racing all they knew, and mixed up with them was Powell sending Shikast along on what he felt was their last hope. It takes a very good man to stand up to the rush of seven crazy ponies in the last quarters of a Cup game, when men are riding with their necks for sale, and the ponies are delirious. The Archangels' back missed his stroke and pulled aside just in time to let the rush go by. Bamboo and Who's Who shortened stride to give the Cat room, and Lutyens got the goal with a clean, smooth, smacking stroke that was heard all over the field. But there was no stopping the ponies. They poured through the goalposts in one mixed mob, winners and losers together, for the pace had been terrific. The Maltese Cat knew by experience what would happen, and, to save Lutyens, turned to the right with one last effort, that strained a back-sinew beyond hope of repair. As he did so he heard the right-hand goalpost crack as a pony cannoned into it—crack, splinter, and fall like a mast. It had been sawed three parts through in case of accidents, but it upset the pony nevertheless, and he blundered into another, who blundered into the left-hand post, and then there was confusion and dust and wood. Bamboo was lying on the ground, seeing stars; an Archangel pony rolled beside him, breathless and angry; Shikast had sat down dog-fashion to avoid falling over the others and was sliding along on his little bobtail in a cloud of dust; and Powell was sitting on the ground, hammering with his stick and trying to cheer. All the others were shouting at the top of what was left of their voices, and the men who had been split were shouting too. As soon as the people saw no one was hurt, ten thousand native and English shouted and clapped and yelled, and before any one could stop them the pipers of the Skidars broke onto the ground, with all the native officers and men behind them, and marched up and down, playing a wild Northern tune called "Zakhme Bagan," and through the insolent blaring of the pipes and the high-pitched native yells you could hear the Archangels' band hammering, "For they are all jolly good fellows," and then reproachfully to the losing team, "Ooh, Kafoozalum! Kafoozalum! Kafoozalum!"

Besides all these things and many more, there was a commander in chief, an an inspector general of cavalry, and the principal veterinary officer of all India standing on the top of a regimental coach, yelling like schoolboys; and brigadiers and colonels and commissioners, and hundreds of pretty ladies joined the chorus. But the Maltese Cat stood with his head down, wondering how many legs were left to him; and Lutyens watched the men and ponies pick themselves out of the wreck of the two goalposts, and he patted the Maltese Cat very tenderly.

"I say," said the captain of the Archangels, spitting a pebble out of his mouth, "will you take three thousand for that pony—as he stands?"

"No thank you. I've an idea he's saved my life," said Lutyens, getting off and lying down at full length. Both teams were on the ground too, waving their boots in the air, and coughing and drawing deep breaths, as the *saises* ran up to take away the ponies, and an officious water carrier sprinkled the players with dirty water till they sat up.

"My aunt!" said Powell, rubbing his back, and looking at the stumps of the goalposts. "That was a game!"

They played it over again, every stroke of it, that night at the big dinner, when the Free-for-All Cup was filled and passed down the table, and emptied and filled again, and everybody made most eloquent speeches. About two in the morning, when there might have been some singing, a wise little, plain little, gray little head looked in through the open door.

"Hurrah! Bring him in," said the Archangels; and his *sais,* who was very happy indeed, patted the Maltese Cat on the flank, and he limped into the blaze of light and the glittering uniforms, looking for Lutyens. He was used to messes, and men's bedrooms, and places where ponies are not usually encouraged, and in his youth had jumped on and off a mess table for a bet. So he behaved himself very politely, and ate bread dipped in salt, and was petted all round the table, moving gingerly; and they drank his health, because he had done more to win the Cup than any man or horse on the ground.

That was glory and honor enough for the rest of his days, and the Maltese Cat did not complain much when the veterinary surgeon said that he would be no good for polo any more. When Lutyens married, his wife did not allow him to play, so he was forced to be an umpire; and his pony on these occasions was a flea-bitten gray with a neat polo tail, lame all round, but desperately quick on his feet, and, as everybody knew, Past Pluperfect Prestissimo Player of the Game.

Charles A. Stephens

TREADING DOWN THE HERD'S-GRASS

It was in haying time, and the weather was so fair that we had mowed all the grass in the south field. We had doubts about cutting down so much, for there were only three of us to take care of it; but the weather had cleared off bright and windy that morning, after a thundershower in the night.

"There are pretty sure to be three or four days of good, hard weather now," said Napoleon, or "Poley," as we called him. "Let's down with it!"

And we did. There were six acres of it, all stout grass, following clover the summer before; two tons and a half to the acre of long-stalked herd's-grass, which, when dry and ready to go into the barn, is about as stiff and hard to pitch and handle as so much wire. Any country boy who has ever "mowed away" knows what such grass is when it is pitched off the cart to him in big forkfuls.

The sun shone hot all that first day, and heavy as the grass was it "made" well. We raked it into windrows with the horse rake during the afternoon. Father was away in the north part of the state, cruising for pine and spruce, in the employ of a lumber company, and Napoleon and I had the haying to do, with the assistance of one hired man.

The next morning, as soon as the dew was off, we turned the windrows. There were about twenty rack-loads of the hay. We planned to haul in ten loads that second day and ten the next.

Seven or eight tons of hay, as every one knows, are about as much as three men ought to handle in one afternoon. It has all to be pitched over twice with forks and trodden down in the haymow: and this latter part of the work, in the case of coarse herd's-grass, is the worst, for the tramping has to be done in a hot, close barn, amid choking dust.

Until noon the second day, when we began hauling, the weather was fair; but immediately after twelve o'clock a change was apparent. A gray haze appeared in the south, soon followed by small shreds of cloud, which increased in size. In Maine we knew those signs only too well during the warm season. Such southern rains come on suddenly.

"It will pour by five o'clock," said Napoleon. "And all this hay out! What's to be done?"

The only thing we could do was to swallow a hasty luncheon and begin hauling as fast as possible.

We sent word of our plight to our next neighbors, the Whitcombs, and as they had finished their haying a day or two previously, they kindly sent over their two hired men, with hayrack and ox team, to help us.

We had been saving what we called the West Bay of the barn in which to put this herd's-grass. The usual cross girders had been taken out of this bay, making one long haymow of it, fifty feet by twenty, and we knew that the crop in the south field would fill it to the great beams of the barn, eighteen or twenty feet above the barn floor.

When we drove in with the first load the hired man started to pitch it off into the bay, and I undertook to stow it. Napoleon had remained out in the field to roll the windrows up into "tumbles," ready to be pitched upon the cart as soon as it returned from the barn.

The hired man was a large, strong fellow. At every fork-ful he flung off about half a hundredweight of that coarse, snarled hay, and I soon found that I was going to have quite as much work as I could manage, for I had to pull the hay back into the long, deep bay, tread it down in the dust and heat, and return to the front in time to take the next tough, snarly forkfuls as they came rolling down off the cart. I could not do it; no one could. My weight, indeed, was not sufficient to tread the coarse stuff down.

This first load was no sooner pitched off and the cart backed out than in drove the Whitcomb rack, piled high with another load. One of the men with this team had remained in the field, rolling up tumbles; the driver was ready to throw off the hay, and they all seemed to think that I could take care of it.

Finding myself worsted, I ran into the house to see if I could not get some of the women to help me tread the hay down, but they had all gone raspberrying.

As I ran back to the barn, however, I happened to see in the lane two three-year-old colts that we were pasturing for Grandfather Adams. They were handsome brown Morgan colts, of which the old gentleman was very fond, for they were well matched, and he expected to exhibit them as a trotting pair at the state fair. He was out nearly every day looking at his pets, giving them salt or tidbits, and seeing to it that we kept the watering trough in the lane pumped full of water. He also made us put brass balls on the horns of all the young cattle, for fear they would hook those colts.

It came into my mind that I might make them tread that hay down in the mow. My need of aid was pressing. I ran out to the lane and called the colts through the yard into the barn, then led them across the barn floor and urged them into the mow. The hay was up just about level with the barn floor when I drove them in, and I put up a board to keep them from coming out. The Whitcomb load was half off by this time; but I pulled a part of it back, and then, bringing a horsewhip from the wagon house, I ran those colts up and down the mow. They were fine, plump, heavy colts, and the way they tramped that herd's-grass down was a joy to behold.

The Whitcomb cart had no sooner backed out of the barn floor than in came our cart with its second load. Napoleon had loaded it hastily, for the sky was darkening.

"Pitch it off! Roll it off!" I exclaimed to the hired man. "I'll take care of it! I'll stow it now as fast as all of you can bring it to me!"

I would wait till I had half a rack-load of it rolled back and distributed about a little; then I would get up on the front girders with the horsewhip and send those colts back and forth, from one end of the long bay to the other. Eight feet are much better than two for treading down hay, and the difference between a hundred and forty pounds of boy and sixteen hundred pounds of colt was at once apparent. It was a great scheme!

Meanwhile the loads came in hurry and haste. One was no sooner pitched off to me than another was ready. We were all working as swiftly as possible. But while throwing off the eighth load our hired man suddenly stopped, leaned on his fork, and began to laugh.

"Say," he drawled, "I s'pose you see that this haymow

is fillin' up pretty fast. It is up to the front beams now. 'Tain't any o' my business, but how are you goin' to git the colts down off'n the mow?''

In the heat and hurry of the emergency I had not thought of that, and they were being elevated higher and higher with every load. In fact, they were up nine or ten feet above the barn floor already; too high for them to jump down without breaking their legs.

The hired man stood and laughed. "Those colts'll be up in the roof of the barn when this field of hay is in," said he.

When he drove out to the field he told Napoleon of the fix I was getting into with the colts, and Poley came running in to see about it.

"That's a pretty go!" he exclaimed. "What will Grandpa Adams say? I don't think you ought to have taken those colts for such a job. The dust is making them cough."

"Well, they might just as well be on the great beams as where they are," said I. "Now they are up here, I am going to keep them at it till this hay is in."

"There'll be the mischief to pay if grandpa finds it out!" replied Napoleon. He hurried back to the field, however, for the cart was waiting.

I felt not a little anxious about the situation; but the loads were coming thick and fast. As I could not get the colts down, I kept them treading, and getting higher with every load. The rain did not begin until nearly five o'clock, and we hauled in eighteen big loads of that herd's-grass; there were only about two loads that became too wet to get in.

But those eighteen loads had filled that haymow quite up to the great beams of the barn. As the hired man had anticipated, the colts were up in the top of that high barn, with hardly room to stand under the roof. Truth to say, too, they were hot and sweaty.

The men from Mr. Whitcomb's went off home, laughing over it; and as for Napoleon and me, the more we studied the problem of getting the colts down, the more difficult it looked. We set a long ladder and carried up two buckets of water to them, and let them stand in the hay and eat what they wanted. In fact, we were tired out with our hard afternoon's work, and there were the cows to milk and all the barn chores to do. It was Saturday night, and our hired man went home.

While we were milking we heard Grandpa Adams calling the colts. It was now raining hard, and he had come over to see that they had opportunity to get under the barnyard sheds.

"Now what shall we tell him?" said Napoleon, anxiously.

Of course I ought to have gone and confessed. I knew it, but I did not want to have him find out what I had done. It disturbed me a good deal to hear the old gentleman out in the rain calling, "Nobby, nobby, nobby!" and "Co-jack, co-jack, co-jack!" up and down the pasture; but I kept quiet, and when at last he came back to the barn and looked for us boys, to ask about the colts, Napoleon and I kept out of sight.

Grandfather at last decided that they must have taken shelter in the woods at the far side of the pasture, as they sometimes did, and although still somewhat disappointed by their nonappearance, he went home without making any further search.

Day had no sooner broken the next morning than Napoleon and I were at the barn. We knew that we must get those colts down in some way even if it were Sunday. It was really work of necessity, but how to manage it and not injure the animals was something of a problem.

We went quietly to Mr. Whitcomb's, called out his two hired men, and held a conference. We hit upon a scheme, and to carry it out we were obliged to go to a sawmill half a mile distant and bring four sticks of timber, two by eight inches, and each twenty-four feet in length.

These we set up aslant, close together, reaching from the barn floor to the top of the haymow, and forming a kind of chute. Taking halters and bits of rope, three of us then climbed on the mow, and by pushing against their sides suddenly as they stood in the snarly hay, threw down first one, then the other, of the colts, and tied their legs securely, to prevent them from struggling. Then we dragged them forward to the top of the chute.

While we were thus employed Napoleon had gone to bring the long, large rope from a set of pulley blocks, and also an old buffalo skin. Having wrapped the skin round one of the colts to prevent injury to its sides, we then let the animal slide down the chute, steadying it with the large rope passed round its body.

We were fortunate enough to get both of them down without accident, and we then untied their legs and turned them out.

The colts were in the pasture, feeding as if nothing had happened, when Grandfather Adams came at eight o'clock. He looked them all over, but could not find a scratch or a mark on either of them. They did cough a little for several days afterward, but he did not chance to hear or notice that.

That winter, however, in December, when father began to take the hay out of the mow, he had some difficulty. Napoleon and I were from home at the time, teaching district schools several miles away, but he wrote to us:

"I should like to know how you two boys stowed that herd's-grass hay last summer, and what you did to it; you must have used a pile driver. No living man can pitch it out with a hand fork. I have sent for a grip fork, and I want you both to come home Saturday and help me pull out two or three tons of it with a tackle and block."

Shelly Rider Meyer

A MISTAKE
IN IDENTITY

*A Tale of a Devil That Was
Cast Out and Came Again*

It was too hot a day for riding, anyway. I wished I had not come so far. The Mexican sun was on my head like a weight. My horse was dripping with sweat, though he had been taking his time. But he was a big horse— too big for endurance—and he fretted nervously all the time. I was not enjoying my ride, and I resolved to take the shortest road home—through the gate and around by the "stony field."

When I rode up to the gate, after a shortcut along the top of an irrigating dam, old Chavez, the gatekeeper, was nowhere to be seen. I had to whistle for him. He came running with apologetic haste.

I might have known better than to let my horse stand directly in front of the bars. The old man was in a hurry and in pulling out the lowest bar his felt sombrero fell from his head. The immense hat tumbled into the road with an ungainly flop. With a snort like a locomotive my horse reared under me, straight up on his hind legs, then tipped over backward!

How I got free of saddle and stirrups I don't remember—the merciful Providence that protects novices must have had an eye out for me—but I distinctly recall sitting in the dust where I had tumbled and watching, fascinated, as my mount of a second before landed on his back in the road with shocking force. I thought at the moment that the crack, like a pistol shot, was the breaking of his back, but I soon saw that it was only the smashing of the saddle. The beast lay for a minute with all four legs waving in the air, like a beetle on his back. Then he rolled over on his side, got on his feet in the most good-natured way in the world, and stood waiting tranquilly—for me to mount, I supposed, that he might do it all over again! I couldn't see it that way, myself. The "big house" of my Mexican host was six miles away, but I would have walked sixty before trusting myself again to that seventeen hundred pounds of equine destruction.

Old Chavez had picked up his sombrero, and now he caught the bridle. I must say that the matter-of-fact way in which he took the whole affair was a credit to his good taste. So far as his manner was concerned, it might have been a daily occurrence for a big horse to gallop up to his gate, stand on his hind legs a moment, then turn turtle while an "Americano," after taking an humble part in the performance, sat in the dust and looked on. I trust I did not betray my fear. I merely asked him to send to the stable for another mount and saddle—that I would wait its coming.

"I will receive you into your house," said Chavez, using the quaint and courteous Spanish phrase, "and you shall wait there. You do well not to mount again. One of the vaqueros shall ride him to the stable—their necks are cheap."

He summoned from the quarters a leather-faced son of the saddle, whom I suspected of having seen my accident and discomfiture, for his face wore a suspicious grin. The vaquero cinched up a crazy old saddle on the bay in place of the broken one, swung himself astride, and plunged his two-inch spurs into the horse's flanks. This last was an unnecessary humiliation to me; but who can blame a man who can do one thing well for showing it when he gets a chance? The bay reared again, but he didn't get far, for the butt of the vaquero's heavy whip met the top of his head between the ears with a thud that was sickening—doubtless to the brute. To me it sounded undeniably sweet.

The bay must have thought he had hit the top of the road, but he took a couple of jumps and tried it again. This time he was evidently convinced that there was no mistake, and started on a furious run, which was just what his rider wanted. In a moment the pair were a cloud of dust down the road.

"When he gets to the stable," said Chavez, "that horse will be too tired to think of any more tricks for many days."

I said nothing, but I remembered with satisfaction that horses sometimes run till they drop dead in their tracks.

We retreated into the cool interior of Chavez's 'dobe house, where a little serving maid offered me in due course the native drinks and dainties. When at last the cigarettes were lit Chavez, all of his own accord, told me the story I will try to repeat. I only wish I could tell it in the old man's vivid Spanish, using all the little tricks with words that cannot be put into English.

"Señor," he said, with that simple directness unmixed

with insolence that the unspoiled native will assume toward a foreigner whom he respects, "you nearly met the death there in the road. You did well to fall free. Why did they let you take that bay? We all know him. You thought he was handsome? And he is handsome, indeed. Once only have I seen a horse more beautiful—and more wicked. But this bay that threw you, he is not wicked truly. He does not have blame. He did not care to kill you. He had a fright, that is all. This other horse I speak of—he had no fear. It was hate he had. He could hate like a man. How we feared him! Let me tell you of him.

"He was black, this other horse—and great—more great yet than the bay. His name? He could have but one name. El Diablo—that was his name, and I will tell you why they called him the Devil, and why they feared him more than the one for whom he was named.

"But first I will tell you how beautiful this horse was. His skin was like a baby's cheek. His tail and mane—they were not like a horse's hair. It was for this beauty that El Señor, your host, bought him—for his blood in the stock. He did not buy him to ride, no, señor. For Diablo was well known in three states—that none might mount him. More, it was dangerous to go near him. He was like a tiger.

"Yet there was a reason for this. A horse, like a man, is not bad without reason. Is it not so? If only we know the reason. I will tell you how this horse became a devil in fact, and earned his name. I was told by one who knows—who saw.

"When the horse was but a colt—wild as any colt is but no worse—he kicked a hostler and broke his arm. A mistake for which the stableboy was to blame, not the horse. But the boy, like a fool, hated the young horse for his broken arm, and when he was well he teased the horse until the brute, too, learned what hate was. Then the boy teased him no longer. For one day the young horse, maddened, broke his stall and came out. If he had caught the lad before he got inside the harness room there would have been much worse business than a broken arm.

"Thus it was. The horse was taught hate by a man. And he learned his lesson well.

"Even then it was not too late. If he had been rightly trained and broken. He was commenced to be broken—that was all. His training was short. I know the trainer that had him—he is a friend of mine. Break the spirit—that is his word. And he does it—with most horses. For he is a strong man, and heavy. But when he came to this horse, it was his own neck that was nearer being broken. I was told about it by one who was there.

"After three falls (and it was a very stony corral) and after being bitten once, kicked also, my friend the trainer said he would return later to finish breaking the horse. He never went back to that hacienda again, though before he had had much business there. I saw him in Guadalajara a week after he had his little turn with Diablo. I did not speak of the affair—he was my friend. But he could not then walk without limping. Yet he is a good man with a horse. He was never thrown before, or since. His method—it is all right. Break the spirit—if you can. But Diablo—my friend did not get him soon enough. That was it. Diablo had already been taught his lesson, and he knew but one—hate!

"Thus it was when the horse came to us. He was very dangerous. We made a corral for him alone, with high bars and very thick. Outside of this we would stand and watch him. It was like looking at the bulls in the pen at the plaza, the day before the bullfight. Not that Diablo looked so terrible, there in the corral with the high bars. He knew as well as we that he could do nothing. But he was waiting. He did not roll his eyes and show the white, or run up and down, or rear against the bars. He was not foolish like that. He was wise, as wise as a man.

"But as we watched him we knew that he was only waiting. When we looked at him we knew he was *thinking—about us*! And it was war he was thinking. For he looked on all men as his enemies, and felt himself stronger than us all. To be sure, we treated him like an enemy—but what would you have? We were afraid for our lives. A bull—he is stupid; he shuts his eyes when he runs at you. But this devil horse—one would dream about him and be afraid. So we cleaned him with a hose from between the bars, and when we cut his hooves it cost us two broken ribs and Lupe sprained his shoulder; the horse-shoer was kicked in the stomach and the ground in the corral was as though plowed.

"And El Señor would bring his guests out to show them the horse, for he had many guests then, the same as now. And all spoke their wonder of Diablo. And those who did not know would say, 'Oh, señor! Do you ride him?' And my patron would say, 'No, I love life!' And then they would be surprised that a horse so beautiful and that stood so quietly should be spoken of thus. One day a lady, who did not believe, put her hand through the bars as if to reach him. And because the horse did nothing, but stood still and let her wave her arm at him, he could not be bad! That was plain—to her. But those who knew of horses did not talk thus. Diablo would stand very quiet, but if he snapped at a fly one could see that he was ready with his teeth and quick as a snake.

"One day there came with El Señor to the corral a great blond man, blond as a Spaniard. He was a countryman of yours, an Americano; a guest of my patron, like yourself. And I do not think this man had to be told why the bars about Diablo were high and strong. But he looked a long time at the horse, and talked much with El Señor there by the corral.

"The next day a few of us watched from where we were hidden to see this Americano get killed. For everyone knew of the orders. All of us were to keep away from the corrals in the morning; only Pascual, the chief hostler, was to be ready. That is why we all came, well hidden, and watched. And, from underneath a wagon, I saw what was done. Anyone might have done it. When the horse was in his shed Pascual closed the gate into the corral—it was a heavy gate for one man, and I knew Pascual must be swearing. Then the tall Americano went into the corral, and the corral gate was shut behind him. El Señor did this, and then he, too, ran and hid, while Pascual opened the shed gate again.

"Out came Diablo into the corral, very quick. The man stood by the fence, as still as wood. It was a surprise. Diablo stood still and looked, and in his surprise he forgot his evil ways. And he didn't even remember them when, after a bit, the Americano slowly opened the corral gate and slipped out. Simple, was it not? I will tell you what it was. It was a new thing to Diablo. He had never seen a man who did not fear him, and hate him, and who did not show him his fear and hate. When he met a man who did not treat him like a wild beast, Diablo did not know what to do. So he did—nothing.

"But however that may be, that which happened is as I tell you. In a week the tall Americano was feeding and petting the horse. We who looked on thought that we were dreaming. In two weeks he had a saddle on him, then a bridle. In a month he was riding El Diablo about just as the little boys ride the burros. We who had known the horse said it was a miracle. There were many who held that the man must be a greater devil than the horse. Others thought that Diablo had gone crazy—had lost his mind. But he gave us proof that he was the same Diablo. For one day the Americano left saddle and bridle on when he turned him into the corral—he was to return presently, for none but he could saddle or unsaddle the horse. In the meantime the bravest of the vaqueros made the effort. We spurred him on, for it was a shame to us that it was an Americano that had mastered the black.

"The vaquero entered the corral, went up to the horse, and got into the saddle. So far, most good. We had great joy—for a moment. Then the boy went into the air, like a stone from a sling. How was it done? It was too quick for me, and I was watching with great care. The vaquero was too angry to explain to us how it was done—and too sore! Diablo was making up lost time—that was all. But when the Americano came the great horse arched his neck like the back of a cat and whinnied and whickered. I tell you, it looked as though he was telling his friend the joke.

"Oh, Diablo loved his master, now that he had found one. There was nothing the Americano could not do with him. He never rode with whip or spurs, but I think the horse would have suffered even this after a while. But to all other men he was dangerous as before. It is true he would let himself be held, by a few of us. But not until the Americano had walked many times with us, his hand on the bridle rein with ours. And even then holding him was a task we feared. For though the black would not break away he would do all else that he could think of in the way of villainy, and that was much. I had to hold him more than any. In those days I did not keep the gate, but rode behind El Señor the times that he went out on horse. And when the Americano went out with Diablo I went with them. For they trusted me with the horse—little joy I had of the trust!

"Strange, is it not, that the horse did not become better and more tame with other men? Perhaps if another one had treated him in the same manner—but no one cared to try. We did go into the corral with him, which we had not done before—without a pitchfork, but no one dared to touch him, nor would he take food from our hands. Diablo had always hated us. I think he hated all Mexicans. I think he knew there was a difference.

"No, that is not all the story—I wish it was. Many times we wondered what Diablo would do when his friend went away. Possibly the Americano would have taken the horse with him if it had not happened different.

"One evening, when the summer had passed, I heard that we were to ride over to the hacienda of Espíritu Santo. It gave me little pleasure, for I know the weather, and while at sunset all was beautiful I knew very well that it would change. But as we set out after supper the moon was up and it was still and quiet. Too quiet! It is said that when there are no winds about it is because they are all away arranging mischief. It was like the deep, still breath a man takes before fighting.

"But El Señor and the Americano rode careless, the Americano on Diablo. And who was I to speak to them unasked about the weather?

"On the going journey the Americano was showing to my master how Diablo obeyed him. He made the black horse trot, and pace, and amble—oh, Diablo was a clever horse. That was why he made such a good villain. Such a good friend, too. El Señor watched—I think he was a little jealous. Still, he and this Americano were great friends, and my master would have nothing against him.

"All this was very well. But I knew the horse was nervous. Was I not unquiet myself? It was the night. And when we got to the hacienda, and I led Diablo into the box stall in the stables, a cursed hen flew up out of the straw. Thanks to the Virgin, I got the door closed, very quick. Diablo kicked a few bars loose, that was all. I hoped he would kill the hen, for I had had a great fright. The stableboys who had followed me ran for their lives. He was a very strong horse, and his heels made a great noise on the wood in the dark stable.

"Now, while the gentlemen were at the dance in the great house it is true that I passed the time with my friends, and I will not deny that we took of the mescal. But I was most careful—I took but enough to warm me on the road home. For I knew it was getting ready to storm, and that I should need my head.

"When the call came for the horses and I led Diablo out,

it was late, and the storm was near. A chilly wind had risen, coming from the hills. There were a few drops of rain in the dust, just enough to smell.

"I had thought that the gentlemen might stay the night at the great house, and had hoped so. But El Señor loves his own bed and neither he nor the Americano were men to stop for weather. They had no families dependent on their bones.

"As we waited in the courtyard I prayed that we might not have to wait long, for Diablo was worse than ever to hold. He backed into one of the other horses, and this other horse he jumped quick, for Diablo was quick with his heels. When a still flash of lightning cut into the sky I thought I would lose him. I was off my feet as he reared, but I dared not let go—and the bridle held. It was a heavy bridle, made after many had been broken.

"At last they came. The gentlemen had not been as careful as I with the mescal. When they stepped out of the door and saw the clouds and how near the storm was, they went back. I hoped again that they would stay the night. I likewise hoped to know soon, as Diablo would not stay with me much longer.

"When the gentlemen came out again I did not know them, for a minute. For they had on borrowed sombreros and great capotes for the rain, and the people in the doorway were laughing at them and calling them rancheros.

"Just then the rain started, suddenly. El Señor and the Americano said good-bye quickly and came hurriedly for their horses. My master was in the saddle first—he was eager for home. I stood a little apart from the other horses with Diablo.

"When the Americano took the bridle and flung it over the black's head I was so glad to be rid of the horse that I thought of nothing else. But when I stepped back for my own mount I turned, for I could hear Diablo's feet dancing in the gravel. That was strange—it was not his way to be wild in the hands of the Americano. Yet wild the horse was as I stood and watched—and different. I remembered afterward that before mounting he had not spoken to the horse, or petted him, as he always did. It must have been the wine in his head—and he was so sure of Diablo! But the horse jumped so that he could hardly mount him. He was a skillful rider, or he never could have got astride him.

"The people were watching in the doorway, and this must have made the Americano angry—that he had to fight to mount. For he dug his heels into Diablo's flanks—perhaps he did so to keep his balance. The black reared, but he often did that. Yet as he reared and wheeled the light from the open door fell on his face and breast and in his eyes. And I saw, as quick as that, that everything was wrong. For this horse, with ears tight back and spread nostrils, was Diablo the killer of men, twice as terrible in the night and the storm. And at the same time I understood it all. There are times when one thinks quickly. The horse did not know his rider, in the changed hat and cloak!

"Maybe I shouted, but for what good? The horse had never had an ear for me. He came down on his forefeet, and for a second I hoped. But the next instant he stood up straight. It was bright with the lightning. The crowd in the doorway screamed and my master shouted in terror. The great black poised for a moment, stretched high. Then backward they went, like a tree falling in the storm!

"Diablo was on his feet a second after. The Americano lay quiet in the light from the open door. The borrowed sombrero was rolled away from his face. And as the horse Diablo plunged to his feet and turned he must have seen, and known. It seems impossible. But he stopped and started to tremble all over, like a horse ridden to death, before it falls. And then he put down his head as slowly and gently as I put down my hand—thus—with his muzzle close to the face of the man. Thus he stood, sniffing with wide nostrils for a moment before they lifted the body up and carried it into the house. And as the people made a way through the door I watched the horse. May God judge me if what I say is not so! Diablo started to follow! A step he went, and stopped and trembled. And his eyes were on the open door, and his neck was strained toward it. Thus he stood, the wind blowing and tangling his mane and tail. And he trembled.

"I took his bridle. I was not afraid of him—now. And when I pulled he came with me, without pulling against me. As I walked him slowly to the stable it was thundering overhead in the black clouds, but I think it might have been dynamite at our feet and Diablo would not have known. I had no fear of him—it was pity I felt. Indeed, it is so. When we got to the stall where I put him he went in like a burro, and stood, trembling and in a sweat. I had to leave him to go to the house.

"No, the Americano was not killed. They say that a man in liquor cannot die from a fall. It must be so—even if a horse falls on him. But he lay in bed for months with a broken hip.

"But let me tell you of the horse. Before the Americano was on his feet again, Diablo was dead! The doctor of horses, whom we brought from Guadalajara for him, said his back was hurt by the fall. Perhaps that was why he had trembled on that night. Perhaps that was why he stood for days in his shed, like a sick calf, getting weaker and thinner. It is possible. I am no doctor of horses, though I have seen and known many. For my part I do not think it was all his back.

"We would have seen had the Americano got well quicker, to come and see the horse. How else could Diablo know he was not dead? But this is crazy talk.

"Of one thing I am certain—that which I have told you. I do not know if the Americano knew. I did not see him again—he went away as soon as he was able. But he must have known that Diablo did not know him that night. Nervous the horse was, with the night, and the storm, and the light from the open door. But that was not it. It was that he did not know whom he had on his back. He thought he carried one of those he hated, and he wished to kill him. He was in that moment the old wicked Diablo. But this was not the same Diablo as the horse that trembled when he saw who it was that lay so still in the driveway. It was not Diablo the man-killer that died—of a twisted back! At least, according to the doctor of horses, it was his back. And he should know.

"Your horse has not yet come, señor. It is a long time to wait—I trust I have not made it longer with my talking. But every word I have said is true.

"Ah, I hear them now. They are here. They have sent you the gray—a great horse, and a good one. You may be glad when you are on him that it is not Diablo you have between your knees. Only one man ever rode him. And he did not ride him for long."

Arthur Conan Doyle

SILVER BLAZE

"I am afraid, Watson, that I shall have to go," said Holmes as we sat down together to our breakfast one morning.

"Go! Where to?"

"To Dartmoor; to King's Pyland."

I was not surprised. Indeed, my only wonder was that he had not already been mixed up in this extraordinary case, which was the one topic of conversation through the length and breadth of England. For a whole day my companion had rambled about the room with his chin upon his chest and his brow knitted, charging and recharging his pipe with the strongest black tobacco, and absolutely deaf to any of my questions or remarks. Fresh editions of every paper had been sent up by our newsagent, only to be glanced over and tossed down into a corner. Yet, silent as he was, I knew perfectly well what it was over which he was brooding. There was but one problem before the public which could challenge his powers of analysis, and that was the singular disappearance of the favorite for the Wessex Cup, and the tragic murder of its trainer. When, therefore, he suddenly announced his intention of setting out for the scene of the drama, it was only what I had both expected and hoped for.

"I should be most happy to go down with you if I should not be in the way," said I.

"My dear Watson, you would confer a great favor upon me by coming. And I think that your time will not be misspent, for there are points about the case which promise to make it an absolutely unique one. We have, I think, just time to catch our train at Paddington, and I will go further into the matter upon our journey. You would oblige me by bringing with you your very excellent field glass."

And so it happened that an hour or so later I found myself in the corner of a first-class carriage flying along en route for Exeter, while Sherlock Holmes, with his sharp, eager face framed in his earflapped traveling cap, dipped rapidly into the bundle of fresh papers which he had procured at Paddington. We had left Reading far behind us before he thrust the last one of them under the seat and offered me his cigar case.

"We are going well," said he, looking out of the window and glancing at his watch. "Our rate at present is fifty-three and a half miles an hour."

"I have not observed the quarter-mile posts," said I.

"Nor have I. But the telegraph posts upon this line are sixty yards apart, and the calculation is a simple one. I presume that you have looked into this matter of the murder of

John Straker and the disappearance of Silver Blaze?"

"I have seen what the *Telegraph* and the *Chronicle* have to say."

"It is one of those cases where the art of the reasoner should be used rather for the sifting of details than for the acquiring of fresh evidence. The tragedy has been so uncommon, so complete, and of such personal importance to so many people that we are suffering from a plethora of surmise, conjecture, and hypothesis. The difficulty is to detach the framework of fact—of absolute undeniable fact—from the embellishments of theorists and reporters. Then, having established ourselves upon this sound basis, it is our duty to see what inferences may be drawn and what are the special points upon which the whole mystery turns. On Tuesday evening I received telegrams from both Colonel Ross, the owner of the horse, and from Inspector Gregory, who is looking after the case, inviting my cooperation."

"Tuesday evening!" I exclaimed. "And this is Thursday morning. Why didn't you go down yesterday?"

"Because I made a blunder, my dear Watson—which is, I am afraid, a more common occurrence than anyone would think who only knew me through your memoirs. The fact is that I could not believe it possible that the most remarkable horse in England could long remain concealed, especially in so sparsely inhabited a place as the north of Dartmoor. From hour to hour yesterday I expected to hear that he had been found, and that his abductor was the murderer of John Straker. When, however, another morning had come and I found that beyond the arrest of young Fitzroy Simpson nothing had been done, I felt that it was time for me to take action. Yet in some ways I feel that yesterday has not been wasted."

"You have formed a theory, then?"

"At least I have got a grip of the essential facts of the case. I shall enumerate them to you, for nothing clears up a case so much as stating it to another person, and I can hardly expect your cooperation if I do not show you the position from which we start.''

I lay back against the cushions, puffing at my cigar, while Holmes, leaning forward, with his long, thin forefinger checking off the points upon the palm of his left hand, gave me a sketch of the events which had led to our journey.

"Silver Blaze," said he, "is from the Somomy stock and holds as brilliant a record as his famous ancestor. He is now in his fifth year and has brought in turn each of the prizes of the turf to Colonel Ross, his fortunate owner. Up to the time of the catastrophe he was the first favorite for the Wessex Cup, the betting being three to one on him. He has always, however, been a prime favorite with the racing public and has never yet disappointed them, so that even at those odds enormous sums of money have been laid upon him. It is obvious, therefore, that there were many people who had the strongest interest in preventing Silver Blaze from being there at the fall of the flag next Tuesday.

"The fact was, of course, appreciated at King's Pyland, where the colonel's training stable is situated. Every precaution was taken to guard the favorite. The trainer, John Straker, is a retired jockey who rode in Colonel Ross's colors before he became too heavy for the weighing chair. He has served the colonel for five years as jockey and for seven as trainer, and has always shown himself to be a zealous and honest servant. Under him were three lads, for the establishment was a small one, containing only four horses in all. One of these lads sat up each night in the stable, while the others slept in the loft. All three bore excellent characters. John Straker, who is a married man, lived in a small villa about two hundred yards from the stables. He has no children, keeps one maidservant, and is comfortably off. The country round is very lonely, but about half a mile to the north there is a small cluster of villas which have been built by a Tavistock contractor for the use of invalids and others who may wish to enjoy the pure Dartmoor air. Tavistock itself lies two miles to the west, while across the moor, also about two miles distant, is the larger training establishment of Mapleton, which belongs to Lord Backwater and is managed by Silas Brown. In every other direction the moor is a complete wilderness, inhabited only by a few roaming gypsies. Such was the general situation last Monday night when the catastrophe occurred.

"On that evening the horses had been exercised and watered as usual, and the stables were locked up at nine o'clock. Two of the lads walked up to the trainer's house, where they had supper in the kitchen, while the third, Ned Hunter, remained on guard. At a few minutes after nine the maid, Edith Baxter, carried down to the stables his supper, which consisted of a dish of curried mutton. She took no liquid, as there was a water tap in the stables, and it was the rule that the lad on duty should drink nothing else. The maid carried a lantern with her, as it was very dark and the path ran across the open moor.

"Edith Baxter was within thirty yards of the stables when a man appeared out of the darkness and called to her to stop. As she stepped into the circle of yellow light thrown by the lantern she saw that he was a person of gentlemanly bearing, dressed in a gray suit of tweeds, with a cloth cap. He wore gaiters and carried a heavy stick with a knob to it. She was most impressed, however, by the extreme pallor of his face and by the nervousness of his manner. His age, she thought, would be rather over thirty than under it.

" 'Can you tell me where I am?' he asked. 'I had almost made up my mind to sleep on the moor when I saw the light of your lantern.'

" 'You are close to the King's Pyland training stables,' said she.

" 'Oh, indeed! What a stroke of luck!' he cried. 'I understand that a stableboy sleeps there alone every night. Perhaps that is his supper which you are carrying to him. Now I am sure that you would not be too proud to earn the price of a new dress, would you?' He took a piece of white paper folded up out of his waistcoat pocket. 'See that the boy has this tonight, and you shall have the prettiest frock that money can buy.'

"She was frightened by the earnestness of his manner and ran past him to the window through which she was accustomed to hand the meals. It was already opened, and Hunter was seated at the small table inside. She had begun to tell him of what had happened when the stranger came up again.

" 'Good evening,' said he, looking through the window. 'I wanted to have a word with you.' The girl has sworn that as he spoke she noticed the corner of the little paper packet protruding from his closed hand.

" 'What business have you here?'' asked the lad.

" 'It's business that may put something into your pocket,' said the other. 'You've two horses in for the Wessex Cup— Silver Blaze and Bayard. Let me have the straight tip and you won't be a loser. Is it a fact that at the weights Bayard could give the other a hundred yards in five furlongs, and that the stable have put their money on him?'

" 'So, you're one of those damned touts!' cried the lad. 'I'll show you how we serve them in King's Pyland.' He sprang up and rushed across the stable to unloose the dog. The girl fled away to the house, but as she ran she looked back and saw that the stranger was leaning through the window. A minute later, however, when Hunter rushed out with the hound he was gone, and though he ran all round the buildings he failed to find any trace of him.''

"One moment," I asked. "Did the stableboy, when he ran out with the dog, leave the door unlocked behind him?"

"Excellent, Watson, excellent!" murmured my companion. "The importance of the point struck me so forcibly that I sent a special wire to Dartmoor yesterday to clear the matter up. The boy locked the door before he left it. The window,

I may add, was not large enough for a man to get through.

"Hunter waited until his fellow grooms had returned, when he sent a message to the trainer and told him what had occurred. Straker was excited at hearing the account, although he does not seem to have quite realized its true significance. It left him, however, vaguely uneasy, and Mrs. Straker, waking at one in the morning, found that he was dressing. In reply to her inquiries, he said that he could not sleep on account of his anxiety about the horses, and that he intended to walk down to the stables to see that all was well. She begged him to remain at home, as she could hear the rain pattering against the window, but in spite of her entreaties he pulled on his large mackintosh and left the house.

"Mrs. Straker awoke at seven in the morning to find that her husband had not yet returned. She dressed herself hastily, called the maid, and set off for the stables. The door was open; inside, huddled together upon a chair, Hunter was sunk in a state of absolute stupor, the favorite's stall was empty, and there were no signs of his trainer.

"The two lads who slept in the chaff-cutting loft above the harness room were quickly aroused. They had heard nothing during the night, for they are both sound sleepers. Hunter was obviously under the influence of some powerful drug, and as no sense could be got out of him, he was left to sleep it off while the two lads and the two women ran out in search of the absentees. They still had hopes that the trainer had for some reason taken out the horse for early exercise, but on ascending the knoll near the house, from which all the neighboring moors were visible, they not only could see no signs of the missing favorite, but they perceived something which warned them that they were in the presence of a tragedy.

"About a quarter of a mile from the stables John Straker's overcoat was flapping from a furze bush. Immediately beyond there was a bowl-shaped depression in the moor, and at the bottom of this was found the dead body of the unfortunate trainer. His head had been shattered by a savage blow from some heavy weapon, and he was wounded on the thigh, where there was a long, clean cut, inflicted evidently by some very sharp instrument. It was clear, however, that Straker had defended himself vigorously against his assailants, for in his right hand he held a small knife, which was clotted with blood up to the handle, while in his left he clasped a red-and-black silk cravat, which was recognized by the maid as having been worn on the preceding evening by the stranger who had visited the stables. Hunter, on recovering from his stupor, was also quite positive as to the ownership of the cravat. He was equally certain that the same stranger had, while standing at the window, drugged his curried mutton, and so deprived the stables of their watchman. As to the missing horse, there were abundant proofs in the mud which lay at the bottom of the fatal hollow that he had been there at the time of the struggle. But from that morning he has disappeared, and although a large reward has been offered, and all the gypsies of Dartmoor are on the alert, no news has come of him. Finally, an analysis has shown that the remains of his supper left by the stable lad contained an appreciable quantity of powdered opium, while the people at the house partook of the same dish on the same night without any ill effect.

"Those are the main facts of the case, stripped of all surmise, and stated as baldly as possible. I shall now recapitulate what the police have done in the matter.

"Inspector Gregory, to whom the case has been committed, is an extremely competent officer. Were he but gifted with imagination he might rise to great heights in his profession. On his arrival he promptly found and arrested the man upon whom suspicion naturally rested. There was little difficulty in finding him, for he inhabited one of those villas which I have mentioned. His name, it appears, was Fitzroy Simpson. He was a man of excellent birth and education, who had squandered a fortune upon the turf, and who lived now by doing a little quiet and genteel bookmaking in the sporting clubs of London. An examination of his betting book shows that bets to the amount of five thousand pounds had been registered by him against the favorite. On being arrested he volunteered the statement that he had come down to Dartmoor in the hope of getting some information about the King's Pyland horses, and also about Desborough, the second favorite, which was in charge of Silas Brown at the Mapleton stables. He did not attempt to deny that he had acted as described upon the evening before, but declared that he had no sinister designs and had simply wished to obtain firsthand information. When confronted with his cravat he turned very pale and was utterly unable to account for its presence in the hand of the murdered man. His wet clothing showed that he had been out in the storm of the night before, and his stick, which was a penang-lawyer weighted with lead, was just such a weapon as might, by repeated blows, have inflicted the terrible injuries to which the trainer had succumbed. On the other hand, there was no wound upon his person, while the state of Straker's knife would show that one at least of his assailants must bear his mark upon him. There you have it all in a nutshell, Watson, and if you can give me any light I shall be infinitely obliged to you."

I had listened with the greatest interest to the statement which Holmes, with characteristic clearness, had laid before me. Though most of the facts were familiar to me, I had not sufficiently appreciated their relative importance, nor their connection to each other.

"Is it not possible," I suggested, "that the incised wound upon Straker may have been caused by his own knife in the convulsive struggles which follow any brain injury?"

"It is more than possible: it is probable," said Holmes. "In that case one of the main points in favor of the accused disappears."

"And yet," said I, "even now I fail to understand what the theory of the police can be."

"I am afraid that whatever theory we state has very grave objections to it," returned my companion. "The police imagine, I take it, that this Fitzroy Simpson, having drugged the lad, and having in some way obtained a duplicate key, opened the stable door and took out the horse, with the intention, apparently, of kidnapping him altogether. His bridle is missing, so that Simpson must have put this on. Then, having left the door open behind him, he was leading the horse away over the moor when he was either met or overtaken by the trainer. A row naturally ensued. Simpson beat out the trainer's brains with his heavy stick without receiving any injury from the small knife which Straker used in self-defense, and then the thief either led the horse on to some secret hiding place, or else it may have bolted during the struggle, and be now wandering out on the moors. That is the case as it appears to the police, and improbable as it is, all other explanations are more improbable still. However, I shall very quickly test the matter when I am once upon the spot, and until then I cannot really see how we can get much further than our present position."

It was evening before we reached the little town of Tavistock, which lies, like the boss of a shield, in the middle of the huge circle of Dartmoor. Two gentlemen were awaiting us in the station—the one a tall, fair man with lionlike hair and beard and curiously penetrating light blue eyes; the other a small, alert person, very neat and dapper, in a frock coat and gaiters, with trim little side-whiskers and an eyeglass. The latter was Colonel Ross, the well-known sportsman; the other, Inspector Gregory, a man who was rapidly making his name in the English detective service.

"I am delighted that you have come down, Mr. Holmes," said the colonel. "The inspector here has done all that could possibly be suggested, but I wish to leave no stone unturned in trying to avenge poor Straker and in recovering my horse."

"Have there been any fresh developments?" asked Holmes.

"I am sorry to say that we have made very little progress," said the inspector. "We have an open carriage outside, and as you would no doubt like to see the place before the light fails, we might talk it over as we drive."

A minute later we were all seated in a comfortable landau and were rattling through the quaint old Devonshire city. Inspector Gregory was full of his case and poured out a stream of remarks, while Holmes threw in an occasional question or interjection. Colonel Ross leaned back with his arms folded and his hat tilted over his eyes, while I listened with interest to the dialogue of the two detectives. Gregory was formulating his theory, which was almost exactly what Holmes had foretold in the train.

"The net is drawn pretty close round Fitzroy Simpson," he remarked, "and I believe myself that he is our man. At the same time I recognize that the evidence is purely circumstantial, and that some new development may upset it."

"How about Straker's knife?"

"We have quite come to the conclusion that he wounded himself in his fall."

"My friend Dr. Watson made that suggestion to me as we came down. If so, it would tell against this man Simpson."

"Undoubtedly. He has neither a knife nor any sign of a wound. The evidence against him is certainly very strong. He had a great interest in the disappearance of the favorite. He lies under suspicion of having poisoned the stableboy; he was undoubtedly out in the storm; he was armed with a heavy stick, and his cravat was found in the dead man's hand. I really think we have enough to go before a jury."

Holmes shook his head. "A clever counsel would tear it all to rags," said he. "Why should he take the horse out of the stable? If he wished to injure it, why could he not do it there? Has a duplicate key been found in his possession? What chemist sold him the powdered opium? Above all, where could he, a stranger to the district, hide a horse, and such a horse as this? What is his own explanation as to the paper which he wished the maid to give to the stableboy?"

"He says that it was a ten-pound note. One was found in his purse. But your other difficulties are not so formidable as they seem. He is not a stranger to the district. He has twice lodged at Tavistock in the summer. The opium was probably brought from London. The key, having served its purpose, would be hurled away. The horse may be at the bottom of one of the pits or old mines upon the moor."

"What does he say about the cravat?"

"He acknowledges that it is his and declares that he had lost it. But a new element has been introduced into the case which may account for his leading the horse from the stable."

Holmes pricked up his ears.

"We have found traces which show that a party of gypsies encamped on Monday night within a mile of the spot where the murder took place. On Tuesday they were gone. Now, presuming that there was some understanding between Simpson and these gypsies, might he not have been leading the horse to them when he was overtaken, and may they not have him now?"

"It is certainly possible."

"The moor is being scoured for these gypsies. I have also examined every stable and outhouse in Tavistock, and for a radius of ten miles."

"There is another training stable quite close, I understand?"

"Yes, and that is a factor which we must certainly not neglect. As Desborough, their horse, was second in the betting, they had an interest in the disappearance of the favorite. Silas Brown, the trainer, is known to have had large bets upon the event, and he was no friend to poor Straker. We have,

however, examined the stables, and there is nothing to connect him with the affair."

"And nothing to connect this man Simpson with the
interests of the Mapleton stables?"

"Nothing at all."

Holmes leaned back in the carriage, and the conversation
ceased. A few minutes later our driver pulled up at a neat little
red-brick villa with overhanging eaves which stood by the
road. Some distance off, across a paddock, lay a long gray-tiled
outbuilding. In every other direction the low curves of the
moor, bronze-colored from the fading ferns, stretched away
to the skyline, broken only by the steeples of Tavistock, and
by a cluster of houses away to the westward which marked the
Mapleton stables. We all sprang out with the exception of
Holmes, who continued to lean back with his eyes fixed upon
the sky in front of him, entirely absorbed in his own thoughts.
It was only when I touched his arm that he roused himself
with a violent start and stepped out of the carriage.

"Excuse me," said he, turning to Colonel Ross, who had
looked at him in some surprise. "I was daydreaming." There
was a gleam in his eyes and a suppressed excitement in his
manner which convinced me, used as I was to his ways, that
his hand was upon a clue, though I could not imagine where
he had found it.

"Perhaps you would prefer at once to go on to the scene
of the crime, Mr. Holmes?" said Gregory.

"I think that I should prefer to stay here a little and go
into one or two questions of detail. Straker was brought back
here, I presume?"

"Yes, he lies upstairs. The inquest is tomorrow."

"He has been in your service some years, Colonel Ross?"

"I have always found him an excellent servant."

"I presume that you made an inventory of what he had
in his pockets at the time of his death, Inspector?"

"I have the things themselves in the sitting room if you would care to see them."

"I should be very glad." We all filed into the front room and sat round the central table while the inspector unlocked a square tin box and laid a small heap of things before us. There was a box of vestas, two inches of tallow candle, an ADP brierroot pipe, a pouch of sealskin with half an ounce of long-cut Cavendish, a silver watch with a gold chain, five sovereigns in gold, an aluminum pencil case, a few papers, and an ivory-handled knife with a very delicate, inflexible blade marked Weiss & Co., London.

"This is a very singular knife," said Holmes, lifting it up and examining it minutely. "I presume, as I see bloodstains upon it, that it is the one which was found in the dead man's grasp. Watson, this knife is surely in your line?"

"It is what we call a cataract knife," said I.

"I thought so. A very delicate blade devised for very delicate work. A strange thing for a man to carry with him upon a rough expedition, especially as it would not shut in his pocket."

"The tip was guarded by a disk of cork which we found beside his body," said the inspector. "His wife tells us that the knife had lain upon the dressing table, and that he had picked it up as he left the room. It was a poor weapon, but perhaps the best that he could lay his hands on at the moment."

"Very possibly. How about these papers?"

"Three of them are receipted hay-dealers' accounts. One of them is a letter of instructions from Colonel Ross. This other is a milliner's account for thirty-seven pounds fifteen made out by Madame Lesurier, of Bond Street, to William Derbyshire. Mrs. Straker tells us that Derbyshire was a friend of her husband's, and that occasionally his letters were addressed here."

"Madame Derbyshire had somewhat expensive tastes," remarked Holmes, glancing down the account. "Twenty-two guineas is rather heavy for a single costume. However, there appears to be nothing more to learn, and we may now go down to the scene of the crime."

As we emerged from the sitting room a woman, who had been waiting in the passage, took a step forward and laid her hand upon the inspector's sleeve. Her face was haggard and thin and eager, stamped with the print of a recent horror.

"Have you got them? Have you found them?" she panted.

"No, Mrs. Straker. But Mr. Holmes here has come from London to help us, and we shall do all that is possible."

"Surely I met you in Plymouth at a garden party some little time ago, Mrs. Straker?" said Holmes.

"No, sir; you are mistaken."

"Dear me! Why, I could have sworn to it. You wore a costume of dove-colored silk with ostrich-feather trimming."

"I never had such a dress, sir," answered the lady.

"Ah, that quite settles it," said Holmes. And with an apology he followed the inspector outside. A short walk across the moor took us to the hollow in which the body had been found. At the brink of it was the furze bush upon which the coat had been hung.

"There was no wind that night, I understand," said Holmes.

"None, but very heavy rain."

"In that case the overcoat was not blown against the furze bushes, but placed there."

"Yes, it was laid across the bush."

"You fill me with interest. I perceive that the ground has been trampled up a good deal. No doubt many feet have been here since Monday night."

"A piece of matting has been laid here at the side, and we have all stood upon that."

"Excellent."

"In this bag I have one of the boots which Straker wore,

one of Fitzroy Simpson's shoes, and a cast horseshoe of Silver Blaze."

"My dear Inspector, you surpass yourself!" Holmes took the bag, and, descending into the hollow, he pushed the matting into a more central position. Then stretching himself upon his face and leaning his chin upon his hands, he made a careful study of the trampled mud in front of him. "Hullo!" said he suddenly. "What's this?" It was a wax vesta, half burned, which was so coated with mud that it looked at first like a little chip of wood.

"I cannot think how I came to overlook it," said the inspector with an expression of annoyance.

"It was invisible, buried in the mud. I only saw it because I was looking for it."

"What! You expected to find it?"

"I thought it not unlikely."

He took the boots from the bag and compared the impressions of each of them with marks upon the ground. Then he clambered up to the rim of the hollow and crawled about among the ferns and bushes.

"I am afraid that there are no more tracks," said the inspector. "I have examined the ground very carefully for a hundred yards in each direction."

"Indeed!" said Holmes, rising. "I should not have the impertinence to do it again after what you say. But I should like to take a little walk over the moor before it grows dark that I may know my ground tomorrow, and I think that I shall put this horseshoe into my pocket for luck."

Colonel Ross, who had shown some signs of impatience at my companion's quiet and systematic method of work, glanced at his watch. "I wish you would come back with me, Inspector," said he. "There are several points on which I should like your advice, and especially as to whether we do not owe it to the public to remove our horse's name from the entries for the cup."

"Certainly not," cried Holmes with decision. "I should let the name stand."

The colonel bowed. "I am very glad to have had your opinion, sir," said he. "You will find us at poor Straker's house when you have finished your walk, and we can drive together into Tavistock."

He turned back with the inspector, while Holmes and I walked slowly across the moor. The sun was beginning to sink behind the stable of Mapleton, and the long, sloping plain in front of us was tinged with gold, deepening into rich, ruddy browns where the faded ferns and brambles caught the evening light. But the glories of the landscape were all wasted upon my companion, who was sunk in the deepest thought.

"It's this way, Watson," said he at last. "We may leave the question of who killed John Straker for the instant and confine ourselves to finding out what has become of the horse. Now, supposing that he broke away during or after the tragedy, where could he have gone to? The horse is a very gregarious creature. If left to himself his instincts would have been either to return to King's Pyland or go over to Mapleton. Why should he run wild upon the moor? He would surely have been seen by now. And why should gypsies kidnap him? These people always clear out when they hear of trouble, for they do not wish to be pestered by the police. They could not hope to sell such a horse. They would run a great risk and gain nothing by taking him. Surely that is clear."

"Where is he, then?"

"I have already said that he must have gone to King's Pyland or to Mapleton. He is not at King's Pyland. Therefore he is at Mapleton. Let us take that as a working hypothesis and see what it leads us to. This part of the moor, as the inspector remarked, is very hard and dry. But it falls away toward Mapleton, and you can see from here that there is a long hollow over yonder, which must have been very wet on Monday night. If our supposition is correct, then the horse must have crossed that, and there is the point where we should look for his tracks."

We had been walking briskly during this conversation, and a few more minutes brought us to the hollow in question. At Holmes's request I walked down the bank to the right, and he to the left, but I had not taken fifty paces before I heard him give a shout and saw him waving his hand to me. The track of a horse was plainly outlined in the soft earth in front of him, and the shoe which he took from his pocket exactly fitted the impression.

"See the value of imagination," said Holmes. "It is the one quality which Gregory lacks. We imagined what might have happened, acted upon the supposition, and find ourselves justified. Let us proceed."

We crossed the marshy bottom and passed over a quarter of a mile of dry, hard turf. Again the ground sloped, and again we came on the tracks. Then we lost them for half a mile, but only to pick them up once more quite close to Mapleton. It was Holmes who saw them first, and he stood pointing with a look of triumph upon his face. A man's track was visible beside the horse's.

"The horse was alone before!" I cried.

"Quite so. It was alone before. Hullo, what is this?"

The double track turned sharp off and took the direction of King's Pyland. Holmes whistled, and we both followed along after it. His eyes were on the trail, but I happened to look a little to one side and saw to my surprise the same tracks coming back again in the opposite direction.

"One for you, Watson," said Holmes when I pointed it out. "You have saved us a long walk, which would have brought us back on our own traces. Let us follow the return track."

We had not to go far. It ended at the paving of asphalt which led up to the gates of the Mapleton stables. As we approached, a groom ran out from them.

"We don't want any loiterers about here," said he.

"I only wished to ask a question," said Holmes, with his finger and thumb in his waistcoat pocket. "Should I be too early to see your master, Mr. Silas Brown, if I were to call at five o'clock tomorrow morning?"

"Bless you, sir, if anyone is about he will be, for he is always the first stirring. But here he is, sir, to answer your questions for himself. No, sir, no, it is as much as my place is worth to let him see me touch your money. Afterward, if you like."

As Sherlock Holmes replaced the half-crown which he had drawn from his pocket, a fierce-looking elderly man strode out from the gate with a hunting crop swinging in his hand.

"What's this, Dawson!" he cried. "No gossiping! Go about your business! And you, what the devil do you want here?"·

"Ten minutes' talk with you, my good sir," said Holmes in the sweetest of voices.

"I've no time to talk to every gadabout. We want no strangers here. Be off, or you may find a dog at your heels."

Holmes leaned forward and whispered something in the trainer's ear. He started violently and flushed to the temples.

"It's a lie!" he shouted. "An infernal lie!"

"Very good. Shall we argue about it here in public or talk it over in your parlor?"

"Oh, come in if you wish to."

Holmes smiled. "I shall not keep you more than a few minutes, Watson," said he. "Now, Mr. Brown, I am quite at your disposal."

It was twenty minutes, and the reds had all faded into grays before Holmes and the trainer reappeared. Never have I seen such a change as had been brought about in Silas Brown in that short time. His face was ashy pale, beads of perspiration shone upon his brow, and his hands shook until the hunting crop wagged like a branch in the wind. His bullying, overbearing manner was all gone too, and he cringed along at my companion's side like a dog with its master.

"Your instructions will be done. It shall all be done," said he.

"There must be no mistake," said Holmes, looking round at him. The other winced as he read the menace in his eyes.

"Oh, no, there shall be no mistake. It shall be there. Should I change it first or not?"

Holmes thought a little and then burst out laughing. "No, don't," said he, "I shall write to you about it. No tricks, now, or—"

"Oh, you can trust me, you can trust me!"

"Yes, I think I can. Well, you shall hear from me tomorrow." He turned upon his heel, disregarding the trembling hand which the other held out to him, and we set off for King's Pyland.

"A more perfect compound of the bully, coward, and sneak than Master Silas Brown I have seldom met with," remarked Holmes as we trudged along together.

"He has the horse, then?"

"He tried to bluster out of it, but I described to him so exactly what his actions had been upon that morning that he is convinced that I was watching him. Of course you observed the peculiarly square toes in the impressions, and that his own boots exactly corresponded to them. Again, of course, no subordinate would have dared to do such a thing. I described to him how, when according to his custom he was the first down, he perceived a strange horse wandering over the moor. How he went out to it, and his astonishment at recognizing, from the white forehead which has given the favorite its name, that chance had put in his power the only horse which could beat the one upon which he had put his money. Then I described how his first impulse had been to lead him back to King's Pyland, and how the devil had shown him how he could hide the horse until the race was over, and how he had led it back and concealed it at Mapleton. When I told him every detail he gave it up and thought only of saving his own skin."

"But his stables had been searched?"

"Oh, an old horse-faker like him has many a dodge."

"But are you not afraid to leave the horse in his power now, since he has every interest in injuring it?"

"My dear fellow, he will guard it as the apple of his eye. He knows that his only hope of mercy is to produce it safe."

"Colonel Ross did not impress me as a man who would be likely to show much mercy in any case."

"The matter does not rest with Colonel Ross. I follow my own methods and tell as much or as little as I choose. That is the advantage of being unofficial. I don't know whether you observed it, Watson, but the colonel's manner has been just a trifle cavalier to me. I am inclined now to have a little amusement at his expense. Say nothing to him about the horse."

"Certainly not without your permission."

"And of course this is all quite a minor point compared to the question of who killed John Straker."

"And you will devote yourself to that?"

"On the contrary, we both go back to London by the night train."

I was thunderstruck by my friend's words. We had only been a few hours in Devonshire, and that he should give up an investigation which he had begun so brilliantly was quite incomprehensible to me. Not a word more could I draw from him until we were back at the trainer's house. The colonel and the inspector were awaiting us in the parlor.

"My friend and I return to town by the night express," said Holmes. "We have had a charming little breath of your beautiful Dartmoor air."

The inspector opened his eyes, and the colonel's lip curled in a sneer.

"So you despair of arresting the murderer of poor Straker," said he.

Holmes shrugged his shoulders. "There are certainly grave difficulties in the way," said he. "I have every hope, however, that your horse will start upon Tuesday, and I beg that you will have your jockey in readiness. Might I ask for a photograph of Mr. John Straker?"

The inspector took one from an envelope and handed it to him.

"My dear Gregory, you anticipate all my wants. If I might ask you to wait here for an instant, I have a question which I should like to put to the maid."

"I must say that I am rather disappointed in our London consultant," said Colonel Ross bluntly as my friend left the room. "I do not see that we are any further than when he came."

"At least you have his assurance that your horse will run," said I.

"Yes, I have his assurance," said the colonel with a shrug of his shoulders. "I should prefer to have the horse."

I was about to make some reply in defense of my friend when he entered the room again.

"Now, gentlemen," said he, "I am quite ready for Tavistock."

As we stepped into the carriage one of the stable lads held the door open for us. A sudden idea seemed to occur to Holmes, for he leaned forward and touched the lad upon the sleeve.

"You have a few sheep in the paddock," he said. "Who attends to them?"

"I do, sir."

"Have you noticed anything amiss with them of late?"

"Well, sir, not of much account, but three of them have gone lame, sir."

I could see that Holmes was extremely pleased, for he chuckled and rubbed his hands together.

"A long shot, Watson, a very long shot," said he, pinching my arm. "Gregory, let me recommend to your attention this singular epidemic among the sheep. Drive on, coachman!"

Colonel Ross still wore an expression which showed the poor opinion which he had formed of my companion's ability, but I saw by the inspector's face that his attention had been keenly aroused.

"You consider that to be important?" he asked.

"Exceedingly so."

"Is there any point to which you would wish to draw my attention?"

"To the curious incident of the dog in the nighttime."

"The dog did nothing in the nighttime."

"That was the curious incident," remarked Sherlock Holmes.

Four days later Holmes and I were again in the train, bound for Winchester to see the race for the Wessex Cup. Colonel Ross met us by appointment outside the station, and we drove in his drag to the course beyond the town. His face was grave, and his manner was cold in the extreme.

"I have seen nothing of my horse," said he.

"I suppose that you would know him when you saw him?" asked Holmes.

The colonel was very angry. "I have been on the turf for twenty years and never was asked such a question as that before," said he. "A child would know Silver Blaze with his white forehead and his mottled off-foreleg."

"How is the betting?"

"Well, that is the curious part of it. You could have got fifteen to one yesterday, but the price has become shorter and shorter, until you can hardly get three to one now."

"Hum!" said Holmes. "Somebody knows something, that is clear."

As the drag drew up in the enclosure near the grandstand I glanced at the card to see the entries.

> Wessex Plate [it ran] 50 sovs. each h ft with 1,000 sovs. added, for four- and five-year-olds. Second, £300. Third, £200. New course (one mile and five furlongs).
> 1. Mr. Heath Newton's The Negro. Red cap. Cinnamon jacket.
> 2. Colonel Wardlaw's Pugilist. Pink cap. Blue and black jacket.
> 3. Lord Backwater's Desborough. Yellow cap and sleeves.
> 4. Colonel Ross's Silver Blaze. Black cap. Red jacket.
> 5. Duke of Balmoral's Iris. Yellow and black stripes.
> 6. Lord Singleford's Rasper. Purple cap. Black sleeves.

"We scratched our other one and put all hopes on your word," said the colonel. "Why, what is that? Silver Blaze favorite?"

"Five to four against Silver Blaze!" roared the ring. "Five to four against Silver Blaze! Five to fifteen against Desborough! Five to four on the field!"

"There are the numbers up," I cried. "They are all six there."

"All six there? Then my horse is running," cried the colonel in great agitation. "But I don't see him. My colors have not passed."

"Only five have passed. This must be he."

As I spoke a powerful bay horse swept out from the weighing enclosure and cantered past us, bearing on its back the well-known black and red of the colonel.

"That's not my horse," cried the owner. "That beast has

not a white hair upon its body. What is this that you have done, Mr. Holmes?"

"Well, well, let us see how he gets on," said my friend imperturbably. For a few minutes he gazed through my field glass. "Capital! An excellent start!" he cried suddenly. "There they are, coming round the curve!"

From our drag we had a superb view as they came up the straight. The six horses were so close together that a carpet could have covered them, but halfway up the yellow of the Mapleton stable showed to the front. Before they reached us, however, Desborough's bolt was shot, and the colonel's horse, coming away with a rush, passed the post a good six lengths before its rival, the Duke of Balmoral's Iris making a bad third.

"It's my race, anyhow," gasped the colonel, passing his hand over his eyes. "I confess that I can make neither head nor tail of it. Don't you think that you have kept up your mystery long enough, Mr. Holmes?"

"Certainly, Colonel, you shall know everything. Let us all go round and have a look at the horse together. Here he is," he continued as we made our way into the weighing enclosure, where only owners and their friends find admittance. "You have only to wash his face and his leg in spirits of wine, and you will find that he is the same old Silver Blaze as ever."

"You take my breath away!"

"I found him in the hands of a faker and took the liberty of running him just as he was sent over."

"My dear sir, you have done wonders. The horse looks very fit and well. It never went better in its life. I owe you a thousand apologies for having doubted your ability. You have done me a great service by recovering my horse. You would do me a greater still if you could lay your hands on the murderer of John Straker."

"I have done so," said Holmes quietly.

The colonel and I stared at him in amazement. "You have got him! Where is he, then?"

"He is here."

"Here! Where?"

"In my company at the present moment."

The colonel flushed angrily. "I quite recognize that I am under obligations to you, Mr. Holmes," said he, "but I must regard what you have just said as either a very bad joke or an insult."

Sherlock Holmes laughed. "I assure you that I have not associated you with the crime, Colonel," said he. "The real murderer is standing immediately behind you." He stepped past and laid his hand upon the glossy neck of the Thoroughbred.

"The horse!" cried both the colonel and myself.

"Yes, the horse. And it may lessen his guilt if I say that it was done in self-defense, and that John Straker was a man who was entirely unworthy of your confidence. But there goes the bell, and as I stand to win a little on this next race, I shall defer a lengthy explanation until a more fitting time."

We had the corner of a Pullman car to ourselves that evening as we whirled back to London, and I fancy that the journey was a short one to Colonel Ross as well as to myself as we listened to our companion's narrative of the events which had occurred at the Dartmoor training stables upon that Monday night, and the means by which he had unraveled them.

"I confess," said he, "that any theories which I had formed from the newspaper reports were entirely erroneous. And yet there were indications there, had they not been overlaid by other details which concealed their true import. I went to Devonshire with the conviction that Fitzroy Simpson was the true culprit, although, of course, I saw that the evidence against him was by no means complete. It was while I was in the carriage, just as we reached the trainer's house, that the immense significance of the curried mutton occurred to me. You may remember that I was distrait and remained sitting after you had all alighted. I was marveling in my own mind how I could possibly have overlooked so obvious a clue."

"I confess," said the colonel, "that even now I cannot see how it helps us."

"It was the first link in my chain of reasoning. Powdered opium is by no means tasteless. The flavor is not disagreeable, but it is perceptible. Were it mixed with any ordinary dish the eater would undoubtedly detect it and would probably eat no more. A curry was exactly the medium which would disguise this taste. By no possible supposition could this stranger, Fitzroy Simpson, have caused curry to be served in the trainer's family that night, and it is surely too monstrous a coincidence to suppose that he happened to come along with powdered opium upon the very night when a dish happened to be served which would disguise the flavor. That is unthinkable. Therefore Simpson becomes eliminated from the case, and our attention centers upon Straker and his wife, the only two people who could have chosen curried mutton for supper that night. The opium was added after the dish was set aside for the stableboy, for the others had the same for supper with no ill effects. Which of them, then, had access to that dish without the maid seeing them?

"Before deciding that question I had grasped the significance of the silence of the dog, for one true inference invariably suggests others. The Simpson incident had shown me that a dog was kept in the stables, and yet, though someone had been in and had fetched out a horse, he had not barked enough to arouse the two lads in the loft. Obviously the midnight visitor was someone whom the dog knew well.

"I was already convinced, or almost convinced, that John Straker went down to the stables in the dead of the night and took out Silver Blaze. For what purpose? For a dishonest one, obviously, or why should he drug his own stableboy? And yet

I was at a loss to know why. There have been cases before now where trainers have made sure of great sums of money by laying against their own horses through agents and then preventing them from winning by fraud. Sometimes it is a pulling jockey. Sometimes it is some surer and subtler means. What was it here? I hoped that the contents of his pockets might help me to form a conclusion.

"And they did so. You cannot have forgotten the singular knife which was found in the dead man's hand, a knife which certainly no sane man would choose for a weapon. It was, as Dr. Watson told us, a form of knife which is used for the most delicate operations known in surgery. And it was to be used for a delicate operation that night. You must know, with your wide experience of turf matters, Colonel Ross, that it is possible to make a slight nick upon the tendons of a horse's ham, and to do it subcutaneously, so as to leave absolutely no trace. A horse so treated would develop a slight lameness, which would be put down to a strain in exercise or a touch of rheumatism, but never to foul play."

"Villain! Scoundrel!" cried the colonel.

"We have here the explanation of why John Straker wished to take the horse out on to the moor. So spirited a creature would have certainly roused the soundest of sleepers when it felt the prick of the knife. It was absolutely necessary to do it in the open air."

"I have been blind!" cried the colonel. "Of course that was why he needed the candle and struck the match."

"Undoubtedly. But in examining his belongings I was fortunate enough to discover not only the method of the crime but even its motives. As a man of the world, Colonel, you know that men do not carry other people's bills about in their pockets. We have most of us quite enough to do to settle our own. I at once concluded that Straker was leading a double life and keeping a second establishment. The nature of the bill showed that there was a lady in the case, and one who had expensive tastes. Liberal as you are with your servants, one can hardly expect that they can buy twenty-guinea walking dresses for their ladies. I questioned Mrs. Straker as to the dress without her knowing it, and, having satisfied myself that it had never reached her, I made a note of the milliner's address and felt that by calling there with Straker's photograph I could easily dispose of the mythical Derbyshire.

"From that time on all was plain. Straker had led out the horse to a hollow where his light would be invisible. Simpson in his flight had dropped his cravat, and Straker had picked it up—with some idea, perhaps, that he might use it in securing the horse's leg. Once in the hollow, he had got behind the horse and had struck a light; but the creature, frightened at the sudden glare, and with the strange instinct of animals feeling that some mischief was intended, had lashed out, and the steel shoe had struck Straker full on the forehead. He had already, in spite of the rain, taken off his overcoat in order to do his delicate task, and so, as he fell, his knife gashed his thigh. Do I make it clear?"

"Wonderful!" cried the colonel. "Wonderful! You might have been there!"

"My final shot was, I confess, a very long one. It struck me that so astute a man as Straker would not undertake this delicate tendon-nicking without a little practice. What could he practice on? My eyes fell upon the sheep, and I asked a question which, rather to my surprise, showed that my surmise was correct.

"When I returned to London I called upon the milliner, who had recognized Straker as an excellent customer of the name of Derbyshire, who had a very dashing wife, with a strong partiality for expensive dresses. I have no doubt that this woman had plunged him over head and ears in debt, and so led him into this miserable plot."

"You have explained all but one thing," cried the colonel. "Where was the horse?"

"Ah, it bolted, and was cared for by one of your neighbors. We must have an amnesty in that direction, I think. This is Clapham Junction, if I am not mistaken, and we shall be in Victoria in less than ten minutes. If you care to smoke a cigar in our rooms, Colonel, I shall be happy to give you any other details which might interest you."

Mary Wilkins Freeman

THE DOCTOR'S HORSE

The horse was a colt when he was purchased with the money paid by the heirs of one of the doctor's patients, and those were his days of fire. At first it was opined that the horse would never do for the doctor: he was too nervous, and his nerves beyond the reach of the doctor's drugs. He shied at every wayside bush and stone; he ran away several times; he was loath to stand, and many a time the doctor in those days was forced to rush from the bedsides of patients to seize his refractory horse by the bridle and soothe and compel him to quiet. The horse in that untamed youth of his was like a furnace of fierce animal fire; when he was given rein on a frosty morning the pound of his ironbound hoofs on the rigid roads cleared them of the slow-plodding country teams. A current as of the very freedom and invincibility of life seemed to pass through the taut reins to the doctor's hands. But the doctor was the master of his horse, as of all other things with which he came in contact. He was a firm and hard man in the pursuance of his duty, never yielding to it with love, but unswervingly staunch. He was never cruel to his horse; he seldom whipped him, but he never petted him; he simply mastered him, and after a while the fiery animal began to go the doctor's gait, and not his own.

When the doctor was sent for in a hurry, to an emergency case, the horse stretched his legs at a gallop, no matter how little inclined he felt for it, on a burning day of summer, perhaps. When there was no haste, and the doctor disposed to take his time, the horse went at a gentle amble, even though the frosts of a winter morning were firing his blood, and every one of his iron nerves and muscles was strained with that awful strain of repressed motion. Even on those mornings the horse would stand at the door of the patient who was ill with old-fashioned consumption or chronic liver disease, his four legs planted widely, his head and neck describing a long downward curve, so expressive of submission and dejection that it might have served as a hieroglyphic for them, and no more thought of letting those bounding impulses of his have their way than if the doctor's will had verily bound his every foot to the ground with unbreakable chains of servitude. He had become the doctor's horse. He was the will of the doctor, embodied in a perfect compliance of action and motion. People remarked how the horse had sobered down, what a splendid animal he was for the doctor, and they had thought that he would never be able to keep him and employ him in his profession.

Now and then the horse used to look around at the empty buggy as he stood at the gate of a patient's house, to see if the doctor were there, but the will which held the reins, being still evident to his consciousness even when its owner was absent, kept him in his place. He would have no thought of taking advantage of his freedom; he would turn his head, and droop it in that curve of utter submission, shift his weight slightly to another foot, make a sound which was like a human sigh of patience, and wait again. When the doctor, carrying his little medicine chest, came forth, he would sometimes look at him, sometimes not; but he would set every muscle into an attitude of readiness for progress at the feel of the taut lines and the sound of the masterly human voice behind him.

Then he would proceed to the house of the next patient, and the story would be repeated. The horse seemed to live his life in a perfect monotony of identical chapters. His waiting was scarcely cheered or stimulated by the vision and anticipation of his stall and his supper, so unvarying was it. The same stall, the same measure of oats, the same allotment of hay. He was never put out to pasture, for the doctor was a poor man, and unable to buy another horse and to spare him. All the variation which came to his experience was the uncertainty as to the night calls. Sometimes he would feel a slight revival of spirit and rebellion when led forth on a bitter winter night from his stolidity of repose, broken only by the shifting of his weight for bodily comfort, never by any perturbation of his inner life. The horse had no disturbing memories, and no anticipations, but he was still somewhat sensitive to surprises. When the flare of the lantern came athwart his stall and he felt the doctor's hand at his halter in the deep silence of a midnight, he would sometimes feel himself as a separate consciousness from the doctor, and experience the individualizing of contrary desires.

Now and then he pulled back, planting his four feet firmly, but he always yielded in a second before the masterly will of the man. Sometimes he started with a vicious emphasis, but it was never more than momentary. In the end he fell back into his lost state of utter submission. The horse was not unhappy. He was well cared for. His work, though considerable, was not beyond his strength. He had lost something undoubtedly in this complete surrender of his own will, but a loss of which one is unconscious tends only to the degradation of an animal, not to his misery.

The doctor often remarked with pride that his horse was a well-broken animal, somewhat stupid, but faithful. All the timid womenfolk in the village looked upon him with favor; the doctor's wife, who was nervous, loved to drive with her husband behind this docile horse, and was not afraid even to sit, while the doctor was visiting his patients, with the reins over the animal's back. The horse had become to her a piece of mechanism absolutely under the control of her husband, and he was in truth little more. Still, a furnace is a furnace, even when the fire runs low, and there is always the possibility of a blaze.

The doctor had owned the horse several years, though he was still young, when the young woman came to live in the family. She was the doctor's niece, a fragile thing, so exposed as to her network of supersensitive nerves to all the winds of life that she was always in a quiver of reciprocation or repulsion. She feared everything unknown, and all strength. She was innately suspicious of the latter. She knew its power to work her harm, and believed in its desire to do so. Especially was she afraid of that rampant and uncertain strength of a horse. Never did she ride behind one but she watched his every motion; she herself shied in spirit at every wayside stone. She watched for him to do his worst. She had no faith when she was told by her uncle that this horse was so steady that she herself could drive him. She had been told that so many times, and her confidence had been betrayed. But the doctor, since she was like a pale weed grown in the shade, with no stimulus of life except that given at its birth, prescribed fresh air and, to her consternation, daily drives with him. Day after day she went. She dared not refuse, for she was as compliant in her way to a stronger will as the horse. But she went in an agony of terror, of which the doctor had no conception. She sat in the buggy all alone while the doctor visited his patients, and she watched every motion of the horse. If he turned to look at her, her heart stood still.

And at last it came to pass that the horse began in a curious fashion to regain something of his lost spirit, and met her fear of him, and became that which she dreaded. One day as he stood before a gate in late autumn, with a burning gold of maple branches over his head and the wine of the frost in his nostrils, and this timorous thing seated behind him, anticipating that which he could but had forgotten that he could do, the knowledge and the memory of it awoke in him. There was a stiff northwester blowing. The girl was huddled in shawls and robes; her little pale face looked forth from the midst with wide eyes, with a prospectus of infinite danger from all life in them; her little thin hands clutched the reins with that consciousness of helplessness and conviction of the horse's power of mischief which is sometimes like an electric current firing the blood of a beast.

Suddenly a piece of paper blew under the horse's nose. He had been unmoved by firecrackers before, but today, with that current of terror behind him firing his blood, that paper put him in a sudden fury of panic, of self-assertion, of rage, of all three combined. He snorted; the girl screamed wildly. He started; the girl gave the reins a frantic pull. He stopped. Then the paper blew under his nose again, and he started again. The girl fairly gasped with terror; she pulled the reins, and the terror in her hands was like a whip of stimulus to the evil freedom in the horse. She screamed, and the sound of that scream was the climax. The horse knew all at once what he was—not the doctor, but a horse, with a great power of blood and muscle which made him not only his own master, but the master of all weaker things. He gave a great plunge that was rapture, the assertion of freedom, freedom itself, and was off. The faint screams of the frightened creature behind him stimulated him to madder progress. At last he knew, by her terrified recognition of it, his own sovereignty of liberty.

He thundered along the road; he had no more thought of his pitiful encumbrance of servitude, the buggy, than a free soul of its mortal coil. The country road was cleared before him; plodding teams were pulled frantically to the side; women scuttled into dooryards; pale faces peered after him from windows. Now and then an adventurous man rushed into his path with wild halloos and a mad swinging of arms, then fled precipitately before his resistless might of advance. At first the horse had heard the doctor's shouts behind him, and had laughed within himself, then he left them far behind. He leaped, he plunged, his iron-shod heels touched the dashboard of the buggy. He heard splintering wood. He gave another lunging plunge. Then he swerved, and leaped a wall. Finally he had cleared himself of everything except a remnant of his harness. The buggy was a wreck, strewn piecemeal over a meadow. The girl was lying unhurt, but as still as if she were dead; but the horse which her fear had fired to new life was away in a mad gallop over the autumn fields, and his youth had returned. He was again himself—what he had been when he first awoke to a consciousness of existence and the joy of bounding motion in his mighty nerves and muscles. He was no longer the doctor's horse, but his own.

The doctor had to sell him. After that his reputation was gone, and indeed he was never safe. He ran with the doctor. He would not stand a moment unless tied, and then pawed and pulled madly at the halter, and rent the air with impatient whinnies. So the doctor sold him, and made a good bargain. The horse was formed for speed, and his lapse from virtue had increased his financial value. The man who bought him had a good eye for horseflesh, and had no wish to stand at doors on his road to success, but to take a beeline for the winning post. The horse was well cared for, but for the first time he felt the lash and heard curses; however, they only served to stimulate to a fiercer glow the fire which had awakened within him. He was never his new master's horse as he had been the doctor's. He gained the reputation of speed, but also of vicious nervousness. He was put on the racecourse. He made a record at the county fair. Once he killed his jockey. He used to speed along the road drawing a man crouched in a tilting gig. Few other horses could pass him. Then he began to grow old.

At last when the horse was old he came into his first master's hands again. The doctor had grown old, older than the horse, and he did not know him at first, though he did say to his old wife that he looked something like that horse which he had owned which ran away and nearly killed his niece. After he said that, nothing could induce the doctor's wife to ride behind him; but the doctor, even in his feeble old age, had no fear, and the sidelong fire in the old horse's eye, and the proud cant of his neck, and haughty resentment at unfamiliar sights on the road, pleased him. He felt a confidence in his ability to tame this untamed thing, and the old man seemed to grow younger after he had bought the horse. He had given up his practice after a severe illness, and a young man had taken it, but he began to have dreams of work again. But he never knew that he had bought his own old horse until after he had owned him some weeks. He was driving him along the country road one day in October when the oaks were a ruddy blaze, and the sumacs like torches along the walls, and the air like wine with the smell of grapes and apples. Then suddenly, while the doctor was sitting in the buggy with loose reins, speeding along the familiar road, the horse stopped. And he stopped before the house where had used to dwell the man afflicted with old-fashioned consumption, and the window which had once framed his haggard, coughing visage reflected the western sunlight like a blank page of gold. There the horse stood, his head and long neck bent in the old curve. He was ready to wait until the consumptive arose from his grave in the churchyard, if so ordered. The doctor stared at him. Then he got out and went to the animal's head, and man and horse recognized each other. The light of youth was again in the man's eyes as he looked at his own spiritual handiwork. He was once more the master, in the presence of that which he had mastered. But the horse was expressed in body and spirit only by the lines of utter yielding and patience and submission. He was again the doctor's horse.

THE OLD
JIM HORSE

The Superintendent of Horses in the New York Fire Department sent a substitute to Thirty-three Engine one day a year or two ago, and took away a big roan horse which had served there for eighteen years and nine months. "Horse registered No. 60, unfit," is the way this act was reported officially. But the men, passing the news around the house, and thence from company to company all over town, said:

"They've taken the old Jim horse. They're going to sell Thirty-three's old Jim."

Now the firemen all knew that the old Jim horse was unfit

for duty. Captain Nash, the foreman of Thirty-three, had been watching secretly for two or three years the growth of a film over the animal's big, intelligent eyes. No expert superintendent of firehorses was needed to see that Jim was going blind. But what of that? There wasn't a horse in the service that knew the business so well as Jim. There wasn't a fireman who loved a big fire more than the roan that ran in the middle of Thirty-three's team of three.

"He learned what he had to do in five minutes after he was bought and delivered here," said Captain Nash. "He caught on the first time they showed him. We never locked him in a stall. It wasn't necessary; for he never left it without permission, except to get a drink or to respond to an alarm of fire. At the first tap of the gong, he sprang forward to his place. Sometimes he came so fast that he had to slide to stop himself under the harness; and when we let him out in the street to wander around, he'd run at the call of the gong, stop on the sidewalk, turn about, and back into his place at the pole. Why, we used to put boxes and chairs in his way from the stall, but he jumped over them and would still be first in the collar. They oughtn't to have condemned Jim. He never cost the city a cent for doctor's bills. Once he fell down on the way to a fire and was dragged a block over the Broadway cobbles; but he got up without our stopping, and though he was pretty sore, we never reported him, and he got over it. Sometimes a hose would burst, but Jim didn't care if only he could turn his head out of the way. Many a shower of falling glass he has stood without flinching, as the scars on his back show, but he was never laid off a day. Half a dozen horses that were mated to him have lived their day and died, trying to pull up even with old Jim. It isn't so long ago they sent us up a spare horse to take the place of one of Jim's mates that was off being shod. There was one run, and Jim chewed the young horse's neck to make him keep up his end, afraid we'd lose first water. He was a great firehorse, was Jim. The only trouble he gave was at mealtimes, which he knew like a clock; and if his feed wasn't set down before him on the minute, he made a fuss, pawing at the side of his stall and starting all the other horses to kicking."

Possibly Captain Nash was prejudiced. He and Jim had served together in the same house for eleven years. But if there was anything so very wrong in concealing Jim's aging weaknesses, the captain was not the only one to blame. Hugh Bonner, the Chief of the Department, had his downtown quarters in Thirty-three's house, and he knew all about Jim, and all about Captain Nash, too, for that matter. Yet he kept mum. Then there was the Superintendent of Horses: why didn't he do something before? It is true he had condemned Jim five years ago. This, however, is the way he did it. After inspecting the horse, he walked up to the captain and said:

"Nash, the old Jim horse is getting unfit. I guess I'll have to send you a substitute."

Captain Nash did not say anything. The substitute came, and he accepted the new horse, but he didn't send Jim away. He handed over another horse. Now the stableman did not know the difference, perhaps, but the Superintendent did. He must have found that he had been fooled; and the captain, liable to punishment for disobeying orders, worried for a week. But nothing came of it. Possibly the Superintendent reported the case to the Chief. If he did, it is curious the Chief never mentioned the matter to Captain Nash. At any rate, the Chief must have known that the Jim horse had been condemned, and he certainly saw the Jim horse afterward first at many a fire.

A year or two later, the Superintendent condemned Jim again, and he did it rather sharply this time. He did not say, "Nash, the old Jim horse," and so on. He commanded Captain Nash to deliver "registered horse No. 60"; but after he was out of the door, he paused, turned half around, and said:

"He isn't fit to run to fires, Nash. You better trade him

off to me for a good, strong, young horse. Anyhow, I'm going to do my duty, and if you want—"

The rest was nothing but a grumble which no one could be expected to understand. The new horse arrived. The Captain hesitated, till at last he thumped on his desk, and shouted down to the man on watch to transfer to the training stables the worst horse in the house. The fireman who received the order grinned, and delivered the next-to-the-oldest horse, an animal that "never was no good, nohow." And when the trampling of the departing hooves had died away, the men upstairs who heard the order stopped the game of cards while one of them went below. He walked, around the engine to Jim's stall, told him to get back, though the horse was not more than half a foot over the line, then returned to the game. He did not report anything verbally, but the others looked in his face, and resumed the play in great good humor. Just as they were forgetting the incident, the Captain came out of his room and passed downstairs. He had to get something out of the feed room, which is back of the horses. Old Jim tried to attract the Captain's attention, but the Captain wouldn't notice him.

The third time the Superintendent acted, he did not give the Captain a chance for any of his tricky horse-trading. He had "registered horse No. 60" removed without talking about it, and Captain Nash was at a loss.

"I knew what it meant," said the Captain afterward. "We had a horse here once, the Buck horse. He was a good fire-horse, too; nothing like Jim, but he served faithful for years, and then went lame in his off hind leg. We did what we could for him till the inspector got onto it and took him away and sold him at auction. About a year after that, when we were all standing out in front of the house one day, an old, broken-down, lame horse came along the street, pulling one of those carts that go around collecting clamshells. He balked right opposite the door. We thought at first he was tired, and I guess he was. Maybe some of the younger firemen laughed when the crazy old driver licked his horse. But all of a sudden we took notice of the horse's sore leg, and somebody said:

" 'It's the old Buck horse, boys.'

"And it was. He had stopped because he wanted to come in home, the old Buck horse did. And his leg was worse."

So Captain Nash remembered the Buck horse when they took away the Jim horse. He waited till the Chief came to the house.

Then he told him. "Chief," he said, "they've come and got the old Jim horse at last."

The Chief did not answer.

"I'd just as lief keep him, Chief," the Captain continued. "He's the best horse I had. A little film over his eyes, and pretty old, but he's—he's the old Jim horse, Chief."

Another pause.

"They'll sell him into some old ash cart or to a Polish peddler. And Jim's served long enough to have a pension."

Then the Chief answered:

"Why don't you write his record up to the Board? I'll endorse it."

"I ain't much on the write," said Nash, "but I'll try it, if you say so."

That was on a Saturday. Captain Nash took Sunday for the job, and here is his formal report to the Board of Fire Commissioners:

> I respectfully forward a brief history of the roan team of horses formerly used in the engine of this company. Of the original Jack horse I have not much to write, he being killed while responding to an alarm for fire at station 236 on May 30, 1881, by colliding with the shaft of Engine 13 tender. The point of the shaft entered his breast. . . . As to the horse Jim, who was received at these quarters on January 14, 1879, and performed duty therein until November 4, 1897, a period of eighteen years and nine months, the first eleven years of which

Jim and his mate had to draw a heavy first-class engine, when the runs were more frequent and much longer than those of the present day, when the same identical engine is drawn by three horses. The Jim horse, in the opinion of all the officers and members ever connected with this company, and the many distinguished persons who visited these quarters, was such that they expressed the belief that there never was a horse that showed more intelligence than the Jim horse.

Here followed a recital of Jim's distinguishing traits in much the same language as that already quoted from Captain Nash.

Chief Bonner wrote something, too:

> I take great pleasure in transmitting for your consideration the history of the Jim horse of Engine Thirty-three, for a period of nearly twenty years. . . . He was about seven years old when purchased, which would make him nearly twenty-seven years of age. I appeal to the Board in behalf of this faithful animal, that he be retained in the service of the department, and assigned to some company where the duties will be light, and that the Superintendent of Horses be directed to not include in his sale registered No. 60, which is the number assigned to this faithful animal.

"This worked," said the Captain. When these communications were read at the Board meeting, the commissioners were silent a moment. Then the president said that he thought Jim had earned his pension and should be retired. No one objected; so the Superintendent of Horses was directed to keep Jim for such light work as might turn up, if there was any such. At any rate, he was not to be sold. This was the first time in the history of the department that a horse was retired like a fireman; but it paid. For example, it put a stop to Captain Nash's grumbling about the new middle horse that runs now with Thirty-three Engine.

Alvah Milton Kerr

IN FRONT OF
THE STAMPEDE

*A Story of the Frontier Railroad
and the Plains*

As claim adjuster in the department of lost, over, and short freight, I was, for the most part, "on the wing," knocking about over all divisions and branches of the road, at the head or tail of problems involving the company's money or the want of it. Old Perth, roundhouse foreman at Wandon, had helped me in fixing the responsibility of a shortage in the freighting of engine oil from an Eastern firm, and perhaps on that account, or from some sort of affinity, we became fast friends. Of course, and quite naturally, an ex-dispatcher like myself and an old engineer like Perth could hardly escape feeling an interest in each other; besides, Perth was a man of good intellect and eminently worthy of cultivation. I rarely passed through Wandon without going over to the roundhouse and shops to see him.

Sitting one day in his little office, which looked on the one hand into the engine room, with its sixteen stalls, and on the other into the repair shop, with its cranes, steam hammers, lathes, and litter of engine parts, he told me the story of Katie Lyon's great ride during Long Blanket's raid, and her race for life in the buffalo stampede.

"It was the first trip I ever fired an engine," he said. "I was then a green lump of a boy, only a couple of years off the farm. Most railroaders, you know, come from the cornfields, especially in the West. Eighteen months in the shops at Omaha had given me an ambition to push my way toward the throttle as fast as possible, and wipers and firemen being plenty in my quarter, I came on out to the mountain division, and went into the roundhouse at Ludder. That was way back in the sixties, when the first road was being pushed across the western half of the continent. Indians and buffalo and soldiers were very much in evidence in those days, and the line, instead of running clean and well ballasted through a civilized land, wormed its way across five hundred miles of bunchgrass and sagebrush, and through another five hundred of mountains, a world of solitude peopled only by creatures of solitude.

"There was some question as to whether Ludder would continue as a divisional point, and, partly on account of its possible removal, the roundhouse had been constructed of wood instead of brick. The building contained stalls for eight engines, and stood some two hundred feet from a creek. Into the creek emptied an eighteen-inch drain, carrying off the wastewater when we washed out the engine boilers. But for this drain it is probable that Katie Lyon would never have taken her memorable ride.

"Jack Lyon, Katie's father, handled the throttle of the old Forty. Jack was a middle-aged man then, and the Forty was young. Both are in the scrap pile now, God bless them! The advanced front of construction was nearly a hundred miles west of us, and such rolling stock as we boasted was chiefly employed in hauling rails, ties, machinery, men, and supplies toward the front. The rather indefinite homes of the company's employees at Ludder consisted, in most instances, of sod huts and flimsy pine cottages. Lyon's home lay a quarter of a mile down the creek, where he found it convenient to have a garden, irrigated from the stream by means of a lifting waterwheel, and where a Jersey cow and calf and a young white mare, brought from Iowa, found pasturage close at hand. The engineer's family consisted of a wife and three children—Katie, fourteen or fifteen years of age, and twin boys in their tenth summer.

"Katie was a restless creature, boyish, and as whimsical and lively as thistledown. I remember—you can hardly fancy how clearly—of often looking down from the enginehouse and seeing the girl and the two little chaps playing at all sorts of pranks in the pasture below the house. One day it would be 'circus,' with Katie on the mare, sometimes standing up, urging the animal round a circle, with one twin as ringmaster and the other as clown or tumbler; another day it would be 'cowboy,' with one of the twins or Katie on the mare and roping the Jersey calf or cow or one of the children. Once, when nine years old, Katie had been to a circus, back in Iowa, and memory of it still flamed in her mind with something of the glory of a great torch seen against the sky. In eastern Nebraska, afterward, she had seen the knights of the sombrero and lariat at work, and had found them picturesque and remarkable. Imitation is the child's part, so they played at that which seemed most fanciful in their world. Lyon occasionally asked his daughter, in teasing vein, if she had yet decided which she was best cut out for, a circus rider or a cowboy. But Katie's equestrian weakness ultimately served the little community a very good turn indeed.

"During those days Indians were plentiful; not quite so thick as grasshoppers, but uncomfortably numerous, and not yet corralled on reservations; as now. Buffalo in uncounted thousands grazed on the plains and in the wide entrances of the mountain valleys all the way from Texas to Montana. Wild horses roamed in freedom, and the antelope and coyote were not afraid. It was beautiful.

"But that order of things had been touched with change; the roar of the locomotive began to reverberate in the solitudes, and the first criminal slaughterers of the bison herds had begun their awful work. The Indians grew resentful and troublesome, and details of United States troops had often to be called out to guard the railroad and defenseless settlements. Then came the general attack led by Chief Long Blanket on the north and by Black Calf from the south. That brought to light the real stuff of most of us, and it was then I found out the true-blue steel of which Katie was made. She used to come up to the station almost every time that her father came in with his engine, and would usually climb into the cab and mount the fireman's seat, and ring the bell while I run the engine into the house. When Lyon wasn't looking, I remember I used to let her hold the throttle as we went down to the roundhouse switch. She could always do almost anything with me.

"Well, one September morning a report came from the front that the men on construction had been having a warm time with the redskins and wanted help. Three troops of the Third Cavalry were in camp on the creek a mile or so from Ludder, and a messenger was sent all speed to notify them. Old Fort Chandler lay off to the southwest of us about fifteen miles, and the blueshirts had been brought near the track in order that they might strike quickly, for disturbing rumors had been coming in for some weeks of a general uprising of the Indians. Major Holme had gone west from Fort Chandler in search of Black Calf and his band, leaving the troops at the fort reduced to a small number—three companies, under the command of Captain Pope, having been detached to guard the railroad and settlement at Ludder. Black Calf, however, had given Holme the slip, and was making a long detour to the south and east to strike us at the division station; but all were ignorant of this. Reports had come in that Long Blanket, with a band of warriors, had been seen in the low foothills north of the track, some twenty miles west of us, and Pope was preparing to swing his force against them, when word came that his men were needed at the front, eighty miles west.

"The superintendent of construction, who was at the front, had sent the message. It came by wire, early in the morning, and within the hour Pope was at the station with his troops. The horses and luggage were hurriedly loaded into boxcars, most of the boys boarded other boxcars, while two flat cars were thrown into the center of the train, each bearing a mounted howitzer and a staked breastwork of railroad iron and a complement of soldiers. Engine Forty was brought out, and hooked on ahead. Her fireman being sick, I was ordered to go with Lyon and fire the engine. That met my wish precisely, for I was anxious to begin firing; besides, there was the enticing vision of a battle at the front. I was young then. It wouldn't entice me now.

"Nearly every one in the straggling village of Ludder came out to see us off. Lyon's wife, with the twins and an anxious face, was there; and while Lyon was oiling round, Katie climbed up into the cab and slipped a revolver under the cushion of the fireman's seat. 'It's father's; you may need it, Joe,' she said, and laughed over her shoulder to me as she jumped to the ground from the gangway. I grinned and blushed, little realizing how and where I should next meet this madcap maid.

"About nine o'clock we rolled out of the station, with a crowd of women and children and eight or ten men cheering us, and began swinging away toward the west. The track was new and in poor shape for fast running; but Lyon let the Forty have her head, his dark eyes glistening as he watched the rails ahead. The country swept away to north and south in scarcely perceptible swells—an ocean of fading grass, yellow-green and dreamy in the tender heat. Vast masses of snow-pure clouds drifted in the sky, while before us, in the west, and curving toward the northeast, rose the lilac-colored heaps of the Rockies. I didn't have much time to poetize, however, for I had my hands full in trying to keep the Forty hot.

"We got on swimmingly for perhaps twenty miles, then we struck a break—two rails had been pried loose from the ties and thrown by the right-of-way. It looked bad. By the merest chance we escaped being ditched. On the north side of the track, and extending for miles toward the west, began a series of low foothills—so low that they seemed much like the gentle swells of a lazy sea. Here and there through this undulating plateau sharp coulees had been cut by the summer waters of the distant mountains, though the streambeds were now dry or carrying little fluid. Pope mounted to the top of a boxcar and scanned the region with his glass, but no Indians or other marauders were in sight. Away to the south we all saw what appeared to be a black lake, a sweep of living liquid, miles in length, and stirring faintly like something moved by a gentle wind.

" 'Buffaloes,' said Lyon laconically, setting the injector pumps to work and jumping to the ground. 'That sort of thing is as common as jackrabbits: but this tearing up of the track is different. Long Blanket and his gang must be over among the hills there somewhere.'

"The conductor and two brakemen were ahead, inspecting the ground. Tracks of both men and horses were thick near the break in the track. Captain Pope promptly ordered a squad of soldiers forward; the rails were brought back and put into place; spikes and a maul were brought from the caboose, and the rupture mended. Then we pulled forward again, but cautiously, Lyon watching the track ahead of us like a hawk, his hand on the throttle lever, while Pope and every boy in blue on the train stood on the alert for a whack at the unseen enemy. Soon we found another break: a half-dozen rails had been pulled up. After we had repaired that, we found another break, and another, and another, and time slipped away into the afternoon, and we were making no progress.

"Pope came and rode in the engine. 'There's a wooden trestle about three miles from here,' said Lyon. 'If they've burned that, then the game is up; we'll never get to the front. The trestle is beyond the big bend ahead there. Hello! there's some more rails pulled up.'

" 'Long Blanket and his band are going west,' said the captain. 'Evidently the chief's idea is to destroy so much track that it will take the company several days to make repairs; meanwhile he will try to connect with the Indians at the front and strike the construction men a heavy blow. I'm of half a mind to mount the boys and go after him. If the trestle is burned, I will do so. Yellow Sky of the Shoshones is the chap who is leading the deviltry, I fancy, out at the front.'

"Now, as later information revealed, the men at the front were taking care of themselves, and also of Yellow Sky, in fine style, while we, the rescuers, were in peril; and affairs back at Ludder, where we thought everything quiet and secure, were alarming to the last degree. Within an hour after our leaving the division station, Black Calf, with a band of two hundred painted braves, appeared south of the town.

"All told, there were something like twenty-five men and boys and perhaps a hundred women and children in the village. All these, in wild excitement, hurried to the round-house, as being the only possible place of defense, and where they might be together. The husbands and grown-up sons of many of the women were at the front, or out on construction trains, or working at points along the line. The place was practically helpless.

"The first thing that Black Calf and his warriors did was to burn the station and several of the houses; then they attacked the roundhouse. The men in the building had barricaded the great doors and cut holes through the board walls; and as several of the men and women had guns and revolvers, the bucks and their leader were held in check, several of their number receiving wounds and two being killed. The Indians poured bullets into the building's walls and doors, but beyond a few slight wounds among the men no casualties had occurred by noon. Laner, the roundhouse foreman, was a stern, gritty fellow, and he and the station agent took command. They put all the children and most of the women—for some of the latter fought side by side with the men—into the ash pits, so that bullets coming through the walls or doors passed over their heads. Mrs. Lyon held her place with the fighters, while, at her command, Katie and the twins crouched in one of the pits. There were two engines in the house, one with steam up.

"A little after noon the redskins massed against the big doors, making a mad attempt to crush their way in. It was then that Laner did a remarkable thing. He suddenly jumped up into the cab of the Fifty-three, the engine with steam on, and yelled to the men to open the doors before her. As the doors swung back he jerked the throttle wide open and leaped off. The engine swept the savages out of the doorway, plowed through the mass of bucks before the building, shot across the turntable and main track, and rolled over on her side, two hundred feet away. Twenty-odd Indians were killed or maimed by this master-stroke. The rest scattered in all directions, but presently returned, fearful, though furious. However, they kept at a safe distance from the front of the building after that.

"The men began to hope then that the bloodthirsty wretches might be beaten off for a time, at least during daylight. But when night should come, what then? The building would certainly be burned by the Indians, and the lives of all the whites be lost in massacre! If there were only some means of getting word to the fort, or to Pope and his men. Katie heard this, and five minutes later disappeared.

"Presently a boy in the ash pit cried that someone was halloing through the drainpipe. A man bent down and listened, then called Mrs. Lyon. 'Katie's in there,' he said, breathlessly. Mrs. Lyon sprang down in the pit, and with white face knelt at the end of the drain. 'I'm going to the fort,' came a shrill, but faraway voice. 'I'm going to wade down the creek to the house. I'll hide along under the bank. I'm going to take White Bess, and see if I can't get help.'

"Mrs. Lyon screamed for Katie to come back, but the voice that came through the drain only said, 'Good-bye, Ma; don't worry about me. There isn't an Indian pony on the plains that can catch White Bess. Tell Mr. Lancr I'll bring the soldiers. Good-bye, Ma.' Mrs. Lyon wrung her hands and implored, but no answer came back. Katie had slipped into the creek from the mouth of the drain and had started on her dangerous mission.

"For three hundred feet or more she crept on her hands and knees close along under the bank; then, getting somewhat out of the range of view, hurried in crouching posture on down the creek to their little home. Stooping low and keeping behind a fence, she reached the stable. Slipping a bridle on the white mare, and strapping a folded blanket on the animal's back, she turned her into the pasture. The animal went at once to the creek to drink, and Katie again crept along the fence and escaped from sight under the bank. A moment later she was leading White Bess down the bed of the shallow stream and away from the town. When the village lay a half-mile or more behind her, she led the mare out through a clump of cottonwoods onto dry ground and mounted. The big soft eyes of the animal were shining with eagerness; the fine September air tasted nice, and the wide yellowish floor of the plain invited her feet. Katie leaned forward, and patted the horse's arched neck. 'We must bring the soldiers, Bessie,' she said imploringly. 'Don't fall, and don't ever give up if they chase us. Mommy and little Dan and Jimmy may never see the light of morning if we fail.' The mare blinked her big eyes and chewed impatiently at the bit; the girl drew in a long, tremulous breath, cried out sharply, and they shot away across the plain.

"To Katie the strong light and broad openness of the prairie were terrible. She looked back across her shoulder to the town, hearing yells and the crack of rifles and the noise of fighting. She rode straight south, selecting the lowest ground, and intending to turn southwest toward the fort when at a safe distance. She had progressed perhaps a mile, when, looking back, she saw a party of Indians on horseback shoot out from the edge of the town, ranging a little west to south. The girl's ruddy cheeks whitened, and her brown fingers clutched the rein nervously. 'We've got to outrun them, Bess,' she cried. 'We've *got* to do it!'

"The lithe, white mare, with her light burden, went like an antelope, breathing softly, and taking the ground with a long, sweeping, steady lope. The girl pulled on the bit a little. 'Let them do their fast running first,' she said, looking back through her flying hair. 'We'll set the pace at the end.'

"The tough Indian ponies, urged by quirt and many a pealing yell, followed her like excited hounds, but kept to the west of her in their course. Clearly the Indians purposed getting between the girl and the fort before attempting to run her down. The racers were probably four miles out from Ludder when Katie realized the intention of the Indians. She at once turned the mare straight toward the fort, and bending low over the animal's neck, urged her with a series of startling screams. The Indians, seeing the move, put their horses to top speed, and riding across the inside of the angle made by Katie's course, sought to cut her off.

"But White Bess ran like a deer, and the Indians crossed her course an eighth of a mile to the rear. They fired no shots and ceased yelling, evidently not wishing to frighten or press the girl until they could get the advantage of position. They now pointed their course slightly to the south, plainly hoping to allay the girl's fears and gradually drive her northwest and away from the fort. Evidently they felt that a straight race after the fleet mare would end in their defeat.

"In spite of her intention, Katie drew gradually toward the west in trying to keep away from her pursuers. She must have been twelve miles from Ludder, and White Bess was wet and breathing hard, when she struck the buffalo herd, the eastern end of that living lake which we had seen from the train when repairing the track.

"It was a terrible blow to Katie's hopes, for she saw that she could not reach the fort unless she could get on the south side of the mighty herd, and such a course would throw her well-nigh into the arms of her pursuers. For a moment she pulled the mare up, looking wildly in all directions. For miles away to the south and west that hairy, awful sheet of dark forms stretched before her. Panting and horrified, she set the tired mare on the gallop again, riding straight toward the west. She must pass clear around the herd and come into the fort from the south or west. Yelling wildly, the Indians came after her, the hardy ponies sticking to the chase like dogs. Katie's face grew drawn and white; her red lips turned ashen and parched. She patted the neck of the dripping mare, praying her not to fail. 'We *must* beat them, Bess! Oh, we must! We must!' she kept pleading.

"That was about the hour in the afternoon when we of the train were repairing the last break before we should turn the bend beyond which lay the trestle of which Lyon had spoken. We had scarcely completed the repairs, when we suddenly saw that the whole black mass of life stretching across the southeast was rolling toward us like a mighty wave. 'Pull ahead, Lyon! Get on the trestle, if it is still standing!' shouted the conductor. Lyon gave the Forty steam, and we whirled away toward the bridge.

"I fancy that there was not a man on the train who did not feel his skin creep with fear and horror at sight of that resistless avalanche of animal life sweeping toward us. The dark billow was miles wide, and its rear was lost in clouds of dust. A band of Indians, by Long Blanket's order, or in attempting to break through to join the chief, had stampeded the mightiest herd of bison ever seen upon the plains. The front of the herd was like a long, uneven wall of rushing water, from the lower edge of which gushed out a curling surf of dust, and beneath which all life that fell or was overtaken was drawn and trampled into fragments. Hundreds of thousands of hooves beat the earth, and the roar from that rushing sea of flesh was like a strange new thunder. Coyotes, antelopes, and wild horses ran before it for their lives; and at one point, near the extreme front of a wedge-shaped pack of riderless horses, we saw what was apparently a child on a gray horse, leaning forward over the animal's neck, and riding madly in the race with death. East of this astonishing figure we saw eight or ten Indians, on ponies and in war paint, straining toward the north, with the hurling black mass not five hundred feet behind them. Even while we looked we saw one of the ponies fall, and the Indian rider leap to his feet and run, only to be drawn under in a moment and disappear from sight.

"In the thrill and horror of the prospect, I did not regard my immediate surroundings, until we suddenly rushed upon the trestle and stopped. Then I saw that a large body of Indian horsemen were riding at a gallop westward on the north side of the track. Long Blanket and his braves, caught in their work of tearing up the track, were trying to get beyond the range of the stampede.

"The trestle was some fifty feet in length, and apparently stretched across the almost dry bed of what had once been a small river. The stringers and ties at the highest point were not more than ten or twelve feet above the ground. Upon these the engine and two cars stood, the balance of the train reaching out along the grade eastward. All along the train I heard shouting and stern orders as the thunder of the stampede grew in volume and rolled toward us. I cannot now say what I thought or felt, the situation was so appalling. Whether the rushing sea of frightened animals would sweep the train away and go over it, leaving us all lifeless, or would break and eddy round us, no man could say. I was hanging out from the gangway, quivering in every nerve, while Lyon's face looked white and strange as he leaned from the window of the cab, his dry lips moving as he watched the gray horse and child coming toward us. Suddenly a wild cry broke from him, and his grimy fingers knotted involuntarily. 'It's Katie, Joe! My God, it's Katie!' he cried.

"A kind of fire swept through me at that, such a leap of the pulses as I had never felt before. I sprang down upon the ends of the ties, and reached my hands toward her, shouting in a sort of frenzy; then, suddenly, as by inspiration, the only possible course of action was revealed to me. I slipped down between the outer ends of the ties, and hung full length from the outside stringer. I saw that Katie was guiding the jaded mare straight toward us. In truth, her eyes had been fastened upon her father's smoking engine for more than a mile.

"As I hung there, with my face toward the oncoming ocean of hairy forms, I felt Lyon's hands gripping my wrists and heard him appealing to God for help. As all that horrible mass came thundering toward us I could see that Katie kept the lead. She was lying low and close over the mare's neck, one hand wound in the animal's mane, the other clutching the rein. Her hair was blown back, and her face looked small and white. The mare looked slim and wet and strange. Her nose was stretched out, her eyes were glassy and red, her lips scarlet and open. At her heels the pack of wild horses came galloping, with manes blowing and heads outstretched; behind them that rushing wall of frenzied buffalo. The panting of the strange multitude of unreasoning brutes was horrifying, rising like an indescribable gasp through the thunder of their hooves.

"When the front of the stampede was perhaps five hundred feet away, I saw a stream of fire leap out from every car along the train, the howitzers crashed, and again the carbines roared. Instantly the wave of buffaloes seemed to double under at the base, then roll into the air like a kind of black and indescribable billow. In that maze of tumbling forms I saw the Indians who had chased poor Katie sink, crushed by bullets and swallowed up in the remorseless mass. I saw this with a glance, for the white, upturned face of Katie was not fifty feet away, and both Lyon and myself were shouting to her to stand up and jump. It was an awful moment. I saw it all as vivid as lightning, yet somehow it had the color of a dream. In Katie's eyes I could see terror mingled with resolution as she got to her feet on the horse's back. An instant she wavered, then straightened up, and as the panting mare shot under us she jumped. For a second I saw her pale face and wide-open eyes flying toward me through the air, then her arms shut about my pendent body with a shock. My arms seemed torn from their sockets by the blow, but Lyon was holding my wrists like a vise. In a moment he loosened his grip, and bending low, caught the girl by the arms and drew her up. By his aid I then scrambled back upon the ties.

"All about us roared a living storm. Dust covered the scene like battle smoke. Through it we saw the incessant flashing of carbines along the train: east and west a vague brown torrent of brutes poured across the track. Under us the press and struggle of hulking forms choked the pass and shook the bridge. When the air cleared, we saw that the work of the soldiers had divided the mighty pack; it was flowing north and northwest in two dark streams. Before us were swaths of slain bison; piles of the bodies lay against the train, and somewhere in that appalling slaughter lay Katie's pursuers.

"Weak and trembling, I climbed up into the engine cab. Lyon sat on the floor, and across his lap lay Katie, limp and panting. 'Mommy—little Dan and Jim—we must go back!' she was gasping. 'All the folks are in the roundhouse—the Indians are there! I was going to the fort for help!'

"Lyon placed her on the fireman's cushion, and jumped to the reversing lever and threw it over, opened the throttle, and whistled 'off brakes.' There was a clanking of couplings, and the train started eastward. In a few minutes Pope and the conductor came scrambling over the foot of the tender.

"'Where are you going?' they demanded.

"'To save my wife and babies,' said Lyon. 'Black Calf and his war party are at Ludder; they've got the folks shut up in the roundhouse: there'll be a massacre!'

"'That's where we are needed, then,' cried Pope.

"Lyon pushed the Forty hard, and at the end of an hour the military train dashed into the division station. At sight of us Black Calf's forces broke and fled, followed and stung by showers of bullets. The soldiers began unloading their horses at once, and mounting for the chase. The overjoyed prisoners poured out from the great doors of the enginehouse, and fairly overwhelmed us in their gratitude. Mrs. Lyon came running toward the Forty to tell Lyon that Katie had probably perished, when, to her amazement and joy, her husband jumped to the ground with Katie in his arms. What followed I couldn't hardly describe, for, tough chap though I was, I couldn't see very plainly for the tears that filled my eyes. I only know that Katie had a reception fit for a princess.

"What became of White Bess? Well, sir, she was found

next morning standing, feeble and badly used up, in a gully about two miles north of the trestle; but we brought her back and turned her into Lyon's pasture, and a few weeks afterward I saw the animal and the children again playing circus. As for the Indians, Major Holme struck Yellow Sky at the front, and beat off his followers, and took the old chief prisoner, while Pope chased Long Blanket and Black Calf into the northwestern hills and gave them a fine drubbing."

"What became of Katie, the heroic little girl?" I asked.

Perth smiled contentedly. "Well," he said, "if you'll come over to the house and take dinner with me, you will meet her. We've been married a good many years, and her hair is gray; but I think you will find her about the sunniest and most motherly woman that ever made a poor railroader feel equal to a millionaire."

Alfred Stoddart

OVER THE JUMPS

A Steeplechase Sketch

I

Dick Madison was trying a new leader in his tandem cart.

"Can he jump?" he asked of Stebbins, the dealer, who sat beside him.

"I'm sure I don't know, sir. I never tried him, but he's built for it. He ought to jump."

"He ought indeed," said Madison, cracking the thong of his whip and causing the leader to break into a canter. "Suppose we try him?"

The white-painted gate which stood at the entrance to Cedarcroft Farm, Madison's sporting bachelor quarters, was closed, and before the dealer realized what he was doing

Madison had straightened the tandem out and headed for it at a gallop.

"You're not going to—"

But Stebbins didn't finish the sentence. He was too busy picking himself up from the grassy bank upon which he was fortunate enough to land when the crash came.

Madison had leapt the fence and stood by the trembling leader's head. The latter, a good-looking chestnut colt, had actually cleared the gate in good style. The wheeler had brought up against it with such force that Stebbins and Madison were both pitched from the cart.

"It's all right—no bones broken," cried Madison gaily to the astonished and outraged horse dealer, "and he *can* jump, can't he?"

"I declare, Mr. Madison, you are—"

"Never mind what I am—I'll take the colt. Just bear a hand with these traces, will you, and we'll drive to the house and I'll write you a check."

The word *check* had a soothing influence upon the indignant dealer. He recalled instantly the very comfortable figure which he had asked Madison for the chestnut colt, and he thought, as there was no harm done, he might as well laugh at Mr. Madison's rash conduct.

This was the manner in which the four-year-old chestnut colt Outrider became the property of Dick Madison—Daredevil Dick—of the Meadowthorpe hunting set. This, however, was in the early fall, and it was not until the fox hunting was well under way, two months later, that Fate and Miss Dorothy Meade began to take an interest in the chestnut colt and his owner.

Outrider was one of those out-of-the-ordinary horses which dealers sometimes get possession of in out-of-the-ordinary ways. Stebbins, whose regular trade was in hunters and heavy harness horses, took this one in a trade from a man who frankly confessed he was afraid of him. Although the colt had been used entirely in harness, he had a good deal the look of a thoroughbred about him, but Stebbins was careless about asking the animal's breeding and history until it was too late. The man from whom he got him went abroad for an extended stay and the horse dealer could learn absolutely nothing about the colt except that he was not quite thoroughbred, though his conformation showed him to be very nearly so.

Outrider had only been in Stebbins's stable at Meadowthorpe a few days when Dick Madison happened in. His eyes fell upon the good-looking chestnut at once, and when he found that Stebbins knew almost nothing about him he determined to try him.

"You say he goes well in harness," he said to the dealer. "Let's rig him in the lead of my dogcart, which is standing outside, and see what he's good for."

Stebbins hesitated. But he knew that caution was not a popular attribute with Dick Madison, so he unwillingly gave the order to his men to put tandem leader's harness on the chestnut.

If he expected the colt to behave badly, he was agreeably disappointed. Madison was a good whip and possessed the knack of handling a tandem with ease. In a few moments they were bowling merrily along the Meadowthorpe Pike, never stopping until, as has been recorded, they brought up precipitately at the gate of Madison's farm.

Madison kept half a dozen hunters and a string of polo ponies at Cedarcroft Farm. No one who rode with the Meadowthorpe Hounds was better mounted as a general thing. But when the hunting season opened he found that his favorite mount was the chestnut colt, Outrider, his latest purchase, who had taken as kindly to jumping as the proverbial duck to the water.

Not only did the colt jump well, but he developed quite an astonishing turn for speed, so much so that Bradbury, the M.F.H., half laughingly said to Madison that he supposed he was only riding that fellow for a certificate—meaning the evidence which must be furnished by the master of some recognized pack of hounds that a horse has been hunted regularly, which is necessary in many steeplechases.

Madison did not venture a reply, but as a matter of fact the M.F.H.'s pleasantry put an idea into his head which clung there so tenaciously that when the entries closed for the Great International Hunters' Steeplechase the name of Outrider, chestnut colt, breeding unknown, owned by Richard Madison, was found to be among them.

II

One day Dick Madison was late for the meet. He galloped Outrider unmercifully over the roads and got both himself and the colt into a very bad humor.

When he reached Rogers's Crossing, the place where the hounds met, he found they had gone on to cover and were drawing the big woodland some three-quarters of a mile away. This meant another hard gallop for Outrider, and the colt was tired already when he came in sight of the red coats of the huntsmen.

They had "found," and the hounds were already streaming out of cover, proclaiming with glad tongue that they were on the line of their fox. There was a high fence and a stiff gate between Madison and the rest of the now galloping field. Most men would have gone round or given up the run. Not so Daredevil Dick. He sent the chestnut colt at it full tilt, and the plucky animal, who had never yet refused, rose at it gamely. But his tired muscles were not equal to the task. He struck with his forefeet and came down badly on the landing side. Madison, who knew to perfection the trick of falling, rolled over and out of harm's way, and in a moment both he and the colt were on their feet. But as he hoisted himself into the saddle again he heard a not unmusical laugh. Looking up, he saw on a big black horse a pretty girl who was actually laughing at him.

It was only a momentary vision, for the girl had wheeled the big black and galloped off with the rest of the field before Madison was fairly in his saddle. But Dick Madison did not like the sensation of being laughed at by a pretty girl, and his mouth stiffened with vexation as he galloped in her wake.

However, his troubles were not yet at an end. Never had Outrider fenced so badly nor blundered so often. Try as he might, he could not get the chestnut colt anywhere near the flying black which his attractive tormentor was riding. Once or twice she looked back. Madison fancied she was laughing at him still.

Suddenly he realized that he was asking too much of the chestnut. With a sigh of regret—for the hounds were running well—he pulled the colt up and reluctantly turned his head toward home.

"Good old boy," he cried, patting the colt on the shoulder. "She laughed at us, did she? Well, we'll show her one of these days."

Bradbury, the M.F.H., gave a dinner that night, and there Madison met the Diana of the morning.

Miss Dorothy Meade, whose brother, racing under the assumed name of "Mr. Melville," owned one of the best-known stables of steeplechasers in training, was visiting the wife of the M.F.H. She was in high spirits that evening, having been awarded the coveted brush after the morning's run, and if Madison thought her pretty on horseback, he was absolutely charmed with her now.

She wore a black evening dress which enhanced the whiteness of her skin. Her hair was light chestnut tinged with gold. She had dazzling white teeth which showed when she smiled, as she did constantly. Her deep blue eyes were lightened by a very merry twinkle.

Madison found to his delight that he was to take her in to dinner. They chatted about various things, but it was not until dessert had been served that he accused her of laughing at him.

"I could not help it," she cried. "You rolled away just like a ball. How is the little horse? He tried so gamely to jump."

Madison resented her patronizing air when she spoke of the "little horse." Outrider was anything but little, being full fifteen hands two inches in height, though not so large—to be sure—as the big sixteen-hand black which Miss Meade had ridden.

"Do you know," he said, "that the little horse has cut down everything here at Meadowthorpe? He was tired and out of form today. I could not get near the big black you rode."

"No, you certainly could not," rippled Miss Meade with a twinkle in her eye which incensed Madison. "It takes a good horse to cut down Anthracite."

"What! That wasn't Anthracite?"

"Yes."

Madison whistled. No wonder the chestnut colt was outclassed. Anthracite was a steeplechaser of national reputation, one of the best performers in "Mr. Melville's" string.

"You see, my brother wanted him kept in shape, and as I needed a horse to bring down here with me he lent me Anthracite. I like him so well that I think I shall buy him."

"But you surely wouldn't make a hunter of one of the best steeplechasers in America?"

"Not altogether. If I buy him, I will hunt him this winter and let him go back to the track again in the spring."

"Is he entered for the Great International?"

"Yes, I believe he is. Fancy my owning a steeplechaser. I would give about everything I own in the world to win such a race as that. Have you any steeplechasers?"

"Nothing but the 'little horse' you laughed at today. He too is entered for the Great International."

Miss Meade smiled.

"Oh, I know. You think he wouldn't have a chance with such horses as Anthracite. But we shall see," cried Madison, nettled by Miss Meade's manner.

"I hope they both start," she answered as Mrs. Bradbury signaled the flight of the ladies to the drawing room. "If they do, you and I will have a little side bet on the result."

Madison bowed his assent as he stood by the door for the ladies to pass through.

III

The scene was Morris Park—America's most beautiful race-course—so soon to be spoken of, alas, as a thing of the past. The day was the day of the Great International.

There was a number of the Meadowthorpe hunting set at the course. The M.F.H. had an especially jolly party on his break. For a big steeplechase always appeals to the hunting crowd, and, besides, they were especially interested in the Great International.

Outrider, "well known with the Meadowthorpe Hounds," to use a favorite auctioneer's phrase, was carded to run in the colors of "Daredevil" Dick Madison. Moreover, Mr. Madison himself was going to ride. Then too the Meadowthorpe set was interested in "Mr. Melville's" Anthracite. For although the big black ran in the Melville colors, his real ownership was well known at Meadowthorpe. In fact, a partnership with one "D. Meade" had been duly and formally registered with the Jockey Club. To all intents and purposes the big black steeplechaser was the absolute property of Miss Dorothy Meade.

Anthracite was to be ridden by a professional—Tim Martin. Although half a dozen of the best 'chasers in the country were entered, the big black had been made first favorite in the betting; while Outrider, the chestnut colt, who was still unknown to the racing public, however well he might be known at Meadowthorpe, was quite neglected at the long odds of thirty to one.

Dick Madison, with a light ulster buttoned over his racing colors, was talking to Dorothy Meade on the lawn of the clubhouse.

"Do you know, Dorothy, I have never quite forgiven you for laughing at me and the 'little horse' that day I first saw you at Meadowthorpe?"

"I suppose you are going to take your revenge today?" she answered with a smile.

"It does seem hard to be going against you, but if I can beat the big black I certainly shall. There—you are laughing again!"

"Only because you are so much in earnest," cried Dorothy in soothing tones. "I only hope the best horse may win."

Eight horses sprang like a flight of swallows from the barrier as it flew up, and a roar of "They're off!" rang out from the grandstand.

Dorothy Meade on the upper balcony of the clubhouse watched with straining eyes and tense muscles the contest from its very beginning. And, strangely enough, it was not the big black racing in "Mr. Melville's" pale blue and green cap that held her attention. Anthracite, big, powerful horse that he was, had gone right to the front according to instructions given to his jockey, which were to "get ahead and stay there." The black was a consistent and reliable jumper and he rarely made a mistake.

Thundering along within a few lengths of him galloped Red Cloud, Madcap, and Bravo. The other entries hung farther back, Outrider among them.

But Madison has not begun to ride him yet. He waits until a mile and a half of the two and one half miles has been covered—and then he takes the chestnut colt by the head and starts to work up.

Madcap has gone down at the water jump—one horse has run out—another has lost his rider at a fence. The race has narrowed down to four—Anthracite, Bravo, Red Cloud, and Outrider.

Dick Madison never rode a better race in his life than the one he is riding now. With voice and heel he urges the chestnut on, yet never fails to hold him steadily to his course or to assist him—with precisely the degree of strength required to regain his speed and balance after a jump. Slowly he forges ahead. He has passed Red Cloud. He hangs at Bravo's saddle girth. Now he leaves him too and challenges the big black.

The jockey on Anthracite gathers himself for a struggle. His whip is raised, once only, for the Liverpool lies before them still, and the time for full speed has not yet come.

Outrider, galloping like a perfect machine, now passes the big black and leads toward the Liverpool. Madison's blood leaps exultantly as he forges ahead. He gives his gallant mount a free head to take off for the formidable jump before him. Outrider gathers himself like a cat ready to spring and then—a blank.

Something has happened at the Liverpool. A few moments later a big black horse gallops past the judges an easy winner, but the girl with a white face and nervously clasping hands does not seem to see him. She is watching the group of men around the Liverpool. A carriage is driven out and someone is helped in. Outrider—riderless—now gallops to and fro on the course, resisting every effort to catch him.

"It is only a contusion, Miss Meade. We will pull him through all right," says the doctor reassuringly to her an hour later. But it is three days before Madison regains consciousness.

When he does he finds himself in a pleasant, sunny bedroom in the Westchester home of Duncan Meade, "Mr. Melville." Moreover, he is admirably nursed back to strength by no less a personage than the owner of Anthracite.

The big black's triumph in the Great International was not to be permanent, however. In a steeplechase run at Meadowthorpe that fall he was fairly and squarely beaten by that game "little horse," Outrider, but on that occasion both horses ran in the colors of Dick Madison. A partnership registered with even higher authorities than that august body—the Jockey Club—had been formed by Dick Madison and the onetime D. Meade.

H. C. Bunner

THE CUMBERSOME HORSE

It is not to be denied that a sense of disappointment pervaded Mr. Brimmington's being in the hour of his first acquaintance with the isolated farmhouse which he had just purchased, sight unseen, after long epistolary negotiations with Mr. Hiram Skinner, postmaster, carpenter, teamster, and real estate agent of Bethel Corners, who was now driving him to his new domain.

Perhaps the feeling was of a mixed origin. Indian summer was much colder up in the Pennsylvania hills than he had expected to find it; and the hills themselves were much larger and bleaker and barer, and far more indifferent in their demeanor toward him, than he had expected to find them. Then Mr. Skinner had been something of a disappointment, himself. He was too familiar with his big, knobby, red hands; too furtive with his small, close-set eyes; too profuse of tobacco juice; and too raspingly loquacious. And certainly the house itself did not meet his expectations when he first saw it, standing lonely and desolate in its ragged meadows of stubble and wild grass on the unpleasantly steep mountainside.

And yet Mr. Skinner had accomplished for him the desire of his heart. He had always said that when he should come into his money—forty thousand dollars from a maiden aunt— he would quit forever his toilsome job of preparing Young Gentlemen for admission to the Larger Colleges and Universities, and would devote the next few years to writing his long-projected *History of Prehistoric Man.* And to go about this task he had always said that he would go and live in perfect solitude—that is, all by himself and a chorewoman—in a secluded farmhouse, situated upon the southerly slope of some high hill—an old farmhouse—a Revolutionary farmhouse, if possible—a delightful, long, low, rambling farmhouse—a farmhouse with floors of various levels—a farmhouse with crooked stairs, and with nooks and corners and quaint cupboards—this—this had been the desire of Mr. Brimmington's heart.

Mr. Brimmington, when he came into his money at the age of forty-five, fixed on Pike County, Pennsylvania, as a mountainous country of good report. A postal guide informed him that Mr. Skinner was the postmaster of Bethel Corners; so Mr. Brimmington wrote to Mr. Skinner.

The correspondence between Mr. Brimmington and Mr. Skinner was long enough and full enough to have settled a treaty between two nations. It ended by a discovery of a house lonely enough and aged enough to fill the bill. Several hundred dollars' worth of repairs were needed to make it habitable, and Mr. Skinner was employed to make them. Toward the close of a cold November day, Mr. Brimmington saw his purchase for the first time.

In spite of his disappointment, he had to admit, as he walked around the place in the early twilight, that it was just what he had bargained for. The situation, the dimensions, the exposure, were all exactly what had been stipulated. About its age there could be no question. Internally, its irregularity—indeed, its utter failure to conform to any known rules of domestic architecture—surpassed Mr. Brimmington's wildest expectations. It had stairs eighteen inches wide; it had rooms of strange shapes and sizes; it had strange, shallow cupboards in strange places; it had no hallways; its windows were of odd design; and whoso wanted variety in floors could find it there. And along the main wall of Mr. Brimmington's study there ran a structure some three feet and a half high and nearly as deep, which Mr. Skinner confidently assured him was used in old times as a wall bench or a dresser, indifferently. "You might think," said Mr. Skinner, "that all that space inside there was jest wasted; but it ain't so. Them seats is jest filled up inside with braces so's that you can set on them good and solid." And then Mr. Skinner proudly called attention to the two coats of gray paint spread over the entire side of the house, walls, ceilings, and woodwork, blending the original portions and the Skinner restorations in one harmonious, homogeneous whole.

Mr. Skinner might have told him that this variety of gray paint is highly popular in some rural districts, and is made by mixing lampblack and ball-blue with a low grade of white lead. But he did not say it; and he drove away as soon as he conveniently could, after formally introducing him to Mrs. Sparhawk, a gaunt, stern-faced, silent, elderly woman. Mrs. Sparhawk was to take charge of his bachelor establishment during the daytime. Mrs. Sparhawk cooked him a meal for which she very properly apologized. Then she returned to her kitchen to "clean up." Mr. Brimmington went to the front door, partly to look out upon his property, and partly to turn his back on the gray paint. There were no steps before the front door, but a newly graded mound or earthwork about the size of a half hogshead. He looked out upon his apple orchard, which was farther away than he had expected to find it. It had been out of bearing for ten years, but this Mr. Brimmington did not know. He did know, however, that the whole outlook was distinctly dreary.

As he stood there and gazed out into the twilight, two forms suddenly approached him. Around one corner of the house came Mrs. Sparhawk on her way home. Around the other came an immensely tall, whitish shape, lumbering forward with a heavy tread. Before he knew it, it had scrambled up the side of his mound with a clumsy, ponderous rush, and was thrusting itself directly upon him when he uttered so lusty a cry of dismay that it fell back startled; and, wheeling about a great long body that swayed on four misshapen legs, it pounded off in the direction it had come from, and disappeared around the corner. Mr. Brimmington turned to Mrs. Sparhawk in disquiet and indignation.

"Mrs. Sparhawk," he demanded, "what is that?"

"It's a horse," said Mrs. Sparhawk, not at all surprised, for she knew that Mr. Brimmington was from the city. "They hitch 'em to wagons here."

"I know it is a horse, Mrs. Sparhawk," Mr. Brimmington rejoined with some asperity; "but whose horse is it, and what is it doing on my premises?"

"I don't rightly know whose horse it *is*," replied Mrs. Sparhawk. "The man that used to own it, he's dead now."

"But what," inquired Mr. Brimmington sternly, "is the animal doing here?"

"I guess he b'longs here," Mrs. Sparhawk said. She had a cold, even, impersonal way of speaking, as though she felt that her safest course in life was to confine herself strictly to such statements of fact as might be absolutely required of her.

"But, my good woman," replied Mr. Brimmington, in bewilderment, "how can that be? The animal can't certainly belong on my property unless he belongs to me, and that animal certainly is not mine."

Seeing him so much at a loss and so greatly disturbed in mind, Mrs. Sparhawk relented a little from her strict rule of life, and made an attempt at explanation.

"He b'longed to the man who owned this place first off; and I don' know for sure, but I've heard tell that *he* fixed it some way so's that the horse would sort of go with the place."

Mr. Brimmington felt irritation rising within him.

"But," he said, "it's preposterous! There was no such consideration in the deed. No such thing can be done, Mrs. Sparhawk, without my acquiescence!"

"I don't know nothin' about that," said Mrs. Sparhawk. "What I do know is, the place has changed hands often enough since, and the horse has always went with the place."

There was an unsettled suggestion in the first part of this statement of Mrs. Sparhawk that gave a shock to Mr. Brimmington's nerves. He laughed uneasily.

"Oh, er, yes! I see. Very probably there's been some understanding. I suppose I am to regard the horse as a sort of lien upon the place—a—a—what do they call it?—an incumbrance! Yes," he repeated, more to himself than to Mrs. Sparhawk, "an incumbrance. I've got a gentleman's country place with a horse incumbrant."

Mrs. Sparhawk heard him, however.

"It *is* a sorter cumbersome horse," she said. And without another word she gathered her shawl about her shoulders, and strode off into the darkness.

Mr. Brimmington turned back into the house, and busied himself with a vain attempt to make his long-cherished furniture look at home in his new leaden-hued rooms. The ungrateful task gave him the blues; and, after an hour of it, he went to bed.

He was dreaming leaden-hued dreams, oppressed, uncomfortable dreams, when a peculiarly weird and uncanny series of thumps on the front of the house awoke him with a start. The thumps might have been made by a giant with a weaver's beam, but he must have been a very drunken giant to group his thumps in such a disorderly parody of time and sequence.

Mr. Brimmington had too guileless and clean a heart to be the prey of undefined terrors. He rose, ran to the window and opened it. The moonlight lit up the raw, frosty landscape with a cold, pale, diffused radiance, and Mr. Brimmington could plainly see right below him the cumbersome horse, cumbersomely trying to maintain a footing on the top of the little mound before the front door. When, for a fleeting instant, he seemed to think that he had succeeded in this feat, he tried to bolt through the door. As soon, however, as one of his huge knees smote the panel, his hind feet lost their grip on the soft earth, and he wabbled back down the incline, where he stood shaking and quivering, until he could muster wind enough for another attempt to make a catapult of himself. The veil-like illumination of the night, which turned all things else to a dim, silvery gray, could not hide the scars and bruises and worn places that spotted the animal's great, gaunt, distorted frame. His knees were as big as a man's head. His feet were enormous. His joints stood out from his shriveled carcass like so many pine knots. Mr. Brimmington gazed at him, fascinated, horrified, until a rush more desperate and uncertain than the rest threatened to break his front door in.

"Hi!" shrieked Mr. Brimmington. "Go away!"

It was the horse's turn to get frightened. He lifted his long, coffin-shaped head toward Mr. Brimmington's window, cast a sort of blind, cross-eyed, ineffectual glance at him, and with a long-drawn, wheezing, cough-choked whinny he backed down the mound, got himself about, end for end, with such extreme awkwardness that he hurt one poor knee on a hitching post that looked to be ten feet out of his way, and limped off to the rear of the house.

The sound of that awful, rusty, wind-broken whinny haunted Mr. Brimmington all the rest of that night. It was like the sound of an orchestrion run down, or of a man who is utterly tired of the whooping cough and doesn't care who knows it.

The next morning was bright and sunshiny, and Mr. Brimmington awoke in a more cheerful frame of mind than he would naturally have expected to find himself in after his perturbed night. He found himself inclined to make the best of his purchase and to view it in as favorable a light as possible. He went outside and looked at it from various points of view, trying to find and if possible to dispose of the reason for the vague sense of disappointment which he felt, having come into possession of the rambling old farmhouse which he had so much desired.

He decided, after a long and careful inspection, that it was the *proportions* of the house that were wrong. They were certainly peculiar. It was singularly high between joints in the first story, and singularly low in the second. In spite of its irregularity within, it was uncompromisingly square on the outside. There was something queer about the pitch of its roof, and it seemed strange that so modest a structure with no hallway whatever should have vestibule windows on each side of its doors, both front and rear.

But here an idea flashed into Mr. Brimmington's mind that in an instant changed him from a carping critic to a delighted discoverer. He was living in a blockhouse! Yes, that explained—that accounted for all the strangeness of its architecture. In an instant he found his purchase invested with a beautiful glamour of adventurous association. Here was the stout and well-planned refuge to which the grave settlers of an earlier day had fled to guard themselves against the attack of the vindictive Indians. He saw it all. A moat, crossed no doubt by drawbridges, had surrounded the building. In the main room below, the women and children had huddled while their courageous defenders had poured a leaden hail upon the foe through loopholes in the upper story. He walked around the house for some time, looking for loopholes.

So pleased was Mr. Brimmington at his theory that the morning passed rapidly away, and when he looked at his watch he was surprised to find that it was nearly noon. Then he remembered that Mr. Skinner had promised to call on him at eleven, to make anything right that was not right. Glancing over the landscape he saw Mr. Skinner approaching by a circuitous track. He was apparently following the course of a snake fence which he could readily have climbed. This seemed strange, as his way across the pasture land was seemingly unimpeded. Thinking of the pasture land made Mr. Brimmington think of the white horse, and casting his eyes a little farther down the hill he saw that animal slowly and painfully steering a parallel course to Mr. Skinner, on the other side of the fence. Mr. Skinner went out of sight behind a clump of trees, and when he arrived it was not upon the side of the house where Mr. Brimmington had expected to see him appear.

As they were about to enter the house Mr. Brimmington noticed the marks of last night's attack upon his front door, and he spoke to Mr. Skinner about the horse.

"Oh, yes," said Mr. Skinner, with much ingenuousness, "that horse. I was meaning to speak to you about that horse. Fact is, I've kinder got that horse on my hands, and if it's no inconvenience to you, I'd like to leave him where he is for a little while."

"But it would be very inconvenient, indeed, Mr. Skinner," said the new owner of the house. "The animal is a very unpleasant object; and, moreover, it attempted to break into my front door last night."

Mr. Skinner's face darkened. "Sho!" he said. "You don't mean to tell me that?"

But Mr. Brimmington did mean to tell him that, and Mr. Skinner listened with a scowl of unconcealed perplexity and annoyance. He bit his lip reflectively for a minute or two before he spoke.

"Too bad you was disturbed," he said at length. "You'll have to keep the bars up to that meadow and then it won't happen again."

"But, indeed, it must not happen again," said Mr. Brimmington; "the horse must be taken away."

"Well, you see it's this way, friend," returned Mr. Skinner, with a rather ugly air of decision; "I really ain't got no choice in the matter. I'd like to oblige you, and if I'd known as far back that you would have objected to the animal I'd have had him took somewheres. But, as it is, there ain't no such a thing as getting that there horse off this here place till the frost's out of the ground. You can see for yourself that that horse, the condition he's in now, couldn't no more go up nor down this hill than he could fly. Why, I came over here afoot this morning on purpose not to take them horses of mine over this road again. It can't be done, sir."

"Very well," suggested Mr. Brimmington; "kill the horse."

"I ain't killin' no horses," said Mr. Skinner. "You may if you like; but I'd advise you not to. There's them as mightn't like it."

"Well, let them come and take their horse away, then," said Mr. Brimmington.

"Just so," assented Mr. Skinner. "It's they who are concerned in the horse, and they have a right to take him away. I would if I was any ways concerned, but I ain't." Here he turned suddenly upon Mr. Brimmington. "Why, look here," he said, "you ain't got the heart to turn that there horse out of that there pasture where he's been for fifteen years! It won't do you no sorter hurt to have him stay there till spring. Put the bars up, and he won't trouble you no more."

"But," objected Mr. Brimmington, weakly, "even if the poor creature were not so unsightly, he could not be left alone all winter in that pasture without shelter."

"That's just where you're mistaken," Mr. Skinner replied, tapping his interlocutor heavily upon the shoulder; "he don't mind it not one mite. See that shed there?" And he pointed to a few wind-racked boards in the corner of the lot. "There's hoss shelter; and as for feed, why there's feed enough in that meadow for two such as him."

In the end, Mr. Brimmington, being utterly ignorant of the nature and needs of horseflesh, was overpersuaded, and he consented to let the unfortunate white horse remain in his pasture lot to be the sport of the winter's chill and bitter cruelty. Then he and Mr. Skinner talked about some new paint.

It was the dead vast and middle of Mr. Brimmington's third night in his new house, when he was absolutely knocked out of a calm and peaceful slumber by a crash so appalling that he at first thought that the side of the mountain had slid down upon his dwelling. This was followed by other crashes, thumps, the tearing of woodwork and various strange and gruesome noises. Whatever it might be, Mr. Brimmington felt certain that it was no secret midnight marauder, and he hastened to the eighteen-inch stairway without even waiting to put on a dressing gown. A rush of cold air came up from below, and he had no choice but to scuttle back for a bathrobe and a candle while the noises continued, and the cold air floated all over the house.

There was no difficulty in locating the sounds. Mr. Brimmington presented himself at the door of the little kitchen, pulled it open, and, raising the light above his head, looked in. The rush of wind blew out his light, but not before he had had time to see that it was the white horse that was in the kitchen, and that he had gone through the floor.

Subsequent investigation proved that the horse had come in through the back door, carrying that and its two vestibule windows with him, and that he had first trampled and then churned the thin floor into matchwood. He was now reposing on his stomach, with his legs hanging down between the joists into the hollow under the house—for there was no cellar. He looked over his shoulder at his host and emitted his bloodcurdling wail.

"My gracious!" said Mr. Brimmington.

That night Mr. Brimmington sat up with the horse, both of them wrapped, as well as Mr. Brimmington could do it, in bedclothes. There is not much you can do with a horse when you have to sit up with him under such circumstances. The thought crossed Mr. Brimmington's mind of reading to him, but he dismissed it.

In the interview the next day, between Mr. Brimmington and Mr. Skinner, the aggressiveness was all on Mr. Brimmington's side, and Mr. Skinner was meek and wore an anxious expression. Mr. Brimmington had, however, changed his point of view. He now realized that sleeping out of winter nights might be unpleasant, even painful to an aged and rheumatic horse. And, although he had cause of legitimate complaint against the creature, he could no longer bear to think of killing the animal with whom he had shared that cold and silent vigil. He commissioned Mr. Skinner to build for the brute a small but commodious lodging, and to provide a proper stock of provender—commissions which Mr. Skinner gladly and humbly accepted. As to the undertaking to get the horse out of his immediate predicament, however, Mr. Skinner absolutely refused to touch the job. "That horse don't like me," said Mr. Skinner. "I know he don't; I seen it in his eyes long ago. If you like, I'll send you two or three men and a block and tackle, and they can get him out; but not me; no, sir!''

Mr. Skinner devoted that day to repairing damages, and promised on the morrow to begin the building of the little barn. Mr. Brimmington was glad there was going to be no greater delay, when, early in the evening, the sociable white horse tried to put his front feet through the study window.

But of all the noises that startled Mr. Brimmington, in the first week of his sojourn in the farmhouse, the most alarming awakened him about eight o'clock of the following morning. Hurrying to his study, he gazed in wonder upon a scene unparalleled even in the History of Prehistoric Man. The boards had been ripped off the curious structure which was supposed to have served the hardy settlers for a wall bench and a dresser, indifferently. This revealed another structure in the form of a long crib or bin, within which, apparently trying to back out through the wall, stood Mr. Skinner, holding his toolbox in front of him as if to shield himself, and fairly yelping with terror. The front door was off its hinges, and there stood Mrs. Sparhawk wielding a broom to keep out the white horse, who was viciously trying to force an entrance. Mr. Brimmington asked what it all meant; and Mrs. Sparhawk, turning a desperate face upon him, spoke with the vigor of a woman who has kept silence too long.

"It means," she said, "that this here house of yours is this here horse's stable; *and the horse knows it;* and that there was the horse's manger. This here horse was old Colonel Josh Pincus's regimental horse, and so provided for in his will; and this here man Skinner was to have the caring of him until he should die a natural death, and then he was to have this stable; and till then the stable was left to the horse. And now he's taken the stable away from the horse, and patched it up into a dwelling-house for a fool from New York City; and the horse don't like it; and the horse don't like Skinner. And when he come back to git that manger for your barn, the horse sot onto him. And that's what's the matter, Mr. Skimmerton."

"Mrs. Sparhawk," began Mr. Brimmington—

"I *ain't* no Sparhawk!" fairly shouted the enraged woman, as with a furious shove she sent the Cumbersome Horse staggering down the doorway mound. "This here's Hiram Skinner, the meanest man in Pike County, and I'm his wife, let out to do day's work. You've had one week of him—how would you have liked twenty years?"

Ellis Parker Butler

PETE, THE CIRCASSIAN HORSE

The Story of a Hairy Wonder

My friend Sam was the most enthusiastic boy I ever knew, and I was constantly surprised by the length, breadth, and depth of his knowledge. You could not mention a thing, from the aurora borealis to fish bait, that he did not know more about than any one else, and he always had some plan to make a lot of money out of whatever was mentioned. I remember that once, when our backyard was full of plaintain that had gone to seed, he enthusiastically convinced me that we could make a fortune by gathering the plaintain seed and drying it and selling it as birdseed. We worked a week gathering the seed, and had made about forty dollars, as Sam figured it, which was pretty good profit for two boys, before I thought of trying the plantain seed on our canary. I never saw a living being so indifferent to food as that canary was to that plantain seed. It refused to eat it—it would not even look at it. We lost in one minute the forty dollars we had worked a week for, and all because an ignorant little yellow bird had its own silly ideas about food! When I told Sam he said pshaw; he knew that, but it had got out of his mind somehow, and we would have to look out for some kind of animal that did like plantain seed and then we would sell the seed easily. But we never gathered any more seed.

One day my father went out in the country to collect a debt a farmer owed him, and he came back with a horse that he had taken in payment. The debt was only twelve dollars, but Peter was that kind of a horse, and father said he felt as if he had given the farmer a discount from the amount of the bill at that. He brought Peter in the back way, so as not to excite comment—for father was a dignified man—and put him in the barn. Then he called me and gave Peter to me.

"Edward," he said, "here is a horse for you. And mind you feed him and water him regularly, or I'll give you such a thrashing you will never forget it!"

I thanked father soberly, for there was not, so far as I could see, anything about Peter to grow enthusiastic over. Our town had many horses, but I had never seen one like Peter. I had never seen a horse as old as Peter. I doubt if there ever was another horse quite as old—he was in his second colthood. He had a chipper, frisky manner that suggested a gay-hearted, frolicsome camel. But most of all, I am sure I never saw such a woolly horse as Peter. The horses in our town were mostly clipped, and those that were not were so curried and rubbed that they were as slick and smooth as a silk hat, but Peter was like an old buffalo robe, or a piece of unplucked beaver, if you know what that is. Part of his hair was woolly and curled, and part was long and straight, and he had a few bare patches that had no hair at all, and his fur was mussed and fuzzed in all directions, with little chunks of burdock burrs here and there. He looked as if a strong wind was constantly blowing him.

A boy of the age I was then would take almost any kind of a horse and be proud of it, but I was not proud of Peter. He looked too different from the horses I had known. I felt that his coat must be some kind of a disease—that he must be a very sick horse—and I was ashamed to own him. I did not know that a winter-pastured horse grows a crop of that kind of hair and that all Peter needed was elbow grease applied with a currycomb.

It is hard for a boy to keep from bragging, and of course I could not keep Peter a secret from Sam, so I made a brag of him.

"Ha!" I boasted. "I've got a horse!"

"Say! Is that so?" said Sam. His eyes sparkled with eagerness. "That's bully, Ed! We've needed a horse, bad, all the time. Why, we can make a raft of money with a horse, piles of it! We'll go into the trucking business, and we can hire the horse out! Say, we'll make a lot now we've got a horse!"

I couldn't become enthusiastic over Peter.

"It isn't a very good horse," I said deprecatingly. "I don't believe it is a very strong horse, Sam. It is rather thin and it don't look very nice."

"Pshaw!" Sam cried. "Oats! That's all it needs. Give a horse plenty of oats and it will fat up in no time, and get strong as an ox. I guess your horse has had too much hay. A horse can't get fat and strong on hay, any more than a man can on lettuce. Let's have a look at the horse. I'll tell you what it needs. I know all about horses. I used to have an uncle who had a horse before I was born."

I led the way to the barn rather reluctantly, and as I unfastened the latch I warned Sam again.

"Sam," I said, "I guess this horse is sick. I never saw any well horse like him. He's as fuzzy as a muff."

"That's bad," said Sam, "that's an awful bad sign, but don't worry. I can cure him up. You remember how I cured up my dog?"

I did. The dog died, but Sam always insisted it died of a different disease than the one that was being cured, and I could not dispute it. Sam got a reputation by curing that dog.

I led Sam around to the stall, and threw open the board window so that Sam could see. For a full minute he stood speechless before Peter. I could see disappointment struggling with enthusiasm in his face. Enthusiasm won. His eyes began to sparkle and he turned to me with words bubbling up in him.

"Ed," he said, "we've got a fortune! Has anybody seen this horse yet?"

"No, I guess not. I haven't shown him to anybody."

"Well, don't! Shut that window and keep it shut."

I shut the window.

"He is rather woolly, isn't he?" I said.

"Woolly!" exclaimed Sam. "I should say he is! And mighty good for us, too! Do you know what kind of a horse that is?"

"What kind?" I asked, for Sam's enthusiasm was beginning to work in me, too.

"That's a Circassian horse!" Sam declared. "You can't fool *me*! Look at his hair! Did you ever see a common horse with hair like that? No, you didn't Hardly anybody ever did. But I have."

"Where?" I asked breathlessly.

"In a sideshow," he said. "I paid ten cents to see it: Sultan, the Long-Haired Horse; but that horse only had a long mane and tail. *This* horse of yours, Ed, has long hair all over, all *but* the tail and mane, and that's good, too. People that saw Sultan wouldn't want to see another just like him, but they will want to see this horse. Millions of people will want to. How much is a million people at ten cents apiece?"

"A hundred thousand dollars!" I said.

"Pshaw!" said Sam. "That's nothing! Everybody will want to see this horse. There's eighty million people in America alone, and then we'll take him abroad. We'll go to Europe with him. I'll bet we'll make a million dollars out of this horse before we are through. We can show him for years and years. We won't have to do anything all our lives but show this Circassian horse. But I won't work when I'm past forty. When we're forty we'll sell the horse. We ought to get a lot, cash down, for him."

"Sam," I said, doubtfully, "do you think this horse will live that long? He looks pretty old now."

"That's right!" he said. "I should have thought of that. I *would* have thought of it in a minute or two. I always *do* think of everything. We've got to get right to work showing the horse before he dies. We can't waste any time. Every day is worth a lot of money to us now. We ought to have a tent and one of those big painted banners to string up before it with Pete, the Circassian Horse, on it, but we've got to get along with this barn, and I'll paint up the best show bill I can to tack up. The first thing *you* want to do is to get a currycomb and comb that horse good. We couldn't show him the way he is. You buy a currycomb and a brush and get right to work, and I'll go home and paint up a show bill."

I did not waste any time. I bought a currycomb with some money I had been saving for the opening of the marble season, which was near, and began to curry Peter.

Peter seemed surprised and vexed, especially when I combed out the burr mats, but that did not worry me. What did worry me was that every stroke of the comb brought out a handful of the long hair. Even my coat, where it brushed against Peter, brought away quantities of the long hair. I began to fear that we should have to exhibit Pete as the

Hairless Horse. I then threw down the currycomb and hunted up Sam. I found him painting a very hairy horse on a sheet of Manila wrapping paper. I told him what was the matter. To my surprise he did not seem downcast by the news. If anything, he was pleased.

"Good!" he cried. "That explains it! I was just wondering, when you came, why that farmer let such a valuable horse go for a twelve-dollar debt. I couldn't understand it, but I see it now. He thought the horse was getting bald. I had an uncle who began to get bald just that way when he was forty, and that is just about as old as that horse is. That's where we are better *off* than that farmer. I know how my uncle stopped his hair from coming out. Was there any dandruff when you combed the horse?"

I thought there was, but I was not sure.

"Of course there was!" declared Sam. "There always is. Uncle had it. What we have got to do to that horse is to cure its dandruff, and then the hair will stop falling out. We have got to treat that horse's hair just the way my uncle treated his hair or that horse will be clean bald, and we've got to be quick about it. We've got to shampoo that horse."

Sam rolled up the show bill and went into the house to find a cake of soap. The best he could do was to get a cake of brown laundry soap, but he said that would do, because the horse's hair was coarse.

"I didn't get any towels," he said as we went along, "because it's handier for you to get them. We want a lot of them. Get all you can, and get a lot of hot water. It will take an awful lot of towels."

I would have liked it better had Sam furnished the towels and let me furnish the soap. I had a feeling of diffidence about asking my mother for enough towels to shampoo a horse, and when we reached our barn I asked Sam if we couldn't make some pieces of old rag carpet that lay in the barn serve as towels. He thought they would do. In fact, he decided they would be a great deal better than towels, being rougher.

He looked Pete over and plucked out several handfuls of hair. Pete did not seem to feel it at all.

"It's a pretty bad case," said Sam gladly. "We've got to work like sixty if we want to cure it. We can't get at the shampoo a minute too soon. It's a wonder to me the hair stayed in so long. I never saw such loose hair. It is a great deal looser than my uncle's was. You had better hurry and put some water on to heat. Did you ever see a shampoo?"

I had not.

"It's soapsuds," he explained. "You rub it in with your hands. There are two kinds, a wet shampoo and a dry one. Uncle had both. They both begin the same way, but in a wet shampoo the man puts his head under a spigot to wash off the suds, and in a dry shampoo you wipe them off with a towel. This is going to be a dry shampoo."

It took a good while to heat the water, for we needed a wash boiler full, and it was lots of work to pump it, quite like washday. But Sam stood by and encouraged me, which made it easier. When the water was warm we carried the boiler out to the barn and began shampooing.

I don't believe the soap was the right kind of soap for shampooing. It was very hard to make suds on Pete, and it was awkward getting at him. We had to lean over the sides of the stall, and he moved around so much that he was usually out of our reach. Otherwise he did not seem to mind it, but if you ever want to know how much surface there is to a horse just try shampooing one. It is a large job, and by the time we had sudsed him and rubbed the suds in, and rubbed him dry with the old carpet, we were tired out; and he had much less long hair than when we began. It came out by handfuls as we shampooed him.

The next day Sam said a dry shampoo was too much work—that a wet shampoo was every bit as good, and that, in his opinion, heating the water was all nonsense. He said he was strong as any man in town, but that there was no use wasting strength, and that we would take Pete down to the creek and give him a wet shampoo.

We covered Pete with a blanket, so that no one would get a free view of the Circassian horse, and took him to the creek the back way. Pete went willingly enough, but when we got to the swimming hole he looked anxious, and he seemed much relieved when we began to shampoo him. We had a bucket with us, and we gave him a good cold shampoo and got him all lathered and then invited him to step into the pool and wash off the lather.

I took hold of the halter and pulled, and Sam encouraged Pete by saying "Ged-dup!" But he refused to enter the water. The bank sloped gradually enough, but Pete would not move. Sam said he would push, and he got behind Pete and tried that while I pulled, and we did move him a little, but Pete sat down, and looked around so resentfully that Sam said it touched his heart. He said he could easily push Pete in single-handed, if he wanted to, but that when a horse looked at him that way he didn't have the heart to do it, so we took the bucket and soused water over Pete, and rubbed him down thoroughly, and by the time we got through the horse had hardly any hair left except the usual short kind.

Sam was very sober on the way home, and whenever he thought I was not looking he felt the muscles of his arms. I know how mine ached! When we had tied Pete in his stall, Sam sat down and let me know what he had been thinking about. He looked sick.

"Ed," he said. "I don't mind this shampoo business a bit, so far as the muscle part goes. You know how strong my muscles are. It isn't half a job for anybody as strong as I am, and I could keep it up for a year, but I don't want to tire you all out. You might get sick, and then where would we be? What I was thinking was that this shampoo business is taking all the Circassian hair off Pete, and even if it does start a new crop, like it did on my uncle, we can't afford to wait. It may take years for Pete to grow another crop. Pete isn't a young horse any more, and maybe he hasn't enough vitality left to grow much hair. My uncle was an awful vital man, and it took him a couple of years to get a good crop growing. What we want is to keep his hair in, and we've got to do it. Now don't you shampoo Pete any more tonight, and tomorrow I'll tell you what to do."

"How are you going to find out, Sam?" I asked.

"Well," he said, "it's your horse and you have a right to know. I'm going to ask Billy Smitt, the barber. I won't say it's for a horse. I'll just ask as if it was my uncle, or anybody. Billy will tell me."

I said it was a good idea.

The next day Sam was stiff but happy when he came to the barn.

"It's all right," he said. "Billy told me. We can do any one of four things—they are all good."

"Go ahead and tell me, why don't you?" I asked when he hesitated.

"Well," he said, "first, Billy says that there is nothing better than a good hair tonic to keep the hair in, and he says the one he makes is best of the lot. It is clean and nice and smells dandy. He let me smell it. That is what I would use if it was my horse, but you have to do the saying."

"What do *you* say, Sam?" I asked. "What would you do if you was me?"

"I'll tell you, Ed," he said. "We are going to make a lot of money out of Pete if we can keep his hair on him, so it is worth spending a little to keep it on. It's just whether you want to spend it or not. Billy's hair tonic is a dollar a bottle, but he says, seeing that I always get my hair cut there twice a year, he will let me have twelve bottles for ten dollars. You would save two dollars right there on every dozen bottles, and in the long run you would save a lot that way, for it will take a lot to cure Pete. About ten dozen, I should say."

I shook my head. I had only twelve cents.

"Oh, well," said Sam, "I didn't think you would want to use the hair tonic. That's why I asked Billy if there was any other way. He says an egg shampoo is good."

"How do you do it?" I asked.

"I guess it's like a soap shampoo, only with eggs," Sam explained.

I looked at Pete. I hated to think how many eggs I would have to rub into him to give him an egg shampoo. Sam did not wait for me to say it.

"I don't recommend it," he said. "He wouldn't have any hair left when we got through, and the third way isn't any better. Billy says when he has a bad case of hair falling out he shaves the head, but it would be an awful job to shave Pete. And we would have to wait until the hair grew in. But there is one other way that is good. Billy says the latest thing is to singe."

"Singe? What's that?" I asked.

"They burn off the ends of the hairs," explained Sam, "and that closes the pores and keeps the roots healthy. I think it's just what Pete needs. You catch up some of the hair in a comb and burn just the ends."

I got a comb—my mother missed it the next morning—and some matches, and we began. Pete watched the preparations suspiciously and gazed at us over his shoulder as if doubtful of our intentions. He had never been singed before, and he had an idea he was too old to begin being singed now. As soon as Sam struck the first match, Pete doubled himself up in the opposite corner of the stall, and the match burned down and burned Sam's fingers before I could get the comb in the hair again. We backed Pete all around the stall and burned twenty matches and did not singe one hair. Sam quit in disgust.

"If you are so anxious to singe this horse, Ed," he said reproachfully, "go ahead and do it. I won't. I think it's cruel."

"What shall we do then?" I asked.

"It's no go!" said Sam. "We can't show this horse as a Circassian horse. What we've got to do is to get at him with the currycomb and brush, and brush all of the hair off of him, and in a while all his hair will fall out and he'll be as bald as an egg."

He got up and walked around Pete.

"That's it!" he exclaimed, his enthusiasm rising. "We'll exhibit him as Pete, the Bald Horse, the Only One in Captivity. It will be a great hit. I never thought much of that Circassian idea, anyway. Pete never was woolly enough. A Circassian horse ought to have hair a foot long. But a bald horse is new. I never even heard of one. As soon as Pete is bald we will begin raking in the money. You get at him with the currycomb and I'll go and paint a poster. Ten cents was enough to charge to see the Circassian horse, but a bald horse—! We'll charge a quarter! I would give a quarter any day to see a horse as bald as Pete will be."

He went away and I curried. I worked three days, and the long winter hair came off Pete until there was left only his shiny brown summer coat. This did not come off at all, and I began to foresee that it would be long before Pete was a hairless attraction.

I was rubbing away with the brush at Pete's side when my father entered the barn. He walked around Pete and examined him carefully.

"Huh!" he said. "He looks better."

He went out and a little later he returned with Miggs, our grocer, and before me he completed a bargain by which Miggs became the owner of the recent Circassian horse for fifteen dollars.

As my father rolled up the money and put it in his pocket,

Miggs glanced around the barn, and his eye alighted on the currycomb.

"Does the currycomb go with the bargain?" he asked.

"Oh, yes!" said my father very good-naturedly. "Take it along!"

And I had paid for it!

F. R. Weir

THE TALE OF
A CAYUSE

The two men met on the trail and eyed each other with native suspicion, then the younger slipped his arms from his pack straps and eased his bundle to the ground while he asked his question.

"Pardner, can you tell me how far it is to the Madrona mill?"

The elder had no idea of relieving himself of his pack. The straps sank into the cavities in front of his shoulders as though they grew there.

"Goin' by the upper trail?" he inquired, without any show of interest.

"Any old trail to git there," growled the questioner. "I naturally want to patronize the shortest route. I'm not out walking for my health."

"Two mile and a half," and the old man presented the square of his pack to the gaze of his interlocutor and stumped off about his business, which was to carry twelve dozen eggs and a jar of butter to Madrona, and to purchase supplies with the money. But his old mouth was parching for a drink, and it was more than likely that the egg and butter money would go into the pockets of the proprietor of the Mug Saloon before any grocer saw the color of it.

When the rancher disappeared, the traveler sat down to rest a moment and to think. His name was Jim Vessy, and his roll of blankets marked him for a "timber jake" hunting a job. He was, in fact, a "timber faller," and a skillful one, and beside the superb length of limb and lumps of muscle, the good judgment, and the alertness, which his trade demanded, Jim possessed a face full of strength and intelligence, and a sidewise glance and grin which were taking, in the extreme.

These last-mentioned attributes were not in evidence now; instead, a misleading frown drew down the corners of his mouth and carved lengthwise wrinkles in his cheeks. He was thoroughly disgusted with himself, the world, and more especially with women.

Womanhood, as he anathematized it, was an embodiment of blond hair, paint, and an insatiable desire for money.

Ten days before he had owned a new suit of clothes and eight hundred dollars; today his worldly possessions consisted of three flannel blankets, seventy-five cents, and a wrinkled costume which spoke loudly of a debauch.

To account for this change in his prospects there was a hazy remembrance of a night "below the line," filled with cheap music, drinking, and fighting, followed by a morning of shame, when he knew he had been drugged and robbed.

He stood up and kicked at his pack viciously. One of the

pack straps was loose, and he felt in his pocket for a knife with which to cut a new hole in the leather. Instead of the knife, he drew forth a small photograph of a woman with yellow hair and a simpering smile. He gazed at it a moment, then laughed and shook his head. "Jim Vessy, you blamed fool!" he said aloud. "And the worst of it is, you ain't in the habit of doing this sort of thing. But you pitied her! You thought there might be good in her. You didn't know, but you've found out. Cheap, too. It only cost you eight hundred dollars; two years' wages, that's all. It might have cost you more: your life, or your liberty. You might have married the—"

He did not finish the sentence, but tossed the photograph into the bushes, took up his pack, and prepared to move on.

"Start again, Jim, and if a woman comes sniveling to you to right a wrong, say to yourself: 'She's a fraud—they're all frauds—grin at her, and pass by on the other side.' "

"You've dropped suthin'," said a voice at his back.

Jim turned to face his surly acquaintance of a few moments before. He was pointing to the card Jim had thrown away. He must have witnessed the act, and the remark was in the nature of a taunt.

"It's all right; I just laid it there expectin' to take it aboard again when I come along back. Got sick of packin' it."

The old man stopped and picked up the photograph. His bleary old eyes seemed to eat it up.

"Say, you didn't happen to see a Siwash ridin' a buckskin cayuse around Seattle when you was there, did you?"

"How do you know I've been to Seattle?"

The old man did not answer, but looked at the picture in his hand with a chuckle. He was an unpleasant rascal, with a bushy white beard, above which his red nose and cheekbones shone fiercely. He wore his shirt open in front, and his old hat cocked over one eye with an exasperating assumption of youth.

"I say, you didn't, did you?"

"Didn't what?"

"See a Siwash on a buckskin cayuse, branded with three letters, *N-a-t,* on his flank?"

"On the Siwash's flank?"

"No, the—say, you're funny, ain't ye? Can't you answer a civil question when a man asks you one? For a nickel I'd wipe the trail with ye!"

Vessy laughed. "I've only got six bits," he said, "and I can't afford to buy luxuries when I need the necessities of life. Know of anyplace handy where I could buy a dinner?"

Speculation shone in the old man's eyes.

"Yes, for six bits you can get a good dinner at my ranch just around the bend. Tell Natura that you paid me and that she's to git you up a good dinner."

"All right. Who is Natura? Your wife?"

"Not yet; I s'pect she will be, though, in time. She's my stepdaughter just now—old woman ain't been dead long."

"All right; I'll tell Natura I've paid you and she's to get my dinner. I don't see what's the use of lying that way, though."

"How lyin'?"

"Why, I haven't paid you, have I?"

"No, but you're a-goin' to, ain't you?"

"Not by a long sight! Natura might not be home. If she is, and gets dinner for me, I'll just settle with Natura."

The old man began to swear. His little eyes and red nose blazed fury. "For two bits I'd kill ye!" he snarled.

Vessy leaned his pack against a fir and grinned.

"If I was sure you'd make a good job of it, I don't know but it would pay. They'd hang you, and the world would be the wider for bein' shy two fools. Well, good day to you; I'm going to see Natura."

"Say, now, on the straight, if you give her the money, she'll keep it. I can't trust the girl. I'm in hard luck, I tell you. You see, she's been cranky ever since her mother died. I've been wantin' to git money enough together to go north, but if I go north, who'll run the ranch?''

"Why don't you sell it?''

"Well—hum—there are family reasons why I don't sell it. I don't care about six bits, though; give it to Natura if you want to. Tell her it's to buy another cayuse. He, he, he. Better not tell her that till after you've had your dinner. Makes a regular fool of herself over the cayuse.''

"Was it hers?''

"Well, she called it hers, you know. That's the way with women—want all they can git.''

"Yes, I know,'' owned Vessy.

"Yes, she called it hers. I rode it down to Madrona one night and got to joshing with a Siwash and made him a present of the pony. Come to in the mornin' under the bar—pony gone—hat gone, and head stove in.''

"Two of a kind!'' muttered Vessy in self-abasement.

"Eh? What say?''

"Nothing.''

"And worst of all was the way Natura acted about the cayuse. Blame a cayuse anyhow! And blame a woman!'' Then he showed the square of his pack once more, as he disappeared, for good, this time.

Vessy, burdened with his blankets and reflections, sought Natura, whom he found sitting in the doorway of a dilapidated shack behind a rail fence. She was not particularly young, and she had never been pretty. What good looks she had were sadly marred by weeping. Tears are not becoming to red-haired women.

She arose from the step and pushed a straggling tress from her forehead with a shapely hand, and, as she stood against the homely background disclosed by the open door, there was a suggestion of purity and womanliness about her which roused a dormant memory in Vessy's heart—the memory of a mother and sister who had slept under the Michigan mosses for ten long years—an atmosphere of home and home comforts surrounded her and crept into the heart of the man-tramp at his first sight of her.

He took off his hat and stood silent a moment, while Natura surveyed him sullenly.

"Could I get a bite to eat here?"

"I don't know; we've just had dinner."

"Anything will do. I've tramped all day."

She went into the house without another word and began to prepare a meal. Vessy threw his pack on the ground and dropped down in the doorway, where Natura had been sitting when he first saw her, and gazed listlessly at the sloping lawn, which melted into a trickling thread of running water between the rail fence and the trail. He noted unconsciously that the ground was unusually free from stumps, and that a flourishing orchard clung to the southern slope like a blanket. It was in bloom now, and flaunted gaudily against the gloom of distant cedar timber. Nearer by there were cherry and plum trees, and fowls of all descriptions waddled or strutted between the house and the shabby stables at the back. Out of doors the place spoke plainly of some sudden check in improvements, a sort of falling from grace, as if the owner had worked mightily up to a certain point, then ceased in despair or failing strength, and allowed Nature to begin to reclaim that which had been wrested from her. These evidences of shiftlessness or defeat stopped at the door of the shack, however. Inside the house law and order reigned.

Presently the odor of ham and coffee stole out over Jim's head. It made him faint with hunger.

"Don't get up too much of a spread; I've only got six bits," he said to the girl, over his shoulder, and squandered one of his rare smiles upon her. This smile of Vessy's was his one charm. He did not know it, but the woman paused with a dish and a spoon in her hand to gaze at him.

"Oh, it won't founder you," she said.

"I saw your father down the trail," he ventured.

"Stepfather," she prompted.

"Well, stepfather, if you like that better. He was telling me he had lost a horse."

"He lost a horse!" she said contemptuously. "He lost a horse! Little he cares!"

She fumbled for her handkerchief and, not finding it at once, grew desperate at the threatened disgrace of shedding tears for a cayuse before a man and threw her apron over her head, thereby concealing her tears, but not her sobs.

Vessy arose hastily. Here it was again; woman and tears!

He stepped inside and stood with his hands in his pockets, surveying the shrouded figure.

"Are you crying on account of the cayuse?"

"Yes, I'm crying on account of the cayuse!" she sobbed. "Oh, poor old Ginger! My mother's old pony gone to be tortured to death by a Siwash!"

"Perhaps the Siwash will sell him," soothed Vessy.

"What difference would that make? Some other brute would finish him! You are all alike; you drink and swear and swagger, and kill horses and women!"

Natura sobbed on while the ham frizzled temptingly on the stove, and the coffee steamed to the spoiling point. An old rooster, with male inquisitiveness, craned his neck in at the door and batted an eye for crumbs.

Suddenly Natura recovered her self-possession, pulled the apron from her head, wiped her face with the restored handkerchief, and announced coldly that dinner was ready. Vessy slunk into a seat at the table, and Natura placed the dinner before him. He took a mouthful of ham and potato and a big gulp of coffee.

"Who did that cayuse really belong to?" he asked at length. "Your father—stepfather—said you called it yours."

"I called it mine because it was mine."

"Then he stole the horse?"

"I don't see how you could call it anything else."

A hopeful look flitted across the woman's face. She came to the side of the table opposite Vessy and sat down facing him. Vessy smiled at her.

"Your stepfather gave me to understand you was goin' to marry him someday."

Her face grew red with anger. "I'm a good sight more likely to kill him someday! Oh, I hate him! He killed my mother, and now he has given away my poor old horse, the only last living friend I had in the world—and to a Siwash!"

She was almost in tears again, but restrained herself.

"I—I was going to say, I've been saving up a little money to get rid of old Jap Ward with, but—I'd be willing to stand old Jap Ward a little while longer if I could only get my horse back again. I don't suppose you would like a chance of earning some money by looking him up, would you?"

She eyed him beseechingly. He was still smiling.

"What will you give?"

"I will give you ten dollars to start with, and if you find him and bring him back, I will give you forty more."

"Not enough," he said.

She brought a picture of the horse from the clock shelf and laid it beside his plate. "You would know him if you found him. He has a big, brown spot around one eye, and he is branded with the first three letters of my name."

"T'aint enough," he repeated.

Natura sighed. "How much would you ask?" she inquired, but the inquiry was mechanical. She felt the hopelessness of her appeal and was prepared for its failure. "I'll give you ten to start on and sixty-five if you bring him home safe and sound."

"Not enough."

"Then your services are too high for me," she said with anger.

"How long since your stepfather stole the horse?"

The form of the question pleased her. "It will be two weeks tomorrow."

"All right. I'll tell you what I'll do. I'll hunt your cayuse for you on one condition."

Natura's eyes were again riveted on his face.

"And if I start for him, I'll bring him, if he is in the State of Washington!"

Natura went to the cupboard and brought out the half of a blackberry pie and replenished the plate of fried cakes.

"You've got a mighty poor opinion of men—and if that old sample I met in the road is what you go by, I can't blame you—and I've got a mighty poor opinion of women. I've had some triflin' examples to judge from, too. But my opinion of women has changed a little since I came in here. A girl who can cry on account of a buckskin cayuse two weeks after it is lost would get to think a good deal of a man, I should imagine, if he was halfway decent. Now, I'll make these terms, and you can take 'em or not, as you like. I want the chance to make you think better of men than you do now. I've got seventy-five cents and three red blankets; you've got seventy-five dollars and a red-and-white stepfather. Now, I find the cayuse and bring him back, then I'll have seventy-five dollars, and you'll have a buckskin cayuse. That'll be quite a start, and we'll shake the stepfather."

She was red now to the roots of her hair, but he was still smiling.

"Don't be silly," she said.

"You won't accept my terms, then?"

"Of course not; you're making fun of me."

"I was not. But, of course, I ain't going to force you to accept. I offered you a good bargain, a horse and a husband for seventy-five dollars and a third-rate old stepfather. Well, how much do I owe you for my dinner? I must be packing. Twenty-five cents! Go on! Twenty-five cents for a whole ham and a bushel of potaters, say nothin' of the pie and dough-nuts?"

He threw a fifty-cent piece and a quarter on the table. "You lose money at six bits. I've coaled up for a week."

She laughed and attempted to thrust the fifty-cent piece into his vest pocket. He caught her hands and held them while he threw the money under the table; then he shouldered his blankets, strode down the path, and took the trail once more, with a backward grin and a wave of the hand.

Natura watched him out of sight, and once she sighed, and once she smiled; then she picked up the money from under the table and stood a long time with it in her hand, and before she put it in her purse, she kissed it.

Strange that so young a woman should love money so.

That night Vessy slept in his red blankets on the ground in the deep, green woods some ten miles beyond the Madrona mill for which he had inquired so anxiously the day before. He was hugging the riverbed and making for the reservation which lay twenty miles to the west.

The next day he breakfasted at twelve o'clock, on three eggs which he borrowed from a rancher's henhouse and boiled in a tomato can over a fir-bough fire. At night he supped with a lone rancher on underdone salt pork and boiled potatoes. He also spent the night and "coaled up" on the same fare in the morning, leaving one of his new red blankets to pay for his entertainment. He was close to the end of his journey now and felt that he needed to be in good trim for whatever lay ahead of him.

Two miles farther on he saw a man hauling logs with a team consisting of a mule and a buckskin cayuse.

The driver was using a goad stick in place of a whip, and the yellow sides of the little cayuse reeked with sweat.

Vessy made his way through the slashing. He saw the letters branded on the yellow flank; he saw the brown spot about the right eye, and he knew he was face to face with the much-lamented Ginger.

The time for action had come, and Vessy was "coaled up" and ready.

"My friend, hold on a minute. Where'd ye git that team?"

"None o' yer blame business. G' lang there! He' up!"

Vessy slipped his pack and went closer to the rancher.

"Say, hold on a minute. You stole that cayuse from a Siwash, and that Siwash stole him from me. I'm out for cayuses today, and you'll untackle right here and now, or I shall be obliged to thrash you."

Without warning, the rancher made a lunge at Vessy with the goad stick; but Vessy, who was on his guard against just such a demonstration, avoided the blow, then closed with his assailant.

His blood was up. He had the length of reach, the muscle, and the disposition of a fighter; but his enemy was no child.

The two men rolled upon the ground, with clenched teeth and knotted muscles, gasping and punching with gurgling oaths, while the cayuse, with heaving sides, cast sidelong glances at his champion, and the mule stood sullenly at rest.

Now Vessy, covered with leaves and brambles, was uppermost; and again the rancher, hatless and bloody, crushed his adversary into the soil and punched with all his might. Once he dealt Vessy a blow in the eye which nearly blinded him, but that blow was the signal for the finish. Vessy was thoroughly in trim now; his blood was seething, and when the tide in the affairs of men brought him to the surface again, he rained blows which told fearfully upon the head and neck of the under man.

He was fighting for Natura.

A blow in the neck, a sudden relaxing of tense muscles, a weak cry for quarter, and the victor removed his knee from the chest of the vanquished and staggered to his feet.

"There, damn ye!" spluttered Vessy, wiping the blood from his face and reaching for his hat; "you might have saved yourself that if you'd been decent. Lay down there, now, and if you stir till I'm over the hill, I'll come back and finish ye!"

He broke the goad stick in three pieces across his knee and flung it far into the brush.

"A man that'll use one of them things ain't fit to own even a mule, so I'm goin' to take the mule with me. If you want it, and can prove that you have any better right to it than I have, you can come after it!"

Then he unhitched the team, arranged the blankets across their backs, mounted the mule, and headed in the direction from which he had come.

Once he looked back and saw the man whom he had pounded, and who had pounded him, sitting on the ground rubbing his shoulder. His red shirt made a dazzling spot of color against the dull greens and browns of the slashing.

It was high noon when Vessy sighted the Ward shack, with its rail fence, its smoke-plumed chimney, its clambering vines, like charity, covering the sins of shiftlessness, and Natura, sitting pensively in the door.

When the cavalcade hove in sight, she cried out in joy and ran lightly down the path to meet it. The next moment her arms were around the sweat-stained neck of the buckskin cayuse, and he fumbled lovingly at her cheek with a flopping, velvet lip.

Vessy, astride the mule, grinned down at them. "I was in hopes," he said, "you might mistake me for Ginger; we're marked about the same around the eye."

"You fought for him?" she questioned worshipfully, but he refused to give any details of the fight, and to Natura's inquiries about the mule he only replied that it was borrowed, and the owner might come for it any day.

"Are you hungry?" asked Natura shyly.

Vessy had washed from his face all the black which was outside the skin.

"No, oh no, but one must go through the motions for politeness' sake, you know, and the sooner we begin the motions, the better it'll suit me," said he, with that sidewise glance and smile before which Natura's heart went down in defeat.

There were fresh eggs and jellied chicken and sliced ham; there were canned blackberries from the woods—the spiciest fruit on earth; there were baked apples, fruitcake, and cherry pie.

"If you serve Ginger this way, you'll just have the mule left," grinned Vessy, surveying the table.

"I'll be more careful of Ginger."

After Vessy had finished his dinner, Natura placed four twenty-dollar gold pieces beside his plate.

"That's all I've got," she said. "I can't give you any more."

"It ain't enough, Natura, girl. I told you it wouldn't be enough."

"You said seventy-five wouldn't be enough; there's eighty there, and it's all I've got."

"I don't want your money. I want—you! I'll be good to you and—Ginger."

"And the mule?" she joked.

"He ain't in the contract, but don't worry about the mule. I want to be fair with you, Natura. I'm a poor specimen of a man, but I can do better, and I mean to. I can earn money and save it, too, for your sake, if you'll let me. I'm goin' down to the Madrona mill right now, and I'm pretty sure of work there, and when I have a pocket full again, we'll get married and give the old stepdaddy the slip, you and I—and Ginger."

"And the mule?"

"Well—no, we'll leave the mule to your father. I've got

a notion the less one has to do with that mule, the better. I expect to get another black eye when I come to take you away."

"How do you know you are going to take me away?"

"I'm sure of it."

He drew her to his knee and kissed her, and she hid her face on his shoulder and knew that she had never been happy before in her life.

"Don't go to the mill," she murmured. "Stay and help me with the ranch."

"No, no; I don't want to marry you until I've had time to show you that I can be a man, and until I've got as much money as you have. I am willin' to marry a woman who is worth nine million times as much as I am morally, but financially, Natura, I'm bound to be the boss when we marry."

"How long will it take you?" she asked.

"Well, let me see—eighty dollars cash, a cayuse, a mule—"

"The mule isn't mine."

"Well, then, let the mule stand as one of my assets; it'll shorten the time a few weeks—oh, we'll be married in two months."

"Don't wait," she repeated, "stay with me here on the ranch."

"Why, my dear, I haven't money enough to git the license."

She reached for the gold pieces. "They are yours—you earned them."

He pushed them away, laughing. "This is better pay for what I did," and he kissed her.

"But I am afraid to stay here with my stepfather. He is a wicked old man. We have had an awful quarrel since you went away. He is in town drinking. He may come home drunk at any minute and murder me. He isn't responsible when he is in liquor."

Vessy sprang up. "Come, Natura, get your bonnet. I'll borrow twenty dollars of you for a weddin' blowout, we'll be married, and I'll take you right down to the mill with me!"

They walked to Madrona to be married, and on the way Vessy told Natura all about the yellow-haired girl in Seattle and that wild night when he lost his savings, and went to the altar with a clear conscience.

Not so Natura. She did not confess until after supper that night at the ranch. Jap Ward, unconscious of the cloud which had settled on his future, was still drinking in Madrona. The fire burned dimly, and the firwood in the cook stove popped like firecrackers. The pleasant odor of the wedding feast lingered in the room, as Natura, actually beautiful in her happiness, stole a well-rounded arm about her husband's neck and murmured: "Jim, I have deceived you, and I didn't dare let you go to the mill before we were married, for fear you'd find me out and never come back. You said you'd never marry a woman until you had as much money as she did. It would have taken a long time, Jim."

Jim was holding a wet handkerchief to his discolored eye, but the other bulged with astonishment.

"The ranch is mine. It belonged to mother. Jap Ward hasn't anything to do with it."

"Holy Moses! How much is it worth?"

"About two thousand. Don't leave me, Jim. That is the reason my stepfather wanted to marry me. Every man in the county has asked me, but they all want my property."

"Two thousand dollars isn't so much, Natura. I'll catch up—I'm bound to catch up."

"But that isn't all; there's my timber claim—it's just back of the ranch—don't leave me, Jim."

"How much?"

"I've been offered six thousand for it, but when the railroad goes through—it is surveyed now—and the sawmill is built this fall, it will double in value—I am afraid."

"Great governor, Natura, how I have been deceived! The only chance I have in the world is in being such a good husband you can't get along without me! Two—six—double—fourteen thousand dollars! Well, the mule is mine, Natura. You shall never own the mule!"

Sewell Ford

SKIPPER

Being the Biography of
a Blue-Ribboner

At the age of six Skipper went on the force. Clean of limb and sound of wind he was, with not a blemish from the tip of his black tail to the end of his crinkly forelock. He had been broken to saddle by a Green Mountain boy who knew more of horse nature than of the trashy things writ in books. He gave Skipper kind words and an occasional friendly pat on the flank. So Skipper's disposition was sweet and his nature a trusting one.

This is why Skipper learned so soon the ways of the city. The first time he saw one of those little wheeled houses, all windows and full of people, come rushing down the street with a fearful whirr and clank of bell, he wanted to bolt. But the man on his back spoke in an easy, calm voice, saying, "So-o-o! There, me b'y. Aisy wid ye. So-o-o!"—which was excellent advice, for the queer contrivance whizzed by and did him no harm. In a week he could watch one without even pricking up his ears.

It was strange work Skipper had been brought to the city to do. As a colt he had seen horses, dragging plows, pulling big loads of hay, and hitched to many kinds of vehicles. He himself had drawn a light buggy and thought it good fun, though you did have to keep your heels down and trot instead of canter. He had liked best to lope off with the boy on his back, down to the Corners, where the store was.

But here there were no plows, no hay carts, nor mowing machines. There were many heavy wagons, it was true, but these were all drawn by stocky Percherons and big Western grays or stout Canada blacks who seemed fully equal to the task.

Also there were carriages—my, what shiny carriages! And what smart, sleek-looking horses drew them! And how high they did hold their heads and how they did throw their feet about—just as if they were dancing on eggs.

"Proud, stuck-up things," thought Skipper.

It was clear that none of this work was for him. Early on the first morning of his service men in brass-buttoned blue coats came to the stable to feed and rub down the horses. Skipper's man had two names. One was Officer Martin; at least that was the one to which he answered when the man with the cap called the roll before they rode out for duty. The other name was "Reddy." That was what the rest of the men in blue coats called him. Skipper noticed that he had red hair and concluded that "Reddy" must be his real name.

As for Skipper's name, it was written on the tag tied to the halter which he wore when he came to the city. Skipper heard him read it. The boy on the farm had done that, and

Skipper was glad, for he liked the name.

There was much to learn in those first few weeks, and Skipper learned it quickly. He came to know that at inspection, which began the day, you must stand with your nose just on a line with that of the horse on either side. If you didn't you felt the bit or the spurs. He mastered the meaning of "right dress," "left dress," "forward," "fours right," and a lot of other things. Some of them were very strange.

Now on the farm they had said, "Whoa, boy," and "Gid a-a-ap." Here they said, "Halt" and "Forward." But Reddy used none of these terms. He pressed with his knees on your withers, loosened the reins, and made a queer little chirrup when he wanted you to gallop. He let you know when he wanted you to stop, by the lightest pressure on the bit.

It was lazy work, though. Sometimes when Skipper was just aching for a brisk canter he had to pace soberly through the park driveways—for Skipper, although I don't believe I mentioned it before, was part and parcel of the mounted police force. But there, you could know that by the coat of arms in yellow brass on his saddle blanket.

For half an hour at a time he would stand, just on the edge of the roadway and at an exact right angle with it, motionless as the horse ridden by the bronze soldier up near the Mall. Reddy would sit as still in the saddle, too. It was hard for Skipper to stand there and see those mincing cobs go by, their pad-housings all aglitter, crests on their blinders, jingling their pole chains and switching their absurd little stubs of tails. But it was still more tantalizing to watch the saddle horses canter past in the soft bridle path on the other side of the roadway. But then, when you are on the force you must do your duty.

One afternoon as Skipper was standing post like this he caught a new note that rose above the hum of the park traffic. It was the quick, nervous beat of hooves which rang sharply on the hard macadam. There were screams, too. It was a runaway. Skipper knew this even before he saw the bell-like nostrils, the straining eyes, and the foam-flecked lips of the horse, or the scared man in the carriage behind. It was a case of broken rein.

How the sight made Skipper's blood tingle! Wouldn't he just like to show that crazy roan what real running was! But what was Reddy going to do? He felt him gather up the reins. He felt his knees tighten. What! Yes, it must be so. Reddy was actually going to try a brush with the runaway. What fun!

Skipper pranced out into the roadway and gathered himself for the sport. Before he could get into full swing, however, the roan had shot past with a snort of challenge which could not be misunderstood.

Oho! You will, eh? thought Skipper. Well now, we'll see about that.

Ah, a free rein! That is—almost free. And a touch of the spurs! No need for that, Reddy. How the carriages scatter! Skipper caught hasty glimpses of smart hackneys drawn up trembling by the roadside, of women who tumbled from bicycles into the bushes, and of men who ran and shouted and waved their hats.

Just as though that little roan wasn't scared enough already, thought Skipper.

But she did run well; Skipper had to admit that. She had a lead of fifty yards before he could strike his best gait. Then for a few moments he could not seem to gain an inch. But the mare was blowing herself and Skipper was taking it coolly. He was putting the pent-up energy of weeks into his strides. Once he saw he was overhauling her he steadied to the work.

Just as Skipper was about to forge ahead, Reddy did a queer thing. With his right hand he grabbed the roan with a nose-pinch grip, and with the left he pulled in on the reins. It was a great disappointment to Skipper, for he had counted on showing the roan his heels. Skipper knew, after two or three experiences of this kind, that this was the usual thing.

Those were glorious runs, though. Skipper wished they would come more often. Sometimes there would be two and even three in a day. Then a fortnight or so would pass without a single runaway on Skipper's beat. But duty is duty.

During the early morning hours, when there were few people in the park, Skipper's education progressed. He learned to pace around in a circle, lifting each forefoot with a sway of the body and a pawing movement which was quite rhythmical. He learned to box with his nose. He learned to walk sedately behind Reddy and to pick up a glove, dropped apparently by accident. There was always a sugarplum or a sweet cracker in the glove, which he got when Reddy stopped and Skipper, poking his nose over his shoulder, let the glove fall into his hands.

As he became more accomplished he noticed that Reddy took more pains with his toilet. Every morning Skipper's coat was curried and brushed and rubbed with chamois until it shone almost as if it had been varnished. His fetlocks were carefully trimmed, a ribbon braided into his forelock, and his hooves polished as brightly as Reddy's boots. Then there were apples and carrots and other delicacies which Reddy brought him.

So it happened that one morning Skipper heard the sergeant tell Reddy that he had been detailed for the Horse Show squad. Reddy had saluted and said nothing at the time, but when they were once out on post he told Skipper all about it.

"Sure an' it's app'arin' before all the swells in town you'll be, me b'y. Phat do ye think of that, eh? An' mebbe ye'll be gettin' a blue ribbon, Skipper, me lad; an' mebbe Mr. Patrick Martin will have a roundsman's berth an' chevrons on his sleeves afore the year's out."

The Horse Show was all that Reddy had promised, and more. The light almost dazzled Skipper. The sounds and the smells confused him. But he felt Reddy on his back, heard him chirrup softly, and soon felt at ease on the tanbark.

Then there was a great crash of noise and Skipper, with some fifty of his friends on the force, began to move around the circle. First it was fours abreast, then by twos, and then a rush to troop front, when, in a long line, they swept around as if they had been harnessed to a beam by traces of equal length.

After some more evolutions a half dozen were picked out and put through their paces. Skipper was one of these. Then three of the six were sent to join the rest of the squad. Only Skipper and two others remained in the center of the ring. Men in queer clothes, wearing tall black hats, showing much white shirtfront and carrying long whips, came and looked them over carefully.

Skipper showed these men how he could waltz in time to the music, and the people who banked the circle as far up as Skipper could see shouted and clapped their hands until it seemed as if a thunderstorm had broken loose. At last one of the men in tall hats tied a blue ribbon on Skipper's bridle.

When Reddy got him into the stable, he fed him four big red apples one after the other. Next day Skipper knew that he was a famous horse. Reddy showed him their pictures in the paper.

For a whole year Skipper was the pride of the force. He was shown to visitors at the stables. He was patted on the nose by the mayor. The chief, who was a bigger man than the mayor, came up especially to look at him. In the park Skipper did his tricks every day for ladies in fine dress who exclaimed, "How perfectly wonderful!" as well as for pretty nursemaids who giggled and said, "Now did you ever see the likes o' that, Norah?"

And then came the spavin. Ah, but that was the beginning of the end! Were you ever spavined? If so, you know all about it. If you haven't, there's no use trying to tell you. Rheumatism? Well, that may be bad; but a spavin is worse.

For three weeks Reddy rubbed the lump on the hock with stuff from a brown bottle, and hid it from the inspector. Then, one black morning, it was discovered. That day Skipper did not go out on post. Reddy came into the stall, put his arm around his neck and said "Good-bye" in a voice that Skipper had never heard him use before. Something had made it thick and husky. Very sadly Skipper saw him saddle one of the newcomers and go out for duty.

Before Reddy came back Skipper was led away. He was taken to a big building where there were horses of every kind—except the right kind. Each one had his own peculiar "out," although you couldn't always tell what it was at first glance.

But Skipper did not stay here long. He was led out before a lot of men in a big ring. A man on a box shouted out a number, and began to talk very fast. Skipper gathered that he was talking about him. Skipper learned that he was still only six years old, and that he had been owned as a saddle horse by a lady who was about to sail for Europe and was closing out her stable. This was news to Skipper. He wished Reddy could hear it.

The man talked very nicely about Skipper. He said he was kind, gentle, sound in wind and limb, and was not only trained to the saddle but would work either single or double. The man wanted to know how much the gentlemen were willing to pay for a bay gelding of this description.

Someone on the outer edge of the crowd said, "Ten dollars."

At this the man on the box grew quite indignant. He asked if the other man wouldn't like a silver-mounted harness and a lap robe thrown in.

"Fifteen," said another man.

Somebody else said, "Twenty," another man said, "Twenty-five," and still another, "Thirty." Then there was a hitch. The man on the box began to talk very fast indeed:

"Thutty-thutty-thutty-thutty—do I hear the five? Thutty-thutty-thutty-thutty—will you make it five?"

"Thirty-five," said a red-faced man who had pushed his way to the front and was looking Skipper over sharply.

The man on the box said "Thutty-five" a good many times and asked if he "heard forty." Evidently he did not, for he stopped and said very slowly and distinctly, looking expectantly around: "Are you all done? Thirty-five—once. Thirty-five—twice. Third—and last call—sold, for thirty-five dollars!"

When Skipper heard this he hung his head. When you have been a $250 blue-ribboner and the pride of the force it is sad to be "knocked down" for thirty-five.

The next year of Skipper's life was a dark one. We will not linger over it. The red-faced man who led him away was a grocer. He put Skipper in the shafts of a heavy wagon very early every morning and drove him a long ways through the city to a big downtown market where men in long frocks shouted and handled boxes and barrels. When the wagon was heavily loaded the red-faced man drove him back to the store. Then a tow-haired boy, who jerked viciously on the lines and was fond of using the whip, drove him recklessly about the streets and avenues.

But one day the tow-haired boy pulled the near rein too hard while rounding a corner and a wheel was smashed against a lamppost. The tow-haired boy was sent head first into an ash barrel, and Skipper, rather startled at the occurrence, took a little run down the avenue, strewing the pavement with eggs, sugar, canned corn, celery, and other assorted groceries.

Perhaps this was why the grocer sold him. Skipper pulled a cart through the flat-house district for a while after that. On the seat of the cart sat a leather-lunged man who roared: "A-a-a-a-puls! Nice a-a-a-a-puls! A who-o-ole lot fer a quarter!"

Skipper felt this disgrace keenly. Even the cab horses, on whom he used to look with disdain, eyed him scornfully. Skipper stood it as long as possible and then one day, while the apple fakir was standing on the back step of the cart shouting things at a woman who was leaning half way out of a fourth-story window, he bolted. He distributed that load of apples over four blocks, much to the profit of the street children, and he wrecked the wagon on a hydrant. For this the fakir beat him with a piece of the wreckage until a blue-coated officer threatened to arrest him. Next day Skipper was sold again.

Skipper looked over his new owner without joy. The man was evil of face. His long whiskers and hair were unkempt and sun-bleached, like the tip end of a pastured cow's tail. His clothes were greasy. His voice was like the grunt of a pig. Skipper wondered to what use this man would put him. He feared the worst.

Far up through the city the man took him and out on a broad avenue where there were many open spaces, most of them fenced in by huge billboards. Behind one of these sign-plastered barriers Skipper found his new home. The bottom of the lot was more than twenty feet below the street level. In the center of a waste of rocks, ash heaps, and dead weeds tottered a group of shanties, strangely made of odds and ends. The walls were partly of mud-chinked rocks and partly of wood. The roofs were patched with strips of rusty tin held in place by stones.

Into one of these shanties, just tall enough for Skipper to enter and no more, the horse that had been the pride of the mounted park police was driven with a kick as a greeting. Skipper noted first that there was no feed box and no hayrick. Then he saw, or rather felt—for the only light came through cracks in the walls—that there was no floor. His nostrils told him that the drainage was bad. Skipper sighed as he thought of the clean, sweet straw which Reddy used to change in his stall every night.

But when you have a lump on your leg—a lump that throbs, throbs, throbs with pain, whether you stand still or lie down—you do not think much on other things.

Supper was late in coming to Skipper that night. He was almost starved when it was served. And such a supper! What do you think? Hay? Yes, but marsh hay; the dry, tasteless stuff they use for bedding in cheap stables. A ton of it wouldn't make a pound of good flesh. Oats? Not a sign of an oat! But with the hay there were a few potato peelings. Skipper nosed them out and nibbled the marsh hay. The rest he pawed back under him, for the whole had been thrown at his feet. Then he dropped on the ill-smelling ground and went to sleep to dream that he had been turned into a forty-acre field of clover, while a dozen brass bands played a waltz and multitudes of people looked on and cheered.

In the morning more salt hay was thrown to him and water was brought in a dirty pail. Then, without a stroke of brush or currycomb he was led out. When he saw the wagon to which he was to be hitched Skipper hung his head. He had reached the bottom. It was unpainted and rickety as to body and frame, the wheels were unmated and dished, while the shafts were spliced and wound with wire.

But worst of all was the string of bells suspended from two uprights above the seat. When Skipper saw these he knew he had fallen low indeed. He had become the horse of a wandering junkman. The next step in his career, as he well knew, would be the glue factory and the boneyard. Now when a horse has lived for twenty years or so, it is sad enough to face these things. But at eight years to see the glue factory close at hand is enough to make a horse wish he had never been foaled.

For many weary months Skipper pulled that crazy cart, with its hateful jangle of bells, about the city streets and suburban roads while the man with the faded hair roared through his matted beard: "Buy o-o-o-o-olt ra-a-a-a-ags! Buy o-o-o-o-olt ra-a-a-a-ags! Olt boddles! Olt copper! Olt iron! Vaste baber!"

The lump on Skipper's hock kept growing bigger and bigger. It seemed as if the darts of pain shot from hoof to flank with every step. Big hollows came over his eyes. You could see his ribs as plainly as the hoops on a pork barrel. Yet six days in the week he went on long trips and brought back heavy loads of junk. On Sunday he hauled the junkman and his family about the city.

Once the junkman tried to drive Skipper into one of the park entrances. Then for the first time in his life Skipper balked. The junkman pounded and used such language as you might expect from a junkman, but all to no use. Skipper took the beating with lowered head, but go through the gate he would not. So the junkman gave it up, although he seemed very anxious to join the line of gay carriages which were rolling in.

Soon after this there came a break in the daily routine. One morning Skipper was not led out as usual. In fact, no one came near him, and he could hear no voices in the nearby shanty. Skipper decided that he would take a day off himself. By backing against the door he readily pushed it open, for the staple was insecure.

Once at liberty, he climbed the roadway that led out of the lot. It was late in the fall, but there was still short sweet winter grass to be found along the gutters. For a while he nibbled at this hungrily. Then a queer idea came to Skipper. Perhaps the passing of a smartly groomed saddle horse was responsible.

At any rate, Skipper left off nibbling grass. He hobbled out to the edge of the road, turned so as to face the opposite side, and held up his head. There he stood just as he used to stand when he was the pride of the mounted squad. He was on post once more.

Few people were passing, and none seemed to notice him. Yet he was an odd figure. His coat was shaggy and weather-stained. It looked patched and faded. The spavined hock caused one hind quarter to sag somewhat, but aside from that his pose was strictly according to the regulations.

Skipper had been playing at standing post for a half hour, when a trotting dandy who sported ankle boots and toe weights pulled up before him. He was drawing a light, bicycle-wheeled road wagon in which were two men.

"Queer?" one of the men was saying. "Can't say I see anything queer about it, Captain. Some old plug that's got away from a squatter; that's all I see in it."

"Well, let's have a look," said the other. He stared hard at Skipper for a moment and then, in a loud, sharp tone, said:

" 'Ten-shun! Right dress!' "

Skipper pricked up his ears, raised his head, and side-stepped stiffly. The trotting dandy turned and looked curiously at him.

"Forward!" said the man in the wagon. Skipper hobbled out into the road.

"Right wheel! Halt! I thought so," said the man, as Skipper obeyed the orders. "That fellow has been on the force. He was standing post. Looks mighty familiar, too—white stockings on two forelegs, white star on forehead. Now I wonder if that can be—here, hold the reins a minute."

Going up to Skipper the man patted his nose one or twice, and then pushed his muzzle to one side. Skipper ducked and countered. He had not forgotten his boxing trick. The man turned his back and began to pace down the road. Skipper followed and picked up a riding glove which the man dropped.

"Doyle," said the man, as he walked back to the wagon,

"two years ago that was the finest horse on the force—took the blue ribbon at the Garden. Alderman Martin would give a thousand dollars for him as he stands. He has hunted the state for him. You remember Martin—Reddy Martin—who used to be on the mounted squad! Didn't you hear? An old uncle who made a fortune as a building contractor died about a year ago and left the whole pile to Reddy. He's got a fine country place up in Westchester and is in the city government. Just elected this fall. But he isn't happy because he can't find his old horse—and here's the horse."

Next day an astonished junkman stood before an empty shanty which served as a stable and feasted his eyes on a $50 bank note.

If you are ever up in Westchester County be sure and visit the stables of Alderman P. Sarsfield Martin. Ask to see that oak-paneled box stall with the stained-glass windows and the porcelain feed box. You will notice a polished brass name-plate on the door bearing this inscription:

SKIPPER

You may meet the alderman himself, wearing an English-made riding suit, loping comfortably along on a sleek bay gelding with two white forelegs and a white star on his forehead. Yes, high-priced veterinaries can cure spavin—Alderman Martin says so.

THE BLACK ROAN
OF 265

The Biography of
a New York Fire Horse

We first met in the hospital and training stables, where men were trying him and other five-year-olds for entrance into the most famous fire department in the world. He was a splendid, handsome, fourteen-hundred-pound, sixteen-and-a-half-hand black roan, "as gentle as a kitten," with eyes set far apart, long, mighty legs of bone and sinew that might have felled a grizzly, and a chest and flanks and shoulders like a young elephant's. He had been rubbed and squeezed and thumped and grabbed by the official veterinary surgeon, and was about to be tried out on a fire engine.

In all his life on the green fields and meadows of the quiet upstate farm he never had seen anything quite so terrible as the gaudy Thing of red paint and glittering brass and nickel. It filled him with fear and terror. Head thrown high, whites of eyes showing and nostrils red and snorting, he was led forth, prancing. But there remained even a more dreadful sight than the glitter-wagon—the leather maze of black, brass-mounted, three-abreast harness that hung open and suspended from the ceiling like a huge spider, ready to be dropped and snapped within two seconds. At sight of this he would have reared and plunged, but a firm and steady hand held him by the head, a firm and steady voice told him he was among friends, and a firm and steady palm patted his neck until at last he trusted himself to be backed under the harness between two veteran grays. Center he was hitched, where the deadweight of the five-ton apparatus pulls heaviest and where all new horses are hooked to show their mettle.

There stood the handsome, kindly beast, trembling with excitement, pawing, and tossing his head with fear and ready to jump out of his harness to escape the dread apparition behind. From the moment the ponderous, smooth-running machine struck the pavement and the tongue of the big spring bell sounded a note, he was seized with a maddening spasm of fear. At a bound and with every ounce of might pent up in his magnificent frame, he threw himself against his collar and tried to bolt. Mouth open and ears laid flat, he struck fire out of the granite. But behind him was the ten-thousand-pound mountain, the grays angrily sat back in their breeching, and his mouth felt a quick, irresistible pull that threatened to land him on his haunches. An iron hand drew rein over him as no hand had ever drawn before. Then came the same familiar, steady voice. And from the hand, along the taut rein into the bloodred, frothy mouth steadily passed a strange current that ran upward inside the skull, between the eyes, where it soothed.

More than an hour the team was driven back and forth, back and forth three blocks, stopping now and then to back the huge apparatus fifty feet in a straight line or in curves and describing figure eights to test quick right and left turns. Lastly came the "balk test," to see what the new horse would do if his engine were stuck in a snowbank. The driver drew his whip and tightened his grip on the lines. "Ge'up!" he cried, and threw the brake hard against the fat rubber tires, where it clung. With a simultaneous bound the three horses jumped forward and dug their toes into the crevices of the pavement. A snap, a sharp crack, a rattle of chains and the roan lurched sharply forward, his whiffletree broken into halves.

Despite the heavy load and the brake and the skillful driver, had the new horse been other than the knowing, gentle beast he was, there would have been trouble. But the roan had found himself. He no longer jumped at sound of the bell nor tried to pull the whole weight of the machine. Neck arched, small head thrown high, and the fire of the late excitement still in his eye, he pranced lightly between the grays that brought in the disabled engine.

But the new horse was a sad sight when, panting, the team drew up and the veterinary man listened for defects in wind. His powerful legs trembled under him. The nervous sweat of fear and excitement had broken out of every pore in his splendid frame and covered his glossy coat with a snowy lather. The surgeon, who annually inspected between thirty and forty horses to replace those killed and crippled in service, listened attentively. Every labored breath out of the strong, young lungs was impelled clear and clean as if out of the cylinder of an air compressor. The man took the soft nose of the horse between his palms and stroked it approvingly.

"Joe," he said, "you're a brick. Ever see a horse 'break in' in one lesson, Hauk?" he continued, addressing a visiting fire captain. "I had only one like that before. Most of 'em take three or four trips just to knock the scare out of 'em. But look at those eyes! See how far they're apart. It won't be a month before that fellow'll know everything you say to him."

"I think we can use him at Two-Sixty-five. You're half a hand taller than the law allows, Joe, but we need you for center. How about it, boy?" asked Hauk. Joe champed his bit and nodded his head, tossing flakes of foam and lather.

Fifty blocks from the hospital and training stables, down in the brand-new granite-front house of Engine Company 265, there were several reasons why Joe should serve thirty days' trial before final enlistment. Despite all indications to the contrary, he might prove too stupid to learn. Like many another fine beast he might lack self-reliance and levelheadedness and might refuse to become reconciled to the stifle of smoke, the roar of the orange flames, and the crashing of falling buildings. He might prove too excitable to use his horse sense and to do his share of the right things at the right time. He might even develop ugliness, or an illness, or a weakness. Or, when hungry or thirsty around mealtime, he might stamp for lunch or for a drink, making sleep overhead impossible for men who fought fires all night.

Company 265 was in the heart of the busiest section of the great city, among gridirons of electric-car tracks, forests of elevated railroad pillars, and throngs of human and animal and wagon traffic. Among the army of fire companies that guarded the town, not one had a better record with its sixty to seventy runs a month. Not one had a more dangerous district. Not one did more business.

Joe struck it lucky the first day. Not even a false alarm came in, and he spent an hour after breakfast giving a reception. Men lined up in front of his stall to visit and inspect. They talked to him and went into his stall and stroked his face and patted his neck and shoulders and quarters and the broad, deep chest where the hard flesh and muscle lay heaped in the shape of a great upside-down heart. He felt very much at home at all this, nibbled silvered buttons and made friends until, finally, he was led forward to another glitter-wagon, only bigger and finer and more glittery than the one the day before. Gently, gently he was led and coaxed and patted, and he recalled the spider harness and allowed himself to be backed under it while Frank and Barney, two magnificent, friendly blacks, were led to either side of him. Lightly the suspended harness was lowered onto the broad backs—then it was raised softly, only to come down heavier, and heavier and heavier, until Joe no longer feared the shiny steel collar and the massive black tangle that swooped and floundered suddenly down upon him.

Some horses hardly object to this ordeal from the first; others require two or three days to become used to it; and some scare-headed animals never become accustomed.

A horse in training for a circus would have been fed sugar and dismissed for the day had he shown half the progress Joe displayed. But in Joe's company there was little sugar and less circus, viewed from the inside. Three times a day, for half an hour, morning, noon, and night, new horses were driven to engines or backed under harness until broken. Often, even before broken to this, the lessons for running from stalls to harnesses were begun.

This training of the new horse took place with the fire gong and every horse in the company, including the two long-legged bays belonging to the big, white tender. With the first tap of each alarm, as the stall chains fell from the bits, the intelligent animals clattered to the front, while Doyle, the engine driver, led the big fellow at a gallop under the center harness. At first the roan was immeasurably panic-stricken. The loud, sonorous stroke of the big gong and the sudden stampede of the other horses startled the very heart in him. But ever there was a kindly voice or a friendly hand. Again and again the gong was struck, and each time, with infinite patience, Joe was urged by the head. Once that day, toward the end of the last lesson, he was lightly flicked from behind with a whip. A gray-black catapult jumped squarely at Doyle, knocked him to one side and brought up snorting pitifully, at the head of the engine. To his dying day none ever put a whip to the roan again.

That night, toward the wee-small hours of morning, while men lay abed asleep and the horses dozed afoot, a weird, wild clash of the gong rent the stillness like the trumpet of Judgment Day. Like the snap of a gigantic spring all was life, the resounding *clang! clang!* of the gong, the sharp, startling tattoo of a score of steel-shod feet on the concrete, the ghostlike slide of dusky, half-clad forms down the brass sliding-rod and the groan of the big front doors thrown wide apart. That was the first time the roan "ran" with his mates. With the note of the big bell he caught the excitement and ran to the pole, where the watch grabbed him and roughly backed him into place. However, the alarm proved for a neighboring company. Within two minutes everything in the magic house was steeped in quiet. Within ten minutes all were asleep except the watch—and Joe.

It took Joe ten days to learn his place under the harness (which is average time for the training of a firehorse); but it was two weeks before he became used to the interruptions of sleep, to eating and sleeping and waking with a bar bit in his mouth, and to eating from the floor instead of out of a manger. It was longer than a month before he ceased to jump at the earsplitting shrieks of whistles, the rattle and bang and clatter of fire apparatuses, the hiss and snort of steam and the thump-thump of his own engine at a hydrant. Solely by kindness and patience he learned all this as he learned to obey implicitly the man on the seat. Through fiery coals sputtered out of the fireboxes of the engines ahead he galloped. On a dead run he and the blacks would come down the crowded thoroughfares, aim into mazes of trucks, cars and wagons, trusting to bell, whistle, and police to clear the road. But a firehorse, like a fireman, must learn to think for himself. More, an intelligent horse, like an expert driver, gathers his own experience. Joe nearly broke his neck gathering his.

The asphalt pavement of 265's street was filled with hollows and depressions flooded by every rainstorm with gray-brown puddles of mud and water. Whistle screeching, bell banging, and smoke belching out of short, black stack, the engine came pell-mell down the street, racing her tender. A puddle that proved a five-inch-deep hole, chopped for repairs, was in front of the roan. He jumped into it, forefeet first, went headlong onto his knees and face, was pushed fifty feet by the frightful impetus of the five tons behind, and scrambled to his feet. The tender swerved by a hair from piling team, wagon, men, and all into the rear of the engine.

That day Hauk had to explain why he was nearly twenty seconds late on a seven-block run. That night, after the engine had been backed into place and the horses had dug into well-earned oats, the captain visited the roan in his stall and patted the scratched face and the skinned knees, while Doyle applied salve. "I thought your neck was broke, poor old fellow," he said, bringing down his hand with resounding slaps that pleased the poor old fellow hugely.

Joe never trusted puddles again. He jumped them. Free and easy as he used to take brooks and creeks on the farm, he cleared every puddle he came across. It is one thing, however, to gallop through a field and to take a ditch at leisure at one's own pace. It is very much another thing to be harnessed to ten thousand mad-whirling pounds, between two giants and a pair of banging, battering poles that anger and excite and make good aim impossible. Yet, one night the roan made a phenomenal jump—one of two that will long be remembered in the company. Doyle himself told the story.

"He's a steeplechaser, he is," the driver said, after giving a little "handshaking and kissing exhibition," which he had taught the new horse during his first six months. "Late last night I was a-rippin' down the avenue at a pretty good clip. The road was clear, far as I could see, and I let 'em out a bit extra, you understand. I had my eyes a block ahead, like I always do, lookin' at the crossin's, when, suddenly, right in the middle of the street, not twenty-five feet away, stuck in an open manhole of a sewer and dead ahead of Joe, I saw a great big sugar barrel. Say! It looked big as a house! I couldn't stop in time and I'd upset the bloomin' engine, trying to pull one side. I just says to myself, Joe, it's up to yourself; and, by the Harry, if he wasn't able for it. I gave him his head and he went at it. Up he reared, sat in the breechin', and between the jump and the racin' five tons, cleared it clean as a whistle. Next second the barrel was knocked to kindlin' against my fire-box."

The second jump of which they will tell you at the big engine-house, got Joe, Frank, and Barney into the newspapers, photographs and all, and was even more spectacular. Like most narrow escapes, this happened at night, when streets were clear, when horses were urged to top speed, when poles and buildings and elevated pillars cast treacherous shadows, and when nothing but a pair of dim red lamps marked a breakneck danger spot. The wheels of the engine were in the streetcar tracks. Doyle had drawn his whip and let it down on the backs of the blacks, and the three angered horses were heading like mad up the dusky avenue. The driver scanned the dark road, never saw two puny danger signals which marked a three-foot-wide ditch thrown clear across the track, and searched the crossing a block ahead. None except the horses knew of the danger until it was passed. Not even Doyle. Suddenly his lines slackened. The great, broad backs of his beasts rose together as if one. A dim red speck flashed by him on either side. With a violent jerk the horses landed back into their collars. They had taken the ditch and so had the engine—running smoothly across on the bridging car tracks. The blacks had learned the roan's trick.

When Joe was a year with the company he might have observed that in his business accidents happen periodically and in bunches of threes, just as they happen in the slow-moving world outside. But he had more important things to attend to during the luxurious hours of idleness between alarms and heartbreaking runs. There were his friends, men and women, who had read of him in newspapers, who came to see him and to whom he need attend; for, the big, good-natured fellow always did his share of the entertaining. He raised his great, mighty forefoot daintily as a kitten and politely "shook hands" with whoever wished. He would stretch forth his soft, pink tongue and give a kiss for the asking. He had other and more complicated tricks in his repertoire, however. He knew how to turn on a water faucet to fill a pail for his drink, though no amount of training could make him see the sense of turning it off again. He could put on his own collar. This steel oval, made to fit his thick neck, might be snapped shut and set upright on the floor and he would manage to stick his small head through it and wriggle it into place.

And so the fine, playful beast lived, the favorite of all who knew him, taking the brunt of the heavy load on his neck and chest, the batter of the two heavy tongues, and passing unscathed with his mates through many a tight place. Once, a surface railroad, changing from cable to electric power, had failed to notify of a temporary bridge which spanned its excavation, and Doyle pulled up in time to drop his team into a six-foot ditch while, brake set, the engine tottered on the brink of the hole and stayed. Again the driver saved his team when, to spare a woman, he had to find an L road pillar. He almost nipped a hind leg off Frank doing the trick; for, instead of putting in head on, he caught the hub of his forewheel and snapped both tongues. Not in a thousand trials could he have repeated the feat; it was a month before he drove again.

Thanks to luck and the driver, for nearly three years the

team remained unscathed before the daring, calculating pilot found himself cornered and bound to sacrifice. The accident happened at two o'clock one morning while running to a three-alarm fire. As the engine drew out of her house the street was lighted bright as day. A mile away, down at the riverfront, red flames leaped mountain high into a jet-black pall. Doyle leaned far forward, gave the animals their heads, and let out a yell. Hard as ever the three long-legged brutes could go they ran, ears laid flat, necks extended and mouths open. With an unearthly din of bell and whistle the engine tore down the street, waking everything along the line, warning two squares ahead.

What happened was past in five seconds. Nearing Broadway, a drunken cabman with two fares bowled leisurely across the street within thirty feet of the racing machine. In another instant it would plow clear through the light vehicle. Doyle dropped one line, grabbed the other with both hands, and threw his full weight on it. Around went three big heads. A wicked, sharp swerve, a startling, grinding crash, and the engine had hit the curb and capsized—the three horses lay tangled on the sidewalk—and Doyle, blood streaming down the side of his head, staggered to his feet and ran for the struggling, kicking beasts. Frank, first up, was grabbed by Hauk. Joe, injured, jumped, frightened, to his feet. Barney, the great, sleek, brave Barney, who had helped break in Joe, had landed under the heap and lay very still. He had made his last run. His neck was broken.

Joe was frightfully hurt. The pole between himself and Barney had snapped short, and the ragged, sharp edge had caught him inside the hind leg and slit it to the bone from knee to near the belly. The dreadful wound stood yawning wide and a torrent of blood escaped. Doyle, bleeding copiously himself, bent under the roan. Almost frantically he clutched the gap and pressed the lips of the wound together while the horse stood dazed, head between forelegs, without a groan but quivering with pain and fright.

In the fire department men do their own wrecking as they do their own animal surgery and about everything else that is required. Not three minutes after the accident three fire companies were at work clearing the street.

Within a minute after the smash the official veterinary in his chief's wagon had rattled out of the hospital and training stables. He drove sharply, with roads clear and gong to warn way. He found they had taken Joe to his stall. A group of anxious-faced men surrounded him. Doyle, still bleeding, had held the rent and stanched the flow of blood. Hauk stood at the big, sick head, stroking the hot, soft nose. The intelligent brown eyes, recently so full of the fire of life, gleamed feverishly and were half closed in pain. It was evident the horse had been very badly hurt. The doctor crawled under the great belly and examined long and earnestly. Then he crawled forth and thoughtfully shook his head.

"Can't you do anything, Mac?" Hauk asked anxiously.

The veterinary shook his head again.

"I'm afraid I can only shoot him for you," he said quietly.

"Shoot nothing!" cried Doyle, almost forgetting his hold on the wound. "That horse saved my life a dozen times!"

"Patch him up for us, Mac," coaxed Hauk.

"Patch him up." "Sew him up, Doc." "Give him a chance, Chief," a dozen gruff voices pleaded. The surgeon gave a doubtful shrug, but took off his coat, rolled up his sleeves, and opened his black leather bag. He washed the wound with scrupulous care and sewed it, drawing the lips neatly together, and then he sprinkled iodoform and bound the leg round and round while the fine animal stood and swayed, faint with pain.

Even before the surgeon finished, the restless wheels within the wonderful department were at work. Wreck or no wreck, Joe or no Joe, Barney or no Barney, the district must be protected. The relief engine and two substitute horses came up the street on a trot and the new machine was backed into place. On the way it had passed the big, red box wagon, the horse ambulance, sent to take Joe. Doyle took the roan by the head, but he never budged. In vain he coaxed and patted and stroked. The big horse simply stretched forth his neck and stood stock-still. It seemed impossible to coax him, and none had heart to use the gad. "Stand by the other horses' heads; I'll move him," said Hauk, and struck the alarm. What happened then brought tears to the eyes of every man. With a heartbreaking half-cry, half-whinny, the gray-black giant tossed his head, darted, and with a pitiful limp galloped through the retreating men, ran to the front of the engine, passed his neck into the open collar and stood under the harness, ready for work. But there was no work just then. Doyle coaxed and patted to get him to move out of the house; but Joe did not want to go. He was perfectly satisfied to stay. He meant to stay. At last they got behind him and in front of him and pulled and shoved and gently urged until he stood in the ambulance, head bowed, tail squeezed tight, a picture of misery at his first ride.

"Good-dy, God dab you—code dack!" cried Doyle, weeping like a woman and waving his hat as the ambulance started away. Many passed thick fingers across their eyes that day, and Hauk, who was a Pennsylvania Dutchman, blew his nose violently.

It was an unending ride for Joe, way up to the hospital, but the wagon ran smoothly and easily, and it took him right into the building, where they lifted him in a sling onto an elevator which hoisted him to the top floor, where all was clean, smelling of tanbark and full of box stalls. He was taken into one of these. A long-wide piece of canvas was passed under his belly, brought together over his back, and hooked to two pairs of block and tackles fastened to roof beams. Then he was hoisted up until his two legs cleared the floor, and there he remained, day in and day out, week in and week out, for a long weary month. Every day the surgeon came and gently squeezed and washed and bandaged. Every day some one of his friends from the granite enginehouse came to visit him, to pat him, to talk to him, and to bring home good news. Twenty other horses, blacks, grays, sorrels, and bays (for in the fire department a good horse is a "good color") were in the stalls. But rarely anyone came to visit them. One of these, swathed to the eyes in bandages, was a victim of flames. Most suffered from sprains or wrenches or cuts or bruises and would recover and be sent back to duty. A few were very sick or very much hurt and, likely, would die or be put out of misery. Several there were that would recover only to be sold to coal dealers, icemen, truckmen, and even ragmen, who insisted not on flawless beasts—for the great city never squandered money on a big farm where its debt to the dumb might be paid.

Joe narrowly missed hauling coal or pulling a beer truck. It was weeks after the wound had healed before the stiffness went out of the leg and the livid red out of the long, hidden scar. It was a full month after this before he was returned to his company, where he had to kiss and shake hands all around, where they patted and petted him and said nice things to him, and where he took his old place, center, next Frank, to whom he talked throughout that blessed night, and next to a new Barney. New Barney was a fiery, scare-headed youngster, with material for a splendid firehorse in him, but he caused Joe a deal of trouble making him behave at hydrants and do his share of backing in the engine.

To tell in detail all Joe saw and experienced in five years in this busy station, where in one year were more accidents and narrow escapes than in fifteen in many another district, would fill quite a book. He saw a wall bulge and fall and bury a water tower, horses, men, wagon, and all. He saw two great, long hook-and-ladders meet head on, and the pole of one bury a foot into the breast of a luckless bay. He saw men and

women jump for their lives and saw them crushed and saw
them burned to death. He saw horses with heads smashed in
against the dreadful L road pillars. He saw others' bones
broken, and policemen stoop over and bring quick ease. He
saw a hundred other things, the most pitifully ludicrous of
all—one of Italy's sons in the rag business hurling invectives
at his steed while the animal pricked his ears to the old music
of gongs and bells, drew a deep breath of beloved coal gas out
of a passing stack, and, whinnying with delight, raced after the
fire engine, rusty stoves, rags, cowbells, and all.

Two blocks east of the firehouse the street dipped into a
steep, ugly decline, crossed an avenue traversed by a trolley-
car line, and graded sharply upward into a long, trying hill.
To take the heavy engine up this hill at a gallop it was necessary to come down the preceding slope on a dead run. There
was an ordinance requiring streetcars to come to a stand at
street crossings of fire companies; but the feat remained haz-
ardous.

Two-Sixty-five was answering an alarm on this street
early one afternoon. All forenoon a wet drizzle of snow had
fallen, covering the city with a white gauze and making the
pavement slippery. Even the three big horses, floundering
angrily, were unable to get a good footing, and as the great,
red, glittering machine rose to the brink of the hill, Doyle
glanced at the basin below and at the steep incline beyond the
tracks. Brake wide off he took the hill, the five tons gaining
more and more headway, horses stretched to their best,
pushed by the mountain behind and traveling at breakneck
speed. Hauk, looking ahead alongside the boiler, screeched
the whistle continuously in short, shrill blasts, and saw the
road was clear.

A great, yellow trolley car stood stock-still, waiting for
the engine to cross. An entire block separated the leviathans.
The car might have moved ahead and passed, with time to

spare. Down thundered the engine, scattering red coals and cinders, belching inky smoke and snorting steam, when the driver was horror-struck. The same impulse which seizes men to leap from precipices had seized a weak-minded man, the motorman. He turned on power and slowly, almost at a snail's pace, he forged his car ahead. A hundred feet away, Doyle saw he must plow through the car. He jammed the brake with all his might. He threw himself frantically on the reins. Upward shot the two tongues of the engine as the weight landed on necks and quarters. The horses fairly crouched to stem the load. Too late! Doyle, helpless, closed his eyes and prayed. Only the roan remained. With a desperate wrench and a frantic plunge, he brought his mates around. Six feet more and all might have escaped, passed the tail of the car. There was a bloodcurdling, grating, rasping crash of wood and glass and iron, like an explosion, the hiss of escaping steam mingled with shrieks of men and women. The big spring bell clanged wildly. The engine lay, turned over, hind wheel spinning in air.

Hauk and the engineer had jumped. Doyle, who never tied himself, had been hurled to the soft back of a horse and slid to the ground. But the team was done for.

Frank, in a tangle of harness, lay cut, dead as a doornail; new Barney, stripped of every vestige but his collar, lay thirty feet away, forelegs splintered; Joe, with a wide, deep cut across his splendid chest, struggled to rise, but fell back bleeding. Doyle and Hauk hobbled to the side of the dying horse. Doyle bent to the prostrate head. The animal had ceased to struggle. He did not seem in pain; but the great sides heaved deeply as his roving eyes riveted on his master, bloodred, his nostrils distended, begging air. The two men pulled off their coats, rolled them, raised the fine, brave head from the wet, icy stones and softly pillowed it. The driver stood gazing hopelessly at his dumb friend. It seemed as if the soft, brown eyes wanted to talk as the brave spirit was fleeing the flesh. They closed, but once again they sought their master. For a minute Doyle gazed—then he broke into tears.

And from the distance came the mad clang and clatter of the fire companies as they drove to clear the wreck.

Richard Harding Davis

THE MAN WHO COULD NOT LOSE

The Carters had married in haste and refused to repent at leisure. So blindly were they in love, that they considered their marriage their greatest asset. The rest of the world, as represented by mutual friends, considered it the only thing that could be urged against either of them. While single, each had been popular. As a bachelor, young "Champ" Carter had filled his modest place acceptably. Hostesses sought him for dinners and weekend parties, men of his own years for golf and tennis, and young girls liked him because when he talked to one of them he never talked of himself, or let his eyes wander toward any other girl. He had been brought up by a rich father in an expensive way, and the rich father had then died leaving Champneys alone in the world, with no money, and with even a few of his father's debts. These debts of honor the son, ever since leaving Yale, had been paying off. It had kept him very poor, for Carter had elected to live by his pen, and, though he wrote very carefully and slowly, the editors of the magazines had been equally careful and slow in accepting what he wrote.

With an income so uncertain that the only thing that could be said of it with certainty was that it was too small to support even himself, Carter should not have thought of matrimony. Nor, must it be said to his credit, did he think of it until the girl came along that he wanted to marry.

The trouble with Dolly Ingram was her mother. Her mother was a really terrible person. She was quite impossible. She was a social leader, and of such importance that visiting princes and society reporters, even among themselves, did not laugh at her. Her visiting list was so small that she did not keep a social secretary, but, it was said, wrote her invitations herself. Stylites on his pillar was less exclusive. Nor did he take his exalted but lonely position with less sense of humor. When Ingram died and left her many millions to dispose of absolutely as she pleased, even to the allowance she should give their daughter, he left her with but one ambition unfulfilled. That was to marry her Dolly to an English duke. Hungarian princes, French marquesses, Italian counts, German barons, Mrs. Ingram could not see. Her son-in-law must be a duke. She had her eyes on two, one somewhat shopworn, and the other a bankrupt; and in training, she had one just coming of age. Already she saw herself a sort of dowager duchess by marriage, discussing with real dowager duchesses the way to bring up teething earls and viscounts. For three years in Europe Mrs. Ingram had been drilling her daughter for the part she intended her to play. But, on returning to her native land, Dolly, who possessed all the feelings, thrills, and heartthrobs of which her mother was ignorant, ungratefully fell deeply in love with Champneys Carter, and he with her.

It was always a question of controversy between them as to which had first fallen in love with the other. As a matter of history, honors were even.

He first saw her during a thunderstorm, in the paddock at the races, wearing a raincoat with the collar turned up and a Panama hat with the brim turned down. She was talking, in terms of affectionate familiarity, with Cuthbert's two-year-old, The Scout. The Scout had just lost a race by a nose, and Dolly was holding the nose against her cheek and comforting him. The two made a charming picture, and, as Carter stumbled upon it and halted, the racehorse lowered his eyes and seemed to say: "Wouldn't *you* throw a race for this?" And the girl raised her eyes and seemed to say: "What a nice-looking, bright-looking young man! Why don't I know who you are?"

So, Carter ran to find Cuthbert, and told him The Scout had gone lame. When, on their return, Miss Ingram refused to loosen her hold on The Scout's nose, Cuthbert apologetically mumbled Carter's name, and in some awe Miss Ingram's name, and then, to his surprise, both young people lost interest in The Scout, and wandered away together into the rain.

After an hour, when they parted at the club stand, for which Carter could not afford a ticket, he asked wistfully: "Do you often come racing?" and Miss Ingram said: "Do you mean, am I coming tomorrow?"

"I do!" said Carter.

"Then, why didn't you say that?" inquired Miss Ingram. "Otherwise I mightn't have come. I have the Holland House coach for tomorrow, and, if you'll join us, I'll save a place for you, and you can sit in our box.

"I've lived so long abroad," she explained, "that I'm afraid of not being simple and direct like other American girls. Do you think I'll get on here at home?"

"If you get on with everyone else as well as you've got on with me," said Carter morosely, "I will shoot myself."

Miss Ingram smiled thoughtfully.

"At eleven, then," she said, "in front of the Holland House."

Carter walked away with a flurried, heated suffocation around his heart and a joyous lightness in his feet. Of the first man he met he demanded, who was the beautiful girl in the raincoat? And when the man told him, Carter left him without speaking. For she was quite the richest girl in America. But the next day that fault seemed to distress her so little that Carter, also, refused to allow it to rest on his conscience, and they were very happy. *And* each saw that they were happy because they were together.

The ridiculous mother was not present at the races, but after Carter began to call at their house and was invited to dinner, Mrs. Ingram received him with her habitual rudeness. As an impediment in the success of her ambition she never considered him. As a boyfriend of her daughter's, she classed him with "her" lawyer and "her" architect and a little higher than the "person" who arranged the flowers. Nor, in her turn, did Dolly consider her mother; for within two months another matter of controversy between Dolly and Carter was as to who had first proposed to the other. Carter protested there never had been any formal proposal, that from the first they had both taken it for granted that married they would be. But Dolly insisted that because he had been afraid of her money, or her mother, he had forced her to propose to him.

"You could not have loved me very much," she complained, "if you'd let a little thing like money make you hesitate."

"It's not a little thing," suggested Carter. "They say it's several millions, and it happens to be *yours*. If it were *mine*, now!"

"Money," said Dolly sententiously, "is given people to make them happy, not to make them miserable."

"Wait until I sell my stories to the magazines," said Carter, "and then I will be independent and can support you."

The plan did not strike Dolly as one likely to lead to a hasty marriage. But he was sensitive about his stories, and she did not wish to hurt his feelings.

"Let's get married first," she suggested, "and then I can *buy* you a magazine. We'll call it *Carter's Magazine* and we will print nothing in it but your stories. Then we can laugh at the editors!"

"Not half as loud as they will," said Carter.

With three thousand dollars in bank and three stories accepted and seventeen still to hear from, and with Dolly daily telling him that it was evident he did not love her, Carter decided they were ready, hand in hand, to leap into the sea of matrimony. His interview on the subject with Mrs. Ingram was most painful. It lasted during the time it took her to walk out of her drawing room to the foot of her staircase. She spoke to herself, and the only words of which Carter was sure were "preposterous" and "intolerable insolence." Later in the morning she sent a note to his flat, forbidding him not only her daughter, but the house in which her daughter lived, and even the use of the United States mails and the New York telephone wires. She described his conduct in words that, had they come from a man, would have afforded Carter every excuse for violent exercise.

Immediately in the wake of the note arrived Dolly, in tears, and carrying a dressing case.

"I have left mother!" she announced. "And I have her car downstairs, and a clergyman in it, unless he has run away. He doesn't want to marry us, because he's afraid mother will stop supporting his flower mission. You get your hat and take me where he can marry us. No mother can talk about the man I love the way mother talked about you, and think I won't marry him the same day!"

Carter, with her mother's handwriting still red before his eyes, and his self-love shaken with rage, flourished the letter.

"And no mother," he shouted, "can call *me* a fortune hunter and a cradle robber and think I'll make good by marrying her daughter! Not until she *begs* me to!"

Dolly swept toward him like a summer storm. Her eyes were wet and flashing.

"Until *who* begs you to?" she demanded. "*Who* are you marrying; mother or me?"

"If I marry you," cried Carter, frightened but also greatly excited, "your mother won't give you a penny!"

"And that," taunted Dolly, perfectly aware that she was ridiculous, "is why you won't marry me!"

For an instant, long enough to make her blush with shame and happiness, Carter grinned at her. "Now, just for that," he said, "I won't kiss you, and I *will* marry you!"

But, as a matter of fact, he *did* kiss her.

Then he gazed happily around his small sitting room.

"Make yourself at home here," he directed, "while I pack my bag."

"I *mean* to make myself very much at home here," said Dolly joyfully, "for the rest of my life."

From the recesses of the flat Carter called: "The rent's paid only till September. After that we live in a hall bedroom and cook on a gas stove. And that's no idle jest, either."

Fearing the publicity of the City Hall license bureau, they released the clergyman, much to the relief of that gentleman, and told the chauffeur to drive across the state line into Connecticut.

"It's the last time we can borrow your mother's car," said Carter, "and we'd better make it go as far as we can."

It was one of those days in May. Blue was the sky and

sunshine was in the air, and in the park little girls from the tenements, in white, were playing they were queens. Dolly wanted to kidnap two of them for bridesmaids. In Harlem they stopped at a jeweler's shop, and Carter got out and bought a wedding ring.

In the Bronx were dogwood blossoms and leaves of tender green and beds of tulips, and along the Boston Post Road, on their right, the Sound flashed in the sunlight; and on their left, gardens, lawns, and orchards ran with the road, and the apple trees were masses of pink and white.

Whenever a car approached from the rear, Carter pretended it was Mrs. Ingram coming to prevent the elopement, and Dolly clung to him. When the car had passed, she forgot to stop clinging to him.

In Greenwich village they procured a license, and a magistrate married them, and they were a little frightened and greatly happy, and, they both discovered simultaneously, outrageously hungry. So they drove through Bedford Village to South Salem, and lunched at the Horse and Hounds Inn, on blue and white china, in the same room where Major André was once a prisoner. And they felt very sorry for Major André, and for everybody who had not been just married that morning. And after lunch they sat outside in the garden and fed lumps of sugar to a charming collie and cream to a fat gray cat.

They decided to start housekeeping in Carter's flat, and so turned back to New York, this time following the old coach road through North Castle to White Plains, across to Tarrytown, and along the bank of the Hudson into Riverside Drive. Millions and millions of friendly folk, chiefly nursemaids and traffic policemen, waved to them, and for some reason smiled.

"The joke of it is," declared Carter, "they don't know! The most wonderful event of the century has just passed into history. We are married, and nobody knows!"

But when the car drove away from in front of Carter's door, they saw on top of it two old shoes and a sign reading: "We have just been married." While they had been at luncheon, the chauffeur had risen to the occasion.

"After all," said Carter soothingly, "he meant no harm. And it's the only thing about our wedding yet that seems legal."

Three months later two very unhappy young people faced starvation in the sitting room of Carter's flat. Gloom was written upon the countenance of each, and the heat and the care that comes when one desires to live, and lacks the wherewithal to fulfill that desire, had made them pallid and had drawn black lines under Dolly's eyes.

Mrs. Ingram had played her part exactly as her dearest friends had said she would. She had sent to Carter's flat, seven trunks filled with Dolly's clothes, eighteen hats, and another most unpleasant letter. In this, on the sole condition that Dolly would at once leave her husband, she offered to forgive and to support her.

To this Dolly composed eleven scornful answers, but finally decided that no answer at all was the most scornful.

She and Carter then proceeded joyfully to waste his three thousand dollars with that contempt for money with which on a honeymoon it should always be regarded. When there was no more, Dolly called upon her mother's lawyers and inquired if her father had left her anything in her own right. The lawyers regretted he had not, but having loved Dolly since she was born, offered to advance her any money she wanted. They said they felt sure her mother would "relent."

"*She* may," said Dolly haughtily. "*I* won't! And my husband can give me all I need. I only wanted something of my own, because I'm going to make him a surprise present of a new motorcar. The one we are using now does not suit us."

This was quite true, as the one they were then using ran through the subway.

As summer approached, Carter had suddenly awakened to the fact that he soon would be a pauper, and cut short the honeymoon. They returned to the flat, and he set forth to look for a position. Later, while still looking for it, he spoke of it as a "job." He first thought he would like to be an assistant editor of a magazine. But he found editors of magazines anxious to employ new and untried assistants, especially in June, were very few. On the contrary, they explained they were retrenching and cutting down expenses—they meant they had discharged all office boys who received more than three dollars a week. They further "retrenched," by taking a mean advantage of Carter's having called upon them in person, by handing him three of four of his stories—but by this he saved his postage stamps.

Each day, when he returned to the flat, Dolly, who always expected each editor would hastily dust off his chair and offer it to her brilliant husband, would smile excitedly and gasp, "Well?" and Carter would throw the rejected manuscripts on the table and say: "At least, I have not returned empty-handed." Then they would discover a magazine that neither they nor any one else knew existed, and they would hurriedly readdress the manuscripts to that periodical, and run to post them at the letter box on the corner.

"Any one of them, *if accepted,*" Carter would point out, "might bring us in twenty-five dollars. A story of mine once sold for forty; so tonight we can afford to dine at a restaurant where wine is *not* 'included.'"

Fortunately, they never lost their sense of humor. Otherwise the narrow confines of the flat, the evil smells that rose from the baked streets, the greasy food of Italian and Hungarian restaurants, and the ever-haunting need of money might have crushed their youthful spirits. But in time even they found that one, still less two, cannot exist exclusively on love and the power to see the bright side of things—especially when there is no bright side. They had come to the point where they must borrow money from their friends, and that, though there were many who would have opened their safes to them, they had agreed was the one thing they would not do, or they must starve. The alternative was equally distasteful.

Carter had struggled earnestly to find a job. But his inexperience and the season of the year were against him. No newspaper wanted a dramatic critic when the only shows in town had been running three months, and on roof gardens; nor did they want a cub reporter when veterans were being laid off by the dozens. Nor were his services desired as a private secretary, a taxicab driver, an agent to sell real estate or automobiles or stocks. As no one gave him a chance to prove his unfitness for any of these callings, the fact that he knew nothing of any of them did not greatly matter. At these rebuffs Dolly was distinctly pleased. She argued they proved he was intended to pursue his natural career as an author.

That their friends might know they were poor did not affect her, but she did not want them to think by his taking up any outside job that they were poor because as a literary genius he was a failure. She believed in his stories. She wanted everyone else to believe in them. Meanwhile, she assisted him insofar as she could by pawning the contents of five of the seven trunks, by learning to cook on a "kitchenette" and to launder her handkerchiefs and iron them on the looking glass.

They faced each other across the breakfast table. It was only nine o'clock, but the sun beat into the flat with the breath of a furnace, and the air was foul and humid.

"I tell you," Carter was saying fiercely, "you look ill. You *are* ill. You must go to the seashore. You must visit some of your proud friends at East Hampton or Newport. Then I'll know you're happy and I won't worry, and I'll find a job. *I* don't mind the heat—and I'll write you love letters"—he was talking very fast and not looking at Dolly—"like those I used to write you, before—"

Dolly raised her hand. "Listen!" she said. "Suppose I leave you. What will happen? I'll wake up in a cool, beautiful brass bed, won't I?—with cretonne window curtains, and salt air blowing them about, and a maid to bring me coffee. And instead of a bathroom like yours, next to an elevator shaft and a fire escape, I'll·have one as big as a church, and the whole blue ocean to swim in. And I'll sit on the rocks in the sunshine and watch the waves and the yachts—"

"And grow well again!" cried Carter. "But you'll write to me," he added wistfully, "every day, won't you?"

In her wrath, Dolly rose, and from across the table confronted him.

"And what will I be doing on those rocks?" she cried. "You *know* what I'll be doing! I'll be sobbing, and sobbing, and calling out to the waves: 'Why did he send me away? Why doesn't he want me? Because he doesn't love me. That's why! He doesn't *love* me!' And you *don't!*" cried Dolly. "You *don't!*"

It took him all of three minutes to persuade her she was mistaken.

"Very well, then," sobbed Dolly, "that's settled. And there'll be no more talk of sending me away!"

"There will *not!*" said Champneys hastily. "We will now," he announced, "go into committee of the whole and decide how we are to face financial failure. Our assets consist of two stories, accepted but not paid for, and fifteen stories *not* accepted. In cash"—he spread upon the table a meager collection of soiled bills and coins—"we have twenty-seven dollars and fourteen cents. That is every penny we possess in the world."

Dolly regarded him fixedly and shook her head.

"Is it wicked," she asked, "to love you *so*?"

"Haven't you been listening to me?" demanded Carter. Again Dolly shook her head.

"I was watching the way you talk. When your lips move fast they do such charming things."

"Do you know," roared Carter, "that we haven't a penny in the world, that we have nothing in this flat to eat?"

"I still have five hats," said Dolly.

"We can't eat hats," protested Champneys.

"We can *sell* hats!" returned Dolly. "They cost eighty dollars apiece!"

"When you need money," explained Carter, "I find it's just as hard to sell a hat as to eat it."

"Twenty-seven dollars and fourteen cents," repeated Dolly. She exclaimed remorsefully: "And you started with three thousand! What did I do with it?"

"We both had the time of our lives with it!" said Carter stoutly. "And that's all there is to that. Postmortems," he pointed out, "are useful only as guides to the future, and as our future will never hold a second three thousand dollars, we needn't worry about how we spent the first one. No! What we must consider now is how we can grow rich quick, and the quicker and richer, the better. Pawning our clothes, or what's left of them, is bad economics. There's no use considering how to live from meal to meal. We must evolve something big, picturesque, that will bring a fortune. You have imagination; I'm supposed to have imagination; we must think of a plan to get money, much money. I do not insist on our plan being dignified, or even outwardly respectable; so long as it keeps you alive, it may be as desperate as—"

"I see!" cried Dolly; "like sending mother Black Hand letters!"

"Blackmail—" began that lady's son-in-law doubtfully.

"Or!" cried Dolly, "we might kidnap Mr. Carnegie when he's walking in the park alone, and hold him for ransom. Or"—she rushed on—"we might forge a codicil to father's will, and make it say if mother shouldn't like the man I want to marry, all of father's fortune must go to my husband!"

"Forgery," exclaimed Champneys, "is going further than I—"

"And another plan," interrupted Dolly, "that I have always had in mind, is to issue a cheaper edition of your book, *The Dead Heat.* The reason the first edition of *The Dead Heat* didn't sell—"

"Don't tell *me* why it didn't sell," said Champneys. "I wrote it!"

"That book," declared Dolly loyally, "was never properly advertised. No one knew about it, so no one bought it!"

"Eleven people bought it!" corrected the author.

"We will put it in a paper cover and sell it for fifty cents," cried Dolly. "It's the best detective story I ever read, and people have got to know it is the best. So we'll advertise it like a breakfast food."

"The idea," interrupted Champneys, "is to make money, not throw it away. Besides, we haven't any to throw away."

Dolly sighed bitterly.

"If only," she exclaimed, "we had that three thousand dollars back again! I'd save *so* carefully. It was all my fault. The races took it, but it was *I* took you to the races."

"No one ever had to drag *me* to the races," said Carter. "It was the way we went that was extravagant. Automobiles by the hour standing idle, and a box each day, and—"

"And always backing Dromedary," suggested Dolly.

Carter was touched on a sensitive spot.

"That horse," he protested loudly, "is a mighty good horse. Some day—"

"That's what you always said," remarked Dolly, "but he never seems to have his day."

"It's strange," said Champneys consciously. "I dreamed of Dromedary only last night. Same dream over and over again."

Hastily he changed the subject.

"For some reason I don't sleep well. I don't know why."

Dolly looked at him with all the love in her eyes of a mother over her ailing infant.

"It's worrying over me, and the heat," she said. "And the garage next door, and the skyscraper going up across the street, might have something to do with it. And *you,*" she mocked tenderly, "wanted to send *me* to the seashore."

Carter was frowning. As though about to speak, he opened his lips, and then laughed embarrassedly.

"Out with it," said Dolly, with an encouraging smile. "Did he win?"

Seeing she had read what was in his mind, Carter leaned forward eagerly. The ruling passion and a touch of superstition held him in their grip.

"He 'wins' each time," he whispered. "I saw it as plain as I see you. Each time he came up with a rush just at the same place, just as they entered the stretch, and each time he won!" He slapped his hand disdainfully upon the dirty bills before him. "If I had a hundred dollars!"

There was a knock at the door, and Carter opened it to the elevator boy with the morning mail. The letters, save one, Carter dropped upon the table. That one, with clumsy fingers, he tore open. He exclaimed breathlessly: "It's from *Plympton's Magazine*! Maybe—I've sold a story!" He gave a cry almost of alarm. His voice was as solemn as though the letter had announced a death.

"Dolly," he whispered, "it's a check—a check for a *hundred dollars*!"

Guiltily, the two young people looked at each other.

"We've *got* to!" breathed Dolly. "*Got* to! If we let *two* signs like that pass, we'd be flying in the face of Providence."

With her hands gripping the arms of her chair, she leaned forward, her eyes staring into space, her lips moving.

"*Come on,* you Dromedary!" she whispered.

They changed the check into five- and ten-dollar bills, and, as Carter was far too excited to work, made an absurdly early start for the racetrack.

"We might as well get all the fresh air we can," said Dolly. "That's all we will get!"

From their reserve fund of twenty-seven dollars, which each had solemnly agreed with the other would not be risked on racehorses, Dolly subtracted a two-dollar bill. This she stuck conspicuously across the face of the clock on the mantel.

"Why?" asked Carter.

"When we get back this evening," Dolly explained, "that will be the first thing we'll see. It's going to look awfully good!"

This day there was no scarlet car to rush them with refreshing swiftness through Brooklyn's parkways and along the Ocean Avenue. Instead, they hung to a strap in a crosstown car, changed to the ferry, and again to the Long Island Railroad. When Carter halted at the special car of the Turf Club, Dolly took his arm and led him forward to the day coach.

"But," protested Carter, "when you're spending a hundred dollars with one hand, why grudge fifty cents for a parlor-car seat? If you're going to be a sport, be a sport."

"And if you've got to be a piker," said Dolly, "don't be ashamed to be a piker. We're not spending a hundred dollars because we can afford it, but because you dreamt a dream. You didn't dream you were riding in parlor cars! If you did, it's time I woke you."

This day there was for them no box overlooking the finish, no clubhouse luncheon. With the other pikers, they sat in the free seats, with those who sat coatless and tucked their handkerchiefs inside their collars, and with those who mopped their perspiring countenances with rice paper and marked their cards with a hatpin. Their lunch consisted of a massive ham sandwich with a top dressing of mustard.

Dromedary did not run until the fifth race, and the long wait, before they could learn their fate, was intolerable. They knew most of the horses, and, to pass the time, on each of the first races Dolly made imaginary bets. Of these mental wagers, she lost every one.

"If you turn out to be as bad a guesser when you're asleep as I am when I'm awake," said Dolly, "we're going to lose our fortune."

"I'm weakening!" declared Carter. "A hundred dollars is beginning to look to me like an awful lot of money. Twenty-seven dollars—and there's only twenty of *that* left now—is mighty small capital, but twenty dollars *plus* a hundred could keep us alive for a month!"

"Did you, or did you not, dream that Dromedary would win?" demanded Dolly sternly.

"I certainly did, several times," said Carter. "But it may be I was thinking of the horse. I've lost such a lot on him, my mind may have—"

"Did you," interrupted Dolly, "say if you had a hundred dollars you'd bet it, *and* did a hundred dollars walk in through the door instantly?"

Carter, reassured, breathed again.

"It certainly did!" he repeated.

Even in his proud days, Carter had never been able to bet heavily, and instead of troubling the clubhouse commissioners with his small wagers, he had, in the ring, bet ready money. Moreover, he believed in the ring he obtained more favorable odds, and, when he won, it pleased him, instead of waiting until settling day for a check, to stand in a line and feel the real money thrust into his hand. So, when the fourth race started he rose and raised his hat.

"The time has come," he said.

Without looking at him, Dolly nodded. She was far too tremulous to speak.

For several weeks Dromedary had not been placed, and Carter hoped for odds of at least ten to one. But, when he pushed his way into the arena, he found so little was thought of his choice that as high as twenty to one was being offered, and with few takers. The fact shattered his confidence. Here were two hundred bookmakers, trained to their calling, anxious at absurd odds to back their opinion that the horse he liked could not win. In the face of such unanimous contempt, his dream became fantastic, fatuous. He decided he would risk only half of his fortune. Then, should the horse win, he still would be passing rich, and should he lose, he would, at least, have all of fifty dollars.

With a bookmaker he wagered that sum, and then, in unhappy indecision, stood, in one hand clutching his ticket that called for a potential thousand and fifty dollars, and in the other an actual fifty. It was not a place for meditation. From every side men, more or less sane, swept upon him, jostled him, and stamped upon him, and still, struggling for a foothold, he swayed, hesitating. Then he became conscious that the ring was nearly empty, that only a few shrieking individuals still ran down the line. The horses were going to the post. He must decide quickly. In front of him the bookmaker cleaned his board, and, as a final appeal, opposite the names of three horses chalked thirty to one. Dromedary was among them. Such odds could not be resisted. Carter shoved his fifty at the man, and to that sum added the twenty dollars still in his pocket. They were the last dollars he owned in the world. And though he knew they were his last, he was fearful lest the bookmaker would refuse them. But, mechanically, the man passed them over his shoulder.

"And twenty-one hundred to seventy," he chanted.

When Carter took his seat beside Dolly, he was quite cold. Still, Dolly did not speak. Out of the corner of her eyes she questioned him.

"I got fifty at twenty to one," replied Carter, "and seventy at thirty!"

In alarm, Dolly turned upon him.

"Seventy!" she gasped.

Carter nodded. "All we have," he said. "We have sixty cents left, to start life over again!"

As though to encourage him, Dolly placed her finger on her race card.

"His colors," she said, "are green cap, green jacket, green and white hoops."

Through a maze of heat, a half-mile distant, at the starting gate, little spots of color moved in impatient circles. The big, good-natured crowd had grown silent, so silent that from the high, sun-warmed grass in the infield one could hear the lazy chirp of the crickets.

As though repeating a prayer, or an incantation, Dolly's lips were moving quickly.

"Green cap," she whispered, "green jacket, green and white hoops!"

With a sharp sigh the crowd broke the silence. "They're off!" it cried, and leaned forward expectant.

The horses came so fast. To Carter their conduct seemed outrageous. It was incredible that in so short a time, at a pace so reckless, they would decide a question of such moment. They came bunched together, shifting and changing, with, through the dust, flashes of blue and gold and scarlet. A jacket of yellow shot out of the dust and showed in front; a jacket of crimson followed. So they were at the half; so they were at the three-quarters.

The good-natured crowd began to sway, to grumble and murmur, then to shout in sharp staccato.

"Can you see him?" begged Dolly.

"No," said Carter. "You *don't* see him until they reach the stretch."

One could hear their hooves, could see the crimson jockey draw his whip. At the sight, for he rode the favorite, the crowd gave a great gasp of concern.

"Oh, you Gold Heels!" it implored.

Under the whip, Gold Heels drew even with the yellow jacket; stride by stride, they fought it out alone.

"Gold Heels!" cried the crowd.

Behind them, in a curtain of dust, pounded the field. It charged in a flying wedge, like a troop of cavalry. Dolly, searching for a green jacket, saw, instead, a rainbow wave of color that, as it rose and fell, sprang toward her in great leaps, swallowing the track.

"Gold Heels!" yelled the crowd.

The field swept into the stretch. Without moving his eyes, Carter caught Dolly by the wrist and pointed. As though giving a signal, he shot his free hand into the air.

"Now!" he shouted.

From the curtain of dust, as lightning strikes through a cloud, darted a great, rawboned, ugly chestnut. Like the Empire Express, he came rocking, thundering, spurning the ground. At his coming, Gold Heels, to the eyes of the crowd, seemed to falter, to slacken, to stand still. The crowd gave a great cry of amazement, a yell of disgust. The chestnut drew even with Gold Heels, passed him, and swept under the wire. Clinging to his neck was a little jockey in a green cap, green jacket, and hoops of green and white.

Dolly's hand was at her side, clutching the bench. Carter's hand still clasped it. Neither spoke or looked at the other. For an instant, while the crowd, no longer so good-natured, mocked and jeered at itself, the two young people sat quite still, staring at the green field, at the white clouds rolling from the ocean. Dolly drew a long breath.

"Let's go!" she gasped. "Let's thank him first, and then—*take me home!*"

They found Dromedary in the paddock, and thanked him, and Carter left Dolly with him, while he ran to collect his winnings. When he returned, he showed her a sheaf of yellow bills, and as they ran down the covered boardwalk to the gate, they skipped and danced.

Dolly turned toward the train drawn up at the entrance.

"Not with me!" shouted Carter. "We're going home in the reddest, most expensive, fastest automobile I can hire!"

In the "hack" line of motorcars was one that answered those requirements, and they fell into it as though it were their own.

"To the Night and Day Bank!" commanded Carter.

With the genial democracy of the racetrack, the chauffeur lifted his head to grin appreciatively.

"That listens good to me!" he said.

"I like him!" whispered Dolly. "Let's buy him and the car."

On the way home, they bought many cars; every car they saw, that they liked, they bought. They bought, also, several houses, and a yacht that they saw from the ferryboat. And as soon as they had deposited most of their money in the bank, they went to a pawnshop on Sixth Avenue and bought back many possessions that they had feared they never would see again.

When they entered the flat, the thing they first beheld was Dolly's two-dollar bill.

"What," demanded Carter, with repugnance, "is that strange piece of paper?"

Dolly examined it carefully.

"I think it is a kind of money," she said, "used by the lower classes."

They dined on the roof at Delmonico's. Dolly wore the largest of the five hats still unsold, and Carter selected the dishes entirely according to which was the most expensive. Every now and again they would look anxiously down across the street at the bank that held their money. They were nervous lest it should take fire.

"We can be extravagant tonight," said Dolly, "because we owe it to Dromedary to celebrate. But from tonight on we must save. We've had an awful lesson. What happened to us last month must never happen again. We were down to a two-dollar bill. Now we have twenty-five hundred across the street, and you have several hundreds in your pocket. On that we can live easily for a year. Meanwhile, you can write the great American novel without having to worry about money, or to look for a steady job. And then your book will come out, and you will be famous, and rich, and—"

"Passing on from that," interrupted Carter, "the thing of first importance is to get you out of that hot, beastly flat. I propose we start tomorrow for Cape Cod. I know a lot of fishing villages there where we could board and lodge for twelve dollars a week, and row and play tennis and live in our bathing suits."

Dolly assented with enthusiasm, and during the courses of the dinner they happily discussed Cape Cod from Pocasset to Yarmouth, and from Sandwich to Provincetown. So eager were they to escape, that Carter telephoned the hallman at his club to secure a cabin for the next afternoon on the Fall River boat.

As they sat over their coffee in the cool breeze, with in the air the scent of flowers and the swing of music, and with at their feet the lights of the great city, the world seemed very bright.

"It has been a great day," sighed Carter. "And if I hadn't had nervous prostration I would have enjoyed it. That race-course is always cool, and there were some fine finishes. I noticed two horses that would bear watching, Her Highness and Glowworm. If we weren't leaving tomorrow, I'd be inclined—"

Dolly regarded him with eyes of horror.

"Champneys Carter!" she exclaimed. As she said it, it sounded like "Great Jehoshaphat!"

Carter protested indignantly. "I only said," he explained, *"if* I *were* following the races, I'd watch those horses. Don't worry!" he exclaimed. "I know when to stop."

The next morning they took breakfast on the tiny terrace of a restaurant overlooking Bryant Park, where, during the first days of their honeymoon, they had always breakfasted. For sentimental reasons they now revisited it. But Dolly was eager to return at once to the flat and pack, and Carter seemed distrait. He explained that he had had a bad night.

"I'm *so* sorry," sympathized Dolly, "but tonight you will have a fine sleep going up the Sound. Any more nightmares?" she asked.

"Nightmares!" exploded Carter fiercely. "Nightmares they certainly were! I dreamt two of the nightmares won! I saw them, all night, just as I saw Dromedary—Her Highness and Glowworm, winning, winning, winning!"

"Those were the horses you spoke about last night," said Dolly severely. "After so wonderful a day, of course you dreamt of racing, and those two horses were in your mind. That's the explanation."

They returned to the flat and began, industriously, to pack. About twelve o'clock Carter, coming suddenly into the bedroom where Dolly was alone, found her reading the *Morning Telegraph.* It was open at the racing page of "past performances."

She dropped the paper guiltily. Carter kicked a hatbox out of his way and sat down on a trunk.

"I don't see," he began, "why we can't wait one more

day. We'd be just as near the ocean at Sheepshead Bay race track as on a Fall River boat, and—"

He halted and frowned unhappily. "We needn't bet more than ten dollars," he begged.

"Of course," declared Dolly, "if they *should* win, you'll always blame *me*!"

Carter's eyes shone hopefully.

"And," continued Dolly, "I can't bear to have you blame me. So—"

"Get your hat!" shouted Carter, "or we'll miss the first race."

Carter telephoned for a cab, and as they were entering it said guiltily: "I've got to stop at the bank."

"You have *not*!" announced Dolly. "That money is to keep us alive while you write the great American novel. I'm glad to spend another day at the races, and I'm willing to back your dreams as far as ten dollars, but for no more."

"If my dreams come true," warned Carter, "you'll be awfully sorry."

"Not I," said Dolly. "I'll merely send you to bed, and you can go on dreaming."

When Her Highness romped home, an easy winner, the look Dolly turned upon her husband was one both of fear and dismay.

"I don't like it!" she gasped. "It's—it's *uncanny*. It gives me a creepy feeling. It makes you seem sort of supernatural. And oh," she cried, "if only I had let you bet all you had with you!"

"I did," stammered Carter, in extreme agitation. "I bet four hundred. I got five to one, Dolly," he gasped, in awe. "We've won two thousand dollars."

Dolly exclaimed rapturously:

"We'll put it all in bank," she cried.

"We'll put it all on Glowworm!" said her husband.

"Champ!" begged Dolly. "Don't push your luck. Stop while—"

Carter shook his head.

"It's *not* luck!" he growled. "It's a gift, it's second sight, it's prophecy. I've been a full-fledged clairvoyant all my life, and didn't know it. Anyway, I'm a sport, and after two of my dreams breaking right, I've got to back the third one!"

Glowworm was at ten to one, and at those odds the bookmakers to whom he first applied did not care to take so large a sum as he offered. Carter found a bookmaker named Sol Burbank who, at those odds, accepted his two thousand.

When Carter returned to collect his twenty-two thousand, there was some little delay while Burbank borrowed a portion of it. He looked at Carter curiously and none too genially.

"Wasn't it you," he asked, "that had that thirty-to-one shot yesterday on Dromedary?"

Carter nodded somewhat guiltily. A man in the crowd volunteered: "And he had Her Highness in the second, too, for four hundred."

"You've made a good day," said Burbank. "Give me a chance to get my money back tomorrow."

"I'm sorry," said Carter. "I'm leaving New York tomorrow."

The same scarlet car bore them back triumphant to the bank.

"Twenty-two thousand dollars?" gasped Carter. *"In cash!* How in the name of all that's honest can we celebrate winning twenty-two thousand dollars? We can't eat more than one dinner; we can't drink more than two quarts of champagne— not without serious results."

"I'll tell you what we *can* do!" cried Dolly excitedly. "We can sail tomorrow on the *Campania*!"

"Hurrah!" shouted Carter. "We'll have a second honeymoon. We'll shoot up London and Paris. We'll tear slices out of the map of Europe. You'll ride in one motorcar, I'll ride in another, we'll have a maid and a valet in a third, and we'll race each other all the way to Monte Carlo. And, there, I'll dream of the winning numbers, and we'll break the bank. When does the *Campania* sail?"

"At noon," said Dolly.

"At eight we will be on board," said Carter.

But that night in his dreams he saw King Pepper, Confederate, and Red Wing each win a race. And in the morning neither the engines of the *Campania* nor the entreaties of Dolly could keep him from the racetrack.

"I want only six thousand," he protested. "You can do what you like with the rest, but I am going to bet six thousand on the first one of those three to start. If he loses, I give you my word I'll not bet another cent, and we'll sail on Saturday. If he wins out, I'll put all I make on the two others."

"Can't you see," begged Dolly, "that your dreams are just a rehash of what you think during the day? You have been playing in wonderful luck, that's all. Each of those horses is likely to win his race. When he does you will have more faith than ever in your silly dreams—"

"My silly dreams," said Carter grinning, "are carrying you to Europe, first class, by the next steamer."

They had been talking while on their way to the bank. When Dolly saw she could not alter his purpose, she made him place the nineteen thousand that remained, after he had taken out the six thousand, in her name. She then drew out the entire amount.

"You told me," said Dolly, smiling anxiously, "I could do what I liked with it. Maybe I have dreams also. Maybe I mean to back them."

She drove away, mysteriously refusing to tell him what she intended to do. When they met at luncheon, she was still much excited, still bristling with a concealed secret.

"Did you back your dream?" asked Carter.

Dolly nodded happily.

"And when am I to know?"

"You will read of it," said Dolly, "tomorrow, in the morning papers. It's all quite correct. My lawyers arranged it."

"Lawyers!" gasped her husband. "You're not arranging to lock me in a private madhouse, are you?"

"No," laughed Dolly, "but when I told them how I intended to invest the money they came near putting *me* there."

"Didn't they want to know how you suddenly got so rich?" asked Carter.

"They did. I told them it came from my husband's 'books'! It was a very 'near' falsehood."

"It was worse," said Carter. "It was a very poor pun."

As in their honeymoon days they drove proudly to the track, and when Carter had placed Dolly in a box large enough for twenty, he pushed his way into the crowd around the stand of Sol Burbank. That veteran of the turf welcomed him gladly.

"Coming to give me my money back?" he called.

"No, to take some away," said Carter, handing him his six thousand.

Without apparently looking at it, Burbank passed it to his cashier. "King Pepper, twelve to six thousand," he called.

When King Pepper won, and Carter moved around the ring with eighteen thousand dollars in thousand-and five-hundred-dollar bills in his fist, he found himself beset by a crowd of curious, eager pikers. They both impeded his operations and acted as a bodyguard. Confederate was an almost prohibitive favorite at one to three, and in placing eighteen thousand that he might win six, Carter found little difficulty. When Confederate won, and he started with his twenty-four thousand to back Red Wing, the crowd now engulfed him.

Men and boys who when they wagered five and ten dollars were risking their all, found in the sight of a young man offering bets in hundreds and thousands a thrilling and fascinating spectacle. To learn what horse he was playing and at what odds, racing touts and runners for other bookmakers and individual speculators leaped into the mob that surrounded him, and then, squirming their way out, ran shrieking down the line. In ten minutes, through the bets of Carter and those that backed his luck, the odds against Red Wing were forced down from fifteen to one to even money. His approach was hailed by the bookmakers either with jeers or with shouts of welcome. Those who had lost demanded a chance to regain their money. Those with whom he had not bet, found in that fact consolation, and chaffed the losers. Some curtly refused even the smallest part of his money. "Not with me!" they laughed. From stand to stand the layers of odds taunted him, or each other. "Don't touch it, it's tainted!" they shouted. "Look out, Joe, he's the Jonah man!" Or, "Come at me again!" they called. "And, once more!" they challenged as they reached for a thousand-dollar bill.

And, when in time, each shook his head and grumbled: "That's all I want," or looked the other way, the mob around Carter jeered. "He's fought 'em to a standstill!" they shouted jubilantly. In their eyes a man who alone was able and willing to wipe the name of a horse off the blackboards was a hero.

To the horror of Dolly, instead of watching the horses parade past, the crowd gathered in front of her box and pointed and stared at her. From the clubhouse her men friends and acquaintances invaded it.

"Has Carter gone mad?" they demanded. "He's dealing out thousand-dollar bills like cigarettes. He's turned the ring into a wheat pit!"

When he reached the box a sunburned man in a sombrero blocked his way.

"I'm the owner of Red Wing," he explained, "bred him and trained him myself. I know he'll be lucky if he gets the place. You're backing him in thousands to *win*. What do you know about him?"

"Know he will win," said Carter.

The veteran commissioner of the club stand buttonholed him. "Mr. Carter," he begged, "why don't you bet through me? I'll give you as good odds as they will in that ring. You don't want your clothes torn off you and your money taken from you."

"They haven't taken such a lot of it yet," said Carter.

When Red Wing won, the crowd beneath the box, the men in the box, and the people standing around it, most of whom had followed Carter's plunge, cheered and fell over him, to shake hands and pound him on the back. From every side excited photographers pointed cameras, and Lander's band played: "Every Little Bit Added to What You've Got Makes Just a Little Bit More." As he left the box to collect his money, a big man with a brown mustache and two smooth-shaven giants closed in around him, as tackles interfere for the man who has the ball. The big man took him by the arm. Carter shook himself free.

"What's the idea?" he demanded.

"I'm Pinkerton," said the big man genially. "You need a bodyguard. If you've got an empty seat in your car, I'll drive home with you."

From Cavanaugh they borrowed a bookmaker's handbag and stuffed it with thousand-dollar bills. When they stepped into the car the crowd still surrounded them.

"He's taking it home in a trunk!" they yelled.

That night the "sporting extras" of the afternoon papers gave prominence to the luck at the races of Champneys Carter.

From Cavanaugh and the bookmakers, the racing reporters had gathered accounts of his winnings. They stated that in three successive days, starting with one hundred dollars, he had at the end of the third day not lost a single bet, and that afternoon, on the last race alone, he had won sixty to seventy thousand dollars. With the text, they ran pictures of Carter at the track, of Dolly in her box, and of Mrs. Ingram in a tiara and ball dress.

"Mother-in-law *will* be pleased!" cried Carter.

In some alarm as to what the newspapers might say on the morrow, he ordered that in the morning a copy of each be sent to his room. That night in his dreams he saw clouds of dust-covered jackets and horses with sweating flanks, and one of them named Ambitious led all the rest. When he woke, he said to Dolly: "That horse Ambitious will win today."

"He can do just as he likes about *that*!" replied Dolly. "I have something on my mind much more important than horse racing. Today you are to learn how I spent your money. It's to be in the morning papers."

When he came to breakfast, Dolly was on her knees. For his inspection she had spread the newspapers on the floor, opened at an advertisement that appeared in each. In the center of a half page of white paper were the lines:

SOLD OUT IN ONE DAY!

ENTIRE FIRST EDITION

THE DEAD HEAT
BY
CHAMPNEYS CARTER

SECOND EDITION ONE HUNDRED THOUSAND

"In Heaven's name!" roared Carter. "What does this mean?"

"It means," cried Dolly tremulously, "I'm backing my dream. I've always believed in your book. Now I'm backing it. Our lawyers sent me to an advertising agent. His name is Spink, and he is awfully clever. I asked him if he could advertise a book so as to make it sell. He said with my money and his ideas he could sell last year's telephone book to people who did not own a telephone, and who had never learned to read. He is proud of his ideas. One of them was buying out the first edition. Your publishers told him your book was 'waste paper,' and that he could have every copy in stock for the cost of the plates. So he bought the whole edition. That's how it was sold out in one day. Then we ordered a second edition of one hundred thousand, and they're printing it now. The presses have been working all night to meet the demand!"

"But," cried Carter, "there *isn't* any demand!"

"There will be," said Dolly, "when five million people read our advertisements."

She dragged him to the window and pointed triumphantly into the street.

"See that!" she said. "Mr. Spink sent them here for me to inspect."

Drawn up in a line that stretched from Fifth Avenue to Broadway were an army of sandwich men. On the boards they carried were the words: "READ *THE DEAD HEAT*. SECOND EDITION. ONE HUNDRED THOUSAND!" On the fence in front of the building going up across the street, in letters a foot high, Carter again read the name of his novel. In letters in size more modest, but in colors more defiant, it glared at him from ash cans and barrels.

"How much does this cost?" he gasped.

"It cost every dollar you had in bank," said Dolly, "and before we are through it will cost you twice as much more. Mr. Spink is only waiting to hear from me before he starts spending fifty thousand dollars; that's only half of what you won on Red Wing. I'm only waiting for you to make me out a check before I tell Spink to start spending it."

In a dazed state Carter drew a check for fifty thousand dollars and meekly handed it to his wife. They carried it themselves to the office of Mr. Spink. On their way, on every side they saw evidences of his handiwork. On walls, on scaffolding, on billboards were advertisements of *The Dead Heat.* Over Madison Square a huge kite as large as a Zeppelin airship painted the name of the book against the sky, on "dodgers" it floated in the air, on handbills it stared up from the gutters.

Mr. Spink was a nervous young man with a bald head and eyeglasses. He grasped the check as a general might welcome fifty thousand fresh troops.

"Reinforcements!" he cried. "Now watch me. Now I can do things that are big, national, Napoleonic. We can't get those books bound inside of a week, but meanwhile orders will be pouring in, people will be growing crazy for it. Every man, woman, and child in Greater New York will want a copy. I've sent out fifty boys dressed as jockeys on horseback to ride neck and neck up and down every avenue. *THE DEAD HEAT* is printed on the saddlecloth. Half of them have been arrested already. It's a little idea of my own."

"But," protested Carter, "it's not a racing story, it's a detective story!"

"The devil it is!" gasped Spink. "But what's the difference!" he exclaimed. "They've got to buy it anyway. They'd buy it if it was a cookbook. And, I say," he cried delightedly, "that's great press work you're doing for the book at the races! The papers are full of you this morning, and every man who reads about your luck at the track will see your name as the author of *The Dead Heat,* and will rush to buy the book. He'll think *The Dead Heat* is a guide to the turf!"

When Carter reached the track he found his notoriety had preceded him. Ambitious did not run until the fourth race, and until then, as he sat in his box, an eager crowd surged below. He had never known such popularity. The crowd had read the newspapers, and such headlines as HE CANNOT LOSE! YOUNG CARTER WINS $70,000! BOY PLUNGER WINS AGAIN! CARTER MAKES BIG KILLING! THE RING HIT HARD! THE MAN WHO CANNOT LOSE! CARTER BEATS BOOKMAKERS! had whetted their curiosity and filled many with absolute faith in his luck. Men he had not seen in years grasped him by the hand and carelessly asked if he could tell of something good. Friends old and new begged him to dine with them, to immediately have a drink with them, at least to "try" a cigar. Men who protested they had lost their all begged for just a hint which would help them to come out even, and everyone, without exception, assured him he was going to buy his latest book.

"I tried to get it last night at a dozen newsstands," many of them said, "but they told me the entire edition was exhausted."

The crowd of hungry-eyed racegoers waiting below the box, and watching Carter's every movement, distressed Dolly.

"I hate it!" she cried. "They look at you like a lot of starved dogs begging for a bone. Let's go home; we don't want to make any more money, and we may lose what we have. And I want it all to advertise the book."

"If you're not careful," said Carter, "someone will buy that book and read it, and then you and Spink will have to take shelter in a cyclone cellar."

When he arose to make his bet on Ambitious, his friends from the club stand and a half-dozen of Pinkerton's men closed in around him and in a flying wedge pushed into the ring. The newspapers had done their work, and he was instantly surrounded by a hungry, howling mob. In comparison with the one of the previous day, it was as a football scrimmage to a run on a bank. When he made his first wager and the crowd learned the name of the horse, it broke with a yell into hundreds of flying missiles which hurled themselves at the bookmakers. Under their attack, as on the day before, Ambitious receded to even money. There was hardly a person at the track who did not back the luck of the man who "could not lose." And when Ambitious won easily, it was not the horse or his jockey that was cheered, but the young man in the box.

In New York the extras had already announced that he was again lucky, and when Dolly and Carter reached the bank they found the entire staff on hand to receive him and his winnings. They amounted to a sum so magnificent that Carter found for the rest of their lives the interest would furnish Dolly and himself an income upon which they could live modestly and well.

A distinguished-looking, white-haired official of the bank congratulated Carter warmly. "Should you wish to invest some of this," he said, "I should be glad to advise you. My knowledge in that direction may be wider than your own."

Carter murmured his thanks. The white-haired gentleman lowered his voice.

"On certain other subjects," he continued, "you know many things of which I am totally ignorant. Could you tell me," he asked carelessly, "who will win the Suburban tomorrow?"

Carter frowned mysteriously. "I can tell you better in the morning," he said. "It looks like Beldame, with Proper and First Mason within call."

The white-haired man showed his surprise and also that his ignorance was not as profound as he suggested.

"I thought the Keene entry—" he ventured.

"I know," said Carter doubtfully. "If it were for a mile, I would say Delhi, but I don't think he can last the distance. In the morning I'll wire you."

As they settled back in their car, Carter took both of Dolly's hands in his. "So far as money goes," he said, "we are independent of your mother—independent of my books; and I want to make you a promise. I want to promise you that, no matter what I dream in the future, I'll never back another horse."

Dolly gave a gasp of satisfaction.

"And what's more," added Carter hastily, "not another dollar can you risk in backing my books. After this, they've got to stand or fall on their legs!"

"Agreed!" cried Dolly. "Our plunging days are over."

When they reached the flat they found waiting for Carter the junior partner of a real publishing house. He had a blank contract, and he wanted to secure the right to publish Carter's next book.

"I have a few short stories . . . ," suggested Carter.

"Collections of short stories," protested the visitor truthfully, "do not sell. We would prefer another novel on the same lines as *The Dead Heat.*"

"Have you read *The Dead Heat?*" asked Carter.

"I have not," admitted the publisher, "but the next book by the same author is sure to— We will pay in advance of royalties fifteen thousand dollars."

"Could you put that in writing?" asked Carter. When the publisher was leaving, he said:

"I see your success in literature is equaled by your success at the races. Could you tell me what will win the Suburban?"

"I will send you a wire in the *morning,*" said Carter.

They had arranged to dine with some friends and later to visit a musical comedy. Carter had changed his clothes, and, while he was waiting for Dolly to dress, was reclining in a huge armchair. The heat of the day, the excitement, and the wear on his nerves caused his head to sink back, his eyes to close, and his limbs to relax.

When, by her entrance, Dolly woke him, he jumped up in some confusion.

"You've been asleep," she mocked.

"Worse!" said Carter. "I've been dreaming! Shall I tell you who is going to win the Suburban?"

"Champneys!" cried Dolly in alarm.

"My dear Dolly," protested her husband, "I promised to stop betting. I did not promise to stop sleeping."

"Well," sighed Dolly, with relief, "as long as it stops at that. Delhi will win," she added.

"Delhi will not," said Carter. "This is how they will finish." He scribbled three names on a piece of paper which Dolly read.

"But that," she said, "is what you told the gentleman at the bank."

Carter stared at her blankly and in some embarrassment.

"You see!" cried Dolly, "what you think when you're awake, you dream when you're asleep. And you had a run of luck that never happened before and could never happen again."

Carter received her explanation with reluctance. "I wonder," he said.

On arriving at the theater they found their host had reserved a stage box, and as there were but four in their party, and as when they entered the house lights were up, their arrival drew upon them the attention both of those in the audience and of those on the stage. The theater was crowded to its capacity, and in every part were people who were habitual racegoers, as well as many racing men who had come to town for the Suburban. By these, as well as by many others who for three days had seen innumerable pictures of him, Carter was instantly recognized. To the audience and to the performers the man who always won was of far greater interest than what for the three-hundredth night was going forward on the stage. And when the leading woman, Blanche Winter, asked the comedian which he would rather be, "the Man Who Broke the Bank at Monte Carlo or the Man Who Cannot Lose?" she gained from the audience an easy laugh and from the chorus an excited giggle.

When, at the end of the act, Carter went into the lobby to smoke, he was so quickly surrounded that he sought refuge on Broadway. From there, the crowd still following him, he was driven back into his box. Meanwhile, the interest shown in him had not been lost upon the press agent of the theater, and he at once telephoned to the newspaper offices that Plunger Carter, the bookmaker breaker, was at that theater, and that if the newspapers wanted a chance to interview him on the probable outcome of the classic handicap to be run on the morrow, he, the press agent, would unselfishly assist them. In answer to these hurry calls, reporters of the Ten o'Clock Club assembled in the foyer. How far what later followed was due to their presence and to the efforts of the press agent only that gentleman can tell. It was in the second act that Miss Blanche Winter sang her topical song. In it she advised the audience when anxious to settle any question of personal or national interest to "Put it up to the Man in the Moon." This night she introduced a verse in which she told of her desire to know which horse on the morrow would win the Suburban, and, in the chorus, expressed her determination to "Put it up to the Man in the Moon."

Instantly from the back of the house a voice called: "Why don't you put it up to the Man in the Box?" Miss Winter laughed—the audience laughed; all eyes were turned toward Carter. As though the idea pleased them, from different parts of the house people applauded heartily. In embarrassment, Carter shoved back his chair and pulled the curtain of the box between him and the audience. But he was not so easily to escape. Leaving the orchestra to continue unheeded with the prelude to the next verse, Miss Winter walked slowly and deliberately toward him, smiling mischievously. In burlesque entreaty, she held out her arms. She made a most appealing and charming picture, and of that fact she was well aware. In a voice loud enough to reach every part of the house, she addressed herself to Carter:

"Won't you tell *me?*" she begged.

Carter, blushing unhappily, shrugged his shoulders in apology.

With a wave of her hand Miss Winter designated the audience. "Then," she coaxed, reproachfully, "won't you tell *them?*"

Again, instantly, with a promptness and unanimity that sounded suspiciously as though it came from ushers well rehearsed, several voices echoed her petition. "Give us all a chance!" shouted one. "Don't keep the good things to yourself!" reproached another. "*I* want to get rich, *too!*" wailed a third. In his heart, Carter prayed they would choke. But the audience, so far from resenting the interruptions, encouraged them, and Carter's obvious discomfort added to its amusement. It proceeded to assail him with applause, with appeals, with commands to "speak up."

The hand-clapping became general—insistent. The audience would not be denied. Carter turned to Dolly. In the recesses of the box she was enjoying his predicament. His friends also were laughing at him. Indignant at their desertion, Carter grinned vindictively. "All right," he muttered over his shoulder. "Since you think it's funny, I'll show you!" He pulled his pencil from his watch chain and, spreading his program on the ledge of the box, began to write.

From the audience there rose a murmur of incredulity,

of surprise, of excited interest. In the rear of the house the press agent, after one startled look, doubled up in an ecstasy of joy. "We've landed him!" he gasped. "We've landed him! He's going to fall for it!"

Dolly frantically clasped her husband by the coattail. "Champ!" she implored. "What *are* you doing?"

Quite calmly, quite confidently, Carter rose. Leaning forward with a nod and a smile, he presented the program to the beautiful Miss Winter. That lady all but snatched at it. The spotlight was full in her eyes. Turning her back that she might the more easily read, she stood for a moment, her pretty figure trembling with eagerness, her pretty eyes bent upon the program. The house had grown suddenly still, and with an excited gesture, the leader of the orchestra commanded the music to silence. A man, bursting with impatience, broke the tense quiet. "Read it!" he shouted.

In a frightened voice that in the sudden hush held none of its usual confidence, Miss Winter read slowly: "The favorite cannot last the distance. Will lead for the mile and give way to Beldame. Proper takes the place. First Mason will show. Beldame will win by a length."

Before she had ceased reading, a dozen men had struggled to their feet and a hundred voices were roaring at her. "Read that again!" they chorused. Once more Miss Winter read the message, but before she had finished half of those in the front rows were scrambling from their seats and racing up the aisles. Already the reporters were ahead of them, and in the neighborhood not one telephone booth was empty. Within five minutes, in those hotels along the White Way where sporting men are wont to meet, betting commissioners and handbook men were suddenly assaulted by breathless gentlemen, some in evening dress, some without collars, and some without hats, but all with money to bet against the favorite. And, an hour later, men, bent under stacks of newspaper "extras," were vomited from the subway stations into the heart of Broadway, and in raucous tones were shrieking "Winner of the Suburban" sixteen hours before that race was run. That night to every big newspaper office from Maine to California was flashed the news that Plunger Carter, in a Broadway theater, had announced that the favorite for the Suburban would be beaten, and, in order, had named the three horses that would first finish.

Up and down Broadway, from rathskellers to roof gardens, in cafés and lobster palaces, on the corners of the crossroads, in clubs and all-night restaurants, Carter's tip was as a red rag to a bull.

Was the boy drunk, they demanded, or had his miraculous luck turned his head? Otherwise, why would he so publicly utter a prophecy that on the morrow must certainly smother him with ridicule. The explanations were varied. The men in the clubs held he was driven by a desire for notoriety, the men in the street that he was more clever than they guessed, and had made the move to suit his own book, to alter the odds to his own advantage. Others frowned mysteriously. With superstitious faith in his luck, they pointed to his record. "Has he ever lost a bet? How do *we* know what *he* knows?" they demanded. "Perhaps it's fixed and he knows it!"

The "wise" ones howled in derision. "A Suburban *fixed*!" they retorted. "You can fix *one* jockey, you can fix *two;* but you can't fix sixteen jockeys! You can't fix Belmont, you can't fix Keene. There's nothing in his picking Beldame, but only a crazy man would pick the horse for the place and to show, and shut out the favorite! The boy ought to be in Matteawan."

Still undisturbed, still confident to those to whom he had promised them, Carter sent a wire. Nor did he forget his old enemy, Sol Burbank. "If you want to get some of the money I took," he telegraphed, "wipe out the Belmont entry and take all they offer on Delhi. He cannot win."

And that night, when each newspaper called him up at his flat, he made the same answer. "The three horses will finish as I said. You can state that I gave the information as I did as a sort of present to the people of New York City."

In the papers the next morning "Carter's Tip" was the front-page feature. Even those who never in the racing of horses felt any concern could not help but take in the outcome of this one a curious interest. The audacity of the prophecy, the very absurdity of it, presupposing, as it did, occult power, was in itself amusing. And when the curtain rose on the Suburban it was evident that to thousands what the Man Who Could Not Lose had foretold was a serious and inspired utterance.

This time his friends gathered around him, not to benefit by his advice, but to protect him. "They'll mob you!" they warned. "They'll tear the clothes off your back. Better make your getaway now."

Dolly, with tears in her eyes, sat beside him. Every now and again she touched his hand. Below his box, as around a newspaper office on the night when a president is elected, the people crushed in a turbulent mob. Some mocked and jeered, some who on his tip had risked their every dollar hailed him hopefully. On every side policemen, fearful of coming trouble, hemmed him in. Carter was bored extremely, heartily sorry he had on the night before given way to what he now saw as a perverse impulse. But he still was confident, still undismayed.

To all eyes, except those of Dolly, he was of all those at the track the least concerned. To her he turned and, in a low tone, spoke swiftly. "I am so sorry," he begged. "But, indeed, indeed, I can't lose. You must have faith in me."

"In you, yes," returned Dolly in a whisper, "but in your dreams, no!"

The horses were passing on their way to the post. Carter brought his face close to hers. "I'm going to break my promise," he said, "and make one more bet, this one with you. I bet you a kiss that I'm right."

Dolly, holding back her tears, smiled mournfully.

"Make it a hundred," she said.

Half of the forty thousand at the track had backed Delhi, the other half, following Carter's luck and his confidence in proclaiming his convictions, had backed Beldame. Many hundred had gone so far as to bet that the three horses he had named would finish as he had foretold. But, in spite of Carter's tip, Delhi still was the favorite, and when the thousands saw the Keene polka dots leap to the front, and by two lengths stay there, for the quarter, the half, and for the three-quarters, the air was shattered with jubilant, triumphant yells. And then suddenly, with the swiftness of a moving picture, in the very moment of his victory, Beldame crept up on the favorite, drew alongside, drew ahead, passed him, and left him beaten.

It was at the mile.

The night before a man had risen in a theater and said to two thousand people: "The favorite will lead for the mile, and give way to Beldame." Could they have believed him, the men who now cursed themselves might for the rest of their lives have lived upon their winnings. Those who had followed his prophecy faithfully, superstitiously, now shrieked in happy, riotous self-congratulation. "At the *mile*!" they yelled. "He *told* you, at the *mile*!" They turned toward Carter and shook Panama hats at him. "Oh, you Carter!" they shrieked lovingly.

It was more than a race the crowd was watching now, it was the working out of a promise. And when Beldame stood off Proper's rush, and Proper fell to second, and First Mason followed three lengths in the rear, and in that order they flashed under the wire, the yells were not that a race had been won, but that a prophecy had been fulfilled.

Of the thousands that cheered Carter and fell upon him

and indeed did tear his clothes off his back, one of his friends alone was sufficiently unselfish to think of what it might mean to Carter.

"Champ!" roared this friend, pounding him on both shoulders. "You old wizard! I win ten thousand! How much do you win?"

Carter cast a swift glance at Dolly. "Oh!" he said, "I win much more than that."

And Dolly, raising her eyes to his, nodded and smiled contentedly.

Zane Grey

THE HORSES
OF BOSTIL'S FORD

I

Bostil himself was half horse. The half of him that was human
he divided between love of his fleet racers and his daughter,
Lucy.

He had seen ten years of hard riding on that wild Utah
border, where a horse meant all the world to a man; and then
lucky strikes of water and gold on the vast plateau wilderness
north of the Rio Virgin had made him richer than he knew.
His ranges beyond Bostil's Ford were practically boundless,
his cattle numberless, and, many as were his riders, he always
had need of more.

In those border days every rider loved his horse as a part

of himself. If there was a difference between any rider of the sage and Bostil, it was that, as Bostil had more horses, so he had more love.

If he had any unhappiness, it was because he could not buy Wildfire and Nagger, thoroughbreds belonging to one Lamar, a poor daredevil rider who would not have parted with them for all the gold in the uplands. And Lamar had dared to cast longing eyes at Lucy. When he clashed with Bostil he avowed his love, and offered to stake his horses and his life against the girl's hand, deciding the wager by a race between Wildfire and the rancher's great gray, Sage King.

Among the riders, when they sat around their campfires, there had been much speculation regarding the outcome of such a race. There never had been a race, and never would be, so the riders gossiped, unless Lamar were to ride off with Lucy. In that case there would be the grandest race ever run on the uplands, with the odds against Wildfire only if he carried double.

If Lamar put Lucy up on Wildfire, and he rode Nagger, there would be another story. Lucy was a slip of a girl, born on a horse, and could ride like a burr sticking in a horse's mane. With Wildfire she would run away from anyone on Sage King—which for Bostil would be a double tragedy, equally in the loss of his daughter and the beating of his favorite. Then such a race was likely to end in heartbreak for all concerned, because the Sage King would outrun Nagger, and that would bring riders within gunshot.

Bostil swore by all the gods that the King was the swiftest horse in the wild upland of wonderful horses. He swore that the gray could look back over his shoulder and run away from Nagger, and that he could kill Wildfire on his feet. That poor beggar Lamar's opinion of his steeds was as preposterous as his love for Lucy!

Now, Bostil had a great fear which made him ever restless, ever watchful. That fear was of Cordts, the rustler. Cordts hid back in the untrodden ways. He had fast horses, faithful followers, gold for the digging, cattle by the thousand, and women when he chose to ride off with them. He had always had what he wanted—except one thing. That was a horse. That horse was the Sage King.

Cordts was a gunman, outlaw, rustler, a lord over the free ranges; but, more than all else, he was a rider. He knew a horse. He was as much horse as Bostil. He was a prince of rustlers, who thought a horse thief worse than a dog; but he intended to become a horse thief. He had openly declared it. The passion he had conceived for the Sage King was the passion of a man for an unattainable woman. He swore that he would never rest—that he would not die till he owned the King; so Bostil had reason for his great fear.

One morning, as was sometimes the rancher's custom, he ordered the racers to be brought from the corrals and turned loose in the alfalfa fields near the house. Bostil loved to watch them graze; but ever he saw that the riders were close at hand, and that the horses did not graze too close to the sage.

He sat back and gloried in the sight. He owned a thousand horses; near at hand was a field full of them, fine and mettlesome and racy; but Bostil had eyes only for the six blooded favorites. There was Plume, a superb mare that got her name from the way her mane swept in the wind when she was on the run; there were Bullet, huge, rangy, leaden in color, and Two-Face, sleek and glossy and cunning; there was the black stallion Sarchedon, and close to him the bay Dusty Ben; and lastly Sage King, the color of the upland sage, a horse proud and wild and beautiful.

"Where's Lucy?" presently asked Bostil. As he divided his love, so he divided his anxiety.

Some rider had seen Lucy riding off, with her golden hair flying in the breeze.

"She's got to keep out of the sage," growled Bostil. "Where's my glass? I want to take a look out there. Where's my glass?"

The glass could not be found.

"What're those specks in the sage? Antelope?"

"I reckon that's a bunch of hosses," replied a hawk-eyed rider.

"Huh! I don't like it. Lucy oughtn't to be ridin' round alone. If she meets Lamar again, I'll rope her in a corral!"

Another rider drew Bostil's attention from the gray waste of rolling sage.

"Bostil, look! Look at the King! He smells somethin'—he's lookin' for somethin'! So does Sarch.'"

"Yes," replied the rancher. "Better drive them up. They're too close to the sage."

Sage King whistled shrilly and began to prance.

"What in the—" muttered Bostil.

Suddenly up out of the alfalfa sprang a dark form. Like a panther it leaped at the horse and caught his mane. Snorting wildly, Sage King reared aloft and plunged. The dark form swung up. It was a rider, and cruelly he spurred the racer.

Other dark forms rose almost as swiftly, and leaped upon the other plunging horses. There was a violent, pounding shock of frightened horses bunching into action. With a magnificent bound, Sage King got clear of the tangle and led the way.

Like Indians, the riders hung low and spurred. In a single swift moment they had the horses tearing into the sage.

"Rustlers! *Cordts! Cordts!*" screamed Bostil. "He sneaked up in the sage! Quick, men—rifles, rifles! No! No! Don't shoot! *You might kill a horse!* Let them go. They'll get the girl, too—there must be more rustlers in the sage—they've got her now! There they go! Gone! Gone! All that I loved!"

II

At almost the exact hour of the rustling of the racers, Lucy Bostil was with Jim Lamar at their well-hidden rendezvous on a high, cedared slope some eight or ten miles from the ranch. From an opening in the cedars they could see down across the gray sage to the alfalfa fields, the corrals, and the house. In Lucy's lap, with her gauntlets, lay the field glass that Bostil's riders could not find; and close by, halted under a cedar, Lucy's pinto tossed his spotted head at Lamar's magnificent horses.

"You unhappy boy!" Lucy was saying. "Of course I love you; but, Jim, I can't meet you any more like this. It's not playing square with Dad."

"Lucy, if you give it up, you don't love me," he protested.

"I *do* love you."

"Well, then—"

He leaned over her. Lucy's long lashes drooped and warm color flushed her face as she shyly lifted it to give the proof exacted by her lover.

They were silent a moment, and she lay with her head on his breast. A soft wind moaned through the cedars, and bees hummed in the patches of pale lavender daisies. The still air was heavily laden with the fragrance of the sage.

Lamar gently released her, got up, and seemed to be shaking off a kind of spell.

"Lucy, I know you mustn't meet me any more. But oh, Lord, Lord, I do love you so! I had nothing in the world but the hope of seeing you, and now that'll be gone. I'll be such a miserable beggar!"

Lucy demurely eyed him.

"Jim, your clothes are pretty ragged, and you look a little in need of some good food, but it strikes me you're a splendid-looking beggar. You suit me. You oughtn't say you have nothing. Look at your horses!"

Lamar's keen gray eyes softened. Indeed, he was immeasurably rich, and he gazed at his horses as if that were the first moment he had ever laid eyes on them.

Both were of tremendous build. Nagger was dark and shaggy, with arched neck and noble head that suggested race, loyalty, and speed. Wildfire was so finely pointed, so perfectly balanced, that he appeared smaller than Nagger; but he was as high, as long, and he had the same great breadth of chest; and though not so heavy, he had the same wonderful look of power. As red as fire, with sweeping mane and tail, like dark-tinged flames, and holding himself with a strange alert wildness, he looked his name.

"Jimmy, you have those grand horses," went on Lucy. "And look at *me*!"

Lamar did look at her, yearningly. She was as lithe as a young panther. Her rider's suit, like a boy's, rather emphasized than hid the graceful roundness of her slender form. Lamar thought her hair the gold of the sage at sunset, her eyes the blue of the deep haze in the distance, her mouth the sweet red of the upland rose.

"Jimmy, you've got me corralled," she continued archly, "and I'm Dad's only child."

"But, Lucy, I *haven't* got you!" he passionately burst out.

"Yes, you have. All you need is patience. Keep hanging round the Ford till Dad gives in. He hasn't one thing against you, except that you wouldn't sell him your horses. Dad's crazy about horses. Jim, he wasn't so angry because you wanted to race Wildfire against the King *for me*; he was furious because you were so sure you'd win. And see here, Jim dear— if ever you and Dad race the red and the gray, you let the gray win, if you love me and want me! Else you'll *never* get me in this world."

"Lucy! I wouldn't pull Wildfire—I wouldn't break that horse's heart even to—to get you!"

"That's the rider in you, Jim. I like you better for it; but all the same, I know you would."

"I wouldn't!"

"You don't love me!"

"I do love you."

"Well, then!" she mocked, and lifted her face.

"Oh, child, you could make me do anything," went on Lamar presently. "But, Lucy, you've ridden the King, and you're the only person besides me who was ever up on Wildfire. Tell me, isn't Wildfire the better horse?"

"Jim, you've asked me that a thousand times."

"Have I? Well, tell me."

"Yes, Jim, if you can compare two such horses, Wildfire is the better."

"You darling! Lucy, did Bostil ever ask you that?"

"About seven million times."

"And what did you tell him?" asked Lamar, laughing, yet earnest withal.

"I wouldn't dare tell Dad anything but that Sage King could run Wildfire off his legs."

"You—you little hypocrite! Which of us were you really lying to?"

"I reckon it was Dad," replied Lucy seriously. "Jim, I can ride, but I haven't much horse sense. So what I think mayn't be right. I love the King and Wildfire—all horses. Really I love Nagger best of all. He's so faithful. Why, it's because he loves you that he nags you. Wildfire's no horse for a woman. He's wild. I don't think he's actually any faster than the King; only he's a desert stallion, and has killed many horses. His spirit would break the King. It's in the King to outrun a horse;

it's in Wildfire to kill him. What a shame ever to let those great horses race!"

"They never will, Lucy, dear. And now I'll see if the sage is clear; for you must be going."

III

Lamar's eye swept the gray expanse. A few miles out he saw a funnel-shaped dust cloud rising behind a bunch of dark horses, and farther on toward the ranch more puffs of dust and moving black specks.

"Lucy, something's wrong," he said quietly. "Take your glass. Look there!"

"Oh, dear, I'm afraid Dad has put the boys on my trail," rejoined Lucy, as she readjusted the glass and leveled it. Instantly she cried: "Three riders and three led horses—unsaddled. I don't know the riders. Jim! I see Sarchedon and Bullet, if ever I saw them in my life!"

"Rustlers! I knew it before you looked," said Jim, with compressed lips. "Give me the glass." He looked, and while he held the glass leveled he spoke: "Yes, Sarch and Bullet—there's Two-Face. The three unsaddled horses I don't know. They're dark bays—rustlers' horses. That second bunch I can't make out so well for dust, but it's the same kind of a bunch—three riders, three led horses. Lucy, there's the King. Cordts has got him!"

"Oh, Jim, it will ruin Dad!" cried Lucy, wringing her hands.

Lamar appeared suddenly to become obsessed by a strange excitement.

"Why, Jim, we're safe hidden here," said Lucy, in surprise.

"Girl! Do you think me afraid? It's only that I'm—" His face grew tense, his eyes burned, his hands trembled. "What a chance for me! Lucy, listen. Cordts and his men—picked men, probably—sneaked up in the sage to the ranch, and run off bareback on the racers. They've had their horses hidden, and then changed saddles. They're traveling light. There's not a long gun among them. *I've got my rifle.* I can stop that bunch—kill some of them, or maybe all—get the horses back. If I only had more shells for my rifle! I've only ten in the magazine. I'm so poor I can't buy shells for my rifle."

"Dear Jim, don't risk it, then," said Lucy, trembling.

"I will risk it," he cried. "It's the chance of my life. Dearest, think—think what it'd mean to Bostil if I killed Cordts and got back the King! Think what it'd mean for me! Cordts is the bane of the uplands. He's a murderer, a stealer of women. Bostil can't sleep for fear of him. I will risk it. I can do it. Little girl, watch, and you'll have something to tell your father!"

With his mind made up and action begun, Jim grew cold and deliberate. Freeing Lucy's pinto, he put her saddle on Nagger, muttering:

"If we have to run for it, you'll be safe on him."

As he tightened the cinches on Wildfire, he spoke low to the red stallion. A twitching ripple quivered over the horse, and he pounded the ground and champed his bit.

"S-sh! Quiet there!" Jim called, louder, and put a hand on the horse.

Wildfire seemed to turn to stone. Next Lamar drew the long rifle from its sheath and carefully examined it.

"Come," he said to Lucy. "We'll go down and hide in the edge of the cedars. That bunch'll pass on the trail within a hundred paces."

Lamar led the way down the slope, and took up a position in a clump of cedars. The cover was not so dense as he had thought it would be. There was not, however, any time to hunt for better.

"Lucy, hold the horses here. Look at Wildfire's ears!

Already he's seen that bunch. Dear, you're not afraid—for once we've got the best of the rustlers. If only Cordts comes up in time!''

As the rustlers approached, Lamar, peering from his covert, felt himself grow colder and grimmer. Presently he knew that the two groups were too far apart for them both to pass near him at the same time. He formed a resolve to let the first party go by. It was Cordts he wanted—and the King.

Lamar lay low while moments passed. The breeze brought the sharp sound of iron-shod hooves. Lamar heard also a coarse laugh—gruff voices—the jingle of spurs. There came a silence—then the piercing whistle of a frightened horse.

Lamar raised himself to see that the rustlers had halted within pistol-shot. The rider on Two-Face was in the lead, and the cunning mare had given the alarm. Jim thought what a fool he had been to imagine that he could ambush rustlers when they had Two-Face. She had squared away, head high, ears up, and she looked straight at the hiding place.

It appeared as if all the rustlers pulled guns at the same instant, and a hail of bullets pattered around Lamar. Leaping up, he shot once—twice—three times. Riderless horses leaped, wildly plunged, and sheered off into the sage.

Lamar shifted his gaze to Cordts and his followers. At sound of the shots, the rustlers had halted, now scarcely a quarter of a mile distant.

"Are y-you all right, Jim?" whispered Lucy.

Lamar turned, to see the girl standing with eyes tight shut.

"Yes, I'm all right, but I'm stumped now. Cordts heard the shots from my rifle. He and his men won't ride any closer. There, they've started again—they've left the trail!"

Lucy opened her eyes.

"Jim, they're cutting across to head off Sarch. He's leading. If they ever catch the other racers, it'll be too late for you."

"Too late?"

"They'll be able to change mounts—you can't catch them then."

"Lucy!"

"Get up on Wildfire—go after Cordts!" cried the girl breathlessly.

"Great Scott, I hadn't thought of that! Lucy, it's Wildfire against the King. That race *will* be run! Climb up on Nagger. girl, you're going with me. You'll be safer trailing after me than hiding here. If they turn on us, I can drop them all."

He had to lift her up on Nagger; but once in the saddle, when the huge black began to show how he wanted to run, her father's blood began to throb and burn in the girl, and she looked down upon her lover with a darkening fire in her eyes.

"Girl, it'll be the race we've dreamed of! It's for your father. It's Wildfire against the King!"

"I'll stay with you—as long as Nagger lasts," she said.

IV

Lamar leaped astride Wildfire, and ducked low under the cedars as the horse bolted. He heard Nagger crash through close behind him. Cordts and his companions were riding off toward the racers. Sarch was leading Bullet and Two-Face around in the direction of the ranch. The three unsaddled mounts were riding off to the left.

One rustler turned to look back, then another. When Cordts turned, he wheeled the King, and stopped as if in surprise. Probably he thought that his men had been ambushed by a company of riders. Not improbably, the idea of actual pursuit had scarcely dawned upon them; and the possibility of any one running them down, now that they were astride Bostil's swift horses, had never occurred to them at all. Motionless they sat, evidently trying to make out their pursuers.

When Lamar stood up in his stirrups, and waved his long rifle at them, it was probably at that instant they recognized him. The effect was significant. They dropped the halters of the three unsaddled horses, and headed their mounts to the left, toward the trail.

Which way they went was of no moment to Lamar. Wildfire and Nagger could run low, stretched out at length, in brush or in the open. It was evident, however, that Cordts preferred open running, and as he cut across the trail, Lamar gained. This trail was one long used by the rustlers in driving cattle, and it was a wide, hard-packed road. Lamar knew it for ten miles, until it turned into the rugged and broken passes. He believed the race would be ended before Cordts had a chance to take to the canyons.

Nagger had his nose even with Wildfire's flank. Lucy rode with both hands at strong tension on the bridle. Her face was pale, her eyes were gleaming darker, and wisps of her bound hair whipped in the wind. Lamar's one pride, after what he felt for his horses, was in Lucy, and in the fact that she could ride them. She was a sweetheart for a rider!

"Pull him, Lucy, pull him!" he shouted. "Don't let him get going on you. Wait till Plume and Ben are out of it!"

As for himself, he drew an iron arm on Wildfire's bridle. The grimness passed from Lamar's mood, taking with it the cold, sickening sense of death already administered, and of impending fight and blood.

Lucy was close behind on the thundering Nagger, and he had no fear for her, only a wild joy in her, that she was a girl capable of riding this race with him. So, as the sage flashed by, and the wind bit sweet, and the quick, rhythmic music of Wildfire's hooves rang in his ears, Lamar began to live the sweetest thing in a rider's career—the glory of the one run ning race wherein he staked pride in his horse, love of a girl, and life.

Wildfire was not really running yet; he had not length- ened out of his gallop. He had himself in control, as if the spirit in him awaited the call of his master. As for the speed of the moment, it was enough for Lamar to see the space between him and Cordts gradually grow less and less. He wanted to revel in that ride while he could. He saw, and was somehow glad, that Cordts was holding in the King.

His sweeping gaze caught a glimpse of Bullet and Two- Face and Sarchedon dotting the blue horizon line; and he thrilled with the thought of the consternation and joy and excitement there would be at Bostil's ranch when the riderless horses trooped in. He looked back at Lucy to smile into her face, to feel his heart swell at the beauty and wonder of her. With a rider's keen scrutiny, he glanced at her saddle and stirrups, and at the saddle girths.

He helped Wildfire to choose the going, and at the turns of the trail he guided him across curves that might gain a yard in the race. And this caution seemed ordered in the fringe of Lamar's thought, with most of his mind given to the sheer sensations of the ride—the flashing colored sage, the speeding white trail, the sharp bittersweetness of the air, the tang and sting of the wind, the feel of Wildfire under him, a wonderful, quivering, restrained muscular force, ready at a call to launch itself into a thunderbolt. For the moment with Lamar it was the ride—the ride!

As he lived it to the full, the miles sped by. He gained on Dusty Ben and Plume; the King slowly cut out ahead; and the first part of the race neared an end, whatever that was to be.

The two nearer rustlers whirled in their saddles to fire at Lamar. Bullets sped wildly and low, kicking up little puffs of dust. They were harmless, but they quickened Lamar's pulse, and the cold, grim mood returned to him. He loosened the bridle. Wildfire sank a little and lengthened; his speed increased, and his action grew smoother. Lamar turned to the girl and yelled:

"Let him go!"

Nagger shot forward, once more with his great black head at Wildfire's flank.

Then Lamar began to return the fire of the rustlers, aiming carefully and high, so as to be sure not to hit one of the racers. As he gained upon them, the bullets from their revolvers skipped uncomfortably close past Wildfire's legs.

Lamar, warming to the fight, shot four times before he remembered how careful he must be of his ammunition. He must get closer!

Soon the rustlers pulled Ben and Plume, half lifting them in the air, and, leaping off the breaking horses, they dashed into the sage, one on each side of the trail. The move startled Lamar; he might have pulled Wildfire in time, but Lucy could never stop Nagger in such short distance. Lamar's quick decision was that it would be better to risk shots as they sped on. He yelled to Lucy to hug the saddle, and watched for the hiding rustlers.

He saw spouts of red—puffs of smoke—then a dark from behind a sage bush. Firing, he thought he heard a cry. Then, whirling to the other side, he felt the wind of bullets near his face—saw another dark form—and fired as he rode by.

Over his shoulder he saw Lucy hunched low in her saddle, and the big black running as if the peril had spurred him. Lamar sent out a wild and exulting cry. Ben and Plume were now off the trail, speeding in line, and they would not stop soon; and out in front, perhaps a hundred yards, ran the Sage King in beautiful action. Cordts fitted the horse. If the King was greater than Wildfire, Cordts was the rider to bring it out.

"Jim! Jim!" suddenly pealed in Lamar's ears. He turned

with a tightening round his heart. *"Nagger! He was hit! He was hit!"* screamed Lucy.

The great black was off his stride.

"Pull him! Pull him! Get off! Hide in the sage!" yelled Lamar.

Lucy made no move to comply with his order. Her face was white. Was she weakening? He saw no change of her poise in the saddle; but her right arm hung limp. She had been hit!

Lamar's heart seemed to freeze in the suspension of its beat, and the clogging of icy blood. He saw her sway.

"Lucy, hang on! Hang on!" he cried, and began to pull the red stallion.

To pull him out of that stride took all Lamar's strength, and then he only pulled him enough to let Nagger come up abreast. Lamar circled Lucy with his arm and lifted her out of her saddle.

"Jim, I'm not hurt much. If I hadn't seen Nagger was hit, I'd never squealed."

"Oh, Lucy!" Lamar choked with the release of his fear and the rush of pride and passion.

"Don't pull Wildfire! He'll catch the King yet!"

Lamar swung the girl behind him. The way she wrapped her uninjured arm about him and clung showed the stuff of which Lucy Bostil was made. Wildfire snorted as if in fierce anger that added weight had been given him, as if he knew it was no fault of his that Sage King had increased the lead.

Lamar bent forward and now called to the stallion— called to him with the wild call of the upland rider to his horse. It was the call that let Wildfire know he was free to choose his going and his pace—free to run—free to run down a rival—free to kill.

And the wild stallion responded. He did not break; he wore into a run that had slow increase. The demon's spirit in him seemed to gather mighty forces, so that every magnificent stride was a little lower, a little longer, a little faster, till the horse had attained a terrible celerity. He was almost flying; and the white space narrowed between him and the Sage King.

Lamar vaguely heard the howling of the wind in his ears, the continuous ringing sound of Wildfire's hooves. He vaguely noticed the blurring of the sage and the swift fleeting of the trail under him. He scarcely saw the rustler Cordts; he forgot Lucy. All his senses that retained keenness were centered in the running of the Sage King. It was so swift, so beautiful, so worthy of the gray's fame and name, that a pang numbed the rider's breast because Bostil's great horse was doomed to lose the race, if not his life.

For long the gray ran even with his red pursuer. Then, by imperceptible degrees, Wildfire began to gain. He was a desert stallion, born with the desert's ferocity of strife, the desert's imperious will; he never had love for any horse; it was in him to rule and to kill. Lamar felt Wildfire grow wet and hot, felt the marvelous ease of the horse's action gradually wearing to strain.

Another mile, and the trail turned among ridges of rock, along deep washes, at length to enter the broken country of crags and canyons. Cordts bent round in the saddle to shoot at Lamar. The bullet whistled perilously close; but Lamar withheld his fire. He had one shell left in his rifle; he would not risk that till he was sure.

He watched for a break in the King's stride, for the plunge that meant that the gray was finished. Still the race went on and on. And in the lather that flew back to wet Lamar's lips he tasted the hot blood of his horse. If it had been his own blood, the last drops spilled from his heart, he could not have felt more agony.

At last Sage King broke strangely, slowed in a few jumps, and, plunging down, threw Cordts over his head. The rustler lcapcd up and began to run, seeking cover.

Wildfire thundered on beyond the prostrate King. Then, with terrible muscular convulsion, as of internal collapse, he, too, broke and pounded slow, slower—to a stop.

Lamar slipped down and lifted Lucy from the saddle. Wildfire was white except where he was red, and that red was not now his glossy, flaming skin. He groaned and began to sag. On one knee and then the other he knelt, gave a long heave, and lay at length.

Lamar darted back in pursuit of Cordts. He descried the rustler running along the edge of a canyon. Lamar realized that he must be quick; but the rifle wavered because of his terrible eagerness. He was shaken by the intensity of the moment. With tragic earnestness he fought for coolness, for control.

Cordts reached a corner of cliff where he had to go slowly, to cling to the rock. It was then that Lamar felt himself again chilled through and through with that strange, grim power. He pulled trigger. Cordts paused as if to rest. He leaned against the face of the cliff, his hands up, and he kept that posture for a long moment. Then his hands began to slip. Slowly he swayed out over the canyon. His dark face flashed. Headlong he fell, to vanish below the rim.

Lamar hurriedly ran back and saw that the King was a beaten, broken horse, but he would live to run another race. Up the trail Lucy was kneeling beside Wildfire, and before Lamar got there he heard her sobbing. As if he were being dragged to execution, the rider went on, and then he was looking down upon his horse and crying:

"Wildfire! Wildfire!"

Choked, blinded, killed on his feet, Wildfire heard the voice of his master.

"Jim! Oh, Jim!" moaned Lucy.

"He beat the King! And he carried double!" whispered Lamar.

While they knelt there, the crippled Nagger came limping up the trail, followed by Dusty Ben and Plume.

Again the rider called to his horse, with a cry now piercing, thrilling; but this time Wildfire did not respond.

V

The westering sun glanced brightly over the rippling sage, which rolled away from the Ford like a gray sea. Bostil sat on his porch, a stricken man. He faced the blue haze of the West, where, some hours before, all that he loved had vanished. His riders were grouped near him, silent, awed by his face, awaiting orders that did not come.

From behind a ridge puffed up a thin cloud of dust. Bostil saw it, and gave a start. Above the sage appeared a bobbing black dot—the head of a horse.

"Sarch!" exclaimed Bostil.

With spurs clinking, his riders ran and trooped behind him.

"There's Bullet!" cried one.

"An' Two-Face!" added another.

"Saddled an' riderless!"

Then all were tensely quiet, watching the racers come trotting in single file down the ridge. Sarchedon's shrill neigh, like a whistle blast, pealed in from the sage. From fields and corrals clamored the answer, attended by the clattering of hundreds of hooves.

Sarchedon and his followers broke from trot to canter— canter to gallop—and soon were cracking their iron shoes on the stony road. Then, like a swarm of bees, the riders surrounded the racers and led them up to Bostil.

On Sarchedon's neck showed a dry, dust-caked stain of reddish tinge. Bostil's right-hand man, the hawk-eyed rider, gray as the sage from long service, carefully examined the stain.

"Wall, the rustler that was up on Sarch got plugged, an' in fallin' forrard he spilled some blood on the hoss's neck."

"Who shot him?" demanded Bostil.

"I reckon there's only one rider on the sage thet could ever hev got close enough to shoot a rustler up on Sarch."

Bostil wheeled to face the West. His brow was lowering; his hands were clenched. Riders led away the tired racers, and returned to engage with the others in whispered speculation.

The afternoon wore on; the sun lost its brightness, and burned low and red. Again dust clouds, now like reddened smoke, puffed over the ridge. Four horses, two carrying riders, appeared above the sage.

"Is that—a gray horse—or am I blind?" asked Bostil unsteadily.

The old rider shaded the hawk eyes with his hand.

"Gray he is—gray as the sage, Bostil—an' so help me if he ain't the King!"

Bostil stared, rubbed his eyes as if his sight was dimmed, and stared again.

"Do I see Lucy?"

"Shore—shore!" replied the old rider. "I seen her long ago. Why, sir, I can see thet gold hair of hers a mile across the sage. She's up on Ben."

The light of joy on Bostil's face slowly shaded, and the change was one that silenced his riders. Abruptly he left them, to enter the house.

When he came forth again, brought out by the stamp of hooves on the stones, his riders were escorting Lucy and Lamar into the courtyard. A wan smile flitted across Lucy's haggard face as she saw her father, and she held out one arm to him. The other was bound in a bloody scarf.

Cursing deep, like the muttering of thunder, Bostil ran out.

"Lucy! For Heaven's sake! You're not bad hurt?"

"Only a little, Dad," she said, and slipped down into his arms.

He kissed her pale face, and, carrying her to the door, roared for the women of his household.

When he reappeared, the crowd of riders scattered from around Lamar. Bostil looked at the King. The horse was caked with dusty lather, scratched and disheveled, weary and broken, yet somehow he was still beautiful. He raised his drooping head, and reached for his master with a look as soft and dark and eloquent as a woman's.

No rider there but felt Bostil's grief. He loved the King. He believed the King had been beaten; and his rider's glory and pride were battling with love. Mighty as that was in Bostil, it did not at once overcome his hatred of defeat.

Slowly the gaze of the rancher moved from the King to tired Ben and Plume, over the bleeding Nagger, at last to rest on the white-faced Lamar. But Bostil was not looking for Lamar. His hard eyes veered to and fro. Among those horses there was not the horse he sought.

"Where's the red stallion?" he asked.

Lamar raised eyes dark with pain, yet they flashed as he looked straight into Bostil's face.

"Wildfire's dead."

"Shot?"

"No."

"What killed him?" Bostil's voice had a vibrating ring.

"The King, sir; killed him on his feet."

Bostil's lean jaw bulged and quivered. His hand shook a little as he laid it on the King's tangled mane.

"Jim—what the—" he said brokenly, with voice strangely softened.

"Mr. Bostil, we've had some fighting and running. Lucy

was hit—so was Nagger. And the King killed Wildfire on his feet. But I got Cordts and three of his men—maybe four. I've no more to say, sir."

Bostil put his arm round the young man's shoulder.

"Lamar, you've said enough. If I don't know how you feel about the loss of that grand horse, no rider on earth knows. But let me say I reckon I never knew your real worth. You can lead my riders. You can have the girl—God bless you both! And you can have anything else on this ranch—except the King!"

Erle Stanley Gardner

CARVED IN SAND

I

Tenderfoot Contraption

When a man lives a great deal in the open, little things some-times stick in his mind. That was the way with the remark the college professor made to me.

"Everything in nature," he said, "has two points of mani-festation."

"Meaning positive and negative?" I asked him, just to let him know that he wasn't going to spring any theory on me that I couldn't at least talk about.

"Not exactly that," he said. "It's something a little more subtle."

I swept my hand in a half circle, including in the ges-

ture the sweep of sun-glittering sand and cacti-studded desert. "What would be the double manifestation of that?" I
asked him.

"I don't know," he said. "I'm not enough of a desert man
to know its manifestations. But you know it. If you'll only
watch it, you'll find that it does have a dual manifestation."

It was only a little thing perhaps, but somehow it stuck
in my mind; and it seemed that I'd found the answer in Pete
Ayers. Pete was desert born and desert bred, and the shifting
sands had got into his blood. He was as restless as a swirl of
loose sand in the embrace of a desert wind. Of course the
desert leaves its mark on everybody who lives in it. Most of
the men who have lived in the desert have gray eyes, firm lips,
a slow, deliberate way of moving about that is deceptive to a
man who doesn't know the breed. When occasion requires
they are as fast as greased lightning, and as deadly as a cornered lion. Ayers was different. He was just a happy-go-lucky
kid who was forever rolling into mischief and stumbling out.
He was always in trouble, always getting out of it by some
fluke.

Now he lay stretched out beside me on the edge of the
rim rock, the hot desert sun beating down on our backs. He
handed me the binoculars.

"Brother," he said, "watch where the bullet strikes. I'm
betting even money that I don't miss him by more than two
inches, and I'll bet on a direct hit for reasonable odds."

That was the way with Pete; always making a bet, always
willing to wager his shirt on the outcome of whatever he
happened to be doing.

"Wait a minute, Pete," I said as he cocked the rifle.
"Let's make certain that it's a coyote. He's acting sort of funny
for a coyote."

"He's going to act a lot funnier," said Pete as he nestled
his cheek against the stock of the rifle, "in just about one
minute."

I focused the binoculars on the slope across the long dry canyon. Ordinarily I don't go in much for binoculars in the desert, because a desert man cannot afford to be cluttered up with a lot of weight. The tenderfoot always carries a camera, binoculars, hunting knife, and compass. They're things that are all right in their way, but the real desert man starts out with a six-gun, a canteen, a pocket knife, a box of matches, and a sack of tobacco. That's about all he needs.

The binoculars were good ones that Pete had won from a tenderfoot in a poker game the night before. They brought up the opposite slope of the canyon with a clearness that made the black shadows transparent.

"Hold everything, Pete!" I said. "It's a police dog!"

I heard Pete's grunt of incredulity, but he lowered the rifle and turned startled blue eyes to me.

"Hell," he said, "you're crazy! There aren't any police dogs out here. Them's tenderfoot binoculars and there's mebbe a sort of tenderfoot influence about 'em."

"Take a look yourself," I said.

Pete put down the rifle and reached for the binoculars. He focused them to his eyes, and then gave a low whistle.

"Hell!" he said. "And I'll bet I'd have hit him!"

I said nothing. We watched the animal for several seconds.

"What the hell's he doing here?" asked Pete.

I didn't know any more than he did—not as much, in fact, so I couldn't say anything. We lay there in silence, with the desert sun beating down on the glittering expanse of waste, making the black rim rock on the other side of the canyon twist and writhe in the heat waves.

After a while Pete passed the binoculars across to me. I found the dog again, steadied my elbows on the hot rock, and watched closely.

"He's running around in little circles, looking for a scent

of some kind," I said. "Now it looks as though he's found it. He runs along straight for ten or fifteen yards, then stops and circles, and then starts going straight. Now, he's found what he wants. He's running close to the ground—and making time."

"Hell," said Pete dryly, "you don't need to tell me everything he's doin', I got eyes, even if they don't magnify eight diameters."

The police dog fascinated me. I couldn't understand what he was doing out here in the desert. I kept the binoculars on him and watched him as he angled down the slope. He was running rapidly now, wagging his tail as he ran, and apparently following the scent without difficulty. He ran down around the edge of the slope, rounded an outcropping of rock, crossed the canyon, and vanished behind a ledge of the rim rock on our side of the canyon.

"Well," said Pete, "the show's over."

"No," I told him, "I'm going to find out what that dog's doing out here."

"That's just the way with you," he said. "Filled full of curiosity."

But I could see from the light in his blue eyes that he was curious, and that he also favored giving the dog a break. A police dog can't live long in the desert. A coyote can get by nicely, but not a dog, no matter how big or how strong he is. It's a question of generations of training, and the coyote has something that no dog has: a certain toughness that enables him to get by.

We moved along the rim rock. I was holding the binoculars by the strap when we reached the next little peak from which we could look down in the canyon.

Pete's exclamation at my elbow showed me that he had seen the camp. I raised the binoculars, and through them saw an automobile, rather battered and dilapidated; a white tent;

a canteen; a cot; a box of provisions. Then I saw a woman's bare arm reach out around the edge of the tent and pick something from the box.

"Looks like a woman down there," I said.

"What the devil would anybody want to camp in that canyon for?" asked Pete.

"Prospector maybe," I told him.

"A woman prospector?" he asked.

"Maybe. She had a white arm. Looked like she was city-bred."

"Just the arm showed?" asked Pete.

"That was all," I said.

"All right," he said. "Keep the binoculars then."

Suddenly the woman came out from around the edge of the tent. I could see at once that she was city-bred. The cut of her clothes, the delicacy of her complexion, the angry red sunburn on the backs of her forearms, all told the story. But the thing that interested me and held me breathlessly watching was the expression on her face. It was an expression of sheer terror.

The police dog had evidently been out with her and had lost her. He had been smelling along the dry sand of the desert, trying to pick up her trail; and now he was trotting along at her side, wagging his tail. Yet the woman's face was twisted and distorted with terror.

She was carrying something in her hand, and she ran twenty or thirty yards back up the slope to the roots of a sagebrush and started digging with her left hand. Her right hand pushed something into the little hole, and then she patted the sand over it, got to her feet, and walked back toward the camp.

I handed the binoculars to Pete, and as my eyes focused on the camp I saw two dots moving from around the slope of the canyon. I saw the police dog grow rigid, and after a few seconds I could hear the sound of his bark.

"Hell," said Pete, "she looks scared."

"She is," I said. "Look at the two dots coming around the slope there, about half a mile down the canyon, Pete."

He raised the glasses and grunted as his eyes took in the two dots. "Two men," he said, "with rifles and six-guns. They've got cartridges in the belts of the six-guns, and they look as though they were getting ready to shoot."

"Are they coming toward the camp?" I asked.

"Toward the camp," he said. "Hell, Bob, after this I think I'm going to carry these tenderfoot contraptions all the time. In the meantime, I'm going down and cut in on that deal."

"Count me in," I told him.

He snapped the binoculars back into the case.

"Going back to get the burros?" I asked him.

"They'll wait," he told me. "Let's go."

The rim rock was a good ten feet in a straight drop. Then there was some loose sand, and the sheer slope of the side of the canyon.

Pete went over the rim rock without hesitation, lit in the sand, threw up a flurry of dust, made two jumps, and started sliding down the ridge. I didn't make quite so clean a leap, and I felt the impact as I struck the sand. My feet went out from under me, I rolled over a couple of times, got to my feet, and started sprinting down the slope, digging my heels into the soil, grabbing at the little clumps of sagebrush and taking long jumps to avoid the patches of rock.

Pete kept gaining on me. I don't know why he didn't go down head over heels, but he managed to bound down as lightly as a mountain goat.

II

Manners in the Desert

Apparently the girl didn't see or hear us. She was looking at two men who were approaching.

The police dog heard us, however, and whirled, starting to bark. With that the woman turned and saw us, of course. She called the dog back and stood staring at us, and once more I caught the expression of terror on her face.

Pete's bronze hand went to his sombrero, swept it off in a bow, and he said, "Pardon me, ma'am, we just dropped in."

There was a ghost of a smile on her face, but it still held that expression of terror.

"It was almost a drop," she said, looking back up the slope where the dust clouds were still drifting about in the hot sun. "Who are you and what do you want?"

Pete jerked his head toward the direction of the approaching figures. "Just thought," he said, "that we'd see if you needed any assistance."

I saw her mouth tighten. "No," she said, "you can't be of any assistance to me."

I didn't beat about the bush at all. "Do you know the men who are coming?" I asked.

"I think so," she said.

"What do they want?" I asked.

"Me," she said.

I waited for an explanation, but there wasn't any. The dog was growling in his throat, but he was lying on the ground where she had ordered him to stay, his yellow eyes glinting from us to the men who were coming up the dry wash.

The two men came up with the tense, watchful attitude

of men who are expecting to engage in gunplay at almost any minute. They looked us over and they looked the girl over. One of them stepped off to one side and said to the girl, "You're Margaret Blake?"

She nodded her head.

"You know who we are and why we are here?" he said.

She said nothing.

He looked from her over to us. "Who are these men?" he asked.

"I don't know," she said.

The man shifted his attention to Pete. "What's your connection with this?" he asked.

Pete grinned at him, a cold, frosty grin. "Don't you know who I am?" he asked.

"No," said the other man, his eyes narrowing, "who are you?"

"I'm the guy," said Pete, "who is going to see that the young woman here gets a square deal."

"This woman," said the man, "is under arrest."

"Arrest for what?" asked Pete.

"As an accessory," said the man.

"To what?"

"Murder."

Pete laughed. "She don't look like she'd be good at murder," he said.

"You can't always tell by looks," said one of the men. "Now, you two fellows get started out of here. I don't like the way you horned in on this party."

"Don't you, now?" said Pete.

The other man said in a low voice, "Make them give up their guns, Charlie. We can't let them go out in the desert with their guns. They might ambush us."

"Yes," said Charlie. "You fellows will have to leave your guns here."

"Now *I'll* tell one," I told him.

I saw grinning devils appear at the corners of Pete's mouth, caught the glint of his blue eyes as he reached slowly to his gun, pulled it out of the holster, and looked at it almost meditatively.

"You don't want me to give *this* gun up?" he asked.

"That's what we want," said Charlie.

"This gun," said Pete, "is a funny gun. It goes off accidentally, every once in a while."

"Pete!" I cautioned him.

The warning came too late. There was a spurt of flame from Pete's gun. I heard the impact of the heavy bullet as it struck the stock of the rifle in the hands of the man nearest Pete.

There was nothing to do but back his play, and so I made what speed I could snaking my six-gun from its holster.

The two men were taken completely by surprise. They had thought that their rifles were sufficient to command the situation. As a matter of fact, at close quarters a rifle is very likely to prove a cumbersome weapon, particularly when a man tries to take in too much territory with it.

"Drop it!" I told the man.

His eyes looked into the barrel of my Colt, and there was a minute when I didn't know exactly what was going to happen. Then the gun thudded to the sand. The bullet had jerked the other's gun from his grasp.

"All right, Bob," said Pete, "they'll get their hands in the air, and you can unbuckle the belts and let their six-guns slip off."

"First, let's make sure they've got their hands in the air," I told him.

Two pairs of hands came up slowly.

"You boys are making the mistake of your lives," said Charlie. "You're going to find yourselves in the pen for this."

"Please don't," the girl pleaded with us. "I'll go with them. It's inevitable."

"No," said Pete, "I don't like their manners—and I always play my hunches."

I unbuckled the guns, let them drop to the ground.

"We're officers," Charlie started to explain, "and you—"

"Sure," said Pete. "I knew you were officers as soon as I saw you. You've got that look about you—and your manners are so rotten. Now turn around and start walking back the way you came. I suppose you've got an automobile staked out around the edge of the slope, haven't you?"

They didn't say anything.

Pete shook his head. "Rotten manners," he said. "You don't answer courteous questions."

"Please!" said the girl. "Don't do this for me. He's right in what he says. You're going to get into serious trouble."

"Miss," said Pete, "getting into serious trouble is something that I'm accustomed to. I get into a new kind of trouble every day. Come on you two, let's march."

We turned them around, but it took a prod with the muzzle of my six-gun to get Charlie started. After they had started they moved along doggedly and steadily.

We rounded the slope and found their car parked in a little draw. Pete's gun pointed the road to town.

"I'm going to be standing here," he said, "until that car is just a little black spot in the middle of a dust cloud, way over on the desert there. And if you should hesitate or turn around and start back, something tells me that you'll have tire trouble right away."

The men didn't say a word. They climbed into the automobile. The starting motor whirred, the engine responded, and the car crept along the sandy wash, struck the harder road, and rattled into speed. Pete and I stood there until the machine had vanished in the distance, leaving behind it nothing but a wisp of dust.

Pete looked at me and grinned. "Sore, Bob?" he asked.

"No," I told him. "I had to back your play, but I wish

you'd use a little discretion sometimes."

"Discretion, hell!" he said. "There's no fun in discretion. Let's go back and talk with the woman. You can figure it out for yourself, Bob. She's okay. Those men were on the wrong track, that's all."

I wasn't so certain, but I holstered my weapon. We started trudging back through the sand. When we rounded the edge of the slope and could look up the canyon, I could see dust settling in the afternoon sunlight.

"Two dust clouds," I told him grimly.

Sure enough, the camp was still there; but the automobile, the young woman, and the police dog had gone.

Pete looked at me, and his face was ludicrous in its crestfallen surprise. "Hell!" he said.

"It's going to take them about two hours to get to town," I said. "Then they'll get some more guns, a couple of others to help them, and start back. The next question is, where can we be in two hours?"

Pete's eyes started to twinkle once more. "I know a swell bunch of country where there's an old cabin," he said, "and I don't think the burros would leave much of a trail getting up there."

"How far can we be on that trail in two hours?" I wanted to know.

"We can be pretty near there."

"Okay," I told him. "Let's go."

We climbed back up to the burros, got the string lined up, and started plodding up the slope toward the old cabin that Pete knew about.

After about an hour the country changed, and we began to run into stunted cedar, glimpsing pines up on the high slopes of the mountain country beyond. Another half hour, and we were well up in the mountains, from where we could look back over the desert.

I paused and pointed back toward the place where I knew the little desert town was situated. "Pete," I said, "you've got those binoculars. Take a look and see if you can see anything that looks like pursuit."

He was focusing the binoculars on the road when I heard a peculiar throbbing sound which grew in volume. I raised my eyes and picked out a little speck against the blue sky—a speck that might have been a buzzard, except that it was moving forward across the sky with steady purpose.

I tapped Pete on the shoulder and pointed with my finger. He raised the binoculars, looked for a minute, and then twisted his face into a grimace.

"They'll pick her up with that," I said, "before she's gone thirty miles."

"There's lots of places she could go inside of thirty miles," Pete said.

"Not with that automobile," I told him, "and not in this country."

Pete shrugged his shoulders. "How the hell did we know they were going to get an airplane to chase her with?"

"How the hell did I know that you were going to start gunplay?" I told him, with some irritation in my voice.

"You should have been able to tell that," said Pete, "by looking at the woman. She was too pretty."

I sighed. "Well," I told him, "I always wanted to know what it felt like to be a fugitive from justice."

"Hell!" said Pete from the depths of his experience. "There ain't no novelty to it—not after the first time or two. It feels just like anything else."

I didn't say anything more. I merely watched the airplane as it diminished in the distance. I was still looking at it when I saw two other planes coming from the west. The plane I had seen first tilted from side to side, making signaling motions, and the other two planes swung in behind it. I focused the binoculars on them and saw them fly in formation, until suddenly they started down toward the desert.

The sun was just setting. The valley was filled with deep purple shadows. In the high places was the hush of coming twilight.

"What did you see?" asked Pete.

"Two more planes," I told him, snapping the binoculars into the leather case.

Pete grinned at me. "That," he said, "isn't going to keep us from eating, is it?"

"Not this meal," I told him, "but I don't know about the next."

III

Accessories to the Crime

Pete had his blankets spread out on the other side of a little ridge. I was careful not to disturb him as I got up and sat there in the moonlight, looking down on the dark mystery of the shadow-filled valleys below. It was cold up here, but I had a blanket wrapped around me, Indian fashion.

Down below, as far as the eye could reach, stretched the desert; a great waste of level spaces, broken by jagged mountain spurs—mountains that were still a part of the desert, dry, arid, covered with juniper, stunted cedar, and an occasional pine. There were no tumbling streams, no dense underbrush—just barren rock and dry trees that rustled in the wind which was blowing from the desert.

Looking down into the black splotches of darkness in the valleys, I knew what was going on in the desert. The wind was stirring the sand into soft whispers, typifying the restlessness of the desert. For the desert is ever restless, ever changing. Its moods change as frequently as the appearance of the desert mountains is changed by sunlight and shadow.

Even up here in this cold, high place the desert seemed to be whispering its mysterious messages; the noise made by drifting sand as it scours against the soft desert rocks, carving them into weird structures, polishing, cutting, drifting, changing, ever changing.

I sat there for three or four hours, watching the moon climb over the eastern rim of the mountains, watching the black pools of mysterious shadow in the canyons gradually recede until the golden surface of the desert glinted up at me from below. Several times I listened to hear Pete's snores, but no sound came from his direction.

After a while I felt somewhat relaxed, and rolled back into my blankets, where it was warmer. In fifteen or twenty minutes I began to feel drowsy, and drifted off to sleep. After all, as Pete had remarked, being a fugitive from justice didn't feel particularly unique, once one had become accustomed to it.

I woke early in the morning and watched the east taking on a brassy hue. It was still and cold. There was not a sound, not a breath. The stars, which had blazed steadily during the night, had now receded to mere needle points of light; and soon they became invisible.

I kicked back the blankets, put on my boots and leather jacket, stamped my feet to get the circulation in them, and walked around the little ledge, to the place where Pete had spread his blankets. The blankets were there, but Pete wasn't.

I looked over the ground, and felt of the blankets. There was frost on the inside of them, where they had been turned back when Pete slipped out. I studied the tracks as well as I could, and then I knew that Pete had slipped one over on me. He had pulled out long before I had got up to watch the moonlight.

Fifty yards from camp I found a piece of paper stuck on a bush. When he had to be, Pete was glib with his tongue, and glib with a pencil if he couldn't talk. He was one of those fellows who expressed himself well.

I unfolded the note and read:

Dear Bob:

I got you into this, and there's no reason why I shouldn't take the blame. You didn't do anything except follow my lead. I don't know how serious it is, but I'm going to find out. You sit tight until I come back.

(Signed) Pete

I should have known that Pete would have done something like that, and I felt irritated that I hadn't guessed it in advance and guarded against it.

It was all right for Pete to claim that I had been blameless and that he was going to take the responsibility. I probably wouldn't have started things if Pete hadn't been there—and then again I might have. But I didn't need a nurse or a guardian, and when I pulled a gun on an officer it was my own free and voluntary act. I didn't like the way Pete was trying to shield me, as though I were a child, instead of a man ten years his senior.

I got some firewood together, got the coffee to boiling, and sat crouched by the fire, warming my hands and waiting for a while before I drank the coffee, hoping that Pete would show up. When he didn't show up, I drank a couple of cups of coffee, but kept the pot hot so that he could have some when he came in.

The sun climbed slowly up the blue-black of the desert sky, and there was still no sign of Pete. I went out on a projecting rock where I could look down into the valley, and kept watch on what was going on. Toward ten o'clock I heard the sound of automobiles, and I could make them out through the glasses, two carloads of men jolting their way along the floor of the valley.

An hour later, I heard them coming back; and the glasses

showed me that which I had dreaded to see, yet expected. In the rear seat of the first automobile was a man and a woman. At that distance I couldn't make out their features, but I didn't have much doubt who they were.

I waited until the machines had gone the length of the valley and turned through the pass into the level desert, then I threw packs on the burros and started back down the mountain. Pete knew exactly where I had been camped, and he also knew that I had the binoculars. I figured that he probably would have a chance to use his pencil once more.

I hit the trail of the automobiles and started following along, keeping my eyes pretty much on the ground. Within half a mile I found what I was looking for, a folded piece of paper lying by the side of the road, catching the glint of the hot desert sun. I unfolded the paper. It was a note from Pete, all right. He hadn't put any heading on it at all, so that if the officers discovered it, it wouldn't give them any clue which would lead to me. The note read simply:

> They caught me. I put up a fight, but they got me, and I guess they got me dead to rights. The woman is the daughter of Sam Blake. Blake killed a prospector named Skinner who had a cabin over in Sidewinder Canyon. They jailed him, and the woman helped him escape. They caught him again and are holding her as an accessory. I don't know what they're going to put against me. I told them you didn't know anything about it and had backed my play with an empty gun. I don't think they're going to look for you.

I knew Bob Skinner, and I also knew the place over in Sidewinder Canyon. It was fifteen or twenty miles over the mountains.

There was nothing much to be done except trail along behind the automobiles, so I plugged along doggedly through the desert sunshine. All the time, I kept thinking about the stuff the woman had buried at the foot of the sagebrush when she saw the two men coming from the direction of the road. When I got near that first camp of hers, I made a detour and went into it. The officers had been all through it, probably looking for evidence.

I climbed back into the shade cast by a spur of rock, and got out the tenderfoot's binoculars again. When I was sure that I had the desert all to myself, I went over to the clump of sagebrush and dug in the sand.

I found a package done up in a newspaper. The package had hacksaw blades and a gun. The hacksaw blades had been used, and I figured that was how Sam Blake had managed to slip out of jail. As far as I could tell, the gun hadn't been fired.

It was a .45 single-action Colt, and it had been carried around quite a bit in a holster.

I looked at the newspaper. It was an extra edition, hurriedly thrown together; one of those little hand-printed efforts put out in small desert towns, usually once a week or once every two weeks.

Ordinarily they contained nothing more exciting than a chronicle of the comings and goings of people who live in a small community.

But this paper was different. Across the top, in big blotchy headlines, black type announced:

BLAKE BREAKS JAIL

Down below:

OFFICERS SUSPECT WOMAN ACCOMPLICE

I sat down on my heels in the sand, and read everything that the paper contained. It was an account of the jailbreak, which didn't interest me particularly, and an account of the crime, which interested me more.

Sam Blake charged that Bob Skinner had jumped a claim which Blake had staked, stripping the claim of the valuable gold that was in a pocket and then skipping out.

I knew Skinner. He was the sort of customer who would be likely to do that very thing. Blake asserted that Skinner had picked up more than five thousand dollars in gold from the pocket, and so Blake had taken his gun and gone down into Sidewinder Canyon.

A lunger by the name of Ernest Peterman had seen him going down toward Skinner's cabin. Peterman had a little cabin up on the summit of a ridge on the east side of Sidewinder Canyon. He'd seen Blake coming along the trail which led to the canyon, and had recognized him. He'd watched him go down to Skinner's cabin. It had been about two-thirty in the afternoon, and Peterman said he knew that Skinner was alive at the time because there was a lot of smoke coming out of the chimney of Skinner's shack. He hadn't paid any particular attention to it, however; he'd just given the scene a casual glance and then gone out to take his afternoon sunbath.

It happened that a ranger had dropped in to see Skinner sometime the next day. He'd found Skinner dead, with a bullet hole in his forehead and a knife wound in his heart. He'd found horse tracks in the trail, and had been able to mark them because of a broken shoe on the right hind foot. He'd trailed the horse into the little settlement, had found it, identified it as belonging to Blake, and had finally forced Blake to admit that he'd been to the cabin.

At first Blake denied it. Later on, he admitted that he'd gone down to have a settlement with Skinner, but he claimed that Skinner was dead when he got there. Things looked black for him because he hadn't reported the murder, and because at first he'd denied that he'd gone down to see Skinner at all. But the thing that clinched the case against him was the testimony of the lunger. If smoke had been coming out of the chimney at the time Blake hit the shack, it was a cinch Skinner had been alive then. Nobody doubted the good faith of the lunger.

I read the paper and frowned. I could see that Pete Ayers had acted on impulse, and the impulse had led him into trouble. We were going to be hooked as accessories, along with the girl. The authorities didn't like the idea of Blake sawing the bars of the jail window and slipping out into the night.

I led the burros over to a nearby spring, saw that they had water, and then started on the long journey over the mountains to Sidewinder Canyon. I didn't dare to strike the main trails. On the other hand, with burros I could keep moving over the desert mountains, particularly after the moon came up.

IV

The Desert Whispers

It was well past daylight when I came out of the jagged mountain formation on the west and into Sidewinder Canyon. I could look down the twisting canyon and see the roof of the prospector's shack. I staked out the burros, and went down on foot.

I could see where the officers and the curious ones had been tramping around the shack. It sat out on a little sandy plateau, and there had been a desert wind in the night which had wiped out most of the tracks; yet they showed as confused indentations in the sand.

It looked as though at least ten or a dozen people had milled around the shack, tracking down the ground.

I went into the cabin. The door was open, of course, as is customary in mountain or desert cabins. There was the damp, musty smell of places which are shaded from the purifying effect of direct sunlight. There was also another musty smell which was more ominous and unforgettable; the smell of death.

I found the bed where Skinner had been sleeping. I found red stains, dry and crusted, on the blankets; stains also on the floor. Lazy flies buzzed in circles over the red stains. It was not a pleasant place to be.

I made but a casual inspection. I knew that others had been there before, and that every inch of the cabin had been searched. Doubtless some of the searchers had been desert men.

I walked out into the sunlight and took a great breath of fresh air, looking up into the clear blue of the cloudless sky, then over at the glittering expanse of jagged, barren ranges which hemmed in the canyon. Everything was still and silent.

Far up in the heavens a black dot marked a circling buzzard.

I started to look around.

It was ten minutes later that I saw something I couldn't explain. That was a fresh break in the little corral back of the house. It was a crazy structure of weather-beaten lumber, held together by rusted nails and supported by posts set into the soft sand at various angles. It was the place where Bob Skinner had kept his prospecting burros; and I could see that a horse had been in the corral recently, and it looked to me as though the break in the corral had been done recently. In one place a board had been splintered, and the splinters hadn't as yet become dulled by the desert sunlight. The clean board showed out from beneath its weather-beaten veneer.

I looked over the stretch of sand around the corral. Useless to look for tracks there. The wind had leveled the sand out and made it into miniature drifts. It was right in line with the opening of a little canyon, down which the night wind would sweep with concentrated force.

I rolled a cigarette and sat looking at that break in the corral fence. After a while I started up the canyon. By the time I had gone a hundred yards I came to a little sheltered place, where there was some soft sand that hadn't been blown by the wind. I saw the tracks of a horse, and to one side the print of a booted foot.

The sun was climbing higher now, and the walls of the little canyon began to radiate heat. I plugged my way along over the rocks, searching for the faintest sign of tracks. A little later on I found more tracks. Then I struck a little trail that ran along the side of the canyon, and in this trail it was easy to follow the tracks. They were the tracks of a horse, and behind the horse, the tracks of a man.

I worked along the little dry canyon, and struck a level place. The horse was running here, and the tracks of the man were heavy on the toes and lighter on the heels.

After a while I got into country that didn't have much sand, but I could follow the tracks better because there hadn't been anything to drift with the desert night wind. I saw the tracks of the horse climb up a ridge, and I followed them.

Near the top of the ridge I struck horse tracks again, and farther on I struck horse tracks and no man tracks. I followed the horse tracks off and on for three or four hundred yards, looking for man tracks. There weren't any.

I went back and tried to pick up the man tracks. I couldn't find them again. They had gone to the top of the ridge and then vanished.

I sat down on my heels, rolled another cigarette, and thought for a while.

There was a spring down the ridge, and three or four miles over toward the head of Sidewinder Canyon. It wasn't a particularly good spring—just a trickle of brackish water, thick with alkali—but it was a spring just the same. I started working down toward that spring.

I didn't see any man tracks until I was within fifty yards of the spring; then I picked up the tracks of booted feet again. As nearly as I could tell, they were the same tracks that I had seen following along behind the horse tracks.

I searched around the spring, and found horse tracks.

These didn't look like the same horse tracks that I had seen earlier in the day. They were the tracks of a bigger horse, and they seemed to be fresher. I went over to the trail which led into the spring, and I could see where the horse had come in along this trail and gone out along it.

I kept poking along, looking in the sagebrush, and finally I found a hole dug in the side of the mountain. It was about a foot deep by two feet long. I poked around in the hole. It wasn't a hole that had been dug with a shovel, but something that had been scooped in the side of the mountain, and half filled in with slag from the side of the bank above. There wasn't anything in the hole.

I went down and followed the tracks of the horse. They went down the trail, evenly spaced and at regular intervals.

I turned back from that trail and went back up the ridges the way I had come into the spring. It was hot now, and the sun was beating down with steady, eye-dazzling fury.

I managed to get back up to the last place where I had found the horse tracks, and started tracking the horse. That was comparatively easy. The horse had worked over toward the west and north, following down a ridge which wasn't quite so rocky, and on which there was a more dusty soil to hold the tracks.

I knew that my burros were trained in the ways of the desert and could shift for themselves until I got back; but I was in need of food, and the inside of my mouth felt raw from drinking the alkali water at the little spring. Nevertheless I kept pushing on, working against time, and at length I found where the horse had started wandering back and forth from a direct line, as though looking for something to graze on.

I followed the tracks until it got dark, and then I built a little fire and huddled over it, keeping warm until the moon came up. Then I began my tracking once more. It was slow work, but I took no chances of getting off the trail. I just worked slowly along the trail, following it along the sides of the ridges; and finally I came to something black lying on the ground.

I saw that it was a saddle, and feeling the tie in the latigo, I could tell that the saddle had been bucked off. The horn was smashed, and there were places where the iron hooves had cut the leather of the saddle. The horse had evidently bucked and twisted, and had walked out from under the saddle. The blankets were off to one side. Rocks were pushed loose from the indentations in the earth which had held them, as though the horse had been standing on his head and striking out with all four feet.

I marked the place where the saddle was, and kept on working down the slope.

It was still dark when I heard a horse whinny.

I called to him. Then I heard his shod feet ringing on the rocks as he came up to me. He was glad to see me. Right then, a man represented food and water to him, and he was eager for human companionship. There wasn't any rope around his neck, but I didn't need any. I twisted my fingers in his mane, and he followed along with me like a dog. When I came back to the place where the saddle lay, I got it back on him, and climbed into it.

He had lost his bridle, but I cut off the strings from the saddle, roped them together, and made a rough hackamore.

The horse was weak, thirsty, and tired; but he was glad to yield to human direction once more, and he carried me back over the ridges.

It was two hours past daylight when I came to the spring, where the horse drank greedily. I let him rest for half or three quarters of an hour, and gave him a chance to browse on some of the greenery which grew around the edges of the water. Then I sent him down the trail and found my burros, standing with full stomachs and closed eyes, their long ears drooping forward.

I got a rope from my pack, slipped it around the neck of

the horse, and started along the trail which led up the east slope of the mountains on the side of the canyon. When I got to the top I poked around, looking for a camp, and after a while I saw the glint of the sun on something white. A man rolled over in the sunlight, pulled a blanket around his nude figure, and got to his feet. He stood grinning at me sheepishly.

I rode over to him. "You're Ernest Peterman?" I asked.

He nodded. He was getting back his health there in the high places of the desert, I knew. That much could be seen in the bronzed skin, the clear eye, and the poise of his head.

Man has devised many different methods for combating various ills, but he has never yet devised anything which is superior to the healing hand of nature in the desert. Let a man get into the high places of the dry desert atmosphere, where the sun beats down from a cloudless sky; let him live a simple life, bathing in sunshine, and resting with the cold night air fresh in his nostrils, and there is nothing which is incurable.

"I wanted you to take a little ride with me," I told him.

"How far?" he asked.

"Just up to the top of the ridge."

"All right. In an hour or so?"

"No," I told him. "Now. I want to get there about a certain time in the afternoon."

"What time?" he asked.

"The same time that you saw Sam Blake go down into Sidewinder Canyon," I told him.

He shrugged his shoulders and shook his head, as though trying to shake loose some disagreeable memory.

"I didn't want to do it," he said.

"Do what?" I asked.

"Testify," he told me.

"I didn't say you did."

"I know," he said. "It isn't that. It's just the thoughts that have been worrying me lately. Have you seen his daughter?"

393

I nodded.

"A wonderful girl," he said. "I don't think her father could be a murderer."

"He went down there with a gun, didn't he?" I asked.

"Yes."

"You don't suppose he just went down there to pay a social call, do you?"

"I don't know. He'd been robbed. Everybody seems to think that Skinner really robbed him."

"Did you know Skinner at all well?" I asked.

He shook his head.

"Ever get up to the top of the ridge much?"

"I've been up there once or twice in the morning."

"How did you happen to be up there on that particular afternoon?"

"I don't know. I was restless, and I just started walking up there. It was a hot day. I took it easy."

"And the shadows were just beginning to form on the western rim of the mountains?" I asked.

He nodded.

"And you could look down on Skinner's little shack?"

He nodded again.

"All right," I said, "I'd like to have you take a ride up there with me."

I let him ride the horse, and he seemed to feel a lot easier when I had a rope around the horse's neck, leading him. I took it that Peterman was pretty much of a tenderfoot in the desert.

"How did you happen to come to the desert country?" I asked him.

"I've tried everything else."

"Are you afraid of it?"

"Yes," he said, "I was dreadfully afraid at first. And then I got so I wasn't afraid."

"How did that happen?" I wanted to know. "Usually when a man sees the desert he either loves it or he hates it. If he hates it his hatred is founded on fear."

"I know," he said. "I hated it at first, and I hated it because I was afraid of it. I'm willing to admit it."

"What changed you?"

"You'd laugh if I told you," he said.

I looked at him, at the bronzed skin, the clear eye, the steady poise of the head, and I smiled. "Perhaps," I said, "I wouldn't laugh."

"It was the whispers," he said. "The whispers at night."

"You mean the sand whispers?" I asked.

He nodded. "There was something reassuring about them," he said. "At first they frightened me. It seemed as though voices were whispering at me; and then, gradually, I began to see that this was the desert, trying to talk; that it was whispering words of reassurance."

I nodded, and we didn't say anything more until we got to the summit of the ridge. I looked over the ridge, and checked Peterman as he started to look over.

"Not yet," I said. "Wait about fifteen minutes."

He sat and looked at me as though he thought I might be a little bit off in my upper story. But already the desert had begun to put its mark upon him; and so he didn't say anything, merely watched me as I smoked a cigarette.

When I had finished two cigarettes, I nodded my head.

"All right," I said. "Now look over."

He got up and looked over the top of the ridge. He looked around for a moment and said, "I don't see anything."

"Look down at Skinner's cabin."

He looked down, and all of a sudden I heard him give an exclamation, his eyes widening in surprise.

I unstrapped the binoculars and handed them to him. "All right," I said, "take another look."

V

Make Way for a Witness

Sun beat down upon the little desert town with its dusty main street and its unpainted board structures squatting in the gray desert which lined either side of the road. A big pile of tin cans marked the two ends of the main street, and these piled-up tin cans were bordered by a nondescript collection of junk which spread out over the desert, interspersed with clumps of sagebrush.

There were occasional automobiles on the street; automobiles, for the most part, of an ancient vintage, innocent of finish and as weather-beaten and dust-covered as the board structures themselves. There were also horses tied to the hitching rack in front of the general merchandise store, and a couple of sleepy burros rested on three legs at a time, casting black shadows on a dusty street.

We rode toward the building where the preliminary hearing was being held. A crowd of people were jammed into the little structure, despite the intense sunlight which beat down upon the roof. Other people crowded around the outside of the building, blocking the windows, craning their necks to listen. Out in the street little groups, recognizing the futility of trying to hear what was going on inside, formed gabbing centers of gossip to discuss the case.

I climbed from the saddle burro and dropped the rope reins over his head. "Make way for a witness," I said.

Men looked around at men. "Hell! It's Bob Zane," someone said. "Make way, you fellows, here comes Bob Zane."

I pushed my way into the courtroom. The tenderfoot clung to my blue shirt. He was sort of frightened and subdued. The atmosphere of the place reeked with the odor of packed bodies and many breaths. People stared at us with cold, curious eyes.

Abruptly, the little space around the judge's desk opened ahead of us, and the two officers stared with startled eyes into my face. One of them went for his gun.

"There he is now!" shouted Charlie, the deputy.

"Order in the courtroom!" yelled a wizened justice of the peace, whose white goatee quavered with indignation.

The officer pulled out the gun and swung it in my direction. "The man who was the accomplice of Pete Ayers, one of the defendants in this case," he shouted.

The judge banged on the desk. "Order in the court! Order in the court! Order in the court!" he screamed in a high piping voice.

I squared myself and planted my feet, conscious of the business end of the gun that was trained at my middle.

"Just a minute," I said. "I came to surrender myself and demand an immediate hearing. I'm charged with being an accessory in a murder case. I can't be an accessory unless there's been a murder, and unless the person I aided is guilty. I've got a witness with me who wants to change his testimony."

I half turned, and pushed forward the tenderfoot.

Peterman looked about him, gulped, and nodded.

"You can't interrupt proceedings this way!" piped the judge.

"Don't you want to hear the evidence?" I asked.

"Of course," he said, "but you aren't a witness."

I held up my right hand and moved a step forward, holding him with my eyes. "All right," I said, "swear me in."

He hesitated a moment, then his head nodded approvingly as his shrill, falsetto voice intoned the formal oath of a witness.

I moved abruptly toward the witness chair. One of the

officers started toward me with handcuffs, but I turned to face the judge. I began to speak rapidly, without waiting to be questioned by anybody.

"The man who killed Bob Skinner," I said, "put a horse in Skinner's corral. When he had finished killing Skinner, there was blood on his hands, and when he tried to catch the horse, the horse smelled the blood, and lunged away from him. The man chased after the horse in a frenzy of haste, and the horse broke through the corral fence and started up the canyon, back of the house. The man followed along behind him, trying to catch the horse.

"A windstorm obliterated the tracks in the sand in front of the corral and around the house, so that the tracks couldn't have been seen unless the officers had appreciated the significance of that break in the corral fence and had gone on up the canyon looking for tracks. I took the course that a horse would naturally have taken, and I picked up the tracks again, up the canyon. And also the tracks of the man who was following."

Having gone that far, I could see that I wasn't going to be interrupted. I looked out over the courtroom and saw eyes that were trained upon me, sparkling with curiosity. I saw that the judge was leaning forward on the edge of his chair. The two officers had ceased their advance and were standing rooted to the spot.

Pete Ayers, who had stared at me with consternation when I pushed my way into the courtroom, was now grinning happily. Damn him! I don't suppose he ever knows what it is to worry over anything. He is as happy-go-lucky as a cloud of drifting sand in the desert. The girl was staring at me with a white face and bloodless lips. She didn't yet appreciate what my coming meant; but Pete knew me, and his face was twisted into that gleeful grin which characterizes him when he is getting out of a tight place.

"All right," snapped the judge in that high, piping voice of his, "go on. What did you find?"

"I followed the horse tracks to the top of the ridge," I said, "and I found where the man had quit chasing the horse. Then I followed the man tracks a way, and lost them. But I figured what a man would do who was out in the desert and hot from chasing a horse he couldn't catch. So I worked on down the ridge to a spring, and once more found the tracks, this time at the spring. I looked around and found where the man had dug a hole and had buried something near the spring. Then I found where he had walked out, secured another horse, ridden back to the spring, pulled whatever had been in the hole out of its place of concealment, and ridden away. He hadn't bothered to look after the horse that had been left in the mountains, figuring that it would die in the desert from lack of water and food.

"I then went back to the place where I had left the horse tracks, and started following the horse. Eventually I found the saddle, and then I found the horse."

There was a commotion in the courtroom. The officers conferred together in whispers, and one of them started toward the door. I quit talking for a little while and watched the officer who was pushing his way through the swirling group of men.

Outside the building a horse whinnied, and the whinny sounded remarkably significant, upon the hot, still air and the sudden silence of that room—a silence broken only by the irregular breathing of men who are packed into the narrow quarters, and who must breathe through their mouths.

"Well?" rasped the judge. "Go on. What happened?"

"I found the saddle," I said, "and I found the horse. I brought the horse back and I brought the saddle back."

"What does all that prove?" asked the judge, curiously.

"It proves," I said, "that the murderer of Bob Skinner wasn't Sam Blake. It proves that Sam Blake came down to call for a showdown with Bob Skinner, but Skinner was dead when he got there. Somebody had murdered Skinner in order to take the gold from his cabin, and the horse had balked at the odor of blood. The murderer had chased the horse for a while, but he couldn't continue to chase him, because he was carrying enough gold to make it difficult for him to keep going after the horse. So he went down to the spring and cached the gold; then he went out to get another horse, and later came back after the gold."

The judge's glittering eyes swung as unerringly as those of a vulture spotting a dead rabbit to the bronzed face of Ernest Peterman, the tenderfoot.

"That man," he said, "swears that he saw smoke coming out of Bob Skinner's cabin just before Sam Blake went in there."

"He *thought* he saw smoke, your honor," I said. "He's a tenderfoot, and new to the desert. He didn't go up on the ridge very often, and he wasn't familiar with Bob Skinner's cabin. Particularly when the afternoon sunlight throws a black shadow from the western ridge."

"What's the shadow got to do with it?" asked the judge.

"It furnishes a black background for the tree that's growing just back of the house, right in line with the chimney on Skinner's cabin."

"A tree?" piped the judge. "What's a tree got to do with it?"

"The tree," I said slowly, "is a blue paloverde tree."

"What's a blue paloverde tree?" the judge inquired petulantly.

"One that you've seen many times, your honor," I said, "in certain sections of the desert. It only grows in a very few places in the desert. It requires a certain type of soil and a certain type of climate. It isn't referred to as a paloverde tree in these parts. Your honor has probably heard it called a smoke tree."

I sat back and let that shot crash home.

The blue paloverde grows in the desert. The Indians

called it the smoke tree because it sends up long, lacy branches that are of a bluish-green; and when the sun is just right, seen against a black shadow, the smoke tree looks for all the world like a cloud of smoke rising up out of the desert.

Peterman was a tenderfoot, and he'd climbed up on the ridge just when the western shadows had furnished a black background for the smoke tree behind Skinner's cabin. He had taken a look at the scene and decided that smoke was coming out of the chimney. No one had ever thought to have him go back and take a look at the cabin under similar circumstances. They had been so certain that Sam Blake was guilty of the murder that they hadn't bothered to check the evidence closely.

The judge was staring at me as though I had destroyed some pet hobby of his. "Do you mean to say that a man mistook a smoke tree for smoke coming from a chimney?" he asked.

I nodded. "Keener eyes than his have made the same mistake, your honor," I said, "which is the reason the Indians called the tree the smoke tree."

"Then who owned the horse?" asked the judge. "Who was it that went in there before Sam Blake called at the cabin?"

I pointed my finger dramatically at the place where the officers had been standing.

"I had hoped," I said, "that the guilty man would betray himself by his actions. I notice that one of the men has left the courtroom hurriedly."

As I spoke, there was the sound of a terrific commotion from outside. A shot was fired, a man screamed, a horse gave a shrill squeal of agony; then there was the sound of a heavy, thudding impact, and the stamping of many feet.

Men turned and started pushing toward the narrow exit which led from the place where the hearing was being conducted. They were men who were accustomed to the freedom of the outdoors. When they started to go through a door, they all started at once.

It was a struggling rush of bodies that pulled and jostled. Some men made for the windows, some climbed on the shoulders and heads of others and fought their way over the struggling mass of humanity. Futilely, the judge pounded his gavel again and again. Margaret Blake screamed, and I saw Pete Ayers slip a circling arm around her shoulder and draw her close to him.

I thought it was a good time to explain to the judge.

"That horse I found, your honor," I said, pushing close to him so that I could make my voice heard above the bedlam of sound, "was a nervous bronco. He made up to me all right because he was thirsty and hungry, but he was a high-strung, high-spirited horse. I left him tied to the rack out in front. I thought perhaps the owner of the horse might try to climb on his back and escape, hoping to take that bit of four-legged evidence with him. But horses have long memories. The last time the horse had seen that man, he had smelled the odor of human blood and had gone crazy with fright."

The crowd thinned out of the courtroom. Here and there a man who had been pushed against a wall or trampled underfoot, cursed and ran, doubled over with pain, or limping upon a bad leg; but the courtroom had emptied with startling speed.

I crossed to the window as the judge laid down his gavel. Impelled by curiosity, he crowded to my side. Outside, we saw, the men were circling about a huddled figure on the sidewalk. The horse, his ears laid back, his nostrils showing red, his eyes rolled in his head until the whites were visible, was tugging and pulling against the rope that held him to the hitching rack. I noticed that there were red stains on one forehoof, and a bullet wound in his side.

Lying on the sidewalk, a rude affair of worn boards, was the crumpled body of the deputy who had helped to make the arrest of Margaret Blake that first time we had seen her. The whole top of his head seemed to have been beaten in by an iron hoof.

The judge looked and gasped. He started for the door, then caught himself with an appreciation of the dignity which he, as a magistrate, owed to himself. He walked gravely back to the raised desk which sat on the wooden platform, raised the gavel, and banged it down hard on the desk.

"Court," he said, "is adjourned!"

It wasn't until after Pete Ayers and Margaret Blake had started out in the desert on their honeymoon that I got to thinking of the words of the college professor.

The desert is a funny place. It's hard to know it long without thinking that there's something alive about it. You get to thinking those sand whispers are not just a hissing of dry sand particles against rock or sagebrush, but real whispers from the heart of the desert.

The desert shows itself in two ways. There's the grim cruelty which is really a kindness, because it trains men to rely upon themselves and never to make mistakes. Then there's the other side of the desert, the carefree dust clouds that drift here and there. They're as free as the air itself.

Pete Ayers was a part of the desert. The desert had branded him with the brand of carefree sunlight and the scurrying dust cloud.

The desert had recorded the telltale tracks that had led to the discovery of the real murderer. Every man is entitled to his own thoughts. Mine are that it's all just two sides of the desert, the grim side that holds justice for murderers, and the happy side that leaves its stamp on men like Pete Ayers.

Pete Ayers clapped me on the back. His bride stared at me with starry eyes.

"We owe it all to you, Bob Zane!" she said, her lips quivering.

But I looked out at the desert. The white heat of an afternoon sun had started the horizons to dancing in the heat waves. Mirages glinted in the distance. A gust of wind whipped up a little desert dust-spout, and it scurried along, the sagebrush bending its head as the dust-spout danced over it.

"No," I told her, "you owe it to the desert. The desert is kind to those who love it. She held the evidence, carved in sand, for the righting of a wrong and the betrayal of a real culprit to justice."

Pete Ayers grinned at me and said, "You're getting so you talk just like that swivel-eyed college professor you guided around last month."

But his smiling eyes shifted over my shoulder and caught sight of the swirling dust cloud scampering merrily over the desert. I watched his expression soften as his eyes followed the swirling sand. And then I knew that college professor was right.

Deborah Moulton

THE WINGÈD FOAL

T orin glanced about quickly to make sure no one was watching. Then he climbed down the rocky hill and ran along the chalk road toward the Transport Compound.

He was late. The afternoon wind had already whipped the sand into biting red clouds. His gold Medallion clanked against his chest as he ran. Sand spattered against his neck and stung his face. He lowered his head and wrapped his cloak close around him. Torin was still in the Unclaimed Zone. He knew the danger of being caught there. For a moment the boy could see the tall granite wall of the Compound. Then the sand clouds swirled again, and the wall dissolved into grainy shadow.

Suddenly the birth siren sliced through the twisting wind and sand with its pulsing call. Squinting, Torin could see the hooded form of his father standing by the stone gate. Would Gen punish him for leaving the Compound without permission? The birth siren sounded again, this time louder and closer. Gen motioned to his son. His sleeves billowed out like black crows in a storm. His hood had blown back, and his gray hair danced wildly in the wind.

"Torin! Come quickly, Saba's going to birth! She's refusing the birth harness!" Even though the wind was churning the sand into noisy vortices, Torin could hear the impatience in Gen's voice. Then, without waiting for his son's reply, the older man strode hurriedly back into the Compound.

Torin broke into a run. "She's not due yet, Father!" he called.

But Gen's cloak was already a blur in the dust. Several attendants muttered nervously among themselves as they flocked toward the huge stone barn. Torin could smell the dirt and rot of their tattered canvas capes as they jostled past him.

A wave of terror washed over Torin's body. His legs refused to run. He pulled in a jagged breath of sand-filled air and pushed his tongue hard against the top of his mouth. He reminded himself it was Saba this time. She would never knowingly hurt him. However, Torin could not stop his dread of transport births, any more than he could stop his dreams.

"Not now!" he whispered as his legs became numb and the vision began.

The image of the huge Egg, still wet, formed before his eyes. Already it rocked and shook in the birthing cage. Soon it was covered by a filigree of tiny cracks. The air was filled with the sound of claws scraping on shell, as the beast inside twitched, panted, and turned. All at once the Egg splintered. There was a hiss as one scaled arm after another climbed out of the broken shell. The claws were long with waiting, and the tail whipped back and forth angrily.

The attendants drew back in horror, forgetting the horse still chained to the birth harness. Unable to escape, the horse screamed and reared, then began to shake violently. The lizard, growing larger by the second, opened its huge black mouth. Its forked tongue rolled from side to side.

The creature began biting the birthing cage. Teeth clanged and rasped against the metal bars. Finally the iron broke. The thing was free!

Slowly the beast turned its reptilian head toward the horse. Its huge black eyes focused on Saba as it stepped carefully, almost daintily, out of the birthing cage. The head rocked from side to side as it eyed the horse, who had become strangely still.

There was a short, empty silence before the hissing began again. Then the thing rose up on its hind feet, flapped its bony wings, and descended hungrily on Saba, who only a few moments ago had sheltered the Egg within her body. There was complete darkness.

Torin shuddered as the vision faded. He looked for his father, but Gen had already entered the barn.

Although Torin was small for his age of fourteen harvests, he had been chosen for a position of authority in the Transport Compound. After all, the Teachers had given him the Medallion, the highest, most coveted honor on all Morn. It was the symbol of responsibility, worn by those selected to rule. He gripped the gold disk about his neck, took a deep breath, and banished the dream from his mind.

"I'm coming," Torin called. But his words were lost in the hot wind.

The inside of the building was strangely silent. Beads of moisture rolled down the stone walls. A crowd had begun to gather. Two attendant men sweated as they pulled taut the transport's reins between two huge tetherings. A third was adjusting the trapdoor on the iron birthing cage. The hinges squeaked as he pulled the door back and let it snap shut. The horse shied and kicked out nervously. Torin shouldered his way through the onlookers. Gen had rolled up his sleeves and stood waiting.

The mare's muscles began to twitch. Yellow mucus dripped from her mouth. She reared angrily as the attendant men tried to force her back into the metal birthing harness.

"Push her back, son," ordered Gen. "You're the one she trusts."

"Easy, Saba, easy," murmured Torin as he reached for her halter.

She pulled away snarling. Torin rubbed her neck gently. Her fur was like velvet, but underneath, her muscles snaked into hard knots. Her eyes dilated as she began the birthing scream. Mindless of the danger of her striking him with her hooves, and the horrible agonized sobbing that seemed to tear into his ears, Torin eased his body against her flank and pushed his shoulder into her. Step by step she backed into the harness. The attendants quickly strapped her to the metal restraining rings. Torin kept rubbing her head and neck. The horse pulled and shivered, and again the scream. The crowd of attendants gasped as the piercing howl cut through the air. Torin tried to will his own strength into the animal. Suddenly the scream ended in a low moaning, as Saba tried unsuccessfully to turn.

"It's done," said Gen with a sigh of relief. His arms were slimy from the birth, and he wiped them on his shirt.

Torin still held Saba's head and stroked her. "Well?" he asked softly.

"Another transport!" answered Gen, smiling. "I was pretty sure from the way she carried it."

The attendants relaxed into murmuring and adjusting their capes. A few peered into the birthing cage.

"Come. The danger's over!" And Gen beckoned for the

attendants to gather round. For a moment everyone stood in a circle. Gen rose. "Praise the Teachers," he said in a solemn voice. The attendants bowed their heads.

"Praise the Teachers," they droned. Saba whinnied peacefully as Torin gave her another pat.

There in the birthing cage lay the newborn transport. He struggled awkwardly to get up. The pink fleshy wings twitched helplessly as he tried to pull first one leg, then the other, under him. Gen smiled at Torin and nodded. Torin felt the bond between him and his father. They had worked as a team in this birth, each needing and relying on the other. Torin rested his hand on his Medallion and smiled proudly back at his father.

Torin knelt down and gathered the foal in his arms. The silver fur was as soft as a rabbit skin. The small foal rocked his head back and forth, his large blue eyes still covered with birth film. Tenderly Torin caressed the newborn transport and set him down in front of Saba.

The attendants unsnapped the harness. Saba nudged the foal until finally it stood wobbling on its four knobby legs. Then, after butting unsuccessfully against Saba's stomach, the foal found the single nipple and began to suckle noisily.

Outside the wind had faded to a gentle whisper. Torin led Saba from the barn to the pasture, with the foal trotting clumsily after. The attendant men began cleaning the birth harness and preparing the new stall. The iron birthing cage was cleaned and put away for the next birth. There would always be the danger of Eggs.

"Father?" Torin tugged at Gen's sleeve.

But Gen only gestured with his hand angrily. "You shouldn't have left the Compound, Torin," he muttered. "You endanger all of us." And he stumped across the stubble grass to shout more orders to the attendants.

The closeness father and son had shared during the transport birth was over. Torin knew Gen would not forgive him for leaving the Compound. It would be useless to try and talk to his father now. More than anything Torin wanted to hear his father say, "Good job, son. You handled Saba well," and maybe rest his hand on the boy's shoulder. Torin felt a rush of self-pity that formed beginning tears behind his eyes. He rubbed his face with his hand. Someday . . .

Slowly Torin climbed the corral fence. Saba whinnied and trotted over to him. She nuzzled his pocket. In spite of himself Torin grinned. Sometimes it seemed the horse was more human than animal. Often he talked to her as if she could understand speech. At any rate she seemed to listen, and Torin always felt comforted when he was with her. He could never share his feelings with Gen, of course. Saba snorted impatiently. Torin dug out some crumbled sugar from his pocket. It was sticky on his palm and glistened in the sun.

The horse picked at the crystals greedily with her soft dark lips. Then she flicked her head, her pale mane rippled, and she pranced back to her foal. For a moment she stretched out her enormous wings, and Torin could see the sun light up the delicate pink veins through the taut skin. Then she tucked her wings up close to her sides and nudged her foal. He whimpered and again began to suckle.

The wind had died, and the afternoon sun was like hot honey on Torin's back. He stretched lazily and pushed his lanky black hair out of his eyes.

In the distance the attendant workers trudged through the Compound, collecting manure for the Reclamation Guild. The Teachers promised that one day all Morn would be green and fertile.

Every week the Guild wagons came and took the precious manure to be tilled into the deserts that covered the planet's surface. The Teachers said it was a project that would take hundreds of years.

Torin always looked forward to the arrival of the Guild

wagons. Sometimes the Guild brought bolts of cloth for clothes. Although everyone wore the same ankle-length gray tunic and cape, attendants' cloth was a coarse woven canvas, while the ruling classes wore fine grade. The cloth, as well as iron pots for cooking and leather for harnesses, were all gifts from the Teachers, who understood all human needs and cared for all people in everything.

Sometimes the Guild merchants spoke of the happenings at other compounds and grain farms. Torin knew that the birth of "Saba's Foal" would be communicated to the neighboring compounds as the wagon traveled its route.

Now that he wore the Medallion, the Guild merchants always bowed before they spoke to Torin. He felt proud to wear a Medallion on a Transport Compound, surely one of the most important projects on all Morn. After all, hadn't he been chosen over countless others to supervise the birth and training of the magnificent flying horses that carried the Teachers through the air?

Of course there was always the unknown danger of a mare producing an Egg instead of a foal. Every Transport Compound had had its share of Eggs. It was rumored that inside the thick shells were huge flying lizards that emerged with an unquenchable thirst for blood. However, the Teachers always came and took away the Eggs. There was no real danger, just empty superstition. Torin felt angry that he had even hesitated at his duty.

Already the attendants had melted back into their daily routines. Gen was probably at the other end of the Compound supervising grounding tethers for the growing herd of flying beasts. Torin's chores for the day were completed.

He yawned luxuriously and lay on the top fence post, his hand resting on his Medallion. The metal warmed to his touch. Torin stared up at the cloud patterns—the air gentle on his face. Soon it would be time for dinner.

The afternoon slowly dwindled to a dull orange. In the

corral Saba and her foal were silhouetted against the gathering night clouds. The Teachers would, in time, choose an appropriate name for it. However, for the moment it would be known only as "Saba's Foal."

Saba arched her wings gracefully and minced over to Torin. She nuzzled her head against his chest. "Saba's Foal" had trotted after her and stood awkwardly on its new legs. Torin slid off the fence and held out his hand to the foal. The foal backed awkwardly away and shook his head from side to side. Torin laughed and reached out his hand again. He loved caring for the new transports, watching them learn first to run, and then to fly. Perhaps Gen would let him train this one. "Saba's Foal" certainly had all the traits of being an exceptional transport—good wing structure, soft thick fur, long legs.

Suddenly Torin withdrew his hand. Was the colt hissing at him? Saba trembled and anxiously butted her nose against her foal. The foal turned and began suckling. Torin relaxed into feeling foolish. It had only been his imagination. But as he started to turn away, he heard the colt squeal angrily.

Saba reared up and cantered to the far end of the field. Left alone the baby transport whimpered helplessly. As Torin approached, the colt began to shake. His tiny wings twitched. Puzzled, Torin glanced at Saba, who was pacing uneasily at the far end of the field. Then he stooped and held out his arms to comfort the animal.

"What's the matter, boy?" he asked the colt gently. But, and now there was no mistaking it, the colt was hissing loudly. Torin took a step back. He now noticed to his horror that the birth film had already cleared from the colt's eyes. Instead of being a soft blue the large round eyes were now a glazed black. Torin backed away slowly. His heart had begun pounding. "Saba's Foal" stood its ground, hissing and rocking its head to and fro. Its black eyes bulged wet. Torin saw a strange network of muscles under the colt's skin rippling and twisting like a bunch of angry snakes pressed under a tight blanket.

Step by step the colt advanced. As the small head wove back and forth, Torin found himself unable to move. All the stories he had ever heard of undestroyed Eggs, cold teeth and hungry things in the night shadows, began racing through his mind. He knew he should run, but his feet were glued to the ground. The colt's eyes seemed to get bigger and bigger, and Torin found himself leaning toward the animal, unable to look away. And soon he didn't want to look away. Somewhere on the edges of his consciousness he heard a steady hiss, like the sound of afternoon wind over dead stubble grass.

Suddenly in the gathering shadows Torin heard the loud clapping sticks that signified dinner. "Saba's Foal" shied from the unexpected sound, and Torin found himself ducking through the corral fence and running toward home. His legs were numb and he stumbled as he ran. The dry stubble grass crunched under his feet.

Ahead candles twinkled in the window of the stone hut. He could already smell the rich sweet steam of stew. The light flickered as his mother passed quickly by the window. Panting he stumbled through the door.

"The colt hissed!"

Gen and Mira stared at him in disbelief. Tentatively Mira put out her hand and touched Torin's cheek. Her fingers were cool and gentle.

"Surely another of your dreams, Torin?" she asked in a low voice.

"No, Mother," he answered.

"Torin, we handled the birth together. There was no sign of a Shell. It was a normal transport birth."

"Something went wrong this time, Father."

Gen turned away and put his hand over his forehead. Torin wished his mother would put her arms around him and stroke his black hair with her gentle, work-worn fingers. But he wore the Medallion now. He was no longer a child. Mira must obey the laws and keep her distance from him.

Torin could feel her wanting to hold him and comfort him. He could always sense what she was thinking. Perhaps this bond was because they looked so much alike—the same cloud-white skin, large black eyes, and frail structure. Like Torin, Mira tired easily. Sleep never seemed to restore her. Torin wondered if she, like him, dreamed. But now that he wore the Medallion, such questions were forbidden.

The fire whispered and crackled in the grate. Finally Gen spoke. "We have only the Teachers. They tell us that what is not an Egg is a transport."

"This is both." Torin broke his thoughts away from his mother. "And, Father, I'm frightened. My dreams have gotten worse since Mordens died."

"Then this was a dream?"

"No, Father. This was no dream."

Gen slumped down in a chair. "I'll have to send for a Teacher," he said in a defeated voice. Mira put her hands on her husband's shoulders.

"There's nothing to worry about," she said quietly. "After all you and Torin both wear the Medallion now."

Gen shook his head sadly and stared into the fire.

The next morning Gen sent a laborer, by transport, to the mountain city of the Teachers. Torin watched the man mount, wave importantly, and spur the horse up. The pale wings opened, flapped noisily, and the transport strained up toward the sky. Far above them, the horse leveled off and began the languorous soaring movements as its wings caught the air currents. Soon transport and rider glided effortlessly through the sky and out of sight. Torin tugged at Gen's sleeve.

"Saba's chest is bleeding, Father. The colt is hurting her."

"I know, Torin. I've separated them." Gen fingered his Medallion nervously.

The messenger returned with the Teacher, Nordeth. Nordeth rode a magnificent transport stallion with black well-boned wings. He was proud and tall and wore the traditional stone mask of the Teachers. The transport saddle he sat in was woven with jewels and gold. His red cape rippled in the hot afternoon wind. Torin and Gen knelt as custom required. Nordeth slowly dismounted, looking first at the fields and paddocks and then at the kneeling men. "Rise," he said coolly, after a long pause.

"Nordeth-on," began Gen, using the correct form of address.

"Yes, yes," broke in Nordeth, "I have the message. Your mare gave birth to a foal that is different. Let me see her and her foal." Nordeth's voice was imperious. Gen bowed and gestured toward the stables. Torin followed a few paces behind.

Saba had been separated from her foal. The tiny transport stood frail in the center of a stall made for grown horses. Nordeth strode quickly in. He ran his hands over the foal's back. The animal hissed. The black eyes grew larger as the Teacher forced open the foal's jaw. Torin gasped. A forked lizard's tongue shot angrily out from between the new white teeth.

"My Lord, we did not keep an Egg!" Gen sounded scared.

"Be quiet, you fool," answered Nordeth angrily. He continued examining the foal. "The sire?"

"One of yours, Lord. Tamweth, I believe. A white stallion. Prendor-on brought him and surveyed the mating."

"And the mare?"

Gen led Nordeth to Saba's stall. The white mare saw Torin and arched her head prettily. Nordeth ran his hands

415

quickly over her. She shied and tried to break away. He wiped his hands distastefully on his cloak. "The mare and foal will have to be destroyed, of course. I'll take them with me."

"Not Saba!" broke in Torin anxiously. Nordeth looked contemptuously at the boy.

"My Lord," soothed Gen in a humble tone, "my son simply meant that, since Saba has so recently given birth, she cannot fly, and for you and your strong steed to carry her and the foal would be asking too much from a noble Teacher."

Nordeth stared hard at Gen. "Very well, I will take only the foal this time. Send Saba in a week, when her milk has gone and she can fly."

"But, my Lord—" began Gen.

"Be thankful I am not charging you with holding an Egg."

Gen bowed. "Yes, Nordeth-on," he answered.

Suddenly Nordeth grabbed Torin by the hair and pulled his head back firmly. He stared at his face, forcing the boy's head to turn first left, then right, as he examined his features critically. Torin flinched as the Teacher's long hard fingers probed his thin cheeks and pulled at the skin around his large dark eyes. "And send your boy too," he added imperiously. Torin could see himself reflected in the Teacher's black eyes behind the stone mask. "We could use him in the Arena. You and Mira produce well."

"Yes, Nordeth-on," said Gen in a low voice.

Nordeth strode to his waiting horse. The attendant men had tied the foal and wrapped it carefully in a sack, which Nordeth fastened quickly to the saddle. The cloth bulged as the foal struggled and bucked. Torin shuddered as he heard the angry hissing and saw the cloth crushed by tiny lizardlike bites. Then Nordeth kicked his stallion hard with his spurs. The horse gave an indignant squeal and climbed quickly into the air. Father and son remained kneeling until the sky was once again empty.

Gen rose and shook Torin hard. "You shouldn't have drawn attention to yourself," he shouted. Then he covered his face with his hands in despair. "How am I going to tell your mother?"

Mira stood motionless, her face white and drawn, her eyes darting back and forth from her husband to her son. "Not Torin!" she said in a low voice. "I won't let him go. He's my son. He's so small for his age. He is not strong enough to serve the Teachers. Gen, please!" She clutched at her husband's arm.

"We exist to serve," Gen said bluntly. Trembling, Mira held out her arms to Torin, but Gen pulled her back. "He is grown now. He wears the Medallion. You know the law."

Torin could see the pain in both their faces as they stared at him. Clutching his Medallion in his fist he turned abruptly and ran to his room.

Alone Torin let the tears slide down his cheeks in hot, salty streams. He stared around the small room as if seeing it for the first time. Soon he would be leaving forever. Those who served the Teachers never returned. He felt he had to memorize every crack in the gray clay wall so that he wouldn't ever forget.

Why did Teacher Mordens have to die? Mordens would have protected him. Mordens was his friend. He remembered the many times they had walked together down the chalky road and talked about cloud pictures and animals, and sometimes just about growing older. Mordens was not like the other Teachers. Mordens had made him promise never to tell the other Teachers about his dreams.

There was a timid knock, and the door to his room creaked open. "I'm still awake, Mother." Although Torin spoke softly, his voice seemed loud and raspy in the silent house. Mira stepped quickly to the bed. Hesitantly she stroked his cheek with her hand. Startled, he looked at her questioningly.

"You're my son," she whispered firmly. "You will always be my son." He closed his eyes, feeling warm and safe.

"Does Father *want* me to go to the Teachers' City? He has been so cold to me ever since I got my Medallion. Does he still . . ." Embarrassed, Torin looked away.

Mira sighed. "Your father does love you, Torin, very much. But the sacred laws—"

"Those laws are wrong. In my dreams, I—" Torin spoke angrily, his voice loud.

Glancing about, Mira raised her hand warningly. "Hush," she whispered. "You mustn't be heard talking like that. Torin, I want you to escape tonight!"

Torin felt his heart pounding. His throat and chest tightened. "Why?" he managed to whisper.

Mira answered slowly. "Mordens made me promise a long time ago that if the Teachers ever summoned you to their City, you were to flee. He said you were to go to the Blue Forest. He said you were special, and that one day you might save all Morn from a terrible fate."

"Me? Does Father know?"

Mira shook her head. "I never told him. Mordens swore me to secrecy. Even from your father."

"What can I do for Morn? I'm not a Teacher, I'm just a human." Torin felt his hands trembling as he fingered the gold chain of his Medallion.

"I don't know, son," said Mira sadly. "But I trust Mordens." She clutched his hands tightly. "I want you to go tonight. That will give you a week's head start."

"But I'll never see you again! I can't bear that, I just can't!"

Mira's voice became brisk. "Take only what you can carry easily. I've prepared food for you. I've known for a long time that today would come. I, too, dream, but not like you, Torin."

"It's almost as if my dreams are swallowing me up,"

Torin whispered hesitantly. "I see things that I know are real, but I don't know if they're past or future. I can't control my dreams anymore. Sometimes I feel so alone."

Mira touched her fingers to Torin's forehead. "Your dreams are much stronger than mine. Just as mine were stronger than my mother's. You are not alone. I wish I had spoken sooner to you. Now there is no time." Mira sighed. "Come. Prepare for your journey and choose a transport from the stables."

"Can I take Saba?" Torin asked. His voice trembled.

"I'd rather you took a transport that could fly. You can cover more ground that way."

"Saba will be able to fly in a week, Mother. If she had produced an Egg, she'd be flying now. It's only her milk that's keeping her grounded."

Mira smiled. "Very well. Saba's a good horse."

"But what about you . . . and Father? Will you be safe when *they* find out?" asked Torin.

Mira took Torin's face in her hands. "Don't worry about us. Just hurry, Torin. Use what's left of the night. The hunt for you will begin soon." Mira turned and left the room, her skirt rustling as she passed through the door.

For a moment Torin sat motionless. How could he leave forever? His parents would be in terrible danger. But somewhere underneath his fears he felt a growing excitement, like a hidden spring. It started bubbling up, washing away his hesitation. He *would* run away, on Saba. Together they would find a new life, away from the Teachers! Someday he would return.

Torin took his saddlebag from under a shelf. It was small and battered, but sturdy. In it he put his knife and some cord. Then he snapped his traveling cape to his shoulders. Mira entered. She carried a bulging sack.

"I've packed bread, cheese, dried meat, and fruit. Eat the food sparingly. Hang this waterskin from the saddle. Try and keep it full. I've also packed a candle and a flint for making fires, a small pot for cooking, and a spoon. It's not much.''

Torin shoved the bundle into his pack. Then he hefted the pack onto his shoulder and took one last look around his room.

Together mother and son passed silently from the house. They walked quickly to the stables. Mira kept glancing over her shoulder to make sure no one saw them.

It seemed as if Saba was waiting. She stood alert in her stall, her graceful wings stretched back. Mira helped Torin saddle her. He slipped the bridle over her head, and she willingly took the bit in her teeth. Mira hooked the water carrier to the saddle. Then Torin led Saba to the field. She pranced lightly. The meadow was flooded with bright silver light from the Sister Planet.

"Oh, Mother . . ." began Torin, not knowing how to say good-bye. Mira embraced him fiercely. He clung to her until she pushed him away, her hands shaking as she gripped his arms. Torin winced as he saw the tears streaming down his mother's face. She nodded and smiled through her tears. "I will always love you."

Torin clung to her a moment longer. Then he sprang upon Saba's back.

For a moment the boy fingered the heavy Medallion around his neck. Then, in a quick angry gesture, he threw it to the ground and spurred Saba hard.

The journey had begun.

James Powell

THE KIDNAP
OF BOUNDING MANE

To mark every Christmas, birthday, or other solemn occasion during his growing up, Ralston Seeley, like many a Canadian boy, received the latest in the "Mounts of the Mounted" adventure books by that lioness of his country's children's literature, Alberta Regina de la Québec. He prized them all, from *Spanish Mane, Star of the Musical Ride,* the exploits of a horse famed on the force for its flashing eyes and the proud, flamencolike tattoo of its hooves when it came to a stop, to the brave antismuggling exploits of *Water Mane, Horse of the Coastal Patrol.*

The sense of high purpose of these loyal animals moved

him and he uttered many a moist sigh over their strength in adversity. But he enjoyed the lighter books in the series, too, like the one about the fat horse who hung around outside the barracks kitchen, *Chow Mane, Horse of the Cookhouse Door,* and would laugh out loud and look around at the furniture as though encouraging it to join in. Was it any wonder, then, that on his graduation from Upper Canada College, Seeley expressed a desire to join the force? When his wealthy father, the fast-food-franchising magnate, objected, young Ralston showed that he'd learned something of Mountie steel from his reading and respectfully held his ground. Their compromise was this: Ralston would get a medical degree from Germany's famous Heidelberg University. If, after that, he persisted in his dream, his father would make no objection.

On graduating from Heidelberg, Seeley returned home at once and presented himself as a candidate for the Mountie Academy. He passed the stiff battery of physical and academic tests with flying colors. But to his astonishment, his application was rejected because of a regulation that said a Mountie could not have a saber scar. Seeley had belonged to a Heidelberg student dueling club and sported a fine memento of that membership across his left cheekbone.

Seeley appealed his case to a special RCMP board of review, but the ruling was upheld. Ralston Seeley could never become a Mountie. As he left the hearing room, his love for the Royal Canadian Mounted Police contorted itself into a deep and implacable hatred. Then and there, he resolved to emigrate to the United States, from where he would dedicate his life to harming and humiliating the force however he could.

Ocean City, Maryland, is hot and crowded in late July. The morning street was a parade of men, women, and children whose angry red backs, outlandish shorts, halters, hats, and cumbersome beach gear marked them as vacationers, all boardwalk-bound. Against this tide came a large, ruddy-faced man with a trim mustache and wearing a blue bowling shirt with I'D RATHER BE PLAYING MINIATURE GOLF printed on the back. Acting Sergeant Maynard Bullock was working undercover.

Up ahead beyond the Pizza Hut, and towering over McDonald's golden arches, stood his destination, the immense statue of a Mountie with arms akimbo and Stetson at a rakish angle. The goggle-eyed monstrosity wore an immense grin, with a tip of the tongue tucked high up in one corner, and sported a scar on the left cheekbone. Bullock gritted his teeth and, passing under the archway formed by the giant bow-legged blue breeks, crossed the Mountie Burger parking lot.

The Mountie Burger was Ralston Seeley's doing. Using skills learned at his father's knee, he launched a new fast-food concept. And, like Pet Rock, like Smurf, like Lava-Light, the bowlegged blue breeks caught the popular imagination. Overnight, giant Mountie caricatures were going up across the United States, each a gaudy, grotesque fire at which Seeley warmed the hands of his vengeance.

Bullock entered the Mountie Burger by a back door. He changed into a T-shirt printed to look like a Mountie tunic and a small cardboard Stetson held on with an elastic chin band. Sour-eyed, he examined himself in the mirror and, as he had for the last ten mornings, he wished he was where he belonged, vacationing with good old Mavis, his wife, at their cabin on Black Fly Lake. Then on the stroke of eleven, Ramon, the morning short-order man, left and Bullock took his place at the grill.

It wasn't long before the loudspeaker squawked and the counter girl's voice said, "One Commissioner in a poncho." Bullock set about assembling the order. The regular Mountie Burger was called a Constable. Two rashers of bacon made it a Corporal, and so on up through the ranks, adding patties and rashers until you got to Commissioner—which was two patties, three rashers, and a slice of bologna. "In a poncho" meant with a slice of cheese.

As he set things sizzling, he heard a loud, uncomfortable voice say, "No, just black coffee for me, miss. I don't eat much when I'm out and about, eh." The "out and about" was uttered "oot and aboot" in finest Canadian style. By godfrey, Seeley's fallen into the trap! thought Bullock, so surprised he almost dropped the slice of bologna on the floor. But when he looked out the food slot, he saw it wasn't Seeley. It was, speak of the devil, his nibs, RCMP Commissioner McNaughton himself.

Chewing thoughtfully on his mustache, Bullock assembled the tall hamburger, holding it together with two long toothpicks topped with little Canadian flags, and sent it through the food slot. Then he went over and looked out the window in the kitchen door. The restaurant was almost empty. McNaughton was sitting at a corner table with a little girl Bullock recognized as Dolly, his granddaughter, the apple of his eye. While she devoured the burger, McNaughton puzzled over his road map.

Bullock took a deep breath, pushed the door open, and crossed to the table. "Food okay, neighbor?" he asked in his version of a loud American voice. But in that complicated language of hand signs which only the Mounties know, he was signaling, It's Acting Sergeant Bullock, Commissioner. I'm down here undercover on the Bounding Mane business.

A month ago, when the force's famed Musical Ride was performing at Toronto's Maple Leaf Gardens, a gypsy fortune-teller with kerchief, bangles, and saber scar had been amusing the Mountie sentries in the stable facilities when suddenly she sprang onto the back of Bounding Mane, the last of the Mounts of the Mounted line. Bounding Mane, whose photograph hung in every grade-school classroom in Canada, galloped out of the building and escaped the city, using side streets. Hoof tracks led the Mounties as far as the border, beyond which they had no mandate to pursue.

Aloud McNaughton said, "Everything's hunky-dory, chef." But his hand signs said, Fill me in, Acting Sergeant.

A bunch of us have given up vacation time to come down and cover as many of Seeley's Mountie Burger outlets as we can, signaled Bullock. He inspects them regularly. Sooner or later he'll show up and lead one of us back to Bounding Mane. Out loud he said, "Need help with that road map?"

"All I can get," said McNaughton, giving Dolly quarters and aiming her at the Pin the Laser on the Mountie electronic game. Then, with a "Take a load off," he nodded Bullock into her chair and whispered, "I'm behind you people a hundred percent. Unofficially, of course. Let's not start a war. If we won, it'd be two in a row and they might make us take possession." They both laughed quietly. This was a Canadian joke.

"What brings you here, sir?" asked Bullock.

"Got a special invitation for Dolly and me to the famous pony roundup in Chincoteague. I guess the Chamber of Commerce wanted to add a Mountie luster to the event. You know about the roundup?"

Bullock nodded. "This small breed of horses runs wild on Assateague Island right across the bay here. The island's about thirty miles long. Once a year, they're rounded up and made to swim this narrow channel—" he tapped the road map to show the place—"between the southern tip of Assateague over to Chincoteague Island on the land side. They auction off some foals and horses to support the local fire company." Bullock paused and looked at McNaughton. What he'd meant to ask was what an RCMP commissioner was doing in a Mountie Burger.

McNaughton folded up the road map. "Well, I guess you're wondering what the heck an RCMP commissioner's doing in a Mountie Burger," he said a bit sheepishly. "You see, the whole way down the Delmarva Peninsula, little Dolly there was singing this song about beer bottles hanging on the wall. By George, she knows her numbers. By the Virginia border, I was close to speaking sharply to her for the first time ever. Then I got a brainstorm.

" 'Dolly,' I said, 'what say we stop for lunch early? You get to pick the place.' That bought me some blessed peace while she studied all the roadside signs. Just before the Ocean City turnoff, she saw the Mountie Burger billboard."

Bullock nodded. "If Your Tummy Can't Go Far, Drive in at the Mountie with the Scar.' "

McNaughton nodded back. "So here's where we had to come," he said. Then he rose and, shaking Bullock's hand, said, "Good luck in your endeavor, Bullock." Then his face turned thoughtful. "Bullock? Bullock? Aren't you the one who slammed the limousine door on the prime minister's hand?"

When Bullock's shift ended, he went over to Golfeteria, the miniature golf course next door to the Mountie Burger. He counted himself lucky to have such a fine off-duty observation post to watch for Seeley. He'd kind of hoped to get a "Lucky dog!" from Inspector McMinn by casually mentioning his miniature golf course during his phone call to announce he was on station. But there was a miniature golf course next to the Mountie Burger in Omaha, too, and McMinn was already buddy-buddy with a Mr. Knee-High, the night manager.

Yes, the jock Mounties with their nude ice hockey might get the headlines, but for those on the force of more intellectual persuasion, miniature golf remained the game of choice. In fact, at the recent International Police Olympics in the old Devil's Island facility, the Mountie miniature golf team crushed the Spanish Guardia Civil and the French Sûreté before edging out the reigning champions—Vatican City's Swiss Guards, whose brief geography had made them masters of the game. (By godfrey, Bullock almost envied them their

Michelangelo uniforms, except for those helmets that looked like fancy-dan Turkish bob skates.)

Marco MacGregor had brought miniature golf back to Scotland from China in 1230 along with the recipe for haggis. (The Scots had immediately diluted the game with space to make it last longer and in this extended, corrupted form the game is most widely played today.) Though he rarely played miniature golf himself, Bullock was drawn by the finesse and strategy of the game. Here in the spectators' gallery of the Ocean City course, Bullock made the acquaintance of another enthusiast, Mr. Theo Necropolis, a stooped and wrinkled old gentleman in a white hat with a transparent green window set in the front of the brim. They talked long and often about the carom and windmill theory, the glory days of the game when you could putt the continent without leaving a miniature golf course, or how the game's decline paralleled that of the whooping crane, whose natural habitat those courses had become.

Necropolis was in miniature-golf supplies. "You know," he said, "green indoor-outdoor carpet remnants and used golf balls I buy from high-school kids. It's kind of a class project. Many a prom and yearbook's been financed by my young people raiding golf-course water traps in the dead of night. Old putters I pick up at yard sales but I don't deal in 'wrap-arounds.' " This last, Bullock knew, referred to putters bent around trees by angry golfers, which the unscrupulous straightened for resale. "It's not much of a living, but every now and then I get to put somebody in the way of a regula-tion-size, five-foot windmill." Then he brightened. "Hey, do you know who makes the windmills?"

"The Dutch?" ventured Bullock.

"The Greeks," said Necropolis proudly.

Yes, the old man was an even bigger fan of the game than Bullock was. At midnight, when the Mountie Burger closed and Bullock went to catch some shut-eye, Necropolis would stay on, talking to Tiny, the manager, or watching the shifty street characters who seemed to draw strength from a late-night game and were masters of the difficult windmill shot.

Today, as soon as he saw Bullock, Necropolis said, "Hey, your guy just left."

Figuring two pairs of eyes were better than one, Bullock had asked the old man to watch out for a man with a saber scar and a Canadian accent, saying the guy owed him money. Had his little white lie paid off? "Which way did he go?" demanded Bullock.

Necropolis shook his hands to show it was too late for that. "He was sitting here watching the play," he said. "When I saw the scar, I moseyed over casuallike and started talking about miniature golf. Well, sir, I soon had him 'ooting' and 'abooting' all over the place. And he's loaded, too, because finally he looked at me and said, 'I count myself a good judge of character, Mr. Necropolis. Would you like to make a quick thousand bucks?'

" 'Who do I have to kill?' sez I. Well, he took that in the comical way it was intended and explained how he had to deliver a horse to a Mr. Emerson down in Chincoteague tomorrow. He said he'd pay me the money to drive the horse down Assateague Island and in the back way. See, the East Coast horse dealers get together down there during pony roundup to show off their choice stock. To hear him tell it, his eye for horseflesh is so sharp that whatever he bids for, so do all the other dealers. So he'd got a mind to sneaking down in a rental car and doing his bidding in a disguise. But he still had this delivery to make, and if anyone saw his truck and horse trailer it'd give the show away. He said he'd meet me on the bridge between Assateague and Chincoteague in a fake beard and give me the thousand there."

By godfrey, thought Bullock, a Canadian with a scar and a horse. The animal had to be Bounding Mane! His luck was changing. He wasn't going to be Bullock who closed the limousine door on the PM's hand any more. He was going to be Bullock who found Bounding Mane and brought Ralston Seeley to justice. But then he frowned. "You took him up on the offer, right?"

"I told him to call me here in an hour. But I may have to give him the big no-can-do. That sand-dune driving's bad enough, but Assateague's a national park and those Park Rangers can be real tough when it comes to unauthorized vehicles. They're your hard-core ecologists. I've heard tell of them pistol-whipping people just for looking cross-eyed at a nesting sapsucker and then covering it up by saying you were attacked by a grizzly. So I'm not sure I want to mess with the Park Rangers—not unless I can partner up with somebody who can lay his hands on a Mountie uniform fast."

As it happened, Bullock was one of those Mounties who bring their uniforms everywhere, even on undercover assignments. He cleared his throat. "What the heck's the uniform for?"

The next morning at the appointed time, Bullock was standing in the Mountie Burger parking lot in full regalia, scarlet tunic and all. Soon a four-wheel-drive pickup pulling a horse trailer paused at the curb with Necropolis stooped over the steering wheel. Before getting in, Bullock went around back and looked inside the trailer. It was Bounding Mane, all right. "It's me, boy!" he said. "You're safe now!" The horse whinnied doubtfully.

Then the old man drove them out of town and southward the few miles to the causeway that took them to Assateague Island. It was another mile of sand dunes, salt grass, and scrub pine to the park's Visitors' Center. At a barrier across the road stood two women and a man in Stetsons and drab park ranger uniforms with automatic weapons. A sign said, PARK CLOSED FOR RENOVATIONS. Beyond the barrier, more armed rangers were formed into ranks around a map on an easel.

Necropolis suggested that perhaps they'd come at a bad time. But it was too late to turn back. Bullock stepped from the pickup, pulled down the skirts of his tunic, ran a knuckle through his mustache, and marched forward. The rangers at the barrier watched him come with uncertain, admiring eyes.

"I am Park Ranger Inspector General Bullock," Maynard announced and was gratified when they came to attention. The barrier rose and Bullock was escorted over to the senior ranger at the easel, a shapely honey-blonde who raised two fingers to the brim of her Stetson and introduced herself. "Thank you, Ranger Wayves," said Bullock as he looked around. "You seem a bit overstaffed. Were you warned of this little surprise inspection?"

"Operation Nip-in-the-Bud, sir."

"Ah," said Bullock wisely. "Proceed, Ranger."

Ranger Wayves turned to the map of Assateague on the easel and used a pointer to indicate a location on the ocean side. "Charlie will have to land here," she said. "His objective, the marsh figwort growths here and here. We will allow Charlie to move inland. Then unit one will cut him off from his boats. Simultaneously, units two and three will open fire. Charlie will only have two routes of escape, here into the quicksand or here into the mine field."

Bullock cleared his throat. "That Charlie sure does give us a lot of bother, eh?"

"The Ladies' Wildflower League of Smyrna, Delaware, sir," said Ranger Wayves, her gray eyes flashing now. "We'll make them an example their kind won't soon forget." Then she added with great feeling, "Would you lead us, sir?"

As Necropolis pulled up beside him right on cue, Bullock said, "For now, these quicky inspections are the best I can do, accompanied by my old trusty retainer here and Yellowstone, my faithful steed." He smiled grandly and got inside the pickup. "Carry on, Ranger Wayves."

But the woman came to the pickup window. "Call me

Amber, sir," she asked breathlessly. Then she reached in and touched his tunic with her fingertips. "Will this be our new uniform, sir? It makes my knees weak."

"Mine, too, Amber," admitted Bullock.

The sandy jeep trail ran close to the ocean side through a landscape of bayberry bushes, marsh grass, dunes, and more scrub pine. After the first few miles, Bullock wondered out loud if they shouldn't do something about Nip-in-the-Bud—what, he didn't know. Necropolis expressed other worries. "Where are the wild horses and the Park Rangers?" he wondered.

"Aren't the horses all rounded up by now?"

"Only those down on the Virginia end of the island make the Chincoteague swim," explained the old man. "I sure hope Wayves hasn't pulled off her people for Nip-in-the-Bud." Frowning, he scanned the horizon with a worried eye.

They drove in silence for several miles. Then Necropolis stopped the pickup. "Listen," he said.

Bullock thought he heard a noisy airplane engine. He stuck out his head and looked skyward. An old World War I Prentiss-Jenkins Hedgehog, a biplane with two open cockpits, lumbered across the sky trailing a banner that read: ASK FOR RALPH BRAND DOG FOOD—YOUR MUTTS DO.

"Oh, brother, let's get out of here!" shouted Necropolis. As they picked up speed and bounced down the road, he added, "You hear talk when you travel around in miniature golf supplies, talk like maybe Ralph, the Dog Food Man, was going to move against the Assateague ponies. Maybe that Smyrna Wildflower business was a setup. We'll never get to Chincoteague if we get caught up in one of Ralph's operations!"

Just then, through the old man's window, Bullock saw three small spotted horses emerge from behind a dune, followed by a rider wearing jeans, a homburg hat, and the navy-pin-striped vest to what must once have been an expensive three-piece suit. Then came more horses and a rider wearing a battered shako which Bullock's browsings in *Jane's Uniforms and Insignia of the World* told him was that of a West Point senior classman, a tragic shako that never got to be tossed in the air at graduation because its owner had washed out in his final year.

"Your regular horse wrangler wouldn't be seen dead working for Ralph," explained Necropolis. "He uses the dregs of Madison Avenue, ex-politicians fresh from the slammer, defrocked clergy, and the like. But don't underrate them. Grinding beautiful horses into dog food can destroy whatever small virtues are left in a man." He looked in the side-view mirror. "More trouble," he said.

Bullock leaned out the window. A Land Rover had appeared on the road behind them and was closing fast. When they'd done a thousand yards, the road turned sharply inland and a second Land Rover blocked their path. Sitting on the hood, a bare-chested man wearing a dirty clerical collar used an automatic weapon to wave them off onto a trail through a stand of tall sea oats. Almost at once they emerged onto a sandy slope leading down to the bay shore, where a tug with a barge lay at anchor. Below them were half a dozen wild horses in a large corral made of rope and oil drums. Men were running everywhere to handle the new arrivals.

The Land Rover following them pulled up on Bullock's side and he felt the muzzle of a pistol behind his ear; he conveyed to Necropolis the orders to stop next to the rustlers at the corral entrance.

A large man, a morbidly fat man with an immense nose and protruding eyes, waddled over as they were dragged from the pickup. He wore a vast butcher's apron with a bloody middle and the name *Ralph* written in cursive script across his heart. Prodding Bullock in the stomach with the butt of an ugly horsewhip, he snarled, "Looks like we got us a leg up on a batch of Ralph's Select Dobie Nuggets.''

Before Bullock could answer, a rustler found Bounding Mane. "Hey, boss!" he shouted, leading the animal out of the trailer.

"The more the merrier," answered the fat man. "Put the critter in with the others."

"That horse is the property of the Canadian government," warned Bullock sternly.

"Mutts can't tell the difference," said Ralph, the Dog Food Man.

Here Necropolis broke his captors' grip. "Leave that horse alone!" he shouted, and tried to fight his way back to where Bounding Mane struggled to get free. Ralph struck the old man down with the butt of his whip, but somehow at that moment Bounding Mane ducked out of his halter and, avoiding all the arms reaching for him, vanished over a sand dune.

In the confusion, Bullock broke loose from his captors, too. Cocking his fists, he struck the Mountie Academy fighting stance with left out and right circling the jaw deceptively. "You! Ralph!" he cried. The fat man turned. But two men grabbed Bullock from behind and the West Point failure and the guy in the clerical collar lunged at him from the front.

Suddenly it was the movie scene Bullock had always wanted to play, the one only the good guy got to do. He threw his weight back onto the two men holding him from behind and cocked his feet in the air. Now he would strike out sharply, kicking the lunging men in their solar plexuses. But "solar plexuses" didn't sound right. He hesitated over the plural for a fraction of a second too long. The two men holding him released their grip and Maynard slammed down hard onto the sand. His attackers grabbed his ankles and dragged him over to their chief.

Ralph looked down at Bullock. "You're dog food, mister," he said, and kicked the Mountie on the side of the head.

When Bullock regained consciousness, the sun had moved in the sky, the corral was full of wild horses, and the men were assembling a ramp up to the barge. He found himself in the shade of the pickup, sitting back to back with Necropolis, their hands tied together behind them. Five feet away, the rustler in the pin-striped vest was leaning against a Land Rover, keeping watch over them. Necropolis whispered, "Glad to have you back, Maynard. I've started on the knots. They'll be child's play. Then—"

Ralph's arrival interrupted him. "Get these two down to the barge," the fat man ordered the guard. As Bullock and Necropolis were pulled to their feet, they heard a muffled explosion in the distance, and then another. Ralph saw Bullock's wondering look. "The Ladies' Wildflower League of Smyrna, Delaware, are tiptoeing through the mine field," he explained with a terrible smile.

"It wasn't just a story you planted, then?" demanded Bullock.

"Why go with a rumor when it's no sweat to pull off the real thing?" said Ralph as more explosions sounded. "My old lady's league president. Hell, the first explosion was probably her." As Bullock sputtered indignantly, the fat man shrugged. "Look, being married to Ralph, the Dog Food Man, wasn't much of a life for her, anyway, right?" He stopped, his attention riveted on a high dune above the corral.

There, silhouetted against the sky, stood Bounding Mane, observing the scene below him. The stallion snorted, whinnied loudly, reared on his hind legs, and whinnied again. The wild horses in the pen heard the call, answered it, and began to churn around in the corral. Rustlers came running from all sides to get the situation under control. Suddenly, Bounding Mane, hair streaming out behind him and nostrils quivering, came galloping down from the dune, followed by two dozen wild horses he'd recruited to his cause.

Ralph cursed and he and the guard charged down the

slope while Bounding Mane and his band made havoc around the corral, tipping over the barrels and tearing down the saddle horses' picket line. Now horses, wild and tame, were streaming off in all directions. By the time Ralph reached the scene, only Bounding Mane remained, fighting a successful rearguard action preventing the rustlers from pursuing the freed animals.

Snapping his horsewhip in the air left and right, Ralph approached Bounding Mane with the nimble Dance of Death grace of the morbidly fat. His exhausted henchmen fell back. It was now the horse against their leader.

The malice in the fat man's eye was matched by the horse's stout determination. Then Ralph sprang forward with the whip and struck Bounding Mane across the shoulder. The horse, which had never felt the lash, stopped dead in his tracks as if too shocked to move. Instantly, six large men flung themselves on Bounding Mane's hindquarters, holding the horse fast. Then, as Bullock remembered it, Ralph shouted, "Blankety-blank you, you blanking horse from blankety-blank hell!" Raising his whip again and flanked by a man carrying a halter, the fat man approached the horse from the front.

Necropolis had freed Bullock's hands by then. The Mountie cupped them around his mouth and shouted, "Bounding Mane, the solar plexuses, the solar plexuses!" The horse looked up as though he did not understand. Suddenly the right plural came to Bullock. "The solar plexi!" he shouted. Now the horse understood. With quickness and surgical delicacy, Bounding Mane shot out both front hooves and struck Ralph and the halter holder square in the solar plexi. Before their bodies hit the sand, Bounding Mane had shaken free and vanished over the dune, following the wild horses of Assateague and the rustlers' saddle horses.

With the keys from the ignitions of the Land Rovers in his pocket, Bullock jumped into the moving pickup with Necropolis behind the wheel. As the truck and tottering horse trailer topped the rise, Bullock looked back at the scene down on the beach. The rustlers were standing around in the wreckage of their corral awaiting the fat man's orders. But Ralph, the Dog Food Man, having managed to prop himself up on one elbow, was too busy flourishing his horsewhip and making a vow to heaven.

"We got to find that horse to get our money," said Necropolis as the pickup regained the jeep trail.

Bullock scanned the horizon. A Mountie horse tended to head north. But Bounding Mane might figure Ralph knew that. "South," he said.

Necropolis turned the steering wheel. "Say," he asked after they'd driven a mile or two, "how come you knew the horse's name back there?"

"I'm afraid I haven't been straight with you, old-timer," said Bullock. "I'm no lowly grill man. I'm Acting Sergeant Maynard Bullock of the Royal Canadian Mounted Police." Then he told of his mission to rescue Bounding Mane and his plan to bring Seeley to justice.

"Does this mean I don't get my money?"

"If this works out," said Bullock, "the youth of Canada will mail you enough nickels and dimes to make you rich beyond your wildest dreams."

They drove on until they found one of the saddle horses, its reins tangled in the branches of a driftwood log. Bullock got out and approached the horse, stroking its neck and freeing the reins. Then he swung up into the saddle and gave the horse its head.

It set off at once for an area of marshland to the south. Necropolis followed as best he could in the pickup. Herons, egrets, and wood ducks fled into the air as the rider passed. After a few minutes' ride, they came to a sign that said they had passed into Virginia and the Chincoteague Wildlife Refuge.

Beyond more marshland, the ground began to rise until they entered a tall grove of pines. Suddenly, there in a clearing soft with pine needles stood Bounding Mane with a pretty piebald mare by his side and the wild horses of Assateague and the saddle horses at his back.

Bullock called the horse to him. The horse whinnied sharply and shook his head. Bullock dismounted and came forward with an understanding smile. "I know. I know, old boy," said Bullock. "You'd like to stay here with your lovely lady and your newfound friends. I can appreciate that. We're both wild, untamed things. But we've let civilization put its harness on us. It's made us symbols of law and order. On top of all that, you're the last of a line made immortal by Alberta Regina de la Québec. Revert to the wild and you'll break the hearts of thousands of young readers."

Bounding Mane heard these words but stood his ground. Trying another tack, Bullock said, "We're a team, you and I, the Mountie and his mount. You've got a maple leaf emblazoned on your flank and so do I." He made double quotation marks with his fingers to show that in his own case he spoke figuratively. "You need us and we need you. Heck," he said, keeping a straight face while spreading it on pretty thick, "when you come right down to it, maybe the Mounties need you more than you need them."

Bounding Mane cocked his head around at the horses and, Bullock would swear to his dying day, shrugged helplessly. Then the animal trotted over to him.

They walked away together, Bounding Mane crunching a lump of maple sugar he had found in the right-hand, maple-sugar pocket of the Mountie's tunic. Out of the corner of his eye, Bullock saw the saddle horse he rode up on trot over and nuzzle the piebald mare's ear. "No, don't look back, old fellow," he warned when Bounding Mane started to turn.

"Remember, the Mountie always gets his man but seldom gets the girl." He walked on in thoughtful silence until they caught up with Necropolis.

The old man had passed them while they'd been in the grove and was parked before a gate in the road about two hundred yards farther south. "Shall we load up or—hey, do you want to arrest the Seeley guy on horseback?" he said.

By godfrey, wouldn't that be a kick, thought Bullock, smiling to himself—arresting Seeley in full uniform and astride Bounding Mane. That'd sure give the Mountie locker room something to talk about. Out loud he said, "Saddle him up." Then he brushed off his uniform and took a kink out of the Stetson brim.

Still smiling, he vaulted into the saddle. Suddenly he heard a sound that took him back to his Mountie Academy days. In Makeup and Disguise, they'd shown them the old trick of turning yourself into a stooped-over codger by buttoning a fly button to the middle buttonhole on your shirt. Every time a superior entered the class, all the Mountie cadets would snap to attention and the buttons would sail across the classroom and rattle against the wall. Bullock had just heard a button bounce off the pickup. Turning in the saddle, he found Necropolis, wigless and erect now, aiming a pistol at him as he stripped latex wrinkles from his left cheekbone to reveal a saber scar. "You?" cried Bullock in astonishment.

At Ralston Seeley's whistle, a very short man rode out from behind the gate, leading a saddle horse. "Squirt here runs my Chincoteague operation," said Seeley, mounting up. Squirt leaned over and took Bullock's reins.

The three rode through the gate and onto a wide road circling a large area of marshland.

Bullock needed a plan, a way to save Bounding Mane. Up ahead, he saw the clump of trees beside the road and knew what he had to do. To put Seeley off his guard, he asked,

"Great job on the accent. How the heck did you get rid of it?"

The shadow of a terrible memory crossed Seeley's brow. It was several minutes before he spoke. Then he said, "Among the crack houses and porno shops of Manhattan are these dark Berlitzlike places run by Canadians who dare never go home again. If you've got the cash, they'll follow you around in teams sixteen hours a day and make you talk, talk, talk. Every time you say 'oot,' 'aboot,' or 'eh' they pummel you with rolled-up newspapers. A week of that'll kill you or cure you."

They had reached the clump of trees. In one sudden motion, Bullock grabbed the reins from a startled Squirt, kicked Bounding Mane forward with his heels, and hurled himself sideways into the trees with all his might. He could get shot as he dodged away among the tree trunks, but at least Bounding Mane would escape back to the wild herd. But something went wrong. The hurling-himself-out-of-the-saddle-into-the-trees part didn't work. In an instant, Squirt grabbed Bullock firmly around the waist, stopping Bounding Mane's forward progress.

"Wonderful, these modern glues," said Seeley with a gloatful smile. "Yes, you're glued to the saddle, old man. There's food for thought."

With a sudden, laboring roar, Ralph's Prentiss-Jenkins Hedgehog appeared, skimming the tops of the trees. The Dog Food Man sat out on the fuselage back behind the pilot, his fat calves stuffed down into the rear cockpit, a wing strut in each hand and the horsewhip between his teeth. "The plot thickens," said Seeley as he watched the plane disappear behind the trees. Then he spurred his horse to a canter and the other two followed.

They rode on quickly across low country spotted with clumps of trees and pools of water. Sika deer and whitetail sprang from their path and birds rose out of the grass. Bullock could hear tatters of noises now, merry-go-round music and the blare of loudspeakers blown to them on the wind.

"By the way," said Seeley, "do you know Commissioner McNaughton was on the board of review that turned down my application for the Mountie Academy? Oh, he was only a superintendent then. The other members of the panel wanted to waive the saber-scar rule and accept me into the academy, I could tell. But McNaughton sat there like God Almighty, and when it came his turn to speak he said: 'If a saber scar, why not a monocle?' I saw the other faces fall and knew my application was doomed."

As he spoke, they emerged from some tall grass and there ahead of them, under the watchful eyes of the village cowboys, were two or three hundred wild horses and foals ready for the quarter-mile swim across the channel to Chincoteague.

"But don't you see McNaughton was right?" insisted Bullock. "After monocles, it'd be heel-clicking, hand-kissing, and dumb steel helmets with those—"

Suddenly the cowboys were shouting and waving their hats. The swim was starting.

The horses took to the water slowly but without fear and swam out strongly between the double row of boats that marked the course. The tide was outgoing and the current slack. Seeley reined in his horse and said, "Here will do nicely, Squirt."

As the small man dismounted, Seeley said, "When it comes to tourists, this pony roundup's good for two days max. But my Mountie Burger and Golfeteria operation pulls in people all year round. So the Chamber of Commerce loves me enough to let me stage a little advertising stunt during this year's swim. Or at least that's what they think you're doing here." Seeley smiled at Bullock. "Even with a late start, a horse like Bounding Mane would finish a swim like this out in front, right?"

"He sure would," agreed Bullock proudly.

"Then picture this," said Seeley. "There's McNaughton and his granddaughter sitting in the VIP bleachers as that first horse reaches shore. What Mountie commissioner, what Canadian schoolgirl wouldn't recognize Bounding Mane? Hurrah, the lost Mount of the Mounted has been found! But hold it. Isn't that a drowned Mountie hanging there upside down under Bounding Mane?"

"Over my dead body!" swore Bullock.

"Heads up, then," advised Seeley and gave Bullock a gentle push. Squirt must have loosened the cinch a notch, for Bullock toppled over, slid down Bounding Mane's side, and came to a stop beneath the animal, hanging upside down from the saddle. "Will that terrible sight and his granddaughter's hysteria trigger McNaughton's fatal apoplectic fit, I wonder? Or will the shameful discovery of a half a million dollars' worth of cocaine in your saddlebags and headlines like MOUNTIE DROWNS IN DRUG SMUGGLING TRY drive McNaughton to blow his brains out?"

Through this, Bullock struggled to right himself by frantically pulling the cinch down with both hands, hoping to hoist himself up onto the horse's back. Seeley looked down at this futile effort with mild interest. "I guess you know they confiscate cars, planes, and boats used for smuggling. But not many know smugglers' horses get sold to Ralph, the Dog Food Man. Good old Ralph W., he's the Mr. Emerson you're going to deliver Bounding Mane to!" Looking pleased with himself, Seeley slapped Bounding Mane on the rump.

During the dash to the water, it took sharp reflexes and head bobbing on Bullock's part to avoid the landscape. Then he had just enough time to grab a deep breath before Bounding Mane was swimming deep in the channel current.

When the initial shock of the water had passed, Bullock set himself to getting out of this little pickle. He'd watched a TV show on the Eskimo and how they righted a capsized kayak. As he remembered it, the trick was all in the hip action. But by the time he got it right in his head, his lungs were bursting—he'd only have enough air for one try. He gave it his best hip shot. Nothing happened. He was a goner. Goodbye, good old Mavis, dear.

Suddenly, as though he understood what Bullock had been trying to do, Bounding Mane duplicated the hip action and swung Bullock and saddle up onto his back. Bullock's head and shoulders broke the surface. He found himself in the midst of a herd of giant sea horses, with their strong necks and handsome heads out of the water, their nostrils flared and ears flatted while beneath the surface mighty tails drove them forward. Bullock saw the cheering boats and heard the roar of the crowd on shore. But he hadn't thought to grab Bounding Mane around the neck and his weight carried him across the horse's back and down the other side. He ended up back under the horse where he'd started.

Expecting Bounding Mane to flip him up again, he waited confidently, arms crossed, marshaling his breath with care. Hanging upside down really sharpened the old wits. Bullock was mulling over the fact that Greeks built the miniature-golf windmills when a variation on the classic Canadian riddle "Who's buried in Sir John A. MacDonald's tomb?" popped into his head: "Why is a miniature-golf windmill like a Trojan Horse?" The answer: "Because the Greeks built it." Was it only the silliness of oxygen deprivation that made the riddle and answer seem important?

At last, and not a second too soon, Bounding Mane repeated the hip action. Bullock broke the surface again, grabbed the horse around the neck, and hung on for dear life. By godfrey, Bounding Mane was out in front by four lengths! That was why he'd been left hanging there so long. The animal had been making his move through the pack. A hundred yards ahead, the crowds on the shore were cheering and clicking their camera shutters.

Bounding Mane's hooves found bottom now. Then Bullock's shoulders and body were out of the water. In the next moment horse and rider were on the shore. Bullock sat tall and straight in the saddle and thrust out his jaw. As Bounding Mane galloped forward between the cheering spectators, Bullock's now steely gaze picked out an astonished McNaughton and his granddaughter standing in the VIP bleachers. By godfrey, this had to be the proudest moment of his career.

As he galloped past the RCMP commissioner, Bullock did a smart eyes-left and saluted. Of course he shouldn't have, for the salute was just enough to tip his delicate balance atop Bounding Mane and he and the saddle swung back down beneath the horse. The last thing Bullock remembered was that he'd forgotten "Heads up!"

Bullock awoke with an aching head and lay there, staring up at the jail-cell ceiling. Then a voice said, "I'm Agent Loomis."

Bullock turned his head and saw a man with hard blue eyes and a crisp tan suit standing at the bars. "Bullock, RCMP," he said, swinging his feet off the cot and trying to stand up. He almost fell. Something terrible had happened to his legs. They were a good foot shorter than they should be. Then he looked down and discovered the saddle was still stuck to his breeks.

"Getting that off's going to be more than the local facilities can handle," predicted Loomis. "The glue's gone through to the skin." Then he said, "Yeah, we've heard about you down here, Bullock. You slam limousine doors on prime ministers' hands. You deal in drugs. Your commissioner's on the phone to Washington right now trying to save that horse from the Dog Food Man. It won't do him any good. Policy's policy."

Bullock waddled over to the bars. "Look, Ralston Seeley planted those drugs. He's a major distributor. He uses his Golfeteria outlets. Don't ask me how."

Loomis shook his head. "Seeley's become very important people down here, spreading money around in all the right places. Talk says he'll be the next secretary of the interior, with big plans to smarten up the park rangers. No, we've had our eye on the Golfeterias. They're owned by a guy called Necropolis. We've raided a couple of outlets but came up dry. Once we sweated one of his night managers with a drug record, a sawed-off shotgun of a runt called Tommy Thumb. But he wouldn't break."

"Good godfrey, that's it!" said Bullock. Then he started counting on his fingers. "Tommy Thumb, Squirt, Tiny, and Mr. Knee-High. Seeley needed them short to work inside the windmills." When Agent Loomis raised an interested eyebrow, Bullock started to pace bowleggedly, one index finger pointing skyward and the other cradling his chin thoughtfully.

"Believe me," he said, "Seeley and Necropolis are the same guy. Suppose he sells these specially marked golf balls to his dealers. That way they can't get caught holding much and a fresh supply's just a putt away. When a marked ball pops inside the windmill, the night manager switches it for one filled with cocaine and drops it out the other side." Bullock wagged his forefinger. "But even as we speak, Seeley's—" But when he turned, Loomis was already out the door.

Bullock frowned. Right now Seeley would be making his escape, riding hellbent for leather back up Assateague Island. He had to be stopped. "Hey, guard!" shouted Bullock. "I've still got my one phone call coming!"

Bullock got his call. Ranger Wayves answered the Visitors' Center phone at the top of Assateague Island. His voice turned husky when Inspector General Bullock identified himself, described Seeley, and ordered her to arrest him when he tried to leave the island.

By godfrey, the story she told him was one he'd treasure

for Mountie campfires. She said they'd been out dumping the bodies of the killed Smyrna ladies into the quicksand. Pounding hoofbeats approached, and suddenly Seeley came barreling over a dune on a horse lathered with sweat. The horse foundered deep in the quicksand, and before Seeley knew what was happening he was up to his waist and sinking fast.

Amber stretched herself out atop the hellish mud and had the others grab her ankles and push her toward Seeley, who was chest-deep in the quicksand and screaming with fear. When her reach fell short of Seeley's outstretched arm, she held out her Stetson. But instead of grabbing the brim and being pulled to safety, Seeley snatched the hat and put it on. Instantly a strange peace spread across the man's face. He threw back his shoulders, tucked in his chin, and gave a bright, boyish smile. And in that instant, so the park ranger witnesses swear, the saber scar vanished from his cheek. Then Ralston Seeley, happy in death, slid beneath the surface of the quicksand.

Black Fly Lake was a silver rink in the moonlight among the black trees. A loon uttered its madman's laughter across the water. Bullock lay on his stomach in the porch hammock and mused on life. He'd been able to put a pretty good face on the Chincoteague business, the Golfeteria bust, Bounding Mane's rescue. Perhaps he'd been less than honest in telling good old Mavis that he'd been personally selected to escort Bounding Mane home.

The fact was, Bullock couldn't have survived the trip to Ottawa sitting on that blasted saddle in the backseat of McNaughton's car, so they'd hoisted him up onto the horse's back and buckled the saddle on. Then they'd cut a hole in the horse-trailer roof for his head and shoulders. The trip had been a grim one, with Dolly McNaughton wide-eyed with wonder all the way. This had obliged Bullock to maintain his formal Mountie expression—"fair but relentless"—through sun, rain, and the rush-hour traffic around Syracuse, New York, until his jaw went numb.

At the Mountie laboratory, technicians had buckled him into a sling and lowered him waist-deep into a vat of acetone. After two hours, he'd been lifted out again. Using a device they described as state of the art but which Bullock thought looked like a large version of those keys you open sardine cans with, they had peeled off the saddle, the seat of his breeks, and a goodly portion of his skin in the same vicinity.

By godfrey, he'd wondered, how was he going to explain his injury to good old Mavis? Then suddenly he got a brainstorm. Laughing darkly, he'd told her he'd gotten it escaping from the grip of one of Seeley's tough adherents.

Bullock could hear her in the kitchen cleaning up the last of the dinner dishes. Soon she'd come out and change his dressing and apply the salve. It was no picnic, lying on your stomach. But what was he grousing about? After a couple of bad starts, he'd finally won the day in Chincoteague. You can lose every battle except the last one. The law-and-order business was just like miniature golf. It was an endgame all the way.

As if it read his thoughts, that loon on Black Fly Lake called out again across the water.

William F. Nolan

SHADOW QUEST

His name was striking: John Shadow. Otherwise, he was a very ordinary fellow. No wife. No family. A drifter, making his way through life as best he could. No goals. No ambitions. He gambled some, losing more than he won. He boxed for pocket money in Dodge City, cut timber in Canada, punched cows along the Cimarron, rode the rods west as a road tramp, served as a bouncer in Santa Fe, and played piano at a fancy house in El Paso. That job ended abruptly when Shadow ran off with one of the house ladies (her name was Margie). But they didn't stay together. Margie left him for a buffalo hunter two weeks later.

He was at loose ends. He owned the clothes on his back, a lump-headed mustang, and a new Winchester he'd won in a Kansas poker game. And not much else.

That was when John Shadow decided to ride into the Sierra Madres after Diablo.

He heard about him in the border town of Los Lobos along the American side of the Rio Grande. A wild stallion. El Diablo Blanco—the White Devil. Fast, smart . . . and mean. Two trappers at the bar were talking about the stallion.

"Has he been hunted?" Shadow asked.

"By the best," said the bartender, a beefy man in a stained apron. "With relays of horses. Sometimes they've run him a hundred miles in one day, but he always outsmarts 'em. Disappears like smoke in the wind. Lemme tellya, if a horse can laugh, he's laughing."

"I'm good with horses," Shadow said quietly.

The barman's smile was cynical. "Got a real *way* with 'em, eh?"

"I'd say so," nodded Shadow.

"Well, then, here's your chance." And he exchanged grins with the two trappers. "Just take yourself a little jaunt up into the Sierras an' fetch out the white."

"I need to think on it," Shadow told him.

He returned to the bar later that same afternoon.

"I'm going after him," he said.

It was a full day's ride into the upper foothills of the Sierra Madres. Shadow was following a crude, hand-drawn map provided by the barman after he'd convinced him he was serious in his quest for the white. The barman had indicated the area where the horse had been most often seen—but Shadow had no guarantee that Diablo had remained in this section of the mountains.

He was well aware of the various methods used in the capture of wild horses. Often, a sizable group of riders pursued the target animals, attempting to force them into a circular run, gradually tightening the circle. Sometimes hunters used relays of horses, constantly maintaining fresh mounts in the hope of running down the winded herd.

There was the story of a legendary hunt by a young Cheyenne warrior in which the Indian had traveled on foot for many hundreds of miles over a period of several months in pursuit of a single horse. The natural speed of a wild horse is reduced by its need to graze each day. Whenever the animal stopped to eat, the Indian's tireless, loping stride would close the distance between them. The Cheyenne lived on water and parched corn, eating as he ran, thus constantly forcing the pursuit.

Eventually, so the story went, both hunter and hunted became gaunt and weakened. The long trail ended on the naked slope of a snowcapped peak high above timberline when the Indian managed to lasso his totally exhausted quarry.

Of course, even if this fanciful tale were true, Shadow had no patience for such an arduous pursuit.

When he was within range of the horse, Shadow intended to bring down the animal with a bullet from his Winchester. The shot would require extreme accuracy, since his bullet must crease the nape of the neck at a spot that would jar the animal's spinal column. This would stun the horse, allowing its capture.

Diablo was unusual in that he ran alone. Most wild horses run with others of their kind, in herds numbering up to fifty or more, but the white stallion had always been a loner, staying well clear of the herds ranging the Sierra Madres. He wanted no young colts or laboring mares to slow his swift progress.

Many attempts had been made to capture him. One group of hunters, led by Colonel Matthew Sutton, had plans for Diablo as an Eastern show horse, and ran the stallion for

six weeks without letup. Eleven horses had galloped themselves to death during that brutal pursuit, while the proud
white drifted ahead of them, beyond their reach, defiant and
strong.

One frustrated hunter claimed that the stallion had never
truly existed—that he was nothing more than an apparition,
a white ghost who galloped like a cloud across the sky.

When John Shadow repeated this last claim to a trapper
he'd met in the high mountains, a one-armed veteran named
Hatcher, the old man declared: "Oh, he's real enough all
right, Diablo is. I've seen him by sun and by moon, in good
weather and bad. There was one time I come up on him close
enough to near touch that smooth silk hide of his, but then
he took off like a streak of white lightning."

The old man cackled at the memory. "A pure wonder,
he is. Ain't no horse like him nowhere in these mountains or
out of 'em, and that's a fact."

"Then you don't think I can catch him?" asked John
Shadow.

"Sure ya can—as easy as you can reach out and catch the
wind." And Hatcher cackled again.

There was a great difference between the arid, sterile mountains around El Paso and this lush terrain of the Sierra Madres.
Here Shadow found water in abundance, and rich grass, and
thickly wooded hills—a veritable paradise that provided Diablo with everything he needed to sustain his wild existence.

Despite the old trapper's firm conviction that the great
horse could never be captured, Hatcher had nonetheless provided solid hope. The trapper had agreed that Diablo did
indeed frequent this particular section of mountain wilderness.

Luck and a keen eye might well reward him here.

Just a day later, as he was riding out of a shallow draw

onto the level of a grassed plateau, John Shadow had his first look at the legendary stallion.

Diablo had been nibbling the green, tender sprouts that tipped a thick stand of juniper and now he raised his head to scent the wind. He nickered softly. Nostrils flaring, he suddenly wheeled about to face the rider at the far end of the plateau.

Shadow had slipped the new Winchester from its scabbard, since the range permitted him to fire, but he slowly lowered the weapon, awed by the animal's size and beauty. Easily seventeen hands tall, deep-chested, sheathed with rippling muscle, and as white as a drift of newly fallen snow, Diablo was truly magnificent.

The horse stood immobile for a long moment, studying his enemy. Then, with a toss of his thick mane and a ringing neigh of defiance, he trotted away, breaking into a smooth-flowing gallop that carried him swiftly out of sight.

Dammit! I could have fired, Shadow told himself; I could have ended it here and now with a single shot.

The light had been ideal and he was certain he could have creased the animal's neck. And there had been ample time for the shot. But the sheer power and majesty of the horse had kept him from firing. What if his bullet had missed its mark and struck a vital area? What if he had killed this king of stallions? Many wild horses have been fatally shot by hunters attempting to stun them.

No, he decided, I need to be closer, a lot closer, to make absolutely *certain* of the shot. And now that he's aware of me, it's not going to be easy.

That night, after a meal of mountain grouse roasted over his campfire, Shadow spread his blanket across a bed of fragrant pine needles on the forest floor. Lying on his back, hands laced behind his head, under a mass of tall pines that crowded the stars, he considered the meaning of freedom.

He had always thought of himself as a free man, yet through much of his life he'd been bound by the commands of others—when he had served in the war, when he was working in bars and brothels, when he'd been a cowpuncher and lumberman. In Diablo, John Shadow had witnessed true freedom. The great horse owed allegiance to no one. The whole wide world of the mountain wilderness served as his personal playground. He ran at no man's bidding, served no master but himself.

And now I'm trying to take that freedom away from him, thought Shadow. I'm trying to saddle and bridle him, bend his will to mine, feed him oats instead of his wild sweet grass, make him gallop at my command.

Did he have the right? Did *anyone* really have the right to own such a glorious animal?

With these melancholy thoughts drifting through his consciousness, Shadow closed his eyes, breathing deeply of the clean mountain air. The faint whisper of wind, rustling the trees, lulled him to sleep.

He awakened abruptly, shocked and wide-eyed, to an earth-shaking roar.

The morning sun was slanting down in dusty yellow bars through the pine branches, painting the forest floor in shades of brilliant orange. At the edge of the clearing, not twenty-five feet from where John Shadow had been sleeping, a huge, brown-black grizzly had reared up to a full-battle position, its clawed forepaws extended like a boxer's hands. The monstrous jaws gaped wide in anger, yellow fangs gleaming like swords in the wide red cave of its mouth.

The mighty bruin, a full thousand pounds of bone and muscle, was not facing directly toward Shadow, but was angled away from him, in the direction of another enemy.

Diablo!

Incredible as it seemed, the tall white stallion was trotting around the grizzly in a wary half-circle, ears flattened, eyes glaring, prehensile upper lip pulled back from its exposed teeth.

The horse was plainly preparing to attack.

Shadow was amazed. He had never known a horse to challenge a grizzly. Even the scent of an approaching bear was enough to send the fiercest stallion into a gallop for safety— yet here was Diablo, boldly facing this forest mammoth with no trace of fear.

Then an even greater shock struck the hunter: Diablo was defending *him*! The bear had apparently been making his forest rounds, overturning rocks for insects, ripping apart dead logs for grubs and worms, when he'd encountered the sleeping figure of John Shadow. He was about to descend on the hunter when the stallion intervened.

It made no logical sense. Yet, somehow, the white horse had felt protective of the man who had been hunting him. That Diablo had come to his rescue was a fact John Shadow accepted, although he was truly stunned by such an act. The scene seemed to be part of a dream, yet Shadow knew he was fully awake. What was happening, *was* happening.

Now Diablo reared up, with a ringing neigh, to strike at the brute's head with his stone-sharpened forehooves. A hoof connected with the bruin's skull like a dropped hammer, and the bear staggered back, roaring horribly, its eyes like glowing sparks of fire.

Then the grizzly counterattacked, lunging ponderously forward to rake one of its great paws across the stallion's neck. This blow, powerful enough to take a man's head off at the shoulders, buckled Diablo's legs, and the stunned animal toppled backward and down, blood running from an open neck wound.

The bear lumbered forward to finish his opponent, but by now Shadow had his Winchester in hand, and he began firing at the dark-shagged beast.

The giant grizzly seemed impervious to bullets. With a frightful bellow of rage, he charged wildly at the hated man-thing.

Shadow stopped firing to roll sideways—barely avoiding the razored claws, which scored the log next to his head. With the huge bruin looming above him like a brown-black mountain, Shadow pumped three more rounds into the beast at heart level.

They did the job.

Like a chopped tree, the monster crashed to the forest floor, expiring with a final, defiant death-growl. It had taken five rifle bullets to kill him.

Diablo lay on his side, only half conscious, breathing heavily, as Shadow tended the stallion's injured shoulder. Using fresh water from his canteen, he cleansed the wound, then treated it with an old Indian remedy: he carefully packed a mix of forest herbs and mud over the wound, and tied it in place with a shirt from his saddle roll.

Amazingly, the animal did not resist these efforts. Diablo seemed to understand that Shadow was trying to help him.

If those claws had gone a half-inch deeper, Shadow knew, the shoulder muscle would have been ruined, crippling the great horse.

He ran his hand soothingly along the stallion's quivering flank, murmuring in a soft voice, "Easy, boy, easy now. You're going to be all right . . . you're going to be fine. . . ."

And Diablo rolled an anxious eye toward John Shadow.

It took more than a week before the white stallion was willing to follow a lead rope. During this entire period Shadow worked night and day to win the gallant animal's trust, talking, stroking, picking lush seed grass for the horse to eat.

The shoulder wound healed rapidly.

On the ninth day after the bear attack, Shadow began his

ride back to Los Lobos, with Diablo trotting behind him on the lead rope.

Shadow was smiling as he rode. Now, suddenly, his life held purpose and meaning. Soon he would teach Diablo to accept him as a rider; he would be the first to guide this glorious beast over valley and plain—and riding him, Shadow knew, would be like riding the wind itself. There would be a mutual trust between them. A deep understanding. A bonding of spirits.

Before he had made this trip into the Sierra Madres John Shadow had never believed in miracles.

Now, looking back at the splendor of Diablo, he knew he had been wrong.

Clay Fisher

THE TRAP

Canady felt the horse beginning to go rough beneath him. He had been expecting it. On this rocky going, no mount could make it for long when he was already ridden out in coming to it.

"Easy, easy," he said to the laboring animal. "It's only a posse." The horse seemed to understand the tone of the words, for it slowed and went better and steadier for a ways. "We'll rest on the rise ahead," Canady said. "I can see back a few miles and you can catch some wind and we'll go on. We'll make it."

He knew they wouldn't. He knew it before they came to

the rise and he got down and walked out on the overhanging spur of gray-black basalt that gave a view down the canyon behind them for ten miles. It wasn't a canyon, really, but a narrowing valley. The canyon proper lay before them. Canady grinned and wiped his streaming face. It was hot, and going to get hotter.

"Hoss," he said, "they're pushing. They mean to take us. They must know the country ahead. They don't ride like there's any hurry."

The horse, now, did not respond with its ears and a turning of its soft eyes, as it had before. It stood, head down, blowing out through its distended nostrils. Canady came back and squatted down and put his hand below the nose of the horse, where the moisture of its pained breathing would strike his palm.

"Damn," he said softly. "Blood."

He got his field glasses from the saddle pocket and examined the pursuers through them. "Eight," he said aloud, "and six ropes. I wonder how come it is that they always fetch so many ropes? Never saw a posse yet didn't feel that each of them ought to have a rope."

His fingers went to his sunburned neck. They felt it tenderly, and he grinned again. "Son of a gun," he said, "it could happen."

Canady's grins were not the grimaces of a fool, or of an unfeeling man. They were the grins of a gambler. And of an outlaw. And a thief. Canady knew where he was and where he had been and, most apparently, where he was going. It did not frighten him. He would grin when they put the loop over his head. That was his kind. He wouldn't curse or revile, and he wouldn't pray. Not out loud, anyway.

"Hoss," he said, "what do you think?"

The animal, slightly recovered, moved its ears and whickered gruntingly. Canady nodded, turning his back to the approaching posse and glassing the country ahead. "Me, too," he agreed. "A grunt and a whicker is all she's worth. We haven't got no place to go." He tensed, as he said it, the glasses freezing on an opening in the rearing base rock of the closing valley.

It was to their right. A good horse, fresh and sound, could take a man up to that gap in the cliff. The spill of detritus and an ages-old fan of boulders and stunted pine that lay below its lip would permit of perilous mounted passage. There was water up there, too, for Canady could see the small white ribbon of the stream splashing down a rainbow falls to mist upon the lower rocks in a spume of red and yellow and turquoise green lights, splendid with beauty in the early sun. "I take it back," he said. "Maybe we do have a place to go. Pretty, too, and handy to town. You can't beat that."

Directly ahead was a level sunlit flat, dotted with tall pines and scrub juniper and house-sized boulders. The clear stream from the high hole in the right-side valley wall watered the flat, growing good mountain hay upon its sandy red loam and making a ride across it a thing to pleasure the heart of any Western man.

"Come on," said Canady to his horse. "You canter me across the flat and I'll climb the fan afoot leaving you to pack up nothing but the saddle and the grub sack. You game? Least we can do is make those birds scratch for their breakfast. And who knows? Our luck might change. We might get up there and into that hole-in-the-wall before they come up to the rise, here, and spot us. If we can do that, there's a chance they'll ride on by, up the valley, and we can double back tonight and make it free."

He was talking to Canady, now, not to the horse. It was the way of men much alone when they needed to do some figuring. They would do it out loud, the way Canady was doing. It sounded better that way, more convincing, and more as though it might really come off. Canady even swung into the saddle believing his own advice, telling himself what he wanted to know, then accepting it as a very good chance indeed. Again, it was his way. A man didn't live by the gun and the good fast horse without acquiring a working philosophy with lots of elastic in it.

"Move out," he repeated to the horse. "It's your part to get us across the flat in time."

The little mustang humped its back and shook itself like a wet dog. Running sweat, and caked as well, flew from its streaked hide. Its gathering of itself in response to the rider's words was a visible thing. The horse was like the man. It wouldn't quit short of the last second, or step, or shot. They were of a kind with the country around them. It was all the edge they had ever needed.

Canady panted. He wiped the perspiration from his eyes and started upward again. Behind him, the little horse came on, unled, the reins looped over the horn so as not to trail and be stepped on. He followed the man like a dog, panting with him, struggling where he struggled, sliding where he slid, and lunging on as he did, after each setback.

They had made it nearly to the top of the fan of fallen rock below and leading into the opening of the side canyon. In another four or five minutes they would be clear of the climb. They would be off the slide and safely into the notch in the high wall of the valley. They would be out of sight of the posse, and the posse still had not come into view of them on the rise back across the pine flat.

"Easy, hoss," gasped Canady. "We're going to make it."

But Canady was wrong. Thirty yards from the top, the mustang put its slender foreleg into a rock crevice and drew back quickly. The movement set the slide moving and caught the leg and crushed it like a matchstick below the knee. When the horse had freed itself and was standing hunched and trembling behind Canady, the shattered leg hung sickeningly a-swing and free of the ground, and Canady cursed with tears in his eyes. It was not the luck of it that brought his angry words, but the shame of it. It was his pity and his feeling for a gallant companion that had given its all and almost found it enough.

The hesitation, the wait there near the top of the slide, near the safety of the hole-in-the-wall, was the natural thing for a Western man. His horse was hurt. It was hopelessly hurt. He would have to leave it, but not like that. Not standing there on three legs hunched up in the middle with pain and fright. Not standing there watching him with those liquid brown eyes. No, he couldn't leave his horse like that.

But how else? He couldn't shoot the mustang, for the noise would key the posse to his location. Had he had a knife, he could cut its throat. Or had he an ax he could have crushed its skull above the eye socket and put the poor devil down painlessly. With a rock he might be able to stun the brave little brute, but he could not be sure of killing it cleanly. The same held true for the butt of his Colt or the steel-shod heel of his Winchester. He could stun the horse, likely put it to its knees, but not, still, be able to go on knowing it would not recover and would try to get up again and go on, and so suffer as no horse-riding man could think to let his mount suffer.

But, damn it, this was *his* life he was arguing with himself about. It wasn't the damned horse's life. If he didn't do something and do it quick, the posse would be over the rise and he and the horse could go to hell together. Well, he would use the Colt butt. He knew he could hit the exhausted animal hard enough with it to put it down for the necessary time for himself to get on into the hole-in-the-wall and for the posse to ride by and on up the valley. That was all the time he needed, or at least it was all he could ask for.

He pulled the Colt and started back to the horse, sliding and stumbling in his hurry to get to the trembling beast and knock it down. But when he got up to its side, when he looked into those dark eyes, he couldn't do it. He had to be sure.

"The hell with the posse," he said to the little horse, and spun the Colt in the air and caught it by the handle and put it behind the ragged ear and pulled the trigger. The smoke from the shot was still curling upward, and the little pony just going slowly down, when the first of the pursuing riders came up over the rise across the flat and yelled excitedly back to his comrades that the game was in sight, and on foot.

Canady went up the little stream. Behind him, where it fed the rainbow falls leaping outward into the main valley, the possemen were just topping the detritus fan and closing in on "the hole."

Back there Canady had made a decision. It was not to stay and fight from the entrance cleft of the hole, where the little rivulet went out of the side canyon. He did not know what lay on up the side canyon, and feared there might be a way by which the possemen, familiar with this territory, could ride a circle and come in behind him. He could not risk that, he believed, and must go on up the creek as far as he could, hoping it would be far enough to find a place where he could put his back to the wall and fight without their being able to get behind him.

Now, going along, the way becoming steeper and narrower and the creek bank little more than wide enough to pass a good horse and rider, he saw ahead of him a basalt dike, or cross dam of rock, which cut across the narrowing floor of the side canyon. Here the stream took another plunge, this of about thirty feet. Above the dike, Canady could see the boles of pine trees and hence knew that the ground above the dike lay fairly level. The cross-laying of rock apparently served as a barrier against which the winter erosions of snow, ice, and thaw had worked with the spring floodings of the creek to bring down soil and build up a tiny flat.

Canady's gray eyes lit up. His brown face relaxed and he said aloud, "By God, maybe this is it," and went on with renewed strength and some hope of keeping his life a little longer. Up there, above that rock cross-bank, a man with a good carbine and plenty of shells could hold down most eight-man posses for several afternoons. Well, two or three, anyway. Or one. For certain, until nightfall. Twelve, fifteen hours, say. It was better than nothing.

His luck held. There was a good angling trail going up that thirty-foot vertical face of rock. It was a game trail, and somewhat of a cow trail, too. He made out the droppings of elk, blacktail deer, range steers, and then, suddenly and strangely, a fairly fresh piling of horse sign. This latter find sent a chill through him. He was on his knees in the instant of the sighting, but then he straightened, grinning. It was all right. The pony was unshod. Moreover, he suspected, from the hard round prints that it left, that it never had been shod and was one of a bunch of broomtails—wild mustangs—that came into this rocky depth for the water that flowed so green and cool in the stream.

Clearing the top of the stone dam, Canady's grin widened. The flat above lay precisely as he had imagined it did. He laughed softly, as a man will who is alone. Now, then, it would be a little different from the way those hungry lawmen had planned it. This was perfect. At the apex of the triangle of the flat he saw the thick stand of sycamore and cottonwood, aspen, laurel and willow, and he knew that the water headed there.

A moment later, he made out the source of the stream, a large artesian spring gushing from the native rock under great pressure. The spring was set above the grove some few feet, its stream falling rapidly to plunge into the foliage. Likely it pooled up there under the trees and at the foot of the down-plunge. That's what lured in the wild horses and the other game and the cattle, too, what few of the latter were hardy enough to come this far into the mountains for feed.

All a man would need to do now, was hole up in those boulders that girded the spring, up there above the trees, and he could command with his Winchester the whole of the small, open flat between the spring grove and the stone cross-dam that Canady had just clambered up.

Taking a deep breath, the fugitive started across the flat, toward the spring and its hole-up boulders. It was not until he had climbed safely into this haven at the canyon head and laid down pantingly to look back on his trail and get ready for the possemen, that he saw where he had come.

Below him in the trees the spring pooled up exactly as he had expected it would. Also the rim of the pool showed the centuries of wear of the hoofed animals coming to its banks for water. But there was something else—two other things—that he had not expected to see there, and his grin faded and his gray eyes grew taut and tired and empty.

The first thing was the wild horse. It had not gone on up out of the little side canyon as Canady had hoped, showing him the way to follow its tracks and escape over the rim where no mounted man might follow. It was still in the grove of trees that sheltered the spring-pool water hole, and it wasn't still there because of its thirst.

Beyond the trees, back where Canady had come from, and so skillfully blended and built into the natural cover of the canyon that even his range-wise eyes had missed them, were the two woven brush-and-pole wings of the second thing Canady had not dreamed to find there. Those were the man-made wings of a mustang corral down there. Canady had stumbled into a wild-horse trap. And he was caught there, with this unfortunate lone mustang that now cowered in the trees and could not get out of the trap any more than could he, and for the same reason—the posse and the box canyon.

"Steady on," Canady called down softly to the terrified horse. "We'll think of something."

Two hours after high noon the sun was gone from the canyon. Canady could see its light splashing the far side of the main valley still, but in the side canyon all was soft shade, and hot. Canady drank enough water to keep himself from drying out, yet not enough to log him. He noted that the wild mustang did the same thing. It knew, as Canady knew, that to be ready to fight or fly called for an empty belly.

"Smart," said Canady, "smart as hell." The horse heard him and looked up. *"Coo-ee, coo-ee,"* Canady called to him reassuringly. "Don't fret; I'll figure something for us." But it was a lie and he knew it was a lie.

He had gone down, right after he first lay up in the spring boulders and saw the trap and the wild broomtail in it, and closed off the narrow gate of the funnel-winged corral with his lariat. He had done that in a hurry, before the posse had worked up into the canyon and taken its position along the top of the cross-dam. His one thought had been that the broomtail was a horse, wild or not, and that so long as a man had a horse he wasn't out of it in that country. And he had wanted to keep hidden from the posse the fact that he did have a horse up there in that headwaters' timber. The mustang had played with him in that last part of it, lying up shy and quiet as a deer in the trees and brush, not wanting any more than Canady wanted for the men to know that it was there.

"It" in this case was a scrubby little stallion, probably too small and old to hold a band of mares. The little horse had not only the fixtures but the temperament of the mongrel stud animal. Watching him lie still in the spring brush, his eyes following every move of the men below him, as well as of the single man above him, Canady knew that he and the trapped horse were friends. The only problem was proving it to the horse.

Sometimes these old scrub studs had been ridden long ago and would remember man's smell and voice. He tried a dozen times to talk the mustang up toward his end of the spring pool. But the animal gave no sign that the sight, scent, or sound of mankind was familiar to him, or welcome. He bared his teeth silently and pinned his ears and squatted on his haunches ready to kick like a pack mule on a cold morning. He did this every time Canady said more than three or four words to him, or accompanied his talk with any movement that might mean he was coming down to see the horse, if the horse would not come up to see him.

What possible good the horse could do him, even if, by some miracle, Canady might gentle him down and put his saddle and bridle on him, Canady didn't know. Then, even in thinking that far, he laughed and shrugged. His saddle and bridle were down there on that rock slide below the hole-in-the-wall. He'd had no time and no reason to take them off his dead mount. So if he went out of there astride that broomtail it would be bareback, and that was about as good a bet as that the crafty old stallion would sprout wings and fly up out of the canyon. A bridle, of sorts, he could rig from splitting and unraveling a short length of his lariat. It would be sort of a breaking hackamore arrangement and might do to give simple directions of right and left and whoa-up.

But even if he rigged this Sioux headstall and got it on the shaggy little horse, then what? That was, even if the rascal wanted to be good, or had been ridden in the past, and remembered it of a sudden? Nothing. Not a damned thing. Canady couldn't ride out of that canyon if he had the best saddle mount in Montana waiting and eager to make the try with him. It was all crazy, thinking of that wild stud. But just finding any horse up there was bound to start a man's mind going. Especially when he had just shot his own mount and was fixing to put his back to the best rock he could find and go down with lead flying.

But it was crazy all the same. All Canady could do was what the old broomtail stud could do—fight the rope to the last breath he had in him, then kill himself, if he could, before the others did it for him.

The afternoon wore on. The heat in the deep-walled

little canyon was enormous. The deerflies swarmed at the spring pool and bit like mad cats. They nearly drove Canady wild, but he fought them with hand and mind and swathed neckband and, when evening came, they lifted up out of the canyon on the first stir of the night wind.

In the early part of the waiting there had been some desultory talk between the posse and Canady, talk of Canady coming out peacefully and getting a fair trial, but the fugitive had not bothered to take that offer seriously. He knew the trial he would get. The posse had its own witnesses with it. They would bring up these two or three men who had "seen" the shooting and say to them, "Is that him?" and the men would say, "Yes, that's him," and the trial would be over. Witnesses! thought Canady. God, how he hated them.

It wasn't that he minded being identified if he was the man. In his business, no feeling was held against the witness who *had* seen something. It was those devils, like the ones with the posse, who had *not* seen the job and yet who were always ready to raise their right hands and be sworn, who were the ones Canady hated.

There had not been any witnesses to what passed between him and that teller. All the other bank people had been on the floor behind the cage, and there had been no customers in the bank, or out in front of it. The shooting had happened and Canady had made it to his horse in back of the bank, and made it away down the alley and into the sagebrush south of town before he had passed a living soul. Then it was two farm wagons, both carrying kids and driven by women, that he had ridden by well out of Gray's Landing. How those good folks—and they were the only real witnesses, save the cashier and the other teller on the bank floor—how they could identify him as anything other than a horseman not of that area, Canady did not know.

As for the three shots that had killed the teller, and they must have killed him or the posse would not have pushed so hard, those shots had been fired *after* both barrels of the .36-caliber derringer that the teller brought up out of the cash drawer had been triggered and put their slugs, one in Canady's chest, and one in the ceiling of the Second National Bank of Gray's Landing, Montana.

But the only witness to that fact was dead. Canady had reacted as all men with guns in their hands react to other men with guns in their hands. He had fired by instinct, by pure conditioned reflex of long experience, when that first .36 bullet went into the pectoral muscles of his left chest.

Armed robbery? Certainly. Twenty years in the Territorial Prison? Of course. A man expected that. But to be run down like a mad dog and cornered and starved out and then strung up on a naked cottonwood like a damned Indian drunk or a common horse thief was not right or fair. Murder? Could you call it murder when the other man was a professional in his business and he could see that you were a professional in yours? When you told him he would be killed if he tried anything funny? Then, when on top of the fair warning, you gave him the first shot? Could you call it murder, then, if you shot in answer to his try at killing you? Self-defense was the actual verdict, but of course an armed robber could not plead self-defense. But he was not guilty of murder, or even of assault with a deadly weapon, or even of intent to commit murder, or of a damned thing, really, but to sack that cash drawer and clear out of Gray's Landing just as fast and peaceably as he and the old horse might manage.

Canady grinned, even as he exonerated himself.

It was no good. He knew it was no good. A man had to be honest with himself. If he was in another business he wouldn't need a gun to conduct his trade. Needing and using a gun, he was always in the peril of being forced to use it. The teller was an honest man. Frank Canady was a crook. The teller was a dead honest man, and Canady was a live dishonest man. Canady was a killer.

"No!" he yelled down to the posse. "I won't do it. I shot second; I didn't mean to harm that fellow. He pulled on me and shot first. But he's dead, ain't he? Sure he is. And you say to me to come on down peaceable and you'll see I get a fair trial? With a dead teller back there on the floor of the Second National? That's rich. Really rich."

The possemen were startled. It had been two hours since the fugitive had made a sound. Previously he had refused to come down and they had thought he meant it. Now, did they detect a change? Was it that he wanted to reconsider and was only protecting his ego by the defiant outburst? What was all this about?

"That's right, you heard us right," the leader of the posse called up to him. "You come down here and we'll guarantee to take you back to Gray's Landing and get you to either Cheyenne or Miles City, wherever the court is sitting, by train and under armed guard. You'll get the trial we promised, and the protection beforehand." He waited a significant moment, then demanded, "What do you say? There's no use any more people getting hurt."

Canady's gray eyes grew tired again.

"That's so," he called back. "It includes me, too. I don't want to see anybody else get it, either. 'Specially me. No thanks, Mr. Posseman. I'll stay up here. I don't fancy that you brung along all them ropes just to tie me up for the ride back to Gray's Landing."

There was a silence from below the cross-dam of rock in the upper throat of the canyon that lasted perhaps two, perhaps three stretching minutes. Then the posseman called back.

"All right," he said, "you'll have it your way. When it's full dark we're going to come for you, and you know what that will mean. There are eight of us, all good shots, and you won't have the chance of a rat in an oat bin. We've got bull's-eye lanterns to light you out. We will set them up behind boulders where you can't snipe them, and yet where they will throw light up there around you like it was bright moonlight. We mean to stomp you out. There will be no trial and no talk of a trial. You're dead right now."

Canady sank back behind his breastwork of basalt and gray-green granite. He hawked the cottony spittle from his throat and spat grimacingly down toward the mustang stud. The animal had been crouching and listening to the exchange of voices intelligently like some big gaunt sandy-maned dog. Seeing him, and noting his apparent interest, Canady managed a trace of his quiet grin.

"What do *you* say, *amigo?*" he asked.

The horse looked up at him. It was the first time in all the long hours that Canady had tried gentle-talking to him that the animal had made a direct and not spooked response to the man's voice. Now he stomped a splayed and rock-split forehoof and whickered softly and gruntingly in his throat, precisely as Canady's old horse had done.

"All right," said Canady, for some reason feeling mightily warmed by the mustang's action, "so we've each got one friend in the world. That isn't too bad. As long as you have a friend you have a chance. Rest easy; let me think. We'll still make it, you and me. . . ."

It was dusk when the old steer came down the cliff trail. He was a ladino, one of those mossy-horned old rascals that had successfully hidden out from the gathers of a dozen years. He was old and crafty and cautious as any wild animal, but he had to have water and he was coming down to the spring pool to get it.

He certainly saw the men of the posse, and winded their mounts, but they did not see him and he knew that they did not. His yellow buckskin hide with the dark *cruz* or cross-stripe on the shoulders, and the dark brown legs and feet, blended perfectly into the weathered face of the cliff, and he made no more sound coming down that hidden trail than a mountain doe might have made. But he had failed to see Canady or to separate his scent, or the scent of the mustang stud, from the other horse and man scents coming from below.

He came on, carefully, silently, yet quickly down the wall of the canyon from the rim above and Canady, seeing him, was suddenly lifted in mind and heart. He had been right in the first place! There *was* a trail up out of that blind box of a side canyon. A track up that dizzy sheer cliff, up there, that would pass a desperate man, or a catlike wild mustang, but not a mounted man or a man going afoot leading his tamed and trained saddle mount.

"Come on, come on," he heard himself whispering to the old outlaw steer. "Come on down here and let me see how you do it. Let me see how and where you get off that damned wall and down here where we are."

He grinned when he said that, when he said "we," meaning himself and the wild stud, without thinking about it. It was funny how a man took to anything for a friend when he had run out of the real McCoy and was in his last corner. He supposed that if a sidewinder crawled along at the final minute and that was all he had to talk to, a man would find some excuse to think kindly of the snake tribe. Well, anyway, he was thinking with deep kindness about the animal kingdom just then. Especially the horse and cow part of it. And extra specially about the latter half.

"Come on, keep coming on, don't slip, for God's sake," he said to the gaunt dun steer. "Easy, easy. Let me see you do it, just don't fall or spook or get a bad smell and change your mind. That's it, that's it. Easy, easy. . . ."

He talked the steer down that cliff trail as though his life depended on it, and it did. And the steer made it. He made it in a way that caused Canady to suck in his breath and shake his head in wonderment. He made it in a way that even caused

Canady to think for a moment about there being something to the idea of a divine providence, for it was the sort of thing no man could have figured out by himself, the weird, crazy, wonderful kind of a last-second reprieve that no force but God Almighty could have sent to a man in Canady's place. It was a miracle.

The dun steer performed it with an easy quickness that defied belief, too. He came to that place on his side of the canyon where it seemed to Canady that the trail must end. The man could see the sheer face of the rock dropping sixty feet to the creek bed. A giant outcropping of granite hid the exact end of the right-side trail, but Canady could see, and with absolute certainty, that the trail did not continue downward past that outcrop that hid its actual terminus.

But as he watched the steer disappear behind the outcrop and as he wondered what would happen next, he saw the lean yellow body lurch itself in a graceful leap from behind the outer edge of the outcrop, and sail outward through the thin air of the canyon's dark throat. It appeared as though the leap would smash the ribby brute into the rearing face of the opposite, left-hand canyon wall, which lay no more than fifteen or twenty feet from the right-side wall. But again the steer disappeared, this time seemingly into the very face of the opposing cliff.

There was a tricky turn in the rock wall of the canyon's left side at just that point, however, and while Canady could see the creek's raggedly broken bottom, he could not see where the steer hit into the wall. All he was sure of for the moment was that the animal had made his landing somewhere other than in the creek bottom. Difficult as it might be to accept, that old outlaw steer had somehow made it from one side of the wall to the other. But, even so, then what? Where was he now? The questions were soon answered when the missing steer appeared to walk right out of the waterfall that came down from Canady's elevated vantage to strike into and begin following the brief section of creek bed into the pool grove. While Canady gaped, the animal stole swiftly to the pool, drank sparingly, returned, and disappeared again behind the curtain of misty water cascading down from the spring above.

So that was it. As simple and as remarkable as that. A trail ran from behind the waterfall up the left-hand wall. At a point opposite the right-side trail's end, it, too, terminated. But it was obvious that there was room enough for a running jump and opposite safe landing, to and from either wall, with both takeoff and landing spots completely masked from the lower canyon.

Gauging the distance of the jump, Canady knew that he could make it. With his boots off and laced about his neck, or better, thrown over with his Colt and the saddlebags with the bank money, the Winchester being slung on his back, alone, he could make that distance through the air. But then, what of that? He made the jump safely and went on up the right-side cliff trail behind the ladino steer and gained the rim; then what? He would still be afoot in a hostile land in midsummer's blazing heat without food, water, or a mount.

That was the rub. Even if he made that jump and the cliff climb beyond it and got to the rim, he would have to have a horse. Otherwise, the possemen, within an hour or two of dark, having come for him and found him gone, would go back out and climb out of the main valley and cut for his sign on both rims of the side canyon, and they would still get him. They would get him, easy, with them mounted and him afoot.

No, he had to take that broomy studhorse with him.

Somehow, he had to get that mustang to go with him up the cliff. If he could do that, could get the little horse to make the jump with him on its back—it would have to be that way for he could never trust the brute to follow him or to wait for him if he allowed it to jump first—if he could make that gap in the canyon on the back of that little wild horse, then stay with him, hand-leading him up the cliff trail, then, oh then, by the dear good Lord, he would make it. He and the horse would make it together. Just as he had promised the raunchy little devil. Up on the rim, he would remount the tough wiry mustang and together they would race away and Canady would have his life and the broomtail stud would have his freedom and the Gray's Landing posse would have their ropes unstretched and their vengeance unadministered and left to God where it belonged.

The thought of the Almighty came very strong to Canady in that moment of desperate hope. He turned his face upward to peer out of the narrow slit of late twilight far above him where the walls of the canyon seemed almost to touch at the top and where, far, far up there, he could now see the yellow steer climbing the last few steps of the steep trail and humping himself over the rim and losing himself to canyon's view.

Canady nodded and said to the dusk-hushed stillness about him: "If you'll let me make it, too, Lord, me and that little hoss down yonder, Lord, the bank don't need it and I won't want it any more after this night, and I will give this money to the widow of that poor teller. I will figure some way to do it, Lord, that she don't know where it came from. And I'll turn loose this little wild hoss, if you will let me gentle him enough to get on him and push him to that jump, up yonder. I'm going to try it, Lord. I'm going down there to the pool and try putting my loop on him right now. You reckon you could help me? I surely hope so, as I think you wouldn't send that ladino steer down here to show a man the way out, and then not help him to make it. Nor likewise do I think you would put that little old mustang studhorse down there in that trap by the pool unless you wanted him used. It looks to me, Lord, as if you truly wanted to pull me out of this here trap, and if that's the way it is, why thank you and I'll do my best. . . ."

473

In the little light remaining, Canady went down from his rocks by the spring to try for the trapped wild horse. He took his rope from the trap gate and closed the gate, instead, with brush and poles, hoping it would turn the stud should he break past him when he came at him with the lariat.

The actual catching went, as such things perversely will, with a strange easiness. Oh, the little horse fought the loop when he felt it settle on him, but he did not do so viciously. The very fact that he permitted Canady to come close enough to dab the loop on him to begin with was peculiarly simple.

It made the matter suspicious to Canady and he thought the little stud was merely stalling on him, was trying to tempt him in close where he could use his teeth and hooves on him. He knew the small mustangs would do this. They would fight like panthers in close, using their teeth like carnivorous animals, and their feet with all the savagery of elk or moose fighting off wolves.

But this was not the case with the tattered broomtail in the mustang trap. When Canady got up near enough to him, he saw the reason why, or thought that he did. The telltale white marks of the cinch and saddle, the places where white hair had grown in to replace the original claybank sorrel hairs, showed clearly in the darkening twilight. Canady's first thought that this horse had been handled before was now assured. And it certainly explained the change in the animal the moment the man snugged the loop high up on his neck, under the jaw, in a way that showed the horse he meant to hold him hard and fast, and to handle him again as he had been handled years before. Memory is a strong force.

The stud made Canady throw him on the ground, using the loose end of the rope to make a figure-eight snake and roll it around the front legs to bring the little pony down, but once he had been thrown and permitted to stand up again, it was all over. This man had gentled many horses. He had spent his life with them. Their smell had become his smell. The very sound of his voice had a horse sound in it. The mustang had heard it in the man's first words. He had sensed his kinship with this particular man, then, and he sensed his mastery of horsekind, now. He submitted to Canady and stood quietly, if still trembling, while the man stroked him and sweet-whispered to him and got him to ease and to stand without shaking, and without dread or apprehension.

Then Canady cut and wove the makeshift breaking halter, the Plains Indians' simple rope rein and bridle arrangement, continuing to talk all the while to the small mustang. When, in half an hour more, it was full dark and the split-ear hackamore bridle and its short reining rope were finished and put upon the horse, the animal was to all practical purposes reduced to a usable saddle horse.

It was a piece of the greatest luck, Canady knew, that he had been able to catch and work the little brute. But it was not so entirely luck that it had no sense or possibility to it, and his success only made the fugitive believe that his hunch of higher help was a true one, and this thought, in turn, strengthened him and made his spirits rise.

"Come on," he murmured to the little horse, "It's time we got out of here. Come along, *coo-ee, coo-ee,* little hoss. That's good, that's real good. Easy, easy . . ."

They went in behind the creek falls, as the yellow ladino steer had done. The mustang pulled back a bit at the water, but once it had hit him he steadied down and followed Canady's urging pull on the lariat as well and as obediently as any horse would have done in similar straits. Beyond the sheet of the falls, the left-hand trail went sharply but safely upward and around the trunklike bulge of the canyon's wall which had hidden it from Canady's view at the spring. Around the turn was the expected straight run at the leap-over.

It was better, even, than Canady hoped. There was some actual soil in its track and, here and there, some clumps of tough wire grass to give footing and power for the jump.

"Steady, now," said Canady, and eased up onto the crouching mustang. The little mount flinched and deepened his crouch, but he did not break. Canady sighed gratefully and nodded upward to that power which clearly was helping him now. He took his grip on the rope rein and put the pressure of his bowed knees to the mustang's ribs. Beneath him, he felt the little horse squat and gather himself. Then he touched him, just touched him, with his left boot heel. The wild stud uncoiled his tensed muscles, shot down the runway of the trail, came up to the jump-across as though he had been trained to it since colthood.

Canady felt his heart soar with the mighty upward spring in the small brute's wiry limbs. He laughed with the sheer joy of it. He couldn't help it. He had never in his life felt a triumph such as this one; this sailing over that hell's pit of blackness down there beneath him; this gliding spring, this arching, floating burst of power that was carrying him high above those deadly rock fangs so far below, and was carrying him, too, up and away from those blood-hungry possemen and their winking, glaring, prying bull's-eye lanterns, which he could just see now, from an eye-corner, coming into view down-canyon of his deserted place at the spring above the pool and the peaceful grove of mountain ash and alder and willow there at the head of Rainbow Creek in Blind Canyon, sixty and more miles from the Second National Bank and that fool of a dead teller in Gray's Landing, Montana.

Oh, what a wondrous, heady thing was life! And, oh! what a beholden and humble man was Frank Canady for this gift, this chance, this answer to his fumbling prayer. He would never forget it. Never, never, never.

They came down very hard at the far end of the jump. The concussion of the horse hitting the ground rattled Canady's teeth and cracked his jaws together as loud as a pistol shot. He saw lights behind his eyes and heard wild and strange sounds, but only for a second or two. Then all was clear again and he and the little horse were going together up the right-side cliff trail, Canady leading the way, the little horse following faithfully as a pet dog behind him. It seemed no more than a minute before they were where it had taken the yellow steer half an hour to climb, and it seemed only a breath later that they had topped out on the rim and were free.

Canady cried then. The tears came to his eyes and he could not help himself. He didn't think that the little mustang would care, though, and he was right. When he put his arms about the shaggy, warm neck and hugged the skinny old stud, the mustang only whickered deep in his throat and leaned into Frank Canady and rested his homely jughead over the man's shoulder. They were of a kind. They belonged to each other, and with each other, and that was true; for that was the way that the possemen found them when they came probing carefully up the bed of the creek in its brief run from the deserted pool grove to the foot of the waterfall.

The horse had fallen with the man beneath him, and neither had known a flash or a spark or a hint of thought in the instant their lives had been crushed out among the granite snags of the creek bed below the jumping place of the yellow ladino steer.

Max Brand

MINIATURE

It was plain to Count Lanskoi, who knew women and horses, that Mariette Willoughby once had been a gem of loveliness, and though time had flawed her deeply, she continued to enshrine herself like a jewel in a rich case. Time, like a hungry fish, begins to swallow us by the head; but Count Lanskoi looked upon Mariette Willoughby as a collector looks upon a Chinese print. He shut the face from his attention and devoted his appreciation to the robes, background, color, and design.

Viewed in this manner, Mrs. Willoughby was quite a satisfactory subject for study, for her Parisian designer kept her imagination under some control and her French maid knew how clothes should be worn. Powerful corseting poured the spacious body of Mrs. Willoughby into a classic mold, which was filmed over by an afternoon dress that had cost several times its weight in gold: it looked like a delicate drapery bestowed upon a statue. Diamonds lighted her hands and clasped the fat of her wrists as she sipped sherry and examined a little miniature.

"You were more beautiful then, Dmitri," said Mrs. Willoughby. She looked up at Lanskoi and rested her eyes on the thin black sheen of his mustache. "But not so manly, my dear," she added.

Count Lanskoi bowed from the hips with youthful suppleness and speed. He had a military way of coming to attention and bowing that American women found entirely irresistible; but until he met Mrs. Willoughby he never had used his graces to get on in the world. It was only when he found himself forty-four, the age of great reason and smaller hope, that he turned at last to the ultimate resource of the poor.

"And what was the regiment again, Dmitri?" asked Mrs. Willoughby.

"The Lancer Guards," said the count.

"Did they use lances?" she asked.

"They did," said Lanskoi.

"Fancy!" said Mrs. Willoughby. "How sweet and medieval! How did they use them?"

"They stuck them into the enemy," said Lanskoi, "and left them there. Then they used the sword."

"Really?" said Mrs. Willoughby. "It's a darling little patent-leather cap, too. I thought that only hussars used them."

Lanskoi answered with another bow, for sometimes he found no words with which he could express himself to his lady. He took a slightly deeper breath and allowed his glance to pass out the window, already blue with the evening, across the yellow lights of Central Park and the naked shimmering of the frosted trees. Then, as though after repose, he returned his smile and his slightly downward regard to Mrs. Willoughby.

She found something enchanting in his lowered head, as though he dared not quite lift his gaze to his queen. She, glancing down in turn, saw the ruby pendant shine and tremble on her bosom. She was beginning to adore Count Lanskoi, because she never felt so well as when she was in his presence.

"But how strange," she said, "to have a blue uniform with a red breast to it!"

"Those are the lapels," he pointed out.

"And such epaulets! Fit for a general, at least!"

"I was only a captain," said Lanskoi, who rarely lied except when he was very hungry.

"Oh, how very odd to wear a red flower on your sword, Dmitri!" cried Mrs. Willoughby, bringing the miniature closer to her eyes.

"It is the scarlet sword knot of St. Anne," said he.

"Ah, does it mean something, then?" she asked.

"It is a decoration," said Lanskoi, with his bow.

"But Dmitri! You never told me about decorations!"

"But you know, Mariette, one does not speak of such things."

"Does one not? Does one not?" said Mrs. Willoughby, almost fiercely. "Well, we shall see about that! . . . Dmitri, kiss me!"

Count Lanskoi bowed, clicked his heels together, lifted her hand, and pressed his lips against a large solitaire diamond.

Mrs. Willoughby continued to gaze upon her hand afterward. "Dmitri," she said, "you are a really sweet . . . boy!" She laughed a little and, laughing, turned her attention to the miniature again. "But ah, ah—what's this?" she asked, putting the picture very close to her nose. "Speaking of decorations, what's this, Dmitri? This red enamel cross on your breast with the crossed swords on it?"

"It is the cross of St. Vladimir," said Count Lanskoi, bowing once more.

"Is it just a part of the uniform, dear?" she asked.

"No," answered the count. "It is not just a part of the uniform."

"But what, then? You know, Dmitri, you have a silly way of holding back. Please tell me about it!"

"It was the second highest decoration that could be awarded to a Russian officer in the Imperial Army," said Lanskoi.

"Dmitri!"

"My dove!" said Lanskoi, and his black mustache bristled with his smile. It was characteristic, when he was with Mrs. Willoughby, that his smile turned on like an electric light and turned off in the same manner.

"But even that isn't all," said Mrs. Willoughby, narrowing her eyes as though for the finest print. "Here is a lamb of a little white cross right over your heart. Does that mean something, too?"

"It does," said Lanskoi.

"What is it, then?"

"It is the Cross of St. George," answered Lanskoi.

"It's a pretty little thing," she remarked. "My dear, what are you looking at on the ceiling?" asked Mrs. Willoughby, with some impatience. "Now, Dmitri, tell me exactly what it means."

He submitted. "It is the highest decoration of the Empire, madame," he said.

"The highest? Oh, Dmitri!" she cried, and rose suddenly from her chair, thrusting herself up with both hands. She stood at her full height and extended her arms.

Count Lanskoi drew a slight breath and embraced her.

"I have made up my mind," said Mrs. Willoughby. "I am going to marry you!"

He tried very hard to make an answer but for the moment his mind was possessed by visions of the country house, the huge, warm, quiet rooms, the servants so perfectly trained, the terraced lawns and their great trees, the stables like a separate mansion, and above all the sheen and silk of the thoroughbreds.

"Dearest, don't be overcome," said Mrs. Willoughby. "I *mean* it. You are going out to the country with me this very evening. . . . Hurry downtown and pay that wretched hotel bill; then meet me here at seven, and we'll motor out. And Sunday, Dmitri, we'll be married in the village church. Don't say a word. My mind is made up. . . . Hand me my purse from that table, Dmitri. . . . Here is five hundred. It will put the miserable hotel out of your mind, at least. And then hurry back—my angel!"

Count Lanskoi did not take a taxicab because he felt that it would be better to walk himself into a clearer understanding of the position which was about to be his. Plainly the five hundred dollars was no more than the first sheaf from the harvest field. But it was not cash that he had in mind; rather he looked forward to the ending of pain than to the beginning of pleasure.

As he walked rapidly down Fifth Avenue, the golden heights of Central Park South shone loftier through the twilight. Men never have built another such face for fairyland as that chain of towers in the half-light of the day. It had been to Lanskoi, since his arrival from Russia, the symbol of all that New York contained which was locked away from him. Now he was to have the key that would open those mysterious doors. As for Mariette Willoughby—when he conceived of her as "Countess Lanskoi," he could not prevent a tremor of cold conscience. The image of another Countess Lanskoi, his mother, was like an eagle in his mind and kept watch over his guiltiness. Russian titles were far too commonly adrift in the world, and even a silly woman like Mrs. Willoughby must know that they could be bought for a song. What she really wanted was the miniature and the count's past life, which the picture represented like a young ghost in an old house.

The walking heated his blood in spite of the evening cold. He began to recall, with the cheerfulness of one who has escaped, all the situations that had imprisoned his spirit in the great city. He had been a doorman, a uniformed dancer in a Russian restaurant, a street laborer, and so on through a dwindling perspective of misery. He was changing all this—and paying his honesty of soul as a price for the alteration. Yet for the moment he was not sold, for the miniature he had presented to Mariette Willoughby was worth at least the five hundred dollars she had given to him. Therefore he walked lightly, one enjoying his last moments of liberty. He left the avenue and headed for his hotel. That was why he came past the entrance of the old riding academy just as half a dozen horses trooped into it. Lanskoi stopped to watch them with an eye trained in the old Russian cavalry school. He was about to step on when he saw the exposed hip of the last of the troop. The blanket had twisted a little awry on the chestnut mare, and he saw on her bright hide a little patch of darkness like the shadow of a crawling beetle.

Lanskoi whistled, for it was the singular birthmark which the great Russian stallion, Bayan, transmitted to his progeny. Strange to find that mark on a horse in America! Bayan had stood for years in the government stud of the Soviets, and this mare was young.

Lanskoi drew near the entrance as the mare walked through, jerking back against the lead rope and dancing sidewise with flattened ears.

"Kassatik!" said Lanskoi.

The mare stopped her dancing. She stood still and turned

her head toward Lanskoi until the groom wrenched her forward.

"Kassatik!" murmured Lanskoi again, as though he were speaking to a woman.

There had been no horses in his life for fifteen years—since the night a battered column dragged through the darkness toward Vladivostok with the guns of the Reds still audible to the rear. A bullet through his left arm had drained much of Lanskoi's strength and brought him to a fever that made him almost glad of the snow that whirled into his face. But his horse was more deeply wounded by weariness, so he walked at the gelding's side, letting it lead him blindly. That had been his last day with a horse; and he remembered the proverb: "A Cossack without a horse is like a man without a soul."

He went suddenly in behind the horses to the big tanbark arena of the riding school. The troop of horses he was following disappeared down a side chute as the count asked the doorman, "Do you know that mare? That last one of the lot?"

The doorman pulled back his cap by its visor. "I know her. I know the devil inside her, too," he said. "But I suppose she'll be knocked down to some damn fool that likes a picture in his stable instead of a horse he can use. Katya is her name, and there's a lot of cat in her, all right."

"She's about to be auctioned off?"

"Here's the list," said the doorman, and gave to the count a thin printed folder.

Lanskoi looked at his watch. It was only a little after five; he still had two hours before he presented himself at the crossroads of his life to take the final way with Mariette Willoughby. He kept remembering the bright head of the mare as she had paused to look him in the face. "I have time," said Lanskoi to himself. But a chilly sense of guilt, and expectation of disaster, worked in his blood and along his nerves.

There were ten or twelve score people in the gallery.

The auctioneer was saying, "Now, my dear friends, I ask you to pause and think again. I conceal nothing from you. I announced in the beginning, and I tell you again, that this gelding is a trifle over in the knees. Gentlemen, do I hear a thousand? To sell him for less is a shame to your intelligence as horsemen and horse lovers."

"Six-twenty-five," said a voice.

A few people laughed, and the auctioneer threw up his hands in despair.

"Six-thirty!" called another bidder. There was louder laughter than before.

"Seven hundred!" called a woman.

"Seven-fifty!"

"Eight hundred!"

"Nine hundred!"

The bidding stopped there, and the gray was knocked down at that price.

A pale young man beside Count Lanskoi said, "The horses know how to sell themselves. Did you see that gray look us in the eye just now?"

"I saw!" agreed Lanskoi. He looked suddenly and hungrily at the pale youth and then sighed, for the man had the dead eye of a professional horse dealer.

A sleek bay mare went for fifteen hundred, and a chunky gelding able to gallop under two hundred pounds brought an even two thousand.

Lanskoi was moved. He held out a gloved hand and said, "They don't want horses; they want safe machines. *That* horse should pull a plow."

He felt his neighbor's eye upon him.

"My name is Hudderson," the stranger said.

"Lanskoi," said the Count.

"Mr. Lanskey," said Hudderson, "when you want some of the right stuff, I hope you'll remember me. I'm in the telephone book."

Lanskoi answered, "I have exactly five hundred dollars in my·pocket—and that's bonanza for me. I would make a poor customer."

Hudderson looked at him with that dead eye and nodded his head with understanding, almost with approval. "But you like to see a gentleman mounted as a gentleman should be," he said.

"Ah—there!" said Lanskoi. "Something like that, I'd say!"

A big dark bay gelding danced into the arena, shaking his bridle-wise head, curving his neck, asking leave to go.

The auctioneer said briefly, "Castleton by Commander out of Serene. I won't insult this horse by describing him. Where shall we start, my friends?"

He began to walk up and down his short platform quietly. No one made an offer. And then Hudderson said in a conversational voice, "Five thousand."

No one turned to look at the bidder. Count Lanskoi felt chilled. The auctioneer said nothing. The silence continued.

"Six thousand," said someone.

"Seven."

"Eight."

"Ten," said Hudderson.

The auctioneer paused for an instant. "I think that's about all," he said. "Going and gone to Mr. Hudderson."

A sound as of a softly blowing wind passed through the gallery, and the gelding was led off.

"Did you waste a thousand in there, perhaps?" asked Lanskoi.

"You see that fat fellow over there?" said Hudderson. "He would have gone to twelve or fourteen, I think. But after my last bid he felt it was no use."

"How high would you have gone?" asked Lanskoi, feeling like a child.

"Not a hundred dollars more," said Hudderson.

"I hope you get your money out of Castleton," remarked Lanskoi courteously.

The pale man laughed. "I know a fat banker in Philadelphia," he said, "who'll pay fifteen thousand for the sake of hacking Castleton along bridle paths."

Lanskoi dipped into his past and rode again over the windy ridges of the Lanskoi estate and saw the birch trees merge with speed on either side of him. In those days he had not even known the prices of the horses that carried him; for money had not counted, then, in his life. It had been an essential, like the air he breathed, unasked-for and always present.

Conscience thrust a cold finger into the small of his back, and he looked at his wristwatch a little later, when a few more horses had passed under the hammer. Amazed to find that it was six-forty, he turned to leave. He walked down to the foot of the gallery as a flashing chestnut mare swept into the riding hall, plunged past the groom who held her, and whirled about as she came to the end of the long rope with which he anchored her.

The auctioneer took a look at the mare and braced back his shoulders. He frowned upon the crowd. "I want to speak seriously to you about this imported mare," he said. "The bloodlines may not be familiar to you, but Bayan is standing in the government cavalry stud in Russia, and Katinka, the dam, is a registered Thoroughbred. You see Katya for yourselves. Flawless lines. Plenty of foot. A bold jumper—"

"So bold she doesn't care where she lands," interrupted a man in the middle gallery, and the crowd laughed heartily.

"I see your minds are set against her," said the auctioneer. "A great pity, too, I would have said," he continued, straightening himself and peering into the gallery.

Lanskoi looked at his watch. The time gap was narrowing with wonderful speed; but he still had time to rush down to

487

the hotel, pay that bill, and arrive at Mrs. Willoughby's apartment house on the stroke of seven. With her, delays were dangerous, he knew; for she had made enough out of three successful marriages to enable her to consult nothing but her pride during the rest of her life. He had a most inward foreknowledge that her automobile would depart punctually at the hour of seven, with or without him.

So he left the gallery and hurried across the riding hall toward the street exit.

He could hear, as he went, further eloquence on the part of the auctioneer: ". . . if I were a younger man, I would want that mare for myself."

Lanskoi turned his head as he walked and saw Katya on her hind legs, striking at the air like a stallion.

"I am open to bids for Katya," concluded the auctioneer in some disgust.

A voice called: "Twenty-five dollars!"

Lanskoi, already at the arched, dark vault of the exit passage, turned suddenly about when he heard that bid. The people still were laughing about it, but not a soul raised the offer. He felt that time was slipping away and was carrying him with it toward disaster. But he could not help calling out. "Fifty!"

The auctioneer, turning toward him, said, "Ah, the gentleman has a proper eye for horseflesh. He cannot endure seeing quality of this sort sacrificed for a song. Friends, Katya is a nervous creature, to be sure, but all she needs is the proper handling."

More laughter and a few shrewd comments from the gallery interrupted him.

"Make it seventy-five!" sang out a voice.

That was the fat man whom Hudderson had pointed out. Lanskoi hated him.

"You amuse yourselves, ladies and gentlemen," said the auctioneer bitterly.

Katya at the moment again was rearing and pawing the air. The mare looked to Lanskoi as wild and tireless as one of those winter storms that rush across the thousand-mile levels of Russia.

"A hundred," said Lanskoi.

He leaned against the wall of the exit passage with his heart going fast. He would have to give up going to the hotel, now, for there was barely time to catch a taxi and get back to Mariette. And if he did not pay the hotel bill, he would be without necessary clothes for the ceremony which—He stopped his mind. He could not allow it to carry him forward into the dark entanglements of the future.

"The gentleman by the door offers a hundred," said the auctioneer, "a hundred for this beautiful, high-blooded—"

"Fifty," said the fat man, yawning.

"Ah, thank you, sir," said the auctioneer. "Thank you very much, Mr. Perkins. I see you all have been amusing yourselves at my expense. I am offered for Katya a hundred and fifty dollars—less than a farmer would have to pay for an old mule."

"Sixty," said Lanskoi, gripping his left wrist to conceal the wristwatch.

"I thank you again, sir," said the auctioneer.

"Two hundred," said the fat man.

"Three," said Hudderson.

The brain of Lanskoi reeled with the successive shocks.

"Three-fifty," said Perkins.

"Seventy-five!" called Lanskoi.

A pause followed. And Lanskoi's heart stood still. The hotel bill was a hundred and fifty-odd dollars; if his bid for the mare stood, his luggage would have to remain unredeemed and he would present himself to his lady with only the single suit in which he stood! He saw fat Mr. Perkins wave his hands and turn one shoulder. He had abandoned the bidding in profound disgust.

"I knew it!" cried the auctioneer. "I knew that there were horsemen in this crowd tonight. Would it be America if the riders were to turn their backs on such a flier as Katya?"

To illustrate his words, she bucked in a flying circle at the end of her rope.

Lanskoi looked at his watch. It lacked one minute of seven o'clock. There was still a hope—

"Going at three-seventy-five," said the auctioneer. "At three-seventy-five going, going, and—"

"Four," said Hudderson.

Lanskoi turned and fled down the exit tunnel with a sick heart.

And then, behind him, he heard the auctioneer saying, "Well, the opposition gives up and withdraws, Mr. Hudderson."

Count Lanskoi reached the edge of the pavement, and the cold night air cut into his face. Above the twinkling, yellow walls of scattered lights he saw the stars like a pale whirl of mist. And it seemed to Lanskoi that he saw the lovely head of Katya at his shoulder, the translucent lens of her eyes clouded by divine blue.

He turned and ran back up the passageway. The rank smell of the horse ring passed up his nose and into his brain like the pungency of whisky.

"Going, going, to Mr. Hudderson," cried the auctioneer briskly.

"Four-ten!" cried Lanskoi.

"Ah-ha, and here we are in a little duel," said the auctioneer.

"Fifty," said Hudderson.

Lanskoi bared his wristwatch and looked down at it. It was five minutes past seven. He could see Mariette leaning back against the cushions of the car while the chauffeur tenderly tucked the robe around her. It was far too late. It seemed to him that the wind of the closing gates of fortune was in his face.

"Sixty!" he called.

"Seventy-five," said the hard, even voice of Hudderson.

Lanskoi cried out, "Five hundred!" and his voice cracked on it just a little. Taking a step out from the shadowy archway into the light of the ring, he peered earnestly up into the gallery to hear his fate pronounced by the pale lips of Hudderson.

"Five hundred offered," said the auctioneer, delighted. "And now let us enter on the real phase of the bidding. Five hundred, Mr. Hudderson; and do I hear—"

Hudderson, a cigarette between his lips, stared at Lanskoi.

"Going at five hundred. Going—"

Hudderson lifted his hand a little as though to signal another bid; but the gesture remained incomplete, and Lanskoi felt the eyes of the horse dealer hold him for an instant of profound understanding.

"Well, let him have her," said Hudderson, and Lanskoi felt that for the first time in his life he had received mercy.

"Too bad," said the auctioneer, shaking his head. "But she is yours, sir!"

Lanskoi took the money from his wallet, the five little hundred-dollar bills, and passed them over. The end of the rope was placed in his hand.

"Hold hard on her!" said the sweating, panting groom. "I'd like to bust her one!"

Katya made a plunge, her ears back.

"*Stoyat!*" called Lanskoi.

The mare stood still with her flanks heaving, her legs braced. Lanskoi gave the rope a slight pull. It was like pulling at a stone pillar.

"Give the gentleman a hand to get her out," said the auctioneer.

"Never mind," said Lanskoi. "She'll come quietly, I think."

"If you'll leave your name and address—" said the auctioneer.

"I'll take her off your hands at once," said Lanskoi. He pulled gently on the rope again. *"Poshli!"* said Lanskoi, and Katya stepped briskly out after him as he turned toward the exit. He felt her breath snuffing at his shoulder as he paused on the sidewalk. The gallery was still applauding.

The doorman called after him, "Are you a horse charmer, sir?"

Lanskoi said nothing, for the cold wind, striking through his clothes, made his sweating body seem naked to the night.

He went up the street with the green light, waited at Fifty-ninth for the traffic to change. Katya crowded him all the way across Central Park South until they entered the bridle path of the park. It dipped down into a darkness under a footpath bridge, and came out on the other side among trees all delicately silvered with frost to the tips of the finest twigs. The beaten snow underfoot was darkened with the soot of New York; but the banks on either side of the path shone like newly cloven marble, all the crystals freshly glistening. Then snow began to fall.

Lanskoi stopped. The shoulder of the mare nudged him as she paused at his side. "Where, Katya?" he asked.

She turned her head, her eyes wide with a lustrous confidence.

"Kassatik!" said Lanskoi, slipping an arm about her neck. He looked about him again and saw a world turned into white iron. It would be long before the spring softened it again to life, for winter was only beginning. The falling snow clouded his future in a smothering mist of white.

Even the miniature, which had been his passport and credential in many a bitter time, was gone now forever. He had come to an end of stratagems and of all gentlemanly resources, and yet in that nakedness of mind he felt a strange comfort, as though his soul had come back to him from exile. As for the future—he could be a groom in some rich man's stable.

A bitter wind out of the north blew against Lanskoi and seemed to freeze and to cleanse him at the same moment.

"Poshli!" he commanded.

The mare stepped forward, and Lanskoi walked at her shoulder with one hand resting on her withers and the lead rope dangling loosely; for he needed to think, and in the meantime it seemed as well for Katya to lead the way.